Bird Study

BIRD STUDY

by ANDREW J. BERGER
Chairman, Department of Zoology,
University of Hawaii

DOVER PUBLICATIONS, INC.
NEW YORK

Published in Canada by General Publishing Company, Ltd., 30 Lesmill Road, Don Mills, Toronto, Ontario.
Published in the United Kingdom by Constable and Company, Ltd., 10 Orange Street, London WC 2.

This Dover edition, first published in 1971, is an unabridged republication of the work originally published by John Wiley & Sons, Inc., in 1961.

International Standard Book Number: 0-486-22699-9
Library of Congress Catalog Card Number: 72-143678

Manufactured in the United States of America
Dover Publications, Inc.
180 Varick Street
New York, N. Y. 10014

To Denny,
John,
and Diana

Bird Study has been written to serve as the basis for a one-semester course in ornithology for liberal arts students. The needs of such students can be met neither by offering them a "watered-down" version of a reference work on ornithology nor by offering them an emasculated text that leaves them with little more accurate information at the end of the course than they had at the beginning. I subscribe to the teaching philosophy that the instructor should not underestimate the ability of his students. This philosophy also recognizes that any really "good" course is the result of constant planning and effort by the instructor. A textbook can only be an aid to learning; it cannot be a substitute for a dynamic teacher. To be most effective, any college course should motivate the student to study independently long after the final grade is known. If this is not the case, then both student and teacher have wasted considerable time.

Not only should the student learn facts; he should also gain a familiarity with the basic principles of the discipline concerned. The facts will be forgotten if not used regularly. The principles and concepts will remain in the form of generalizations for a much longer period and will serve as a frame of reference for related fields of study. The basic principles

Preface

of the conservation of natural resources should be of vital concern not only to the student of birds, or mammals, or wild flowers but to every thinking person in the United States.

The emphasis in this book is on the living bird and primarily on North American birds. The student would gain a faulty impression of the broad scope of ornithology, however, if he were not given the opportunity to be exposed to some of the more technical aspects of the subject, such as structure, function, and systematics. In several places technical language could not appropriately be avoided. Notable in this regard is the elaborate vocabulary developed by ethologists in their study of animal behavior. Regardless of the subject matter, however, the aim has been to present accurate information in a readable manner. If this goal has been achieved, there are others who should find this book useful. It might well serve as a source book for teachers in elementary and high schools and for the parents of inquisitive children. Many college professors would be delighted to see in their students the "inquiring mind" as it is exhibited by children of the ages of six to ten. Such children not only pose many penetrating questions but they are more than eager to increase their knowledge much faster than circumstances usually allow in our society.

Most of the information in this book is common knowledge to ornithologists and therefore needs no documentation, which would be distracting in an elementary text. Where different writers have disagreed on the definition of terms, I have adopted the terms and concepts of Elliott Coues (*Key to North American Birds,* 1903) and of Josselyn Van Tyne and A. J. Berger (*Fundamentals of Ornithology,* 1959). I have planned this book with the thought in mind that it might serve as a text for a course in which Dr. Olin Sewall Pettingill's excellent *A Laboratory and Field Manual of Ornithology* would be used for laboratory instruction. Like Pettingill, I have tried to present material with the student uppermost in mind, for I agree with a friend who wrote that "college textbooks can make interesting reading if the author, instead of trying to impress his colleagues with his breadth of knowledge, will write to make the students enthusiastic learners."

For helpful suggestions I thank Dr. Harrison B. Tordoff (Chapters 1 and 2), Dr. Daniel S. Lehrman (Chapter 5), Dr. Donald S. Farner (discussion of photoperiodism), and Dr. Donald W. Douglass (Chapter 10). I am especially indebted to Dr. Pettingill, who read the entire manuscript. I express my appreciation to David R. Sterrett for preparing the original pen and ink illustrations, and to

Mrs. Delia M. Adams for her expert typing of the manuscript. My wife has contributed immeasurably both in the tedious task of proofreading and in translating my scientific jargon into plain English. I thank the several authors and publishers who granted permission to use published material; acknowledgments appear in the text. For their splendid cooperation and generosity in providing a large supply of photographs I wish to thank especially Samuel A. Grimes, Brooke Meanley, and Walter P. Nickell.

ANDREW J. BERGER

Ann Arbor, Michigan
April, 1961

Contents

Mammals, birds, reptiles (lizards, snakes, turtles, crocodiles), amphibians (frogs, toads, salamanders), and fishes are so distinctive in external appearance that even the uninitiated person can recognize (in most instances) which is which (e.g., hair is characteristic of mammals, feathers are found only on birds). Nevertheless, these five groups of animals share certain basic anatomical similarities and are grouped together as backboned or vertebrate animals. In order to understand the relationships among these classes, however, one must study their ancient history (paleontology), their development from the fertilized egg (embryology), and the anatomy of the adult animals. As a result of such studies, scientists believe that both birds and mammals took their origin, many millions of years ago, from primitive reptiles—reptiles unlike any of those living today. With the passage of eons of time, the succeeding generations of offspring gradually evolved into the kinds of reptiles, birds, and mammals found today (Figs. 1, 2).

Each of these three classes of vertebrate animals has some features peculiar to itself, and each possesses other characteristics that are shared with one or the other of the major classes. Thus one can point out that both reptiles and birds have an egg-tooth on the

1

Introducing the Bird

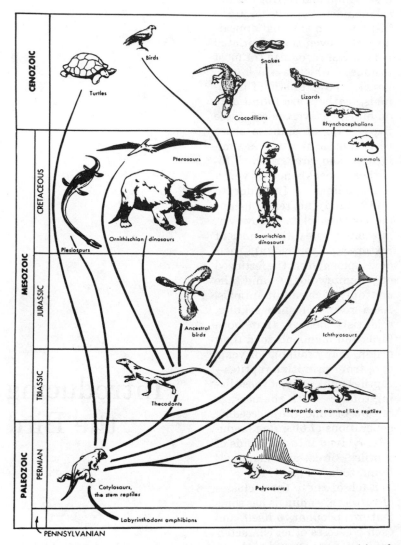

FIGURE 1. The family tree of the reptiles: a pictorial diagram summarizing the history of the reptiles and their relationship to birds and mammals. (By permission from *The Dinosaur Book* by Edwin H. Colbert, published by McGraw-Hill Book Company, Inc. Copyright, 1951, by the American Museum of Natural History.)

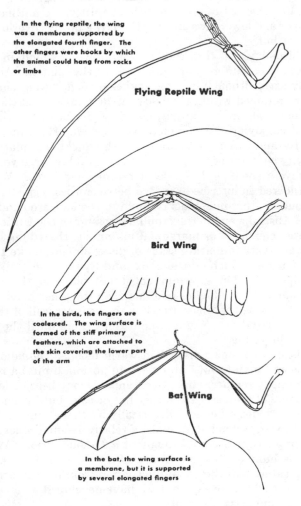

In the flying reptile, the wing
was a membrane supported by
the elongated fourth finger. The
other fingers were hooks by which
the animal could hang from rocks
or limbs

Flying Reptile Wing

Bird Wing

In the birds, the fingers are
coalesced. The wing surface is
formed of the stiff primary
feathers, which are attached to
the skin covering the lower part
of the arm

Bat Wing

In the bat, the wing surface is
a membrane, but it is supported
by several elongated fingers

Drawings by John C. Germann

FIGURE 2. Wing of pterosaur (an extinct flying reptile), bird, and bat. (By permission from *The Dinosaur Book* by Edwin H. Colbert, published by McGraw-Hill Book Company, Inc. Copyright, 1951, by the American Museum of Natural History.)

upper jaw at hatching. This egg-tooth, not really a tooth but a horny protuberance which disappears shortly after hatching, presumably aids the embryo in breaking out of its eggshell. Birds of today, like the turtles (but not other reptiles), do not have teeth; the upper and lower jaws are sheathed by a horny covering to form a beak or bill.

All birds lay eggs (i.e., they are *oviparous*), which, in most instances, are cared for by the adults until they hatch. All reptiles also lay eggs, although in some snakes (*ovoviviparous* snakes) the eggs are retained within the body of the female until they hatch. Most mammals are *viviparous*, i.e., they give birth to living young rather than laying eggs complete with a shell. However, two very primitive and specialized mammals (the duckbilled platypus and the spiny anteater of the Australian region) lay large-yolked eggs that have a shell, as do those of reptiles and birds. What may be considered an intermediate step between these egg-laying mammals and all other mammals is found in the kangaroo and its relatives of Australia and in the familiar opossum of the United States. In these "pouched" or marsupial mammals, the young leave the uterus at a very immature stage of development, make their way to the female's pouch on the belly, and there grasp a nipple with their lips. Further development takes place in the pouch or *marsupium*. In the higher mammals, on the other hand, the very tiny fertilized egg becomes attached to the inner wall of the uterus (the womb) and development continues there until the time for birth of the young.

Birds and mammals are called warm-blooded (*homoiothermic*) animals and maintain (within certain normal limits) a relatively constant body temperature. Such animals may become less active at extremes of temperature, either hot or cold, but in general their activities are not influenced drastically by changes in air temperature. In warm-blooded animals, a relatively small fluctuation in body temperature occurs throughout a 24-hour period. When you and I, as humans, become aware of a rise in body temperature much greater than the usual fluctuation from man's normal temperature of 98.6°, we say that we have developed a "fever," with its various unpleasant symptoms.

By contrast, it is perfectly normal for the body temperature of reptiles to fluctuate considerably with changes in air temperature. They are more active on warm days and sluggish on cold days. Reptiles (as well as fishes and amphibians) are called cold-blooded (*poikilothermic*) animals, which is to say that their body temperature is not maintained at a nearly constant level as in mammals and birds. Another important difference between reptiles and birds is that the newly hatched reptile is independent at once; the young receive no parental care. Most species of birds, on the other hand, protect and feed their newly hatched young. The length of the period of dependency on the parents varies considerably among the families of birds, as will be discussed in Chapter 8.

In summary, one might note that although mammals, birds, and reptiles differ in many respects and form three separate classes, a detailed study of their development and internal structure reveals that birds and reptiles share many more similarities than do reptiles and mammals or birds and mammals.

TOPOGRAPHY OF THE BIRD

In order to facilitate the description of the external appearance of birds, the main anatomical regions are subdivided into named areas or parts. The outer surface of the bird, then, is mapped out in some detail, and the resulting pattern constitutes the topography of the bird. Figure 3 is a generalized sketch of a bird to show these

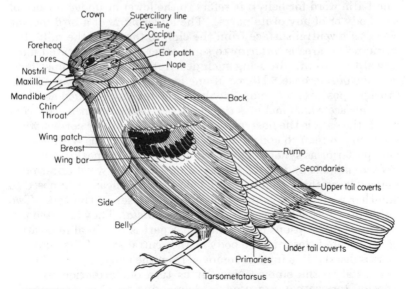

FIGURE 3. Generalized sketch of a bird to show major topographical regions.

areas and the special terms used in describing the plumage and other external features of birds.

Before we define these special terms it seems pertinent to remind the student that the study of any subject involves the learning of some new vocabulary, which may be relatively simple or quite complicated and elaborate. Despite the impression that one sometimes receives when reading "scientific" papers in some fields of study, the purpose of any specialized vocabulary is not to confuse but to insure precise definition of words, which is a prerequisite for exchanging ideas with others. Therefore it is important that the student learn the meaning of special terms early in order that they may become useful "tools," so to speak, rather than a hindrance to learning and understanding.

We need first to consider some words that tell what general part of the body is being discussed. In a sense these are directional terms in that they refer to general areas on opposite sides or ends of the body or one of its members. When we speak of the *dorsum* we mean specifically the bird's back. If we refer to the *dorsal surface,* however, we may mean the upper surface of any part of the bird: the head, the back, the tail, or the wings. The *upper parts* of a bird are, by definition, the entire dorsal surface from the forehead to the tip of the tail. The opposite to dorsal is *ventral* (from the Latin word for belly); it refers to the lower or under surface of the body or of any of its parts. The *under parts* of a bird include the entire ventral surface from the chin to the tip of the tail. If a structure or area is *anterior* to some other part, it is located more toward the front. In using such descriptive terms one must have a plane of reference. Hence, if one is thinking about man and his upright posture, one may speak of the anterior surface as being that surface which includes the face, chest, and abdomen. By contrast, the back is the *posterior* surface. It is perfectly correct when referring to man to consider anterior as synonymous with ventral and posterior as synonymous with dorsal. When speaking of four-footed animals and birds, however, one uses the word anterior to refer to something that is located closer to the head as opposed to another region that is posterior to it, or closer to the tail. Two other descriptive terms are *proximal* and *distal*. They are used primarily in descriptions of the limbs. A part is proximal in position if it is located closer to the body or the central axis of the body. A part is distal if it is further removed from the body; e.g., the fingers are distal to the elbow. Now let us turn our attention to more specific terms that are used in delineating the topography of a bird.

The Head

The head often exhibits special features that aid one in bird identification. We pointed out above that birds lack teeth and that their bills are formed by a horny covering over the jawbones. Anatomically the upper jaw is the *maxilla* and the lower jaw is the *mandible,* but both often are referred to as mandibles in birds. The two *mandibles,* then, form the *bill* or *beak.* The shape of the mandibles is in general correlated with food habits (see Chapter 9), and the members of large families of birds may have bills which are very similar in structure and configuration. Thus, most of the different kinds of American wood-warblers have a thin, delicate, and sharply pointed bill; the vireos have a somewhat heavier bill that is slightly hooked and notched at the bill tip; woodpeckers typically have straight, chisel-like bills; the bill of a hawk or eagle is heavy and strongly hooked at the tip. Parts of the bill are given special names. The *culmen* is the longitudinal ridge along the dorsal surface of the upper mandible or maxilla. The *gonys* is the median ridge along the ventral surface of the anterior fused portion of the lower mandible. The cutting edges of the two mandibles are called the *tomia* (sing., tomium). There are right and left maxillary tomia along the lower free edges of the upper mandible and right and left mandibular tomia along the upper free edges of the lower mandible. The *commissure* is the line along which the maxillary and mandibular tomia meet when the bill is closed. The *commissural point* is simply the angle of the mouth, i.e., the area where the upper and lower mandibles meet posteriorly. The bony skeleton of the mandibles in this area, however, is covered by relatively soft, fleshy tissue in contrast to the hard, horny sheath that forms the cutting edges of the mandibles. The term *rictus* has been used by some authors to denote this fleshy area. The *gape* is the opening or space between the mandibles when the bill is open. When hand-feeding young birds, one is delighted when the bird gapes (opens widely) for food.

The top of the head is divided into three named areas. Beginning anteriorly at the base of the bill, in sequence these areas are: the *forehead* (the front of the head), the *crown* (top of head), and the *occiput* (back of head). The *chin* and the *gular region* form the lower or ventral surface of the head. The chin is the small V-shaped area between the two forks or branches of the lower mandible posterior to the gonys. The gular region is the remaining portion of the ventral surface of the head, but this term usually is reserved for special situations, e.g., in describing the gular pouch (an expansion of the skin of the chin, gular region, and neck) of pelicans. There is no discrete line of demarcation between the gular region of the head and the ventral surface of the neck (called the *jugulum*), so that the two areas together usually are spoken of as the *throat*.

On the side of the head are the *lores* (the space between the base of the bill and the eye), the *orbital region* (the eye, eyelids, and the immediately surrounding skin and feathers), the ear or *auricular patch,* and the *malar* ("cheek") *region* (the area between the throat and the three areas just listed). Birds do not have an external ear flap (auricle or pinna); the opening of the external ear canal is covered by the feathers of the auricular feather patch. Many birds have feathers of contrasting color on the side of the head, which may be useful in describing plumages. These feathers may form an *eye ring* surrounding the eye, a *superciliary line* above the eye, or an *eye line* which may extend both in front of and behind the eyeball itself. Conspicuous eyelashes formed by specialized feathers are present in some birds, such as the ostrich, cuckoos, and hornbills. These eyelashes may be feather-like or they may be "hairlike," in which instance they are classified as bristles. Bristles located at the corners of the mouth are called rictal bristles because they grow from the skin of the rictal area.

Some other special anatomical structures found on the bill or head are a cere, a shield, a comb, and a wattle. A *cere* is a soft, swollen covering of the base of the upper mandible; it is present in hawks, owls, and parrots. A *frontal shield* (as in the Purple Gallinule) is a horny projection extending from the base of the upper mandible onto the forehead. The *cock's comb* of chickens is a specialized, unfeathered, fleshy pad of skin on top of the head. Similar in structure to the comb, *wattles* are fleshy growths that hang downward from the side of the face, the chin, or the throat.

The Neck and Trunk

The neck connects the head to the body; it extends from the base of the skull to the body or trunk. The junction of neck with body is not readily apparent in most birds but it may be located approximately by imagining a line drawn across the back at the level of attachment of the wings to the body. The dorsal or upper surface of the neck is the *nape*. The *jugulum* is, as mentioned above, the little-used term for the ventral or lower surface of the neck. The dorsal surface of the *trunk* (the area between the base of the neck and the base of the tail) is divided into the *back* and the *rump*.

Either of these areas, but especially the rump, may be differently colored from the rest of the upper parts of the bird, and then may be useful as a field mark for identification. A good example is the white rump of the Yellow-shafted Flicker, which is very conspicuous when the bird is flying away from the observer. In most birds one arbitrarily calls the anterior two-thirds of the trunk the back; the posterior one-third is the rump. The ventral surface of the trunk is subdivided into the breast, belly, sides, and flanks. The *breast* is the anterior portion that, strictly speaking, extends from the base of the neck to the posterior margin of the breastbone (the *sternum*). In actual practice the term is often used to denote a somewhat smaller, anterior, and more rounded portion of the ventral surface of the body that does not extend as far back as the posterior margin of the sternum. The *belly* (or abdomen) extends from the breast to an imaginary transverse line which passes through the vent. Both the breast and the belly curve upward to form the *sides of the body,* which, by tradition, are described with the ventral surface or under parts of a bird. As applied to birds, the term "flank" is loosely defined by most writers, and it probably never is comparable to the flank of mammals; it might be preferable to discontinue using the term for birds. For practical purposes, the avian flank is composed of the femoral feather tract and any other feathers growing from the skin covering the thigh, as in the "flank plumes" of the Violet-green Swallow.

The Hind Limb

The entire limb or appendage which supports the body and which has a foot at its extremity is called the "leg" by most people. The word "calf" may be used for the fleshy area between the knee and the ankle, and the portion above the knee may be called the thigh by the layman. The anatomist agrees with that location for the thigh and has called the bony support of the thigh the *femur* (Fig. 4). He uses the word leg or *crus,* however, for only that section between the knee and the ankle. It has two bones, the *tibia* (the major supporting bone) and the *fibula.* This segment of roast chicken or turkey is called the "drumstick." The bony framework of the hind limb of man and other mammals is completed by a series of foot bones (*tarsals, metatarsals,* and *phalanges*).

The hind limb of the bird differs in several respects from the condition found in man. The ankle joint is not located between the two bones of the crus or leg and the most proximal of the foot bones (the talus), as in man, but lies between two rows of foot bones

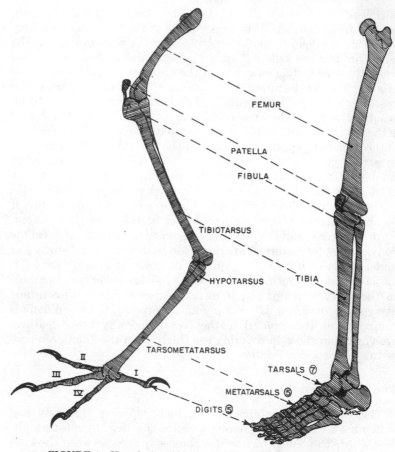

FIGURE 4. Homologies of bones of hind limb of a bird and man.

(tarsal bones). During embryological development, some of the tarsal bones fuse (grow together) with the distal end of the tibia. Hence, the major supporting bone for the bird crus (the drumstick) is not the tibia, as in man, but is more properly called the *tibiotarsus,* a word combining the names of the fused bones: the tibia and some of the tarsal bones. The fibula, the second bone of the crus, is poorly developed in birds; usually it does not extend as far as the distal end of the tibiotarsus. The *tarsometatarsus,* which is roughly comparable to our instep, is formed by the fusion of other tarsal bones with three metatarsal bones (which also fuse with each other). A single, independent metatarsal bone ("accessory metatarsal") is present and serves as a support for the first toe. The foot of the bird, in the broad sense, is composed of the tarsometatarsus and the phalanges (the bones of the toes). It is the tarsometatarsus (and not the leg or crus) that the bird bander encircles with his band or "ring."

In descriptions of birds, the tibiotarsus is usually termed the "tibia" and the tarsometatarsus is called simply the "tarsus." Both terms sometimes are used to include not only the supporting bones but also the muscles and the skin with its covering feathers and/or scales. It may be noted here that in most birds the tarsus (as well as the toes) is more or less completely covered by horny scales, not greatly unlike the scales of some reptiles. These scales are arranged in a number of patterns among the different families of birds. In the Golden Eagle, the grouse, and many owls the tarsus may be wholly or partly feathered, and in the Snowy Owl and ptarmigan even the toes may be almost completely covered by feathers.

The bird's thigh is completely covered by contour feathers and most of it is hidden by the skin of the body. Consequently, the thigh and the knee joint usually are not apparent in the living bird. For this reason, some people think that the bird's knee bends forward, or just the opposite to the way that the knee bends in man. This, of course, is not true. Because the thigh is hidden by feathers and skin, it is the feathered leg that is the first obvious segment of the hind limb, and it is the bird's ankle joint that often is confused with the knee joint.

The ostrich has but two toes, a few birds have three, but most birds have four toes. In the most common arrangement of toes (the *anisodactyl* foot), the first toe (the big toe or *hallux*) points backward whereas the other three toes point forward. Each toe is supported by a series of small bones called phalanges (sing., phalanx). The number of these bones in each toe is relatively constant throughout the many families of birds. There are a few exceptions but the general pattern is as follows: toe I (hallux) has two supporting bones; toe II (the inner front toe) has three bones; toe III (the middle front toe) has four bones; toe IV (the outer front toe) has five bones. The usual practice is to refer to toes (and fingers) by using Roman numerals.

The feet of certain birds have become modified from the pattern described above. In cuckoos, parrots, and woodpeckers, for example, toes I and IV are turned backward and toes II and III are turned forward; these birds have *zygodactyl* feet. In the trogons, which inhabit the tropical regions of both hemispheres, toes I and

II are turned backward and toes III and IV are turned forward, a condition spoken of as *heterodactyl*. A few birds have only three toes (*tridactyl* feet). This specialization has taken place in large flightless birds such as the rheas of South America and the cassowaries and emus of the Australian area. Among North American birds, the auks, guillemots, and their relatives, and all American plovers (except the Black-bellied Plover) are tridactyl, as are a few other species, e.g., Sanderling, Black-backed Three-toed Woodpecker, and Northern Three-toed Woodpecker.

Birds' feet exhibit other specializations. The three front toes of a duck are enclosed by a webbing of skin, a condition described as *palmate*. All four toes are enclosed by a web in cormorants and pelicans; such feet are described as being *totipalmate*. Various degrees of reduction in the amount of webbing between the toes (or the number of toes involved in the web) can be found in such birds as terns, herons, and shorebirds. The surface area of the toes may also be increased by the presence of membranous lobes of varying sizes along the sides of the toes, as in grebes, coots, and phalaropes. Seasonal changes occur in the toes of the Ruffed Grouse. With the approach of winter, a fringe of horny projections grows out along the sides of the toes. These horny "snowshoes" serve to distribute the bird's weight over a wider area as it walks on the snow.

The Forelimb

To the layman, again, the "arm" is the entire upper limb. Anatomically, the *arm* is the most proximal segment of the forelimb, that part which extends from the shoulder to the elbow; the *humerus* is the supporting bone of this segment (Fig. 5). The *forearm,* extending from the elbow to the wrist, contains two bones, the *radius* (on the thumb side) and the *ulna*. A series of eight *wrist* (or *carpal*) *bones* lies between the forearm and the *hand bones* (*metacarpals*). The bony supports for the fingers are called phalanges, as they are in the foot. The anterior limb of the bird has been modified for flight. This modification shows itself both in the fusion and in the apparent loss of bones. For example, only two wrist bones are found in the adult bird. Other carpal bones have fused during development with three metacarpal bones to form the *carpometacarpus,* the bony support for the bird's hand. Moreover, of the typical pattern of five metacarpal bones in the hand of most higher vertebrates, only three remain in the bird and these are mostly fused together. Similarly, of the typical number of five fingers or digits, the bird has only three. Most authors

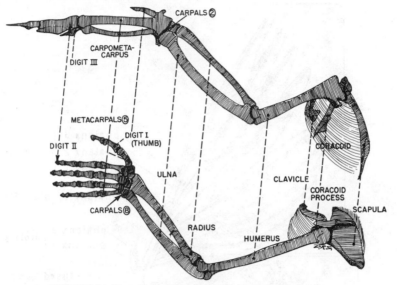

FIGURE 5. Homologies of bones of forelimb of a bird and man.

consider these to be as follows: digit I (the thumb or pollex), digit II (the second or index finger), and digit III (the third or middle finger).

Some of the most important feathers for flight are attached to certain wing bones (Fig. 6). The feathers borne by the carpometacarpus and digits II and III are called *primaries*. The wrist is the starting place for numbering flight feathers. Thus, when referring to the primary feathers by number, one considers the innermost feather (that one closest to the wrist) as number 1. In some birds, the outermost primary (number 10, 11, or 12) is so much reduced in length that one may have to look very closely in order to find and identify it. This reduced outermost primary is called the *remicle*. Among the many bird families the number of primary feathers varies from 9 to 12 in flying birds. Flightless birds may have as few as 3 (the cassowary) or as many as 16 (the ostrich).

The *secondaries* are the feathers that are attached to the dorsal surface of the ulna; no feathers are attached to the radius. The outermost secondary is nearest the wrist and is counted as number 1; the others are numbered in sequence as one proceeds toward the elbow. The number of secondaries varies from 6 (some hummingbirds) to as many as 32 (the Wandering Albatross). Most of the

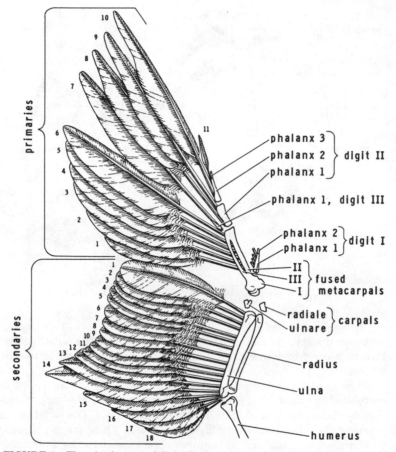

FIGURE 6. The wing bones and flight feathers as seen from below. (By permission from *Fundamentals of Ornithology* by Josselyn Van Tyne and Andrew J. Berger, published by John Wiley & Sons, Inc. Copyright, 1959.)

small passerine birds have 9 secondaries (not 6 as stated in some books).

Primaries and secondaries, which constitute the flight feathers proper of the wing, collectively are called the *remiges* (sing., *remex*). In addition to the remiges there are other groups of named feathers on the wing. The *alula* (also called the spurious wing or bastard wing) is composed of those feathers that are attached to the thumb or pollex. The number of such alula quills in different birds varies from two to at least seven. The alula acts as a wing slot in flight. The *tertiaries* are feathers that grow from the skin overlying the arm (humerus). The number and relative development of these feathers vary considerably among the families of birds. Peculiarities in their length, color, or shape are sometimes used in describing plumages. (Some authors consider the tertiaries to be the third series in the group of flight feathers included under the term of remiges.) The remaining feathers on the wing are grouped together as *coverts* (or tectrices). *Upper primary coverts* and *upper secondary coverts* are located on the dorsal side of the wing. A *greater* (or major) *primary covert* overlies the base of each primary feather. Anterior to these is a row of *middle* (or median) *primary coverts.* The bases of the alula feathers also are overlapped by coverts. The *greater secondary coverts* overlie the bases of the secondaries. Anterior to these are at least two additional rows of feathers: the *middle* (median) *secondary coverts* and one or more rows called the *lesser* (or minor) *secondary coverts.* Finally, along the leading edge of the wing (both in the forearm and in the hand or *manus*) are an indefinite number of *marginal coverts.* Less numerous feathers on the under surface of the wing constitute the *under wing coverts:* collectively they are called the *lining of the wing.*

The Tail

When an ornithologist speaks of the tail of a bird he usually means the well-developed and conspicuous feathers of the tail. These flight feathers of the tail, which serve as a rudder and as a brake in flight, are known as the *rectrices* (sing., *rectrix*). The anatomical tail (*cauda*) also includes the terminal bones (*vertebrae*) of the backbone (spinal column), plus the muscles, nerves, and blood vessels associated with the vertebrae. The last bone in this series, to which the tail feathers are actually attached, is called the *pygostyle.* It is formed by the fusion of several bones during embryological development. A series of *upper* and *lower tail coverts* grow from the skin anterior to the bases of the tail feathers. The under tail coverts are sometimes differently colored from the rest of the feathers on the under surface of the bird (as in the Catbird, Brown Towhee, and Bohemian Waxwing) and they, as a group, are then referred to as the *crissum.*

THE FEATHER

Birds can be characterized by the simple statement that only they among all animals possess feathers. Feathers, like the hair of mammals, develop from the skin (integument) which covers the outer surface of the body. The feather grows from a papilla located within a feather follicle (a small depression or cavity) in the skin. The full-grown feather is completely "dead," as are the ends of our fingernails. A bird does not experience pain when a feather is cut any more than we feel pain when a nail is trimmed or our hair is cut.

Structure of the Feather

The main stem or *shaft* of a typical feather is composed of two continuous parts: the *calamus* and the *rachis* (Fig. 7). The calamus is hard, smooth, cylindrical, and essentially hollow. In the days of quill pens, it was the base of the calamus that served as the pen point after it had been cut on the diagonal. The base of the calamus is embedded in the feather follicle in the skin. There is a small hole (the *inferior umbilicus*) at the base of the calamus; it is through this opening that the growing feather receives its blood supply. A second hole or pit (the *superior umbilicus*) is located at the opposite end, where the calamus continues as the rachis. The somewhat quadrangular-shaped rachis continues from the calamus to the tip of the feather. The rachis bears on either side a large series of branches (*rami*) or *barbs,* which form the web or *vane* of the feather. One may speak also of a narrower outer web and a wider inner web, which together form the vane. Although scarcely visible to the unaided eye, each barb similarly gives rise to a series of small filaments or plates called *barbules;* the barb, in a sense, is constructed like a very small feather. Only by examining the feather under a microscope can one fully appreciate the details of structure that give strength and flexibility to the vane of the feather. Under magnification one can see that the barbules them-selves support a series of small hair-like processes (the *barbicels*), which have been described as a fringe on the barbules. Some of the barbules on the anterior or distal side (i.e., those which point toward the tip of the feather) of the barb have a hooked tip at the end of the barbicels, which are then called *hamuli;* a hamulus, therefore, is a hook-tipped barbicel. These hooks serve to interlock the barbules in the formation of a strong yet remarkably flexible web. The flight feathers of the wing and tail represent the extreme development of the *pennaceous* feather described in this paragraph.

What has variously been termed the "perfect" or the "complete" feather actually consists of two shafts or feathers: the outer main feather and an inner feather called the *aftershaft* (Fig. 8). The aftershaft arises at the junction of the calamus and the rachis on

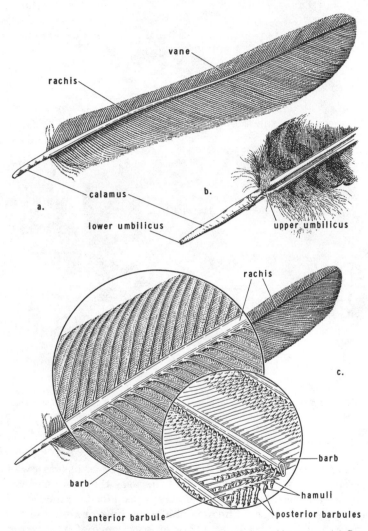

FIGURE 7. A typical flight feather and the nomenclature of its parts. (a) General view. (b) Detail of the base of the feather. (c) Detail of the vane. (By permission from *Fundamentals of Ornithology* by Josselyn Van Tyne and Andrew J. Berger, published by John Wiley & Sons, Inc. Copyright, 1959.)

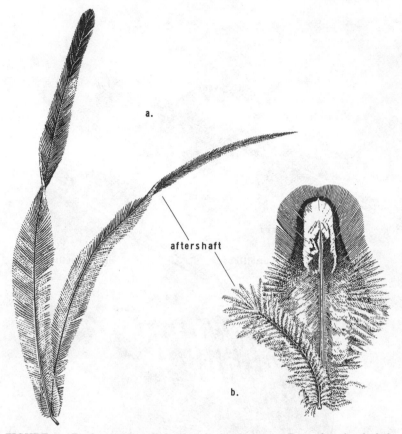

FIGURE 8. Feathers with well-developed aftershaft. (a) Emu; the aftershaft is nearly as large as the main feather. (b) Pheasant (*Phasianus*) back feather. (By permission from *Fundamentals of Ornithology* by Josselyn Van Tyne and Andrew J. Berger, published by John Wiley & Sons, Inc. Copyright, 1959.)

the inner side of the main feather.   In a very few birds (cassowaries and emus), the aftershaft is nearly as large as the main feather; in grouse and pheasants it also is well developed but it is much smaller than the main feather.   The aftershaft is minute or absent entirely in many birds, and rarely is there any evidence of it on a flight feather; it is usually found associated with other kinds of contour feathers.   Whatever its relative development, the aftershaft differs from the main feather in most birds in that it lacks hooklets and barbicels.   Not having a stiff vane, therefore, such a feather is fluffy or downy (*plumulaceous*).

Types of Feathers

1. *Contour feathers* are those that form the outline or contour of the body. The most highly developed contour feathers, as suggested above, are the flight feathers of the wing and tail (remiges and rectrices). Most of the contour feathers that form the outer covering of the body exhibit an intermediate structure between that of the firm-vaned flight feather and the downy aftershaft already described. Most of the body contour feathers are firm-vaned distally but loose-webbed at the base of the rachis. In addition to the well-developed feathers that form the outer covering of the body, many specialized and degenerate types of feathers are generally classified as contour feathers because they are believed to be derived from typical contour feathers. *Semiplumes,* like the aftershaft, lack hooklets on the barbicels and, therefore, are loose-webbed or fluffy in appearance (Fig. 9). *Bristles,* which often look like hairs, are among the most highly modified feathers. They may be found in some birds near the angle of the mouth (rictal bristles), around the nostrils, or above the eye (eyelashes). Bristles were formerly considered a type of filoplume.

Several people have taken the time to count all of the contour feathers on specimens of various species of birds. As one might expect, a large bird has more feathers than a small bird. This variation in number of feathers among different birds can be illustrated by giving three examples. A Ruby-throated Hummingbird was found to have 940 feathers; a Bobolink had 3235 feathers; and a Whistling Swan had 25,216 feathers.

2. *Filoplumes,* also, are very specialized, hair-like feathers, but they usually grow in groups of two to eight around the base of a contour feather. Most filoplumes are completely covered by the overlying contour feathers. One type has a suggestion of a small vane near the tip of the feather. A second type has no vane at all; such a hair-like filoplume may extend beyond the contour feathers, as on the back of a Robin that has recently grown new feathers. They also may be seen on the body of a mature chicken after its feathers have been "plucked."

3. *Down feathers* (*plumules*) are small, soft feathers that lack a vane. Even the rachis may be absent so that the barbs fan out in a tuft at the tip of the calamus. They are found in greatest abundance in penguins, loons, grebes, albatrosses, petrels, cormorants, pelicans, ducks, geese, swans, gulls, terns, puffins, hawks, and owls. The down feathers of adult birds are almost always concealed by the contour feathers. An exception is offered by some Old World

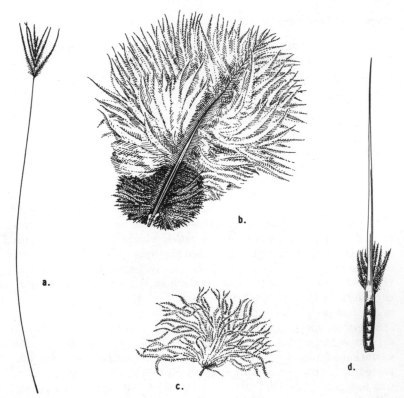

FIGURE 9.   (a) Filoplume, from Edward's Pheasant.   (b) Semiplume, from a curassow.
(c) Down, from a crane (*Grus*).   (d) Bristle: an eyelash, from a Marsh Hawk.   (By permission from *Fundamentals of Ornithology* by Josselyn Van Tyne and Andrew J.
Berger, published by John Wiley & Sons, Inc.   Copyright, 1959.)

vultures in which exposed down is found on the neck.   The young
of certain birds are completely covered by a coat of down when
they hatch.   Familiar examples of these *downy young* are ducks,
chickens, quail, pheasants, hawks, and owls.   This nestling down
differs somewhat in structure and texture from the down found in
adult birds (Figs. 10, 11).

4. *Powder downs* are specialized feathers that produce a waxy
powder that may be used to dress the plumage or to protect it
from moisture.   They differ from all other types of feathers in that
they grow continuously at their base and disintegrate at their tip
(hence the technical name of *pulviplume*) to form a continuous
supply of the powder.   Powder down feathers may grow in solid

patches (on the breast, lower back, etc.) or they may be distributed more or less throughout the plumage (as in parrots). They are seen at their best development in herons, bitterns, and tinamous.

Color of Feathers

All classes of vertebrate animals have some brightly or strikingly colored species but none has so many brilliantly colored repre-

FIGURE 10. A downy Upland Plover chick after leaving the nest. (Courtesy of Brooke Meanley.)

FIGURE 11. Two 18-day-old Turkey Vultures photographed in front of their nesting stump. (Courtesy of Walter P. Nickell.)

sentatives as the birds. In trying to identify the many kinds of "brownish" sparrows the person who begins his bird study in the Temperate Zone may be overly impressed by the number of dull-colored birds. In order to appreciate fully the range of colors in birds, one must see some of the breath-taking colors and color combinations exhibited by many birds that live in the tropical regions of the world (see Gilliard, 1958).

It usually comes as a complete surprise to the beginning student to learn that some of the most colorful of feathers contain only a black or brown pigment and that white feathers have no pigment at all. The colors in such instances are the result of the feather's structure, so that one speaks of these as *structural colors* (or *schemochromes*). "White" light or sunlight is composed of a series of light rays of different wave lengths, which we see as different colors under the proper circumstances. (Infrared and ultraviolet waves do not stimulate the retina of our eye and therefore we do not see them.) The colors of the visible spectrum range from red to violet. These and the intermediate colors are those that one sees in a rainbow; drops of water serve to "separate," in a sense, the rays so that each is visible to our eye. In a selective way, feathers function in a similar manner, except that a white feather "looks white" to us because it reflects all of the light striking it, whereas a feather looks black if it absorbs all of the light rays striking it. Not all white feathers have exactly the same structure, however, and some white feathers have a lustrous appearance while others are "chalky." When certain white feathers are placed in balsam, the feather becomes transparent because the index of refraction of the feather and that of the balsam are so nearly the same that reflection does not occur at the balsam-feather interface.

There seems to be no known blue pigment in feathers. The barbs in the blue feathers of the Blue Jay, for example, are composed of a colorless layer which reflects the blue light rays to our eyes and a deeper layer containing a dark pigment which absorbs all of the other colors.

There is a green pigment found in the feathers of the African touracos, but, so far as is known, none of the green feathers of New World birds contain any green pigment (relatively few of these many types of green feathers have been analyzed chemically, however). The green feathers of New World birds have a structure like that of the blue feathers of the Blue Jay. In addition, the outer sheath of the feather contains a yellow or a dark pigment. This combination of structure and one of these nongreen pigments results in feathers that we see as pure green or olive green.

There are many birds, of course, which have feathers whose color is primarily or entirely due to the pigments they contain. We speak of these as *pigment colors* or *biochromes*. These occur in various shades of yellow, pink, red, and brown. Available evidence suggests that some of these pigments can be synthesized by the bird, which is to say that the physiological processes of the bird can make the pigments from the raw materials in the food it eats. Some pigments, on the other hand, apparently must occur as complete pigments in the bird's food; the bird cannot manufacture them from the raw products in the food. Evidence of this often is obtained when certain birds are raised in captivity, e.g., Pine Grosbeak, Purple Finch, and Red Crossbill. When the birds undergo a molt, the new feathers usually lack the characteristic reddish or pinkish colors of the adult plumage, which is assumed to be due to a deficiency in the diet of the captive birds. It is possible, of course, that the missing element in the diet may not be a complete pigment but rather a single chemical compound that is only one of several needed in a series of steps in the complicated process of synthesizing the pigment.

We have been discussing the "normal" colors of feathers. At rare intervals, changes (mutations) take place in the germ cells (the eggs and sperm) which result in the production of feathers wholly unlike the typical feathers of the bird concerned. This change may affect a single feather, a group of feathers, or all of the feathers. One of the more common mutations produces white feathers. This abnormal absence of color is called *albinism*. A "true" or "total" albino lacks color in all structures derived from the skin as well as in the eye. In addition to having white feathers, therefore, a total albino has pale-colored tarsi, a very pale bill, and pink eyes (because the pigment is absent that ordinarily conceals the red color of the blood circulating in the eyeball). Such albinos are relatively rare in nature, but there are records of "nearly complete" albino Robins, House Sparrows, Traill's Flycatchers, Meadowlarks, etc. (Fig. 12). More common are instances referred to as incomplete, imperfect, or partial albinism.

The white feathers of albino birds appear to be weaker structurally than colored feathers. A pink-eyed albino Robin that I raised had only the barest suggestion of a pale pink suffusion on some of the breast feathers. This bird went through several apparently normal molts in captivity but the wing and tail feathers were unusually brittle. In the space of five or six weeks after the new feathers were full size, the tips of all of the flight feathers would be broken. In time the bird lost such a large part of each of the wing and tail feathers that it was unable to fly for more than a few feet along the ground. The feathers of a normal-plumaged nest mate of the albino, however, did not break at the tip but remained in excellent condition from one molt to the next.

Other mutations result in an increase of black (*melanism*), red (*erythrism*), or yellow (*xanthochroism*) pigment in the feathers. One refers to birds with such plumages as melanistic, erythristic, or xanthochroistic specimens. Melanism occurs especially in some hawks; erythrism occurs in the Prairie Chicken and in the Screech Owl in the eastern part of the United States; xanthochroism is found in parrots, but it is rare.

When such birds as ducks, geese, cranes, and phalaropes inhabit areas where the water and mud contain a high concentration of iron their feathers sometimes develop a reddish tinge. The ferric-oxide stain deposited on the feathers is lost only when the birds lose their feathers and grow new ones. This deposition of extraneous color on the feathers is called *adventitious* staining or coloring.

FIGURE 12. A "nearly complete" albino Traill's Flycatcher, one of two such birds found in a nest near Ann Arbor, Michigan.

FEATHER TRACTS

In only three groups of birds do the feathers grow more or less regularly from nearly all parts of the skin. These three are the ostrich, the penguins, and the peculiar screamers of South America. In all other birds the feathers grow from restricted areas called *tracts* or *pterylae*. The areas of bare skin (sometimes containing down feathers) between the feather tracts are called the *apteria* (sing., *apterium*). Because the apteria are concealed by the feathers, it is necessary to cut the feathers close to the skin in order to study the pattern of the tracts and the apteria that separate them.   The study of the feather tracts is called *pterylography* or *pterylosis.*

Figures 13 and 14 illustrate the feather tracts on the dorsal and the ventral surfaces of the bird.   It will be noted that, in general, the several tracts are named according to the part of the bird that they cover.   The *capital tract* includes all the feathers growing on the dorsal surface of the head.   The *spinal tract* includes all the feathers growing along the midline on the dorsal surface of the neck, back, and rump as far as (but not including) the oil gland; it is subdivided into cervical, interscapular, dorsal, and pelvic regions. The *caudal tract* is composed of the rectrices, their upper and lower coverts, the feathers of the oil gland (when present), and the anal circlet of feathers (those which surround the vent or the external opening of the digestive tube).   The *ventral tract* contains

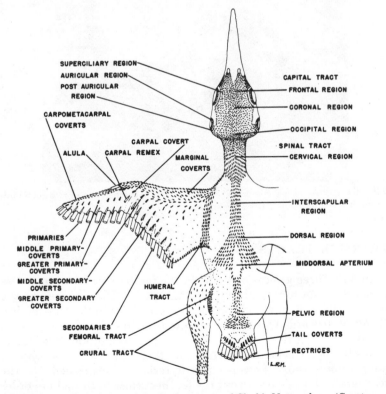

FIGURE 13.   Dorsal view of the feather tracts of Clark's Nutcracker.   (Courtesy of L. Richard Mewaldt and the editor of *The Condor.*)

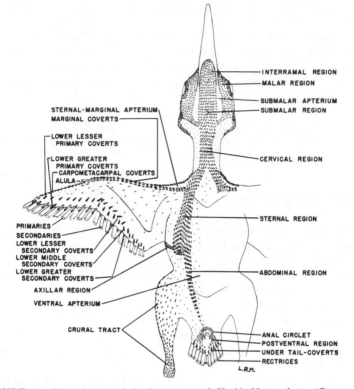

FIGURE 14.   Ventral view of feather tracts of Clark's Nutcracker.   (Courtesy of
L. Richard Mewaldt and the editor of *The Condor*.)

the feathers on the under parts of the bird; it extends from the chin
to the anal circlet; it is subdivided into interramal, malar, submalar,
cervical, sternal, axillary, and abdominal regions.   It may be noted
that the *axillars* (or axillaries) are feathers that grow in the "arm-
pit" region, which is the axillary region.   The *alar tract* is composed
of all of the feathers on the wing exclusive of those growing from
the skin over the shoulder area, which constitute the well-developed
humeral tract.   The feathers that grow from the humeral feather
tract are called the *scapulars* (or scapularies).   The scapulars and
the axillars close the space between the spread wing and the body
of the bird.   The discrete *femoral tract* contains well-developed
feathers that grow from the skin on the lateral surface of the thigh.
The *crural tract,* rather than being a single tract, includes all the
feathers that grow on the leg.

The skin of the bird is notable for the absence of skin glands (sweat and sebaceous glands). Many birds, however, do have a large gland located on the rump just anterior to the base of the tail. This is the *oil gland* or *preen gland.* Its secretion is used in "dressing" the feathers and other epidermal structures (i.e., those derived from the skin). In some birds a circlet of feathers surrounds the opening(s) of the gland to form a conspicuous brush-like tuft of feathers. Such birds have a *tufted oil gland.* In still other birds, no conspicuous feathers grow from the oil gland; these birds have a *nude oil gland.* The oil gland is absent entirely in some birds (e.g., the ostrich, some parrots, some pigeons, and some woodpeckers).

CHANGE OF FEATHERS

The tips of the feathers gradually wear or are broken off as a result of the bird's activities. If this process were to continue indefinitely, a bird eventually would lose the ability to fly and to conserve its body heat. Inasmuch as the fully grown feather is not capable of further growth, the only alternative is to lose the worn feathers and to grow new ones, and all birds grow a new set of feathers at least once each year. It should be noted at the beginning that when one speaks of the *molt* of feathers one is referring to two processes: *ecdysis* or losing the old feathers and *endysis* or growing new feathers.

Available evidence suggests that changes in the ratio of daylight to darkness as the seasons change are an important environmental factor in inducing molt. The actual physiological processes that cause the activity within the papilla at the base of the feather follicle, however, are very imperfectly understood. Once the feather reaches its maximum size and development, the cells of the papilla become quiescent until they are stimulated at the time of the next molt. If, however, a feather is accidentally or intentionally pulled out of its follicle at other times of the year a new feather will begin to grow in a very short time. The development of the new feather takes place within a horny, cylindrical sheath; the growing feather with its shiny sheath is called a *pinfeather* (sometimes also blood quill). After a certain stage of development has been reached, the tip of the sheath splits open (Fig. 15). The feather gradually assumes its definitive form as more and more of the confining sheath breaks away or is pulled off during the preening activities of the bird. The last remaining vestige of the sheath is to be found at the very base of the feather.

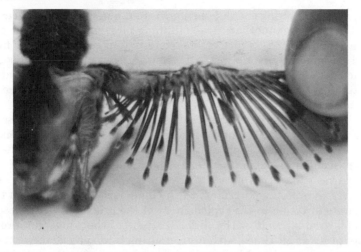

FIGURE 15.   Prairie Warbler 148 hours old, to illustrate the developing wing feathers.
(Courtesy of Val Nolan, Jr., and Duane Carmony.)

The shedding of the old feathers does not take place in a hap-
hazard manner.   It almost invariably proceeds in a definite, orderly
sequence, the pattern varying among different birds, sometimes even
among those that belong to the same family.   It has been learned,
for example, that among the many kinds of owls the large species
lose their tail feathers in pairs over an extended period of time,
whereas the small species lose all their tail feathers in a matter of
hours.   The explanation of this difference in tail molt seems to be
that the larger species are more dependent on a functional tail for
flight and for maneuverability in capturing their prey, and, therefore, that they would not be able to survive for long periods if their
flight ability was seriously handicapped by the absence of all their
tail feathers.

All birds have an even number of tail feathers, unless, of course,
one has been pulled out accidentally.   Half of the tail feathers are
attached to transverse processes on either side of the pygostyle
(the last vertebra in the spinal column).   The tail feathers are
numbered by pairs, beginning with the innermost feathers (pair
number 1).   In most birds, the tail feathers are lost in pairs,
beginning with the innermost pair and followed at fairly regular
intervals by the next succeeding pair, the outermost pair being the
last to be replaced.   This sequence of feather replacement, beginning with the innermost pair and ending with the outermost pair,
is referred to as a *centrifugal* tail molt.   A modification of this

sequence of molting the tail feathers is found in the Brown Creeper and in some woodpeckers, tree-climbing birds which use their tail as a support; in these birds the second pair of rectrices is lost first and the innermost pair is lost last. In a very few birds (such as some toucans and woodpeckers) the sequence of molt progresses from the outermost to the innermost pair of feathers, a pattern described as a *centripetal* tail molt.

Similarly, molt of the wing feathers usually begins by the loss of the innermost primary of each wing. Then, in regular sequence, the other primaries drop out and are replaced by new feathers. The secondaries begin to molt at about the time the molt of the primaries is half completed. The pattern of molt of secondaries progresses from the outermost to the innermost feathers, i.e., in the opposite direction to the replacement of the primaries. As a result of this gradual molt of the flight feathers of the wing, the bird is able to fly at all times, although molting birds characteristically become secretive and less active (especially during the late summer). There is also a fairly regular sequence of molt of the wing coverts and of the contour feathers covering the body, but it is less apparent when the molt of these feathers begins or, especially, has been completed. Exceptions to the general rule that the wing feathers are molted gradually are found among the species of certain families that are primarily aquatic in habit. Loons, grebes, anhingas, flamingos, ducks, geese, swans, most cranes and rails, and many members of the auk family lose all of their remiges at essentially the same time, and therefore are flightless until the new feathers develop to the point at which flight can be maintained.

We have pointed out that all adult birds molt their feathers at least once a year. This *annual molt* takes place at the end of the breeding season and therefore is called the *postnuptial molt*. The plumage thus acquired is the breeding plumage for the following year. In some instances the bright breeding plumage is not evident until the tips of certain feathers are worn off during the winter months. The typical black "bib" of the male House Sparrow, for example, develops as the grayish tips of the throat feathers wear off over a period of several months. The Snow Bunting offers another example of this type of "color change." The tips of the new feathers of the head and rump are brown, whereas most of each feather is white; the tips of the back feathers are brownish or buffy white, whereas most of each back feather is black. The wear of the tips of all these feathers results in a sharply contrasting breeding plumage of white on the head and rump and black on the back. Similarly, the light, speckled postnuptial plumage of the

Starling changes gradually by wear of feather tips during the winter to the iridescent black, purple, and green plumage of the breeding season.

A few species of birds have a second molt in the spring, a *prenuptial molt,* which may be either complete (i.e., involving all of the feathers) or partial (involving only the body feathers). Two examples of birds which have two molts each year are the Sharptailed Sparrow and the White-crowned Sparrow. Finally, some ptarmigan may have as many as three or four molts each year.

Although some birds are completely naked at the time of hatching (Fig. 16), the majority have some *natal* or *nestling down.* The amount of natal down varies from a complete covering (*ptilopaedic young;* as in ducks) to only a few wisps of down on the back and top of the head (*psilopaedic young;* some wrens). Typically in passerine birds, the first contour feathers (which form the *juvenal plumage*) begin their growth within a few days after hatching. As these juvenal feathers grow, remnants of the natal down continue to adhere to their tips. The juvenal plumage is short-lived. Some young sparrows, for example, begin their *postjuvenal molt* before the juvenal tail feathers have completed their growth (Sutton, 1935). The juvenal plumage is replaced by the *first winter plumage.*

FIGURE 16. A Chimney Swift less than 24 hours old. At hatching the bird weighs between 1 and 1.5 grams; it hatches from an egg that averages 1.88 grams. (Courtesy of Richard B. Fischer and the New York State Museum and Science Service.)

Often similar to the winter plumage of adult birds, the first winter plumage in some species may be duller in color or may be different in pattern from that of the adult. The *first nuptial plumage* (that worn for the bird's first breeding season) may be acquired by a partial molt of body feathers or it may result simply from the wear of feather tips. (Selected examples of these plumages and their manner of acquisition are discussed in Chapter 2.)

ECLIPSE PLUMAGE

The males of most Northern Hemisphere ducks undergo a special kind of postnuptial molt that produces an inconspicuous female-like plumage called the "eclipse plumage." During this molt the male Mallard, for example, loses all of the characteristic bright colors that make this one of the most familiar of North American ducks, the green of the head and the chestnut of the breast (see colored illustration in Kortright, 1943). There is not only a complete molt of feathers but all of the flight feathers (remiges and rectrices) are lost in a very short period of time. Consequently, the birds remain flightless until the new flight feathers have grown in. A second molt begins at about the time the bird has functional flight feathers again. This second molt (which does not involve the flight feathers) produces the typical male breeding plumage. There is much variation among the several species of ducks as to the length of time the eclipse plumage lasts and the length of time required to attain the full breeding plumage. Thus, the Mallard retains the eclipse plumage for about one month, the Blue-winged Teal for several months, and the Ruddy Duck retains a dull female-like "winter" plumage from about October to April (not all ornithologists agree that this female-like plumage is a prolonged eclipse plumage). The eclipse molt has been prevented experimentally by castrating ducks or by keeping them at abnormally low temperatures throughout the summer. Although best known in the males of Northern Hemisphere ducks, the eclipse plumage is found in the males of some Southern Hemisphere ducks, in some female ducks of both hemispheres, as well as in a few Old-world families of birds.

The beginning student is confronted by many problems in learning to identify birds in the field. This is so despite the existence of excellent illustrated guides, which actually become increasingly useful as one's experience with birds increases. Moreover, as an observer's competence in identification increases he usually begins to wonder why certain birds are grouped together and called wood-warblers or vireos, or why the Song Sparrow and the House Sparrow are placed in different families. What is the basis for cataloguing or classifying birds? The science of classification or taxonomy is a technical one, which, in its details, is beyond the scope of an introductory book on ornithology. One important goal of classification, however, is to make it easier to learn and remember information, and the student must gain some familiarity with the basic scheme used to suggest the relationships among birds.

We begin with a consideration of the category known as the *species,* or the different kinds of birds, because this is what one actually observes in the field. A bird species is a population of similar individuals that occupies a definite geographical area; the individuals of this population breed among themselves but normally not with the members of any other species. Robins,

Field Identification

Blue Jays, Cardinals, and Song Sparrows are examples of species of birds. It should be noted particularly that a species is not a single bird but rather an entire population of similar birds. The population may be very small (numbering less than 100 individuals) or it may be very large (many thousands of birds). Furthermore, although the individuals that form a species are so similar in external appearance that one can immediately recognize the kind of bird it is, we should call attention to the general "rule" that *variation is characteristic of all animals*. Not even "identical twins" are exactly alike in every respect. It is fortunate for the beginner that most of the variations exhibited by the members of a species cannot be discerned in the field. One does not, for example, encounter difficulty in recognizing a Blue Jay even though no two Blue Jays are identical in size or in the minute details of their plumage. Occasionally, however, one does see a bird that is slightly different from the "typical" representative of the species: it may be lighter or darker in color, it may exhibit larger patches of some contrasting color, etc. Whatever these differences may be, most of them fall within the *normal limits of variation* for that particular species. Therefore, a beginning student should not memorize minute detailed descriptions of birds. Instead, he needs to develop a "feeling" for what a particular species is. An elaborate and detailed technical diagnosis of birds is essential for museum and taxonomic work. For field identification it is unnecessary and, in fact, it may be a real handicap. Consequently, the most successful field guides are designed to emphasize distinctive features or "field marks," which enable one to identify a bird quickly even though it may be some distance away. Some field marks are less conspicuous than others and necessitate closer observation before positive identification can be made. Moreover, the amount of individual variation in plumage within a species varies considerably among species. One soon learns with field experience which are the more variable species (e.g., some hawks) and which species may be confused with very similar species.

The *genus,* as a taxonomic category, is a concept. It is, in part, an aid to memory. The taxonomist groups together in a genus those species of birds which seem to him to be obviously closely related because he believes that they have evolved from a common ancestor during relatively recent times. The several kinds of nuthatches (White-breasted, Red-breasted, Brown-headed, and Pigmy nuthatches), for example, are placed in the genus *Sitta* to suggest that they are closely related and that they have evolved from a common ancestor (Fig. 1). Similarly, the several kinds of crows are placed in the genus *Corvus.*

FIGURE 1. The four species of North American nuthatches. From top to bottom: White-breasted Nuthatch; Red-breasted Nuthatch; Brown-headed Nuthatch; Pigmy Nuthatch.

The next major, and more inclusive, category in the taxonomic hierarchy is the *family* (page 333). Like the genus, it is a concept and a useful cataloguing device; it is not something that one observes in the field. The taxonomist includes in a particular family all of the genera (with their respective species) of birds that he believes have evolved from a common ancestor. This is, of course, a more remote or ancient ancestor than the one mentioned in the discussion of the genus. One might stretch things a point and say that the species contained within a given genus are first cousins and that the species in the different genera that constitute a family are second cousins. Because they have a common ancestry (ancient though it may be), the various species of a family share certain basic similarities or characteristics. No other family of birds has exactly the same combination of characters. The species or kinds of birds are arranged by families in field guides, and it would seem, therefore, that the problem of bird identification must be a simple one. Such, however, is not the case for the beginning student. Some family characters are conspicuous anatomical structures that are obvious even at a distance, but these are the exceptions. More than half of all the birds of the world belong to the large group of passerine or "perching" birds (see Chapter 11). This large number of birds (over 5000 species) has been grouped into about 67 families. The differences among these families often are small, although the problems of identification are reduced when one considers only North American birds (27 families of passerine birds are included in the American Ornithologists' Union's "Check-List" of 1957).

NAMING BIRDS

Birds, as well as many other animals, have both a *common name* and a *scientific name*. The common name is, in a sense, a nickname. It is the name used in conversation and the one most often employed when discussing common birds in the field. It is a perfectly useful and acceptable name for such purposes, especially when talking about local birds. By itself it is unacceptable when writing about birds because some birds have more than one common name, and the same bird may be known by different common names in various parts of the country. To cite only one example, the Yellow-shafted Flicker is (or has been) variously known as the Golden-winged Woodpecker, Pigeon Woodpecker, High-hole, High-holder, Wake-up, Wick-up, Yellow-hammer, etc., and some of these names have also been applied to the Red-shafted Flicker.

The common name may or may not be of assistance to the beginning student as he tries to associate a name with a bird. More often than not the name is not descriptive of the bird. The name "Robin" or "Robin Redbreast" means something to most people simply because this bird is so common in residential areas of cities and towns. A Blue Jay or a Bluebird obviously must be at least partially blue in color. On the other hand, after seeing their first Green Heron, there are few students who have not asked why the bird is called "green." Nor does the name Vesper Sparrow mean much to a student who first sees and hears this bird sing at 5:00 o'clock in the morning. Birds that were named after people also are confusing (e.g., Blackburnian Warbler, Kirtland's Warbler, MacGillivray's Warbler, Townsend's Solitaire, Harris' Sparrow), as are those named after cities or states (Philadelphia Vireo, Connecticut Warbler, Kentucky Warbler, Tennessee Warbler). In instances where the common name offers no clues as to the color or pattern of the bird, Dr. Hickey (1943) has made the very pertinent suggestion that one coin his own name for temporary use until the proper name can be associated with the bird. He points out that "the two water-thrushes, for instance, could almost pass for twins. One has a yellow line over the eye, the other a white one. Many observers can never remember which has which. Try privately calling one the 'white Louisiana' for a while, and the other the 'yellow northern.' In a surprisingly short time, a once-vexing personal problem will have been permanently settled." Similarly, one might refer to Virginia's Warbler as the "pale-breasted, yellow-rumped, rufous-crowned warbler," and Lucy's Warbler as the "pale-breasted, chestnut-rumped, chestnut-crowned warbler." Wilson's Warbler might be called Wilson's "yellow-breasted warbler with the black cap." Any combination of descriptive terms, no matter how clumsy it may seem at first, will do the trick. For some birds the color, color pattern, or other characters are such that one quickly associates the bird with the right name. The process is much slower with other birds, and not all persons have problems with the same bird or group of birds.

A scientific name for each kind of bird insures the exact identity of a species not only for the ornithologists of North America but also for those of all parts of the world. The scientific name is composed of two Latin or Latinized words (often of Greek derivation). The first word of the name is the *genus* or *generic name*. It is always capitalized and italicized. Examples already used in this chapter are *Sitta* (for nuthatches) and *Corvus* (for crows). The second word in the scientific name is the *species* or *specific name;* it is always italicized but not capitalized. It tells what kind of nuthatch, for example, we are talking about. Thus, *Sitta carolinensis* is the White-breasted Nuthatch, *Sitta canadensis* is the Red-breasted Nuthatch, *Sitta pusilla* is the Brown-headed Nuthatch, and *Sitta pygmaea* is the Pigmy Nuthatch.

As is true of the common name, the parts of the scientific name may or may not be descriptive of the bird. The wood-warbler genus *Dendroica* contains a large number of species of common birds. The generic name is actually derived from two Greek words and means "a tree inhabitant." Another wood-warbler genus is *Vermivora,* which means "worm-eating." Inasmuch as many birds are "tree inhabitants" and "worm eaters," the names *Dendroica* and *Vermivora* may be of little help to the beginning student. Similarly, the specific name may give no clues as to the characters of the bird, e.g., *Dendroica pensylvanica* for the Chestnut-sided Warbler. The Latin word *vireo* means "I am green." Unaltered it becomes the generic name *Vireo,* which contains several species of the vireo family. The participial form is often used as the species name: *virens* or *virescens.* Examples are *Empidonax virescens,* Acadian Flycatcher; *Contopus virens,* Eastern Wood Pewee; *Dendroica virens,* Black-throated Green Warbler; and *Icteria virens,* Yellow-breasted Chat. More helpful are those instances where the common name expresses more nearly the meaning of the specific name. A good example is that of the Golden-cheeked Warbler (*Dendroica chrysoparia*). The specific name *chrysoparia* is derived from two Greek words that mean "gold cheek." The specific name *flaviventris* is formed from the Latin words *flavus* (yellow) and *venter* or *ventris* (belly or pertaining to the belly), and is descriptive of the Yellow-bellied Flycatcher (*Empidonax flaviventris*).

GEOGRAPHICAL RANGE

In the fifth edition (1957) of its "Check-List," the American Ornithologists' Union includes 75 families of birds with representatives that live in North America (for the exact area included, see page iv of the "Check-List"). The part of North America inhabited by the species of these families varies greatly (Fig. 2). Some families are represented essentially throughout the entire area. Still other families or genera merit recognition because one or two species are found in Alaska, in southern Texas or Arizona a short distance north of the Mexican border, etc. Furthermore, although a family may be represented by many species of birds in the United States, there may be large areas of the country in which there is a single species, or even none at all. Thus, of the many species of hummingbirds found in the United States, only the Ruby-throated Hummingbird is to be expected (regularly) east of the Great Plains. The problem of hummingbird identification is much different for the student in the Pacific Coast States, therefore, than it is for those who live east of the Mississippi River. This leads up to the simple statement that one of the first steps for the beginning

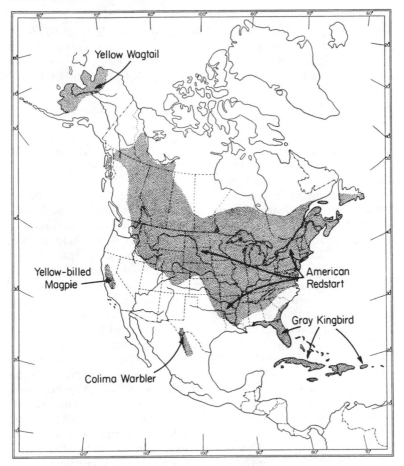

FIGURE 2. Approximate breeding ranges of five selected species. The Yellow Wagtail has a very extensive distribution in the Old World (from Scotland to northern
Siberia). The exact winter range of the Alaskan Yellow Wagtails remains unknown,
but the birds migrate across the Bering Strait and southward down the Pacific coast
of Asia.

student is to find out what birds he should expect to see in his
locality.

The student can learn a great deal by studying the ranges given
for each species in either of Roger Tory Peterson's *Field Guides*
(1941, 1947) and compiling therefrom a list of the species he might
reasonably expect to find in his own area. A second, less time-con-
suming, approach to this problem is to obtain a check-list of the

birds of his state, which usually is published under the auspices of the state university or museum. It may be possible, also, to obtain a list of the birds that have been found in some restricted area within the state. Such lists often are published in the journal of the state Audubon Society (see Pettingill, 1956, Appendix G).

SEASONAL OCCURRENCE

Because many species of birds migrate in the autumn, the beginning student in the northern part of the United States has fewer birds to learn during the winter months. Ideally this might be the best time to begin bird study. Even during this period, however, the student must learn to distinguish between two general groups of birds: *permanent residents* and *winter residents* (or visitants). Permanent residents are those species which do not migrate but remain in a restricted area throughout their lives. If these species are learned during the winter, they will be old friends by the next breeding season. Winter residents are species which have nested in more northern regions (or at higher elevations in mountains), and which may have completed a relatively short migration; these birds will migrate northward again for the next breeding season.

The spring migration may take place over a period of several months, perhaps from February until early June, depending on the part of the country. Some of the many species of returning birds will remain to nest in the locality; these are *summer residents*. These and permanent residents are the birds that the student should first concentrate on learning. Other species will linger for only a few days (or weeks) and then will continue their migration to a nesting ground further north; these species will be known only as *migrants*. Probably the greatest problems in identification will be encountered with some of the migrants because they are seen for such a short period each year. Finally, brief mention should be made of *stragglers* or *accidentals*, individual birds which at rare intervals are found far away from the usual range of the species. The discovery of one of these birds is cause for great excitement among those bird watchers whose primary goal is to compile a large "life list" of birds seen, but the rare appearance of accidentals is not important biologically. Because of the great possibility of misidentification, most professional ornithologists, and especially those who are responsible for compiling accurate lists of the birds of an area, insist that proof of occurrence of accidentals be based on collected specimens.

WHERE TO FIND BIRDS

A check-list, as the name implies, usually consists only of a list of the birds that have been found in a given region. It may, in addition, tell how common or rare each species is and at what time of year it may be expected to occur. It does not tell where to look for the birds. The different kinds of birds found in a locality are not evenly distributed throughout the area. Most of the species exhibit a definite preference for a particular type of environment or habitat in which to live. One does not expect to find a Scarlet Tanager in a corn field nor a Savannah Sparrow in deep woods. Another step for the beginner, therefore, is to learn where to look for birds (Figs. 3, 4).

The field trips conducted as a part of an introductory course in ornithology are scheduled so that the student is introduced to the several major types of bird habitats in his community. In this way he learns what birds generally inhabit open water, cattail marshes, grassy fields, deep woods, desert areas, mountain slopes, etc., de-

FIGURE 3. A slash pine (*Pinus caribaea*) bog with pitcher plants (*Sarracenia flava*) in southern Georgia. This is the breeding habitat for the Red-cockaded Woodpecker, Brown-headed Nuthatch, Bachman's Sparrow, and Pine Warbler. (Courtesy of Brooke Meanley.)

FIGURE 4. A shrub-grown field in southern Michigan, where hawthorn (*Crataegus*) is the dominant plant. Typical nesting birds are Mourning Dove, Traill's Flycatcher, Catbird, Cedar Waxwing, Yellow Warbler, American Goldfinch, and Field Sparrow.

pending on the part of the country concerned. By listing the species seen on each field trip, one begins to realize that some species are restricted to one special habitat, whereas other species may be found in several habitats. In much of southern Michigan, for example, the Cerulean Warbler nests only in heavy deciduous woods; the bird is irregular in distribution, however, and it is not found in every woods that looks suitable to the observer. By contrast, the Song Sparrow is found in nearly all southern Michigan habitats: in towns, in thickets along highways, in bush-grown fields, along fence rows, in marsh areas, and in woods. (A more detailed analysis of bird habitats is presented in Chapter 3.)

WHEN TO FIND BIRDS

Teachers of ornithology traditionally have introduced the beginning student to the subject by insisting that field trips begin at some unreasonably early hour, such as 5:00 o'clock in the morning. The basis for this unappreciated tradition is that most birds are very active for several hours after daybreak and they may be more conspicuous because most species sing persistently during this period. To the neophyte, however, this great chorus of bird song may be confusing and discouraging, especially if there has not been time for breakfast before the field trip. Moreover, during the winter or during the breeding season, one can find birds just as well (and sometimes better) at other times of the day. We may cite as an example Henslow's Sparrow, one of the small, inconspicuous sparrows that is often difficult to locate. The life history of this bird has not been studied intensively, and there are many puzzling features about its breeding biology. Henslow's Sparrow not only tends to move from one breeding habitat to another in succeeding years but it appears to move from one field to another even during the same breeding season. Nevertheless, there is a relatively simple way to find the birds. In addition to some daytime singing, this sparrow characteristically sings persistently at night as well. Perhaps the easiest way to find breeding populations of Henslow's Sparrows is to listen for their distinctive song as one drives slowly along country roads after sundown and well into the night. Two other nighttime singers that may be found in the same way are the Grasshopper Sparrow and the Short-billed Marsh Wren. Owls and other birds that are primarily nocturnal in habit are, of course, most difficult to observe. The nighthawks, however, become active near sundown and some are still active at daybreak; on dark, cloudy days they sometimes fly about in search of food, giving their characteristic calls. The Whip-poor-will and its relatives generally begin their singing after darkness has fallen. Often one may actually see these birds by driving slowly along unimproved rural roads or lanes and watching for the orange "eye shine" as the car lights, piercing the darkness, strike the bird's eyes. It is sometimes possible to get very close to a Whip-poor-will in this way, and even to catch it if one approaches slowly while shining a powerful light on the bird.

LEARNING BIRD SOUNDS

The experienced field ornithologist depends on his ears as well as his eyes to tell him what birds are in an area. In fact, such relatively common birds as the Acadian Flycatcher, Blue-winged Warbler, Grasshopper Sparrow, and Henslow's Sparrow often are very difficult to locate unless one is familiar with their songs. These birds may go virtually unknown as summer residents in areas where bird students depend on their eyes alone. Some other birds, even when seen, may not be identified accurately unless one hears their song or sees their nests (Fig. 5). This is true for three small fly-

FIGURE 5.   An Acadian Flycatcher at its nest.   (Courtesy of Samuel A. Grimes.)

catchers: Acadian Flycatcher, Traill's Flycatcher, and Least Flycatcher.   The difficulty in identifying these flycatchers is not
limited to birds seen in the field.   At one time I raised in captivity
an Acadian, a Traill's, and a Yellow-bellied Flycatcher.   Several
well-known American ornithologists were uncertain as to which was
which as the birds moved about silently less than 10 feet away.   Had
the birds been singing, each species would have been identified in-
stantly.   Similar difficulties must be overcome in learning to
recognize the several species of *Empidonax* flycatchers found in the
western part of the United States (Traill's, Hammond's, Dusky,
Gray, and Western flycatchers).

Perhaps the main prerequisite for learning bird songs is the desire
to know them.   One gets nowhere by saying "I can't learn bird
songs."   It is true that some people are much more attuned to bird
songs than others and seem to learn them both faster and with less
effort.   Some songs are so distinctive that one needs to hear them
only a few times before one can name the unseen bird with assur-

ance. Other songs are much more difficult to learn. In such instances there is no adequate substitute for listening to a particular song for extended periods of time each day until one quickly associates the song with the bird. Phonograph recordings are also helpful for learning confusing songs.

The Robin, the Scarlet Tanager, and the Rose-breasted Grosbeak belong to three different families, are entirely unlike in plumage, but have similar songs. The tanager's song has been characterized, in part, as being like that of a Robin "with a sore throat," and the grosbeak's song as being "Robin-like but sweeter and more liquid." Considerable experience is necessary to separate the three songs when they are heard in the same woods. It may be especially trying for the student who has not yet learned to expect the Robin in the woods as well as in residential areas in towns. Three species of birds that belong to the same family and that sing similar songs are the Mockingbird, the Catbird, and the Brown Thrasher. The songs of all three birds consist of a series of notes and phrases that are similar in quality. The notes and phrases in the Catbird song are not repeated; those of the thrasher usually are given twice; and those of the Mockingbird are repeated rapidly several times. Written or verbal attempts to point out differences or similarities between songs are helpful but they mean little until the student can listen to the songs. Descriptions dealing with differences in quality (e.g., the Scarlet Tanager and the Rose-breasted Grosbeak) are especially unsatisfactory unless the songs can be heard and compared in the field.

I have known students who could recognize most of the summer resident birds by their songs but who had great difficulty separating the songs of the Vesper Sparrow and the Song Sparrow, two birds whose songs seem entirely unlike to my ear. Other students continually are confused by the songs of the Baltimore Oriole, the Indigo Bunting, or the American Goldfinch. Thus it would seem that birds' songs do not sound the same to all of us, and it is partly for this reason that descriptions of bird songs often are of little help to the beginning student. Several methods have been devised to convey such information to others.

Musicians, who automatically visualize a series of sounds as notes on a staff, may benefit by using the method of musical notation for recording bird songs. The method is unsatisfactory for most ornithologists and is used by very few. A. A. Allen (1930: 399) used a series of symbols (circles, lines, dashes, dots), accompanied by words or syllables where possible, to describe songs; Hickey (1943) described this method as a "rough kind of musical shorthand."

Saunders (1951) used a more elaborate graphic method, which included phonetic interpretations and descriptive words (Fig. 6). Although Saunder's method was carefully conceived after studying bird songs for many years, its value for most people is problematical, and some have difficulty interpreting the graphic representation even after they know the bird's song.

Word descriptions and phonetic interpretations are sometimes helpful in learning songs. To some observers the song of the Ovenbird sounds like *teacher, teacher, teacher, teacher,* with each succeeding phrase being louder than the preceding one. *Witchity-witchity-witchity-witch* conveys to some people the nature of the song of some male Yellowthroats in parts of the species' range. Perhaps because we were taught that it is so, most people hear the Bobwhite, the Whip-poor-will, and the Eastern Wood Pewee sing their own names.

Birds utter a large variety of sounds that are shorter than songs and that are referred to as *call notes.* According to the function they serve, these are classified as alarm notes, location notes, greeting notes, intimidation notes, food calls, gathering calls, etc. It is, in general, much more difficult to learn call notes than it is to learn bird songs. The alarm notes given by many birds are nearly identical, and it probably is not possible to identify all of them; others can be learned after one has had considerable experience. Fortunately, there are several welcome exceptions of birds that do have distinctive call notes, e.g., the Veery's *phew,* the Scarlet Tanager's *chick-kurr,* the American Goldfinch's *swi-siieee,* the Rose-breasted Grosbeak's *eek,* the Rufous-sided Towhee's *chewink,* and the Grasshopper Sparrow's peculiar two-syllabled *til-lic* alarm note.

Although of minor importance for purposes of identification, some birds produce mechanical sounds which may be diagnostic for the species. An excellent example is offered by certain sounds produced by the male American Woodcock during its spring courtship flights. The evening flights begin shortly after sundown. The bird follows a spiral course as it flies to a considerable height, there to circle erratically for a short time. Then by a series of zigzag swoops, the return to earth is made very rapidly, the bird alighting very close to the spot from which the performance began. During the upward flight the bird produces a mechanical sound—which has been described as a "chippering trill"—as the air rushes between modified primary feathers. Other sounds accompanying the flight are made by the bird's "voice box." While perched on the ground between flights, the bird gives a nasal "beep" call, which superficially is similar to the call of the Common Nighthawk, and stu-

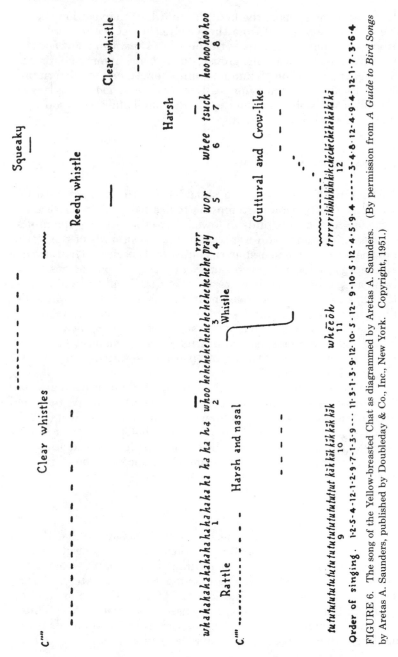

FIGURE 6.   The song of the Yellow-breasted Chat as diagrammed by Aretas A. Saunders.   (By permission from *A Guide to Bird Songs* by Aretas A. Saunders, published by Doubleday & Co., Inc., New York.   Copyright, 1951.)

dents sometimes report the first nighthawk of the year long before
the birds have returned from their winter home.   Other birds that
produce mechanical sounds as the air passes between flight feathers
are ducks, quail, pheasants, grouse, doves, some hummingbirds, and
the nighthawk.   The "Thunder-pump" or American Bittern produces its deep, far-carrying call of *oong-ka-choonk* as it goes
through a series of contortions while alternately filling its esophagus
with air and then releasing it.

VISUAL HELPS

Theoretically, at least, one should learn the characteristics of
each bird family before attempting to use a field guide.   Rarely is
this plan for learning birds followed, however, even by the professional ornithologist whose special interest is in birds of the world.
For the most part, one first learns individual species.   Then as more
and more species of a given family are learned, one begins to develop a concept of the characteristics of that family.   In discussing
the various aids to field identification, therefore, I have often de-
liberately selected examples of birds that are distantly related in
order to demonstrate that one usually does not depend on the
family characters but instead one notes conspicuous color characters (or other features) that often occur repeatedly in different
bird families.
The most commonly used clues for field identification are concerned with size, shape and proportion, color, color pattern, and
special features of the bill, head, wings, tail, and legs or feet (Fig. 7).
Often of equal importance to these external physical characters,
however, is the behavior of the bird; the experienced field ornithologist can identify many birds from a distance by the pattern of
their flight.

Size

Only a little field work is necessary to demonstrate that the size
of a bird is an important field clue.   Size is apt to be one of the most
perplexing matters for the beginning student because one needs
some experience before one can estimate size accurately.   Nearly
everyone is familiar with the House Sparrow, the Robin, and the
Crow, so that these birds often are used as a "yardstick."   Thus, a
particular unidentified bird may be the size of a Robin, or it may
be larger than a sparrow but smaller than a Robin, etc.   When a

bird is some distance away, however, size is often deceptive. A good example is offered by the Greater Yellowlegs and the Lesser Yellowlegs, two birds which are nearly identical except for size. When seen together, the difference in size is conspicuous; but when a single bird of either species is seen in a situation where its size cannot be compared with that of some other bird, positive identification may not be possible unless one knows that the calls of the two species are diagnostic. The Common Raven is almost twice as bulky as the Common Crow, but this difference may not be evident if only one or the other of these species is seen at a distance. The two species can be separated in flight by the shape of the tail and the position of the wings when the birds are soaring: the Raven has a wedge-shaped tail and holds its wings in a nearly horizontal position when soaring; the Crow has a square-tipped tail and holds its wings tilted upward when soaring. Other pairs of species that may present problems when observed under adverse field condi-

FIGURE 7.   A Black-necked Stilt at its nest with eggs; bill, color pattern, and very long red legs make this an easy bird to identify. (Courtesy of Samuel A. Grimes.)

tions because they differ primarily in size are the King Rail and Virginia Rail, the Herring Gull and Ring-billed Gull, the Hairy Woodpecker and Downy Woodpecker, and the Cedar Waxwing and Bohemian Waxwing.

Shape

Many waterbirds, especially during migration, must be identified at such a distance that colors and special field marks are not discernible. Shape, proportions, or posture as seen in silhouette may then be of paramount importance. It seems safe to assume that everyone can recognize a duck, and that it is common knowledge that most ducks are primarily aquatic birds. Not all swimming birds are ducks, however. Therefore, one needs to learn the distinguishing shapes or silhouettes of ducks, loons, grebes, cormorants, coots, murres, phalaropes, etc. (Fig. 8). Following are examples of keys to identification of some of these birds when seen on water. The several species of loons vary in size from that of a large duck

FIGURE 8. Birds of a sea coast. In the air, left to right: Parasitic Jaeger, Black Skimmer, Common Tern, Gannet, Fulmar, Herring Gull. On the water, left to right: Brown Pelican, Cormorant, Common Merganser, Common Loon, Common Eider. (By permission from *A Laboratory and Field Manual of Ornithology* by Olin Sewall Pettingill, Jr., published by Burgess Publishing Company. Copyright, 1956.)

to that of a small goose. Loons are large-bodied birds that float or swim low in the water; they have relatively short, stout necks and their sharply pointed bills are held nearly parallel to the surface of the water. With the exception of the Western Grebe, which has a very long neck, grebes are not only much smaller than loons but they are short-bodied and have relatively longer and more slender necks. When grebes are alarmed, they quickly sink under the surface of the water, sometimes so rapidly that it looks as though they had been pulled under by their feet. Ducks, on the other hand, dive head first into the water, or take flight, when alarmed. The cormorants are large birds that, like loons and unlike geese, swim low in the water, but their longer, snake-like necks are held more erect and the bill is pointed upward rather than being held parallel to the surface. The three species of mergansers have more slender bills than other ducks and sometimes are confused with loons or cormorants. All of the mergansers except the male Common Merganser, however, have a feathered crest on the top of the head, and the bill shape of the mergansers is unlike that of the loons. Each of these groups of birds also can be identified by special characters in flight. Both loons and grebes, for example, have short tails, and both look hunch-backed in flight because their neck and feet slope downward from the curve of the back. However, in addition to being smaller than loons, most grebes display large patches of white in the wings when flying. A merganser holds its head, neck, body, and tail in a horizontal plane in flight; cormorants also fly with extended necks but both neck and tail are much longer than in the mergansers.

Differences in bill size or bill shape often may be important either at close range or at a distance. The White Pelican and the Trumpeter Swan may be confused if they are not flying or are seen from a distance unless one knows that the pelican has a long, flat bill and the swan has a very long neck and relatively small bill. The Downy and Hairy woodpeckers are almost identical in plumage pattern, and when they are seen separately it may be difficult to decide whether the bird is the "large one" or the "small one." The larger Hairy Woodpecker, however, has proportionately a much heavier and longer bill than the Downy Woodpecker. The shrikes and the Mockingbird are superficially alike in plumage pattern, especially in flight. The Mockingbird has a slimmer body, a longer tail, larger wing patches, and a more slender and pointed bill than the chunky, larger-headed, shorter-tailed shrikes, whose thick bills are hooked at the tip.

Color

Color of the plumage may be the only clue necessary for identification. Because most people have not developed their powers of observation and discrimination, however, they tend to see only the brightest color, and often they are not able to report later where the color occurred on the bird. The trained ornithologist knows, and the beginning student soon learns, that the report of a "red" bird means that the untrained observer might have seen a Cardinal, a Scarlet Tanager, a Summer Tanager, a Pine Grosbeak, a Red Crossbill, a Purple Finch, a House Finch, or a Vermilion Flycatcher, depending upon the part of the country concerned. Only after study does one learn that of these "red" birds only the male Summer Tanager is essentially all red and that it does not have a feathered crest on the top of the head. The male Cardinal has a prominent crest as well as a black face patch. The brilliant male Scarlet Tanager has black wings and tail. The male Vermilion Flycatcher, which is found only in the southwestern part of the United States, has a blackish back as well as wings and tail, and it is entirely unlike the Scarlet Tanager in body build, in behavior, and in habitat preference. One could contrast in a similar manner each of the species mentioned above with respect to bill shape, body proportions, behavior, habitat preference, and range of occurrence. By knowing what birds to expect in a given area and by studying colored pictures, one soon learns these "key" characters for identifying the "red" birds. This may seem so obvious as to be ridiculous, but it sums up the typical problem faced by the beginning bird watcher. A similar example is offered by the various "blue" birds: Blue Jay, Steller's Jay, Scrub Jay, Piñon Jay, Mexican Jay, Indigo Bunting, Lazuli Bunting, Blue Grosbeak, Eastern Bluebird, Western Bluebird, Mountain Bluebird, and Cerulean Warbler.

Field Marks

A "field mark," in the broad sense, may be any plumage pattern or any special feature of the head, bill, wings, tail, or "legs," or even a behavior pattern; several examples of such characters have already been mentioned (Figs. 9, 10). In general, however, one commonly thinks of a field mark as being some striking color pattern. Despite the wide variety of colors and color patterns exhibited by birds, pigments of contrasting colors tend to be concentrated in certain areas. The chief areas are the crown of the head, the cheeks, the throat, the sides of the neck, the sides of the

FIGURE 9. A Brown Pelican at nest with young; note the large bill and gular pouch. (Courtesy of Samuel A. Grimes.)

body, the shoulders and wings, and the rump and tail. This list does not exhaust the possibilities, however, and the following special features may be added: eye ring, eye line, superciliary ("eyebrow") line, "mustache" or "whisker" marks, breast color, breast bands, and back color or pattern. Moreover, there are special instances which do not fit precisely into any one of these categories or which combine several of them. Nevertheless, it is the occurrence of feathers of contrasting color in any one or more of these areas which most frequently serves as a field mark.

A brightly colored crown patch that contrasts sharply with the rest of the head is found in a number of unrelated birds. In some birds, the patch is small and it may be concealed by surrounding feathers most of the time, as in the Eastern, Western, Cassin's, and Gray kingbirds. Differences in the tails of these four kingbirds provide good clues for field identification where the ranges of some of them overlap. The Eastern Kingbird has a conspicuous transverse white band across the end of the tail; the Western Kingbird has narrow white margins along the length of the tail; similar to the last species in many respects, Cassin's Kingbird lacks the white

FIGURE 10. A group of Wood Ibises in Florida. Although called an "ibis," this is the only North American representative of the stork family. (Courtesy of Samuel A. Grimes.)

margins on the tail; the Gray Kingbird has a black, notched tail. Two wood-warblers with a usually concealed crown patch are the Orange-crowned and Nashville warblers. In many species, however, the crown patch is conspicuous at all times, as in Swainson's Warbler, Chestnut-sided Warbler, Palm Warbler, Ovenbird, Wilson's Warbler, Green-tailed Towhee, White-crowned Sparrow, Tree Sparrow, Chipping Sparrow, and Swamp Sparrow.

A contrasting rump patch is sometimes useful for identifying birds when on the ground, in a tree, or in flight. Some examples are the Marsh Hawk, Killdeer, the flickers, Cliff Swallow, and Magnolia Warbler. A few species of birds (Virginia's and Lucy's warblers; Colima Warbler; Myrtle and Audubon's warblers) have both bright crown patches and rump patches. If two closely related species have the same crown and rump coloring, as is true for Audubon's and Myrtle warblers, one needs a third character in order to distinguish between the two: the Myrtle Warbler has a white throat; Audubon's Warbler has a yellow throat.

Conspicuous eye rings, eye lines (or patches), superciliary lines, and wing bars frequently provide the necessary clue for separating two or more similar species. The several species of vireos, for example, can be divided into two general groups: (1) those that have conspicuous wing bars—Black-capped, White-eyed, Hutton's, Yellow-throated, and Solitary vireos, and (2) those that either lack wing bars entirely or that have indistinct ones—Bell's, Gray, Black-whiskered, Red-eyed, Philadelphia, and Warbling vireos (Fig. 11). Most of the vireos have either a distinct superciliary line or a combination of an eye ring and an eye line that forms "spectacles." In general, the species that have wing bars also have spectacles; those that lack wing bars have a superciliary line (or an incomplete or inconspicuous eye ring). Final identification of the vireos depends on a knowledge of the distinctive features of each species, which may be the color of the head, eye, throat, spectacles, or superciliary line, or even differences in the habitat occupied during the breeding season.

FIGURE 11. A Black-whiskered Vireo at its nest. (Courtesy of Samuel A. Grimes.)

We have already mentioned wing patches that are conspicuous during flight in most grebes, in shrikes, and in the Mockingbird. Among the many other examples that might be cited are these: the scaup ducks, the Bufflehead, White-winged Dove, the nighthawks, the Pauraque, the magpies, Phainopepla, and the Lark Bunting. The two species of cuckoos frequently are seen in rapid flight across a road or from one thicket to another. Such a brief glimpse of one of these birds usually is sufficient for making an accurate identification because the Yellow-billed Cuckoo displays a large area of rufous color in the wings during flight, whereas the Black-billed Cuckoo does not. An even larger number of species have some contrasting color (often white) in the tail. The best field mark for the Vesper Sparrow is its white outer tail feathers. When in winter plumage, differences in voice and in the pattern of tail coloration offer the only reliable clues to identification of the several species of longspurs.

All birds sometimes raise their crown feathers but only a few land birds have a conspicuous feathered crest on the top of the head, so that it is easy to learn this small group: Scaled Quail, Belted Kingfisher, Pileated Woodpecker, Ivory-billed Woodpecker, Blue Jay, Steller's Jay, the several species of titmice, waxwings, Phainopepla, Cardinal, and Pyrrhuloxia. A few species have tufts of feathers that stand up to form "horns" or "ears" (Great Horned, Long-eared, and Screech owls; Horned Lark), and some have characteristic plumes that project upward from the head (California, Gambel's, and Mountain quail), or that extend backward over the neck (as in some herons).

Behavior

Very often one can identify a species, or can determine what family it belongs to, simply by observing its actions (Fig. 12). In their search for food, woodpeckers, nuthatches, and creepers climb on the trunks or larger branches of trees but each group goes about this in a different manner. Woodpeckers and creepers typically fly from the higher part of one tree to the base of another tree, where they begin to work up the trunk, using their tails for support. Creepers usually follow a fairly tight spiral course around the trunk; woodpeckers climb upward over the bark in a more deliberate manner, sometimes confining their actions to one side of the tree, at other times gradually moving around it. Woodpeckers, unlike creepers, however, frequently stop their ascent and back down the trunk tail first. Nuthatches not only climb or walk up a trunk

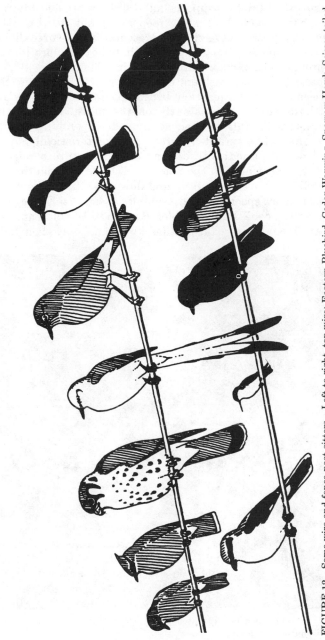

FIGURE 12. Some wire and fence-post sitters. Left to right, top wire: Eastern Bluebird, Cedar Waxwing, Sparrow Hawk, Scissor-tailed Flycatcher, Robin, Eastern Kingbird, Red-winged Blackbird. Bottom wire: Loggerhead Shrike, Ruby-throated Hummingbird, Purple Martin, Barn Swallow, Tree Swallow, Starling. (By permission from *A Laboratory and Field Manual of Ornithology* by Olin Sewall Pettingill, Jr., published by Burgess Publishing Company. Copyright, 1956.)

(without using their tail for support) but also climb head downward, something that woodpeckers and creepers do not do (Fig. 13). One does not have to observe these representatives of three different families of birds very long to realize that they also are totally unlike in proportions, in color pattern, and in bill shape.

Most species of wood-warblers can be distinguished from the vireos, especially during migration, because the wood-warblers are "nervous" birds that are constantly on the move, whereas the vireos are more deliberate in their actions, often perching quietly for a short time. The tyrant-flycatchers characteristically sit on an exposed perch, periodically darting out to capture a passing insect, and then returning to the perch. All birds at some time or other "twitch" or move the tail up and down, but this behavior is exaggerated in a few species. Four examples of such "tail-waggers" are the Eastern Phoebe, Palm Warbler, Kirtland's Warbler, and the Water or American Pipit. Rather than "wagging" only their tails,

FIGURE 13. A Brown-headed Nuthatch at the entrance to its nesting cavity. (Courtesy of Samuel A. Grimes.)

the waterthrushes and the Spotted Sandpiper rapidly lower and raise the entire back end of the body, an action called "teetering." Adult Dippers, as well as young birds recently out of the nest, bob up and down as though their legs were springs; the entire body is lowered and raised as the bird alternately bends and then extends its legs. The phalaropes have a peculiar habit when feeding of swimming rapidly in a very small circle, all the time dabbing their bills into the water.

Differences in the pattern of flight often are of great aid to identification (Fig. 14). Not only does the Chimney Swift look like a "flying cigar" but its relatively long, narrow, and pointed wings are beat very rapidly in what appears to be a jerky manner. The flight of a swallow, with its long but more triangular-shaped wings, is much more graceful. Swifts usually fly at a considerable height above ground, whereas swallows often fly low over fields or bodies of water. One rarely sees swallows in towns and cities during the breeding season, but swifts and nighthawks may be common then and both may be seen flying overhead in the evening. The nighthawk is a much larger bird than the swift and it has a long, rather than a very short, tail; its flight is slow and leisurely. After the wings have been flapped several times, there follows a short glide with wings outstretched, after which the wings are flapped again. The Lesser or Texas Nighthawk, as well as Common Nighthawks that inhabit wilderness areas, often fly very close to the ground (or water), barely skimming over the tops of bushes or shrubs. In any habitat, the flight of the nighthawk is distinctive.

The Eastern Kingbird is one of the tyrant-flycatchers that has a distinctive flight pattern. At times its stiff and rapidly quivering wings are held below an imaginary horizontal plane through the body, which creates an effect that Roger Tory Peterson describes as flying on the "tips of its wings." Some birds swoop up and down through the air as though they were following alternately the crest of a wave and then the trough between waves. Notable examples of birds that have such an undulating flight are most woodpeckers, nuthatches, pipits, and goldfinches. The meadowlarks have an entirely different flight pattern in which there is an alternation of a short series of rapid wing beats followed by a period of gliding. Marsh Hawks and Sparrow Hawks often hover in mid-air before dropping to earth after prey, and kingfishers similarly hover before plunging into water after fish. Storks, ibises, limpkins, and cranes fly with their necks and legs fully extended, whereas herons and bitterns fly with their necks retracted or folded back toward their shoulders.

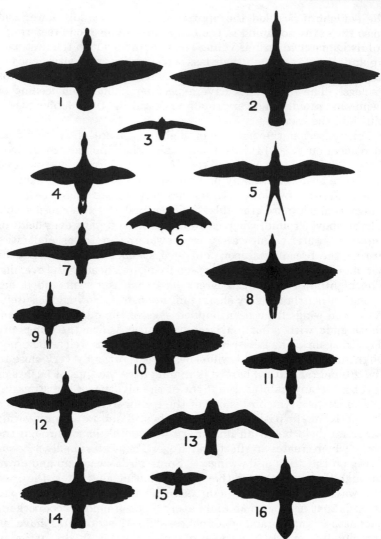

FIGURE 14. Outlines of flying birds. 1. Redhead. 2. Common Merganser. 3. Chimney Swift. 4. Pied-billed Grebe. 5. Forster's Tern. 6. Big Brown Bat. 7. Black-bellied Plover. 8. American Coot. 9. Virginia Rail. 10. Screech Owl. 11. Black-billed Cuckoo. 12. Mourning Dove. 13. Common Nighthawk. 14. Belted Kingfisher. 15. Purple Finch. 16. Common Grackle. (By permission from *A Laboratory and Field Manual of Ornithology* by Olin Sewall Pettingill, Jr., published by Burgess Publishing Company. Copyright, 1956.)

The flight of a cuckoo is swift and direct, as is that of the House Sparrow. It is not uncommon to find House Sparrows and Song Sparrows perched on telephone wires or fences in rural areas; the flight pattern of each species is so distinctive that each can be identified when seen only in silhouette. Four other species of sparrows that sometimes nest in the same field usually can be identified by their flight pattern. When an observer frightens or "flushes" a Vesper Sparrow from the ground, the bird darts upward and flies off in a more or less straight line for a considerable distance, more often than not alighting in a tree or bush rather than returning to the ground. The Grasshopper Sparrow has a peculiar fluttering type of flight, stays much closer to the ground, and, after a short flight, suddenly drops into the grass again. The Savannah Sparrow also drops quickly into the grass but does so after a swift and erratic flight, which is sometimes almost zigzag in pattern. I cannot improve on Dr. George M. Sutton's (1928: 180–181) inimitable description of the flight of Henslow's Sparrow: "The tail and rump twist or twirl in a peculiar and very characteristic way, just a second or two after the bird has flushed or left its perch. This twisting motion seems to be accompanied by a temporary change in the beat of the wings, and gives the impression that the propellant power ceases for an instant, while the bird rearranges its body."

CONFUSING PROBLEMS

In the discussion of field aids, the several species have been treated as though the male and female always are alike in plumage pattern. Although this is true for some birds, there are many species in which this is not the case; these instances add to the student's confusion. Therefore one needs to learn which species exhibit *sexual dimorphism* in plumage, i.e., those in which the male and female are dissimilar in color or other features of the plumage. Among the many species of birds exhibiting sexual dimorphism, the male usually has the brighter plumage but the female phalarope is more brightly colored than the male. Dimorphism also may be expressed as a difference in size; the male often is larger but among hawks, owls, and phalaropes the females usually are larger than the males. The color pattern of young birds may be similar or dissimilar to that of the adults, but in general the juvenal plumage of both sexes is dull or inconspicuously marked and is similar to that of the adult female (Fig. 15).

FIGURE 15.   An adult and several immature White Ibises.   (Courtesy of Samuel A. Grimes.)

Table 1 presents information on plumage patterns.   Such a table is useful as a general summary, but it should be emphasized that the degree of difference between male and female plumages may be very striking or may be very small.   When the dimorphism is striking, it is usually the female plumage that confuses the student.   So many patterns are found among birds that the placement of some species in a reasonably short and simple table is to some extent an arbitrary one.   For example, one may consider the Catbird a "colorful" species (as is done here) or as one that is "never brilliant."   Male and female Robins are similar in plumage but all colors usually are darker in males.   Male and female Belted Kingfishers are *similar* but the female has two breast bands, whereas the male has a single breast band.

Dimorphic Species

In order to understand the plumages of dimorphic species, one must consider the molts by which their plumages are acquired (Table 2).   A good example is the Scarlet Tanager.   In the fully

TABLE 1*
Sexual, Seasonal, and Age Differences in Plumage Coloration

1. Sexes alike throughout the year; never brilliant; immature† birds like adults: Brown Creeper; many tyrant-flycatchers; wrens; most thrashers; Brown Towhee; Grasshopper, Tree, Chipping, Vesper, Fox, Swamp, Lincoln's, and Song sparrows.

2. Sexes similar, colorful or strikingly marked throughout the year:
   a. juvenal plumage dull, inconspicuously marked, and/or unlike adult— Red-headed Woodpecker, waxwings, Verdin, Robin, Eastern Bluebird, Painted Redstart, Green-tailed Towhee, Lark Sparrow, Black-throated Sparrow.
   b. juvenal plumage similar to, and as colorful as, adult plumage— Belted Kingfisher, Great Crested Flycatcher, titmice, chickadees, nuthatches, shrikes, Catbird, Mockingbird, meadowlarks.

3. Sexes similar, both colorful or strikingly marked during breeding season only: Black-bellied and Golden plovers, Dunlin, Short-billed Dowitcher.

4. Male more colorful than female:
   a. more colorful throughout the year—hummingbirds, woodpeckers, Vermilion Flycatcher, American Redstart, Orchard Oriole, Red-winged Blackbird, Brown-headed Cowbird, Summer Tanager, Cardinal, Pyrrhuloxia, Blue Grosbeak, Rose-breasted Grosbeak, Rufous-sided Towhee, Painted Bunting.
   b. more colorful during breeding season only—Bobolink, Scarlet Tanager, American Goldfinch, Indigo Bunting, Lark Bunting, longspurs.
   c. more colorful except when in eclipse plumage—many ducks.

5. Female more colorful than male: phalaropes.

* Modified from Allen (1930) and Pettingill (1956).
† After the postjuvenal molt.

TABLE 2
Sequence of Plumages and Molts

Name of Plumage	Name of Molt*
natal down	postnatal
juvenal	postjuvenal
first winter	first prenuptial
first nuptial	first postnuptial†
second winter	second prenuptial
second nuptial	second postnuptial†

* Name of molt by which preceding plumage is replaced entirely or in part.
† This is the annual molt during which all feathers are replaced.

adult breeding plumage, the male has a brilliant scarlet head and body and jet black wings and tail. However, this plumage is not acquired until the second prenuptial (spring) molt of any individual male. The female Scarlet Tanager is a yellowish-green bird with brownish wings and tail. The juvenal plumage of both sexes is alike and is similar to that of the female in being brownish green or yellowish green above, but the young have dusky streaks on the breast and sides. The young birds undergo a partial postjuvenal molt in which the brownish wing and tail feathers of the juvenal plumage are retained; the first winter plumage of both sexes is like that of the adult female except that young males have some black wing coverts. The first breeding plumage results from a prenuptial molt, during which the male grows the scarlet head and body plumage and a black tail; the brownish wing feathers, however, are retained for the male's first breeding season. The first postnuptial (or annual) molt produces the second winter plumage in which the male assumes the female-like body plumage but black wing and tail feathers. The male attains the fully adult breeding plumage at the second prenuptial molt; the jet black wings and tail are retained but the olive head and body feathers of the second winter plumage are replaced by scarlet feathers. By contrast, the adult male Summer Tanager retains its bright rose-red plumage throughout the year; the female is olive above and yellow below; both have only a postnuptial molt. Only the first-year male has a prenuptial molt, involving body and tail feathers and wing coverts but not the remiges, which are replaced at the postnuptial molt.

Like the male Scarlet Tanager, the male Rose-breasted Grosbeak does not acquire its fully adult breeding plumage until the second prenuptial molt. The sexes are alike in juvenal plumage except that the male has pink (the female, yellow) feathers along the edge of the wing. At the postjuvenal molt, the male retains the brownish wing and tail feathers of the juvenal plumage but grows new body feathers, some of those of the neck and breast, as well as the lining of the wings, being suffused with pink. The first prenuptial molt involves the tail feathers as well as body plumage; the new tail feathers are black and the body feathers are more or less like those of the older males, but the first-year males retain their brownish wing feathers. These are lost at the time of the first postnuptial molt. Entirely unlike the male in color, the adult female Rose-breasted Grosbeak looks more like a striped brownish sparrow but is considerably larger, has a much heavier pale-colored bill, and pale yellow wing linings.

The male Indigo Bunting, when seen in good light, is a brilliant indigo blue; it appears black when seen from below, as is often the case during the breeding season when the male sings from the upper branches of a tree. The female is entirely different, being brown above and dull white and grayish below, with obscure streakings. The adults have a complete postnuptial and a partial prenuptial molt. The male's winter plumage contains much brown but it is unlike that of the female. The first-year breeding male differs from older males in having some brownish secondaries and inner primaries and by having some brown feathers above and white below.

Some families of birds have many species that are very similar in color and pattern (see page 67). The species of other families exhibit a wide variety of plumage patterns. A good example is the troupial or blackbird family, which contains the Bobolink, meadowlarks, orioles, blackbirds, cowbirds, and grackles.

The male Bobolink in breeding plumage is a conspicuous bird with black under parts and large patches of buffy white or white on the back of head, sides of back, rump, and upper tail coverts. The general color of the female is buffy yellow with dark stripes on the crown, upper parts, and sides; she wears this pattern year around. Adult birds have two complete molts (prenuptial and postnuptial) each year. The male's breeding plumage is lost entirely at the postnuptial molt; his winter plumage is like that of the female. The prenuptial molt takes place while the birds are still on the wintering grounds in South America. This molt produces a veiled plumage in which the contrasting black and white feathers of the male are mostly concealed by yellowish and buffy feather margins, which largely wear off before the birds arrive on the breeding grounds. The two sexes are alike in juvenal plumage and in the first winter plumage; the partial postjuvenal molt apparently involves all feathers except the remiges and rectrices; the first nuptial plumage is acquired by a complete first prenuptial molt.

Unlike the Bobolink, the Red-winged Blackbird has a single molt each year; all of the feathers are replaced at the postnuptial molt. The sexes are alike in juvenal plumage, but the complete postjuvenal molt produces dissimilar male and female first winter plumages. The more brightly colored nuptial plumage of both adults and first-year birds is attained simply by the wear of feather tips. The details in pattern of the male plumage vary considerably, especially among first-year males.

The male Orchard Oriole has the head, neck, back, remiges, and rectrices black; the breast, belly, rump, and upper tail coverts are a rich chestnut. The female is yellowish green above, yellow below, and has brownish wings and tail. Adult birds of both sexes have a complete postnuptial molt only. The sexes are alike in juvenal and in first winter plumages. The male's first nuptial plumage is attained by a partial prenuptial molt; it is similar to that of the female except that the male has a black throat patch and often a scattering of chestnut feathers in the plumage. The fully adult male plumage is acquired at the first postnuptial molt. The other four common species of orioles of the United States also exhibit sexual dimorphism (Baltimore, Bullock's, Hooded, and Scott's orioles), but two Mexican species that nest in southern Texas, the Black-headed and Lichtenstein's orioles, do not.

The male and female differ conspicuously in plumage color in these other members of the blackbird family: Yellow-headed Blackbird, Tricolored Blackbird, Rusty Blackbird, Brewer's Blackbird, and Boat-tailed Grackle. The Boat-tailed Grackle is notable because the black iridescent male is much larger (with a very long, keel-shaped tail) than the brown female. The male Brown-headed Cowbird is a black bird with a brown head; the female's plumage is uniformly gray. Both male and female Bronzed (Red-eyed) Cowbirds of southern Arizona, New Mexico, and Texas, however, are uniformly blackish. Male and female meadowlarks (*Sturnella*) are very similar in plumage characters, although males tend to be darker (and larger) than females.

Many of the breeding wood-warblers of the United States show sexual differences in plumage. Among these dimorphic species, the American Redstart will be one of the first to come to the attention of the beginning student. I present here the traditional description of the sequence of plumages in this species; much new information is needed, however. The adult male is black above, white below, and has patches of orange on the wings, tail, and sides of breast. The adult female is gray and greenish gray above, white below, and has light yellow patches where the male has the orange color. The sexes are alike in juvenal plumage, which is unlike that of either adult. Standard references state that the young birds undergo a partial postjuvenal molt, a partial first prenuptial molt, and that the first nuptial plumage of the male is like that of the female except for some black feathers on the head, neck, and breast. The fully adult male plumage pattern is attained at the first postnuptial molt. After that time, adult males and females are believed to have only one molt each year (the postnuptial).

Dimorphism in plumage pattern is characteristic of hummingbirds, and this family offers a different type of problem. The females of western hummingbirds are similar in color pattern and it is not possible to distinguish between certain species in the field, e.g., Black-chinned and Costa's; Allen's and Rufous hummingbirds.

Sexes Similar

More frustrating in some ways are those species in which the male and female are identical, or nearly so, in color pattern (Table 1), because one often wants to know which sex performs certain duties, especially during the breeding season. Each bird must be color-marked if one wishes to make a careful study of such species. The sexes are essentially alike (the female may be slightly duller) in some species of wood-warblers. Typical examples are these: Swainson's, Worm-eating, Orange-crowned, Nashville, Virginia's, Lucy's, Yellow-throated, Grace's, Chestnut-sided, Palm, Kentucky, and Red-faced warblers, the Ovenbird, the waterthrushes, the Yellow-breasted Chat, and the Painted Redstart (Fig. 16). Some families in which the sexes often are alike also have several species that are similar in color pattern: shorebirds, gulls, terns, tyrant-flycatchers, wrens, thrashers, vireos, and sparrows. We have already called attention (page 44) to the difficulty of identifying the species of *Empidonax* flycatchers unless one knows their songs. The

FIGURE 16. A Worm-eating Warbler at nest with young. (Courtesy of Samuel A. Grimes.)

details of the molt of most tyrant-flycatchers are imperfectly known, in part because the postjuvenal and postnuptial molts are completed after the birds leave the breeding grounds. A number of sparrows are small, streaked, brownish birds that require much study by the beginning student; the song of each species is distinctive. The pattern of molt among the sparrows (especially first-year birds) is variable, but the adults of some species (e.g., Swamp, Lincoln's, and Song sparrows) have only a complete postnuptial molt, the following nuptial plumage resulting from the wear of feather tips.

Immature Plumages

Either the juvenal or the first winter plumage may be unlike that of the adults. The adults of the following members of the finch family, for example, have plain under parts, whereas the juvenal plumage of each is streaked below: Grasshopper, Lark, Rufous-crowned, Cassin's, Tree, Chipping, Clay-colored, Brewer's, Field, Black-chinned, White-crowned, Golden-crowned, and White-throated sparrows, the juncos, and the Rufous-sided Towhee. Unlike the adults, young robins and bluebirds are heavily spotted below. In the juvenal plumage, which is worn for some time after the young leave the nest, Red-headed Woodpeckers have the head, neck, and upper breast dusky brown rather than red. Immature gulls and terns may be difficult to identify because the plumage may be unlike that of the adult but similar to that of another species. The unusually long tails of a few species make identification easy, but it is obvious that a period of time must elapse before the stub-tailed fledglings acquire an adult-sized tail. Four examples of long-tailed birds whose young sometimes present problems to the beginning student are the Scissor-tailed Flycatcher, magpies, Boat-tailed Grackle, and Common Grackle.

Fall and Winter Plumages

The most confusing problems in field identification are met in the nonbreeding plumages of shorebirds, gulls and terns, and many wood-warblers; some can be identified only by an expert. Not only do many North American species of wood-warblers exhibit sexual dimorphism in plumage pattern but the winter plumage of both adults and immature birds may be surprisingly unlike the breeding plumage. The general coloration of many species during the winter is yellowish and greenish, and, although some retain vestiges of field marks characteristic of the breeding plumage, few birds seen in the field during fall migration look like the colored illustrations in a book. The beginning student should bide his time before attempting to identify fall shorebirds and wood-warblers. If he is particularly interested in plumages or in wood-warblers, he may embark on a much-needed study because there is little complete and accurate data on the plumages and molts of these birds.

This is a pertinent place to point out that not even the best field ornithologists can identify every bird seen. Some birds in certain plumages are difficult (or even impossible) to identify with certainty. Important, too, are the conditions under which a bird is seen. Light-colored birds look black when seen against the sun; many optical illusions result when a bird is seen in shadows. Every competent field ornithologist probably has had experiences similar to those described by Dr. Hickey—with binoculars trained carefully on a "bird" in the distance, a closer approach reveals it to be a bottle, a stick, or a piece of paper; following a "strange" bird carefully through a thicket for some time, the bird is recognized as a common species as soon as it moves into the open. Such experiences may be hard on the ego but the experienced ornithologist expects to have them; the beginning student should expect them too.

3

Bird Habitats

A bird's habitat is the place where it lives. We speak in terms of the habitat preference for each bird species, for, as mentioned on page 41, birds are not distributed evenly throughout the world or even within their breeding range. We know little about the details of habitat selection by birds, but, in general, it seems "obvious" to ornithologists that each species is best adapted or suited to the habitat it occupies; otherwise it would not survive in that habitat. In a narrow sense, a knowledge of bird habitats is important to the beginning student because he must learn where to look for birds (Fig. 1). In a broad sense, it is essential because the nature of a given habitat determines the type of bird life it can support. A bird's structure, behavior, and evolutionary history all are related to the environment where the bird now lives and where its ancestors lived.

The environment itself is the result of many interacting factors, both physical and biological. The study of these forms the science of *ecology:* the interrelations between living organisms and their environment. Recognizing its all-inclusive nature, Odum (1959) defined ecology as *environmental biology.* The advanced study of bird ecology involves a consideration of all factors related to the life of the

FIGURE 1. Rice field canal and floodgate in southeastern South Carolina; the giant cutgrass at the right provides the nesting habitat for the King Rail and the Purple Gallinule. (Courtesy of Brooke Meanley.)

bird: climate and its influence on both plants and animals, as well as the effect of plants and animals on the environment and on each other. This chapter is an introduction to bird ecology.

PHYSICAL FACTORS

Birds, as warm-blooded animals, can survive over a wide range of climatic or ecological conditions, but differences in physiological tolerance to climatic extremes among birds may play an important role in their distribution and on their behavior in a given habitat. Birds are affected directly or indirectly by air temperature, humidity, precipitation, sunlight, wind (see page 112), and soil (Fig. 2). Plants and lower animals are affected by many other physical conditions that make up their environment. Although any one of these may be the *limiting factor* that determines the distribution of plants or animals, it is in general the interaction of two or more of them that determines the suitability of the environment for any particular living thing. The study of these interrelationships is a

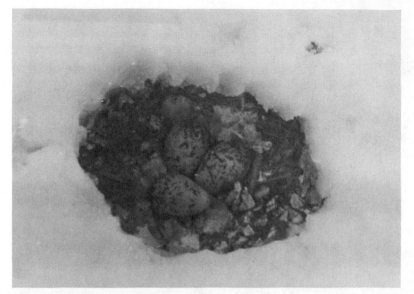

FIGURE 2. A Michigan Killdeer nest in the snow, April 10, 1942. Many early nests of the Killdeer, Horned Lark, and other ground-nesting species are destroyed by heavy snowfall. (Courtesy of Walter P. Nickell and the editor of *The Wilson Bulletin*.)

challenging one; the examples and explanations for birds cited here may be considered, for the most part, to be greatly oversimplified.

Air Temperature

Either low or high temperatures may limit a bird's distribution. Low nighttime temperatures may limit the northern distribution, usually in relation to available food supplies and length of daylight. Penguins in the Antarctic and Snowy Owls in the Arctic must be physiologically adapted to inhabit these frigid areas. In a comparative study of the domestic hen and the Herring Gull, Chatfield et al. (1953) found differences in the sensitivity of leg nerves to cold, which one assumes is related to the gull's ability to stand on ice or to swim in near-freezing water. The majority of North American birds are migratory species. Those that nest at high latitudes (or elevations) may withstand extreme fluctuations in air temperature during a relatively short breeding season, where the days are long and there is an abundant food supply (Fig. 3). During sleep, or on cold days, birds fluff out their feathers, and in so doing form an insulating layer of air between the skin and the feathers. Birds also gain protection from cold, rain, and wind by special roosting habits (page 155). Sutton and Parmelee (1954) discussed problems related to the destruction of young Water Pipits on Baffin Island, where 21 large young were found dead in their nests. The nestlings presumably died of starvation and/or exposure during a five-day period of wet, cold, and windy weather. Temperature also may be a limiting factor in the southward distribution of birds. For example, Ring-necked Pheasants have been introduced in the southern United States with indifferent success. R. E. Yeatter presented evidence suggesting that reproduction fails because the embryos do not survive at the high air temperatures encountered during the egg-laying period, when the eggs are uncovered most of the time.

Humidity and Precipitation

Humidity plays an important role in modifying the effects of air temperature, but little is known about the possible direct effect of humidity on birds. As an observed fact, we may cite *Gloger's rule:* "Intensity of melanin pigmentation tends to decrease with mean temperature; the amount of black pigment tends to increase with increase of humidity; yellowish or reddish-brown pigmentation is characteristic of regions of high temperature and aridity." Species

FIGURE 3. An Arctic Loon on its nest at Churchill, Manitoba. (Courtesy of Samuel A. Grimes.)

which demonstrate these correlations in pigmentation with temperature and moisture are the Bobwhite, Red-tailed Hawk, Horned Lark, Fox Sparrow, and Song Sparrow (page 336). Because both temperature and water are critical factors in the life of plants, it is very difficult to separate the roles of vegetation and of temperature-moisture relations in limiting the distribution of birds. As an approach to this problem, Arthur C. Twomey studied the temperature-moisture relations in the breeding range of the Hungarian Partridge in Europe, and in Missouri and Montana, where the species was introduced. In neither state were the temperature-moisture relations exactly like those in Europe throughout the year, but they were similar in Montana during much of the year, including the entire breeding season. The partridge became established in Montana but not in Missouri, even though the temperature-moisture conditions in Missouri appeared to be suitable during the winter months, thus suggesting that these factors were more critical during the breeding season. Mayhew (1955) found that the production of Mallards in the Sacramento Valley of California was high in years of high spring rainfall and very low in years of spring drought.

Light and Radiation

The most obvious relation between sunlight and bird activities is shown by species which are diurnal, crepuscular, or nocturnal in habit. Among diurnal species, some inhabit open areas and others live in deep woods where light intensity is much reduced. Changing light intensity is related directly to the beginning of song in the morning and the cessation of song in the evening. The duration of day-length and the daily rhythm of light and darkness are important in the lives of both plants and animals. The effect of day-length on endocrine glands (page 301) is discussed in relation to migration (page 124) and the breeding cycle (page 203).

Shelford and Yeatter (1955) discussed the apparent influence and interaction of ultraviolet light, rainfall, and temperature on the biology of several species, particularly during certain periods in the annual cycle. For the Greater Prairie Chicken, these critical periods are the two weeks (approximately) prior to egg-laying, the time of hatching, and when the young birds are between four and eight weeks old. Although the Prairie Chicken is subject to more sunlight on its open grassland breeding range than is the Bobwhite in eastern parts of the United States, available information indicates that ultraviolet light is important for successful reproduction of both these species. Differences in the habitats occupied by these species suggest that physiological sensitivity and/or tolerance to ultraviolet radiation varies among species. It should be noted that, although life is dependent on sunlight as the ultimate source of energy, ultraviolet (and other) radiation is deleterious or fatal to the protoplasm of animal cells in excessive amounts and under certain conditions (see Chapter 14 in Odum, 1959).

Soil

All animals are dependent ultimately on plants. The growth and distribution of plants depend on the amount and kind of soil, and the soil itself is the product of both climate and vegetation. In addition to the part played by soil in providing food and plant cover for birds, soil of the proper composition is needed by some birds that use mud in their nests (e.g., Cliff Swallow, Barn Swallow, Robin). Dirt banks of the proper consistency must be available for such species as the Belted Kingfisher and Bank Swallow, which excavate nesting burrows in the ground. Soil may be important because of the presence or absence of certain chemical elements which are essential for normal physiological processes. Dale and DeWitt (1958), for example, presented evidence indicating that the success of Ring-necked Pheasants may depend on an adequate amount of calcium in the soil. They determined that the effects of calcium deficiency are cumulative. They found that, although the experimental birds' reproduction was fairly good the first year, mortality of the chicks was high. Among the survivors the following spring, 12 hens on the same calcium-deficient diet "produced an average of 22 eggs each, but there was an average of only 2.7 chicks per hen alive at the age of 10 weeks. A control group from these birds fed the standard reproduction diet . . . produced an average of 12.7 chicks per hen." Winter seems to be the critical period for pheasants living in areas with a calcium-deficient soil. Over much of their range in the United States, the winter diet consists largely of corn (a very poor source of calcium), which accentuates any deficiency in calcium from other sources. By contrast, alfalfa and soybeans are rich in calcium, they grow best in calcium-rich areas, and pheasants generally are abundant in soybean- or alfalfa-producing areas. Hence, calcium-deficient soil may be a limiting factor for pheasants when all other habitat requirements seem to be suitable for the species.

FIGURE 4. A Red-cockaded Woodpecker at its nesting hole; this is a typical inhabitant of the fire-type coastal plain pineland. (Courtesy of Samuel A. Grimes.)

Fire

Fire is a significant ecological factor, especially in grassland and woodland areas. Odum (1959: 138) speaks of the large stands of longleaf pines of the coastal plains of southeastern United States as being a "fire climax," in that the pines cannot be maintained in the complete absence of fire (Fig. 4). Under that condition, scrub hardwoods grow more rapidly and choke out the pines, as well as such ground cover as grasses and legumes, which provide essential food for the Bobwhite and other species. A suitable breeding habitat for the Kirtland's Warbler apparently has depended on periodic fires caused by lightning throughout the ages. In this instance, complete fire control on the breeding range presumably would result in extinction of the species (see pages 92, 327).

BIOLOGICAL FACTORS

Vegetation

Although the beginning student should be aware of the intricate interactions of the physical factors summarized above, his first concern is to learn about different bird habitats. In an attempt to explain the distribution of birds, authors have divided North America into various regions (e.g., life zones, biotic provinces, biomes) based on temperature and the characteristic plant growth (see Van Tyne and Berger, 1959). Each system has certain limitations, but the concept of *major biotic communities* or *biomes* (Fig. 5) probably is of the most value for an initial study of bird distribution.

A major biotic community includes all of the plants and animals that are found in a given area. The vegetation of each biotic community is the product of the soil and climatic conditions and has a particular *life form,* e.g., coniferous forest, grassland. The stable or final plant community that develops in a given region is called a *climax community.* Over much of the eastern part of the United States, for example, the climax vegetation is mature deciduous forest. The particular species of trees that form the dominant plants vary from area to area within the deciduous formation: oak-hickory forests are characteristic of the central Atlantic states; beech-maple forests, of the north central region; maple-basswood forests, of Minnesota and Wisconsin. Similarly, the grassland biome (which occurs where rainfall is insufficient to support forest life forms) of the plains states is subdivided into east-west zones of tall grasses (5 to 8 feet), mixed grasses (2 to 4 feet), and short grasses (0.5 to 1.5 feet).

The following brief descriptions of the major biotic communities of North America, with examples of typical bird inhabitants, are based primarily on Pettingill's (1956: 158-164) treatment of the subject.

1. The *tundra biome* is, in a sense, an arctic grassland, characterized by low temperatures and a short growing season (about two months). Only the surface of the ground thaws during the short summer, and vegetation is limited to lichens, sedges, grasses, and dwarfed woody plants. Similar conditions are found at high elevations (above the timber line), so that two types of tundra are described.

a. Arctic tundra: northern Canada, south along the coasts of Hudson Bay, and throughout most of Labrador and Newfoundland. Characteristic breeding birds are: Willow Ptarmigan, Rock Ptarmigan, Snowy Owl, Horned Lark, Water Pipit, Lapland Longspur, Smith's Longspur, and Snow Bunting (Fig. 6).

b. Alpine tundra: discontinuous areas above 10,000 feet* in the

---

* The elevation at which the timber line occurs depends on the latitude, climate, and direction of slopes in the mountain range. The timber line in the western United States varies from about 6000 to 11,500 feet.

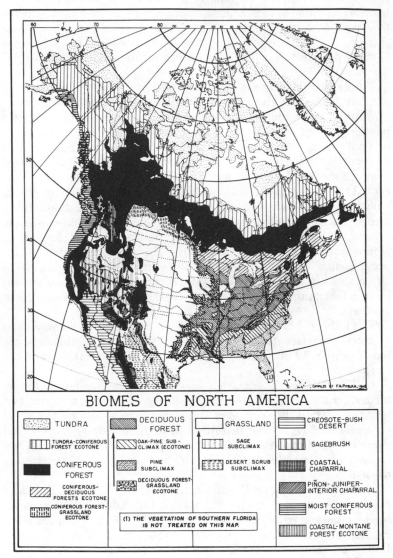

FIGURE 5. Biomes of North America as depicted by Frank A. Pitelka. (Courtesy of Frank A. Pitelka.)

FIGURE 6.   A female Smith's Longspur ready to settle on its ground nest at Churchill, Manitoba.   (Courtesy of Samuel A. Grimes.)

Rocky Mountains and the Sierra Nevada–Cascade system (Fig. 7). Breeding birds: White-tailed Ptarmigan, Water Pipit, and rosy finches.

2. *Coniferous forests* cover vast areas of Canada and the United States.   Three main subdivisions are described.   As in the deciduous forest biome, the species of conifers vary from region to region.

a. The transcontinental coniferous forest of southern Canada parallels the arctic tundra to the north.   Breeding birds: Goshawk, Spruce Grouse, Hawk-Owl, Black-backed Three-toed Woodpecker, Yellow-bellied Flycatcher, Olive-sided Flycatcher, Gray (Canada) Jay, Red-breasted Nuthatch, Brown Creeper, Winter Wren, Hermit Thrush, Golden-crowned Kinglet, several warblers (Tennessee, Magnolia, Cape May, Bay-breasted, Canada), Purple Finch, Pine Grosbeak, Pine Siskin, White-winged Crossbill, and Slate-colored Junco.

b. The eastern montane coniferous forest extends from northeastern United States southward at high elevations in the Appalachian Mountains to North Carolina.   Breeding birds: Goshawk, Olive-sided Flycatcher, Red-breasted Nuthatch, Brown Creeper,

FIGURE 7.   Alpine tundra in the Mt. Evans region of Colorado; elevation about 12,500 feet.

Winter Wren, Hermit Thrush, Golden-crowned Kinglet, Magnolia Warbler, Blackburnian Warbler, Canada Warbler, Purple Finch, Pine Siskin, Red Crossbill, Slate-colored Junco, and White-throated Sparrow.

c. The western montane coniferous forest occupies the area below the alpine tundra in the Rocky Mountains, extending southward to New Mexico, and in the Sierra Nevada–Cascade system into California (Figs. 8, 9).   Breeding birds: Goshawk, Blue Grouse, Black-backed Three-toed Woodpecker, Williamson's Sapsucker, Hammond's Flycatcher, Olive-sided Flycatcher, Gray Jay, Clark's Nutcracker, Mountain Chickadee, Red-breasted Nuthatch, Brown Creeper, Winter Wren, Hermit Thrush, Townsend's Solitaire, Golden-crowned Kinglet, Ruby-crowned Kinglet, Audubon's Warbler, Townsend's Warbler, Hermit Warbler, Cassin's Finch, Pine Grosbeak, Pine Siskin, Red Crossbill, and Gray-headed Junco.

3. *Deciduous forest biome* is found, at elevations below the co-niferous forests, in the eastern United States, from southern New England and the Appalachian Mountains west to the bottom lands and bluffs along the Mississippi River and its tributaries.   Breed-ing birds: Red-shouldered Hawk, Broad-winged Hawk, Barred Owl, Great Horned Owl, Whip-poor-will, Red-bellied Woodpecker, Hairy Woodpecker, Great Crested Flycatcher, Acadian Flycatcher, Eastern Wood Pewee, Carolina Chickadee, Tufted Titmouse, White-breasted

FIGURE 8. A distant view of the timber line and alpine tundra in the Mt. Evans region of Colorado.

Nuthatch, Wood Thrush, Blue-gray Gnatcatcher, Yellow-throated Vireo, Worm-eating Warbler, Cerulean Warbler, and Hooded Warbler.

4. The *grassland biome* (prairie), as mentioned above, is found in the plains states. It extends from the forested bottom lands

FIGURE 9. Timber line in the Mt. Evans region of Colorado to show the relatively sharp break between the alpine tundra and the western montane coniferous forest; elevation about 11,500 feet.

along the Mississippi River west to the Rocky Mountains, and from south-central Texas north into Canada (the prairie provinces). The vegetation changes from east to west with increasing elevation and decreasing annual rainfall. Breeding birds: Swainson's Hawk, Ferruginous Hawk, Greater Prairie Chicken, Sharp-tailed Grouse, Long-billed Curlew, Burrowing Owl, Western Meadowlark, Lark Bunting, Grasshopper Sparrow, and, in the northern regions, Sprague's Pipit, Baird's Sparrow, McCown's Longspur, and Chestnut-collared Longspur.

5. *Southwestern oak woodland* occurs mainly on hills and mountain slopes in New Mexico, Arizona, Nevada, Utah, California, and parts of Colorado and Oregon. Breeding birds: Nuttall's Woodpecker, Arizona Woodpecker, Bridled Titmouse, Hutton's Vireo, Virginia's Warbler, and Black-throated Gray Warbler.

6. *Piñon-juniper woodland* is found on hills and mountain slopes, above the deserts or grasslands and below the coniferous forest, in the Great Basin and the Colorado River region of Colorado, Utah, Nevada, Arizona, New Mexico, and the eastern side of the Sierra Nevada–Cascade system in California. Breeding birds: Gray Flycatcher, Ash-throated Flycatcher, Piñon Jay, Plain Titmouse, Common Bushtit, Blue-gray Gnatcatcher, Bewick's Wren, and Black-throated Gray Warbler.

7. The *chaparral biome* occurs in canyons and on mountain slopes in California and Mexico. Varying with the locality, dominant plants include snowbush (*Ceanothus*), chamiso (*Adenostoma*), manzanita (*Arctostaphylos*), scrub oak (*Quercus*), mountain mahogany (*Cercocarpus*), coffeeberry (*Rhamnus*), poison oak (*Rhus*), and baccharis (*Baccharis*). Breeding birds: Wrentit, California Thrasher, Gray Vireo, Orange-crowned Warbler, Sage Sparrow, Black-chinned Sparrow, and White-crowned Sparrow.

8. The *desert biome* is found, in general, in regions that have less than 10 inches of annual rainfall. Two main types of desert have been classified as "hot" or "low" deserts and "cool" or "high" deserts. Both have typical plants with a characteristic spacing or pattern of vegetation, but there are many intermediate types that result from differences in temperature, rainfall, elevation, and geological nature of the country (compare Figs. 10, 11, 12, 13). Dixon (1959), in a study of desert birds in Brewster County, Texas, found 13 species "that might be considered to comprise a 'standard' desert avifauna" of the hot deserts; some of the species also have been reported from cool deserts and from the chaparral biome. Dixon concluded that, to a considerable extent, the "occurrence of desert species in adjacent formations indicates an attraction to the shrub life form and not to the desert climate *per se*." Pettingill

FIGURE 10. Typical desert east of Tucson, Arizona. A Curve-billed Thrasher's nest can be seen in the center cholla cactus. Dry grama grass of the previous fall occupies the foreground. The low tree in the background is mesquite, and in the distance is a single saguaro cactus, an uncommon plant on the flats of this area. The Tanque Verde Mountains can be seen in the distance. (Courtesy of George Olin.)

FIGURE 11. A typical saguaro cactus forest in the foothills of the Santa Catalina Mountains of Arizona. There is a dense ground cover of scrub mesquite, ocotillo, and desert hackberry. (Courtesy of George Olin.)

FIGURE 12. The sparsely vegetated desert in the extreme southern tip of Nevada a few miles west of Davis Dam and the Colorado River.

(1956) characterized, in part, two chief types of desert communities as follows:

a. Sagebrush communities are found at elevations above the scrub desert between the Rocky Mountains and the Sierra Nevada–Cascade system. Dominant plants include sagebrush (*Artemisia*), shadscale (*Atriplex*), greasewood (*Sarcobatus*), rabbitbrush (*Chrysothamnus*), winterfat (*Eurotia*), and some grasses. Breeding birds: Sage Grouse, Sage Thrasher, Sage Sparrow, Brewer's Sparrow, Black-throated Sparrow.

b. Scrub desert is found in the lowlands and valley floors from western Texas west to southwestern California. Here the plants, 3 to 6 feet high, are widely spaced. Creosote bush (*Larrea*) is often the dominant plant, but other common plants include mesquite (*Prosopis*), paloverde (*Cercidium*), catclaw (*Acacia*), ironwood (*Olneya*), ocotillo (*Fouquieria*), agaves, cacti, and yuccas. Breeding birds: Gambel's Quail, Roadrunner, Elf Owl, Lesser Nighthawk, Costa's Hummingbird, Gilded Flicker, Gila Woodpecker, Vermilion Flycatcher, Verdin, Cactus Wren, Bendire's Thrasher, Crissal Thrasher, Black-tailed Gnatcatcher, and Phainopepla.

Ecological Distribution

It must be emphasized that the delineation of major biomes stresses the *geographical distribution* of plants and associated ani-

mals. Great expanses of the climax vegetational types existed before man began to exploit the land. But, even in undisturbed areas,
local variations in climatic and topographical features (such as
streams, rivers, lakes, cliffs, mountains) resulted in discontinuities
in the climax vegetation so that small "islands" of different plant
forms occurred. In addition, man's activities have altered or destroyed most of the climax vegetational areas from the eastern sea-
board to the Rocky Mountains, as well as many of those west of
the Continental Divide. The effect that cutting the forests in the
Great Lakes area had on the relative abundance and distribution
of the Brown-headed Cowbird and other species has been described
graphically by Mayfield (1960). In considering the distribution of
birds, it is not enough to refer to the major biomes. The nearly
continuous stands of deciduous forest that once covered most of
the eastern part of the United States have been broken up and replaced by urban areas and farming country. Consequently, to say
that a particular species is found throughout the eastern United
States means only that it is to be found where a suitable habitat
exists for that species. The same is true for any other large geographical area. In the detailed study of a bird species, or group of
species, therefore, one must think in terms of *ecological distribution,* or the relationship of the bird to the environment of its particular habitat. Here are two examples that illustrate discontinuities in bird distribution correlated with discontinuities in their
habitat.

FIGURE 13. A view of the Mojave desert near Three Sisters Butte, northeast of
Pearblossom, Los Angeles County, California.

Middleton (1957) studied an interesting area of about 300 acres in southeastern Michigan, in which he found bird species typical of northern coniferous forests and of both northern and southern deciduous forests. He reported that conifers along a spring-fed stream included arbor vitae, tamarack, white pine, hemlock, and black spruce in that order; other boreal tree and shrub species, occurring in lesser numbers, were yellow, cherry, and gray birches, mountain maple, black alder, and American yew. This distinctly northern-type habitat, with its associated ground cover of sphagnum moss, wintergreen, pipsissewa, goldthread, and clintonia, supported such typically northern species as the Magnolia Warbler, Northern Waterthrush, Mourning Warbler, and Canada Warbler. Other parts of the area consisted of swamp forest in which the principal trees and shrubs were red maple, black ash, slippery elm, red-osier dogwood, prickly ash, meadowsweet, and several species of hawthorns. Here the nesting species were those characteristic of deciduous forests in southern Michigan (Wood Thrush, Veery, Redeyed Vireo, Ovenbird, Scarlet Tanager, Rose-breasted Grosbeak). The third major habitat was an upland beech-maple forest, with a scattering of oaks, hickories, basswood, cottonwood, black cherry, and tulip poplar. Southern species that have moved into Michigan within the past 60 years and/or which approach the northern limit of their breeding range in Michigan were found in this upland forest (Acadian Flycatcher, Tufted Titmouse, Yellow-throated Vireo, Cerulean Warbler, and Cardinal), or in the wetter areas (Blue-winged Warbler, Yellow-breasted Chat).

The second example demonstrates the discontinuity of pine-oak woodlands which grow at elevations above 5000 feet in southern Arizona (Fig. 14). The small, steep, and rugged mountains are separated from each other by the desert lowlands, which have a different flora and fauna. In his description of this area, Marshall (1957: 35) said that the "pine-oak woodland is the only kind of vegetation with pines and oaks equally conspicuous. Its pines resemble ponderosa pine of the forest zone next above on a mountain, and its oaks are mostly the same species that compose encinal below. This combination of two forms of tree growth, segregated above and below, constitutes a transition between pine forest and woodland, a unique feature of my study area. Elsewhere . . . the tall pines of the lower border of the forest stand as a wall confronting dwarf growth of chaparral or piñon-juniper woods." Figure 15 shows the effect of altitude and latitude on the vegetation in the areas studied by Marshall. Within the pine-oak biome, he recognized 10 more or less distinct habitats. He noted that the avifauna

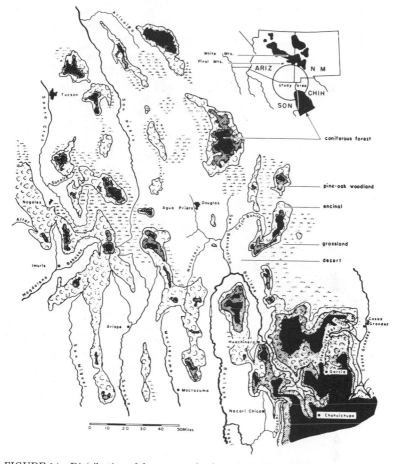

FIGURE 14. Distribution of desert, grassland, encinal, pine-oak woodland, and coniferous forest in the area shown in the insert. (Courtesy of Joe T. Marshall, Jr., and
the Cooper Ornithological Society, from *Pacific Coast Avifauna No. 32.*)

"was apt to reflect the peculiar juxtaposition of vegetation in the
canyon chosen rather than to typify the mountain, its latitude, and
climate." Of the 93 species of birds discussed by Marshall, he reported that aside from Mexican species like the Coppery-tailed
Trogon and the Painted Redstart "the assemblage of breeding birds
at the census stations is similar to that of other foothill areas in
the southwestern United States. For example, the following birds
are conspicuous both in Mexican pine-oak woodland and in the
Digger pine-blue oak woodland of central California": Screech Owl,

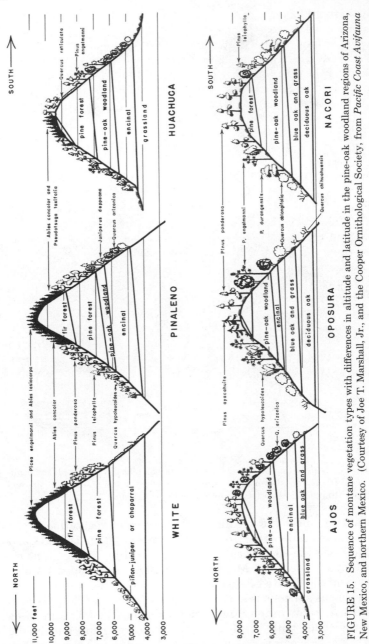

FIGURE 15. Sequence of montane vegetation types with differences in altitude and latitude in the pine-oak woodland regions of Arizona, New Mexico, and northern Mexico. (Courtesy of Joe T. Marshall, Jr., and the Cooper Ornithological Society, from *Pacific Coast Avifauna* No. 32.)

Red-shafted Flicker, Acorn Woodpecker, Ash-throated Flycatcher, Western Wood Pewee, Common Bushtit, White-breasted Nuthatch, Bewick's Wren, Western Bluebird, Blue-gray Gnatcatcher, Hutton's Vireo, Black-throated Gray Warbler, Rufous-sided Towhee, Brown Towhee, Rufous-crowned Sparrow, and Chipping Sparrow. Marshall's discriminating discussion should be studied by all students interested in bird distribution and habitat selection.

Ecotones

Only rarely is there an abrupt change in the vegetation at the boundary between adjacent biomes. Usually there are areas of transition, called *ecotones,* from one type of plant community to another. The ecotones are characterized by having a wide variety of shrubs, trees, and herbaceous plants, which typically provide more food and cover for animals than do areas having a more uniform vegetation. Such areas of transition in vegetational types are found between forests and shrub-grown fields, between forests and grassland, between marshes and upland communities, etc. Ecotones are of special interest to ornithologists because they usually support a larger variety of bird species (as well as of individuals of the species) than either of the communities they separate. This tendency for increased variety and numbers of species in ecotones is called the *edge effect.* Some species are almost entirely limited to these areas of transition. Characteristic birds of shrubby deciduous ecotones are Traill's Flycatcher, Mockingbird, Catbird, Brown Thrasher, Yellow Warbler, Chestnut-sided Warbler, Prairie Warbler, Yellow-breasted Chat, Baltimore Oriole, Bullock's Oriole, Cardinal, Blue Grosbeak, Indigo Bunting, Lazuli Bunting, Painted Bunting, Clay-colored Sparrow, Field Sparrow, and Song Sparrow. Interdigitations of arctic tundra and coniferous forest biomes result in an ecotone consisting of a scattering of low tundra shrubs and stunted conifers. This "timber line" ecotone is the breeding habitat for the Gray-cheeked Thrush, Northern Shrike, Blackpoll Warbler, Common Redpoll, Tree Sparrow, and Harris' Sparrow.

Ecological Succession

When the climax vegetation typical of any of the major biotic communities is destroyed by man or by natural events, the new vegetation passes through a series of stages before the stable climax vegetation is reached again. This replacement process is called *secondary ecological succession. Primary ecological succession*

occurs where life has not existed previously, such as on newly exposed rock, sand bars, new islands, deltas, glacial moraines, or
newly formed ponds or lakes. In either primary or secondary succession, each of the successive, transitory stages has its typical
plants (and animals) and is called a *seral community;* the entire
series of communities is called a *sere.* The example of primary
succession most often cited is that which occurs in lakes in the eastern United States. Aldrich (1945), for example, described five
stages in the succession from open-water vegetation to climax forest in Ohio, characterizing each by the dominant plants. These
stages and the bird inhabitants that he found are:

   1. Water lily: Pied-billed Grebe, and, sometimes, the Mallard.
   2. Loosestrife-cattail: Pied-billed Grebe, Mallard, Virginia Rail,
Long-billed Marsh Wren, Red-winged Blackbird, Swamp Sparrow.
   3. Buttonbush-alder: Red-winged Blackbird, Swamp Sparrow,
Eastern Kingbird, Traill's Flycatcher, Yellow Warbler, Catbird,
American Goldfinch, Yellowthroat, Song Sparrow.
   4. Maple-elm-ash: Yellowthroat, Song Sparrow, Blue Jay, Hairy
Woodpecker, Downy Woodpecker, Eastern Wood Pewee, White-
breasted Nuthatch, Black-capped Chickadee, Tufted Titmouse,
Red-eyed Vireo, Ovenbird.
   5. Beech-maple climax: Hairy Woodpecker, Downy Woodpecker,
Eastern Wood Pewee, White-breasted Nuthatch, Black-capped
Chickadee, Tufted Titmouse, Red-eyed Vireo, Ovenbird.

A similar series of stages occurs in other areas of the deciduous
forest biome (and in other biomes) but the dominant plants and
the bird inhabitants may be different.

   Although each stage in a sere is transitory, the duration of each
of the seral communities varies with many factors, both physical
and biological. A particular stage may persist indefinitely when
exposed to frequent or extreme changes in the physical environment which inhibit the normal replacement process. Certain primary seral communities that are presumed to represent the highest
stage reached in their particular area during the present geological
age provide excellent habitats for special groups of birds (Fig. 16).
These seral communities include the following (see Pettingill,
1956):

   1. Shores: rocky or sandy areas with little or no vegetation bor-
dering large bodies of water.
   2. Fresh-water and salt-water marshes: usually inundated land
with grasses, sedges, and other herbaceous plants.

FIGURE 16. Gulf Coast Marshes at Grand Chenier, Louisiana, the nesting habitat
of the Clapper Rail, Purple Gallinule, and many other water birds. (Courtesy of
Brooke Meanley.)

  3. Swamps: usually inundated land with shrubs and some trees.
  4. Savannas: primarily level, dry grassland with widely spaced
shrubs and trees.
  5. Shrublands: areas in which low woody plants predominate.
  6. Riparian woodlands: woodlands, composed mostly of deciduous
trees, near streams or in bottom lands where there is an adequate
subsurface water supply. These communities are especially prominent in the more arid sections of the western United States.

  Secondary succession occurs as a result of fire, wind, or human
activities. Johnston and Odum (1956) described five stages in secondary succession on upland areas in Georgia (Fig. 17). These
stages and the characteristic birds for each are given in Table 1;
special attention should be paid to changes in densities of the bird
species with changes in the vegetation.

Ecological Tolerance

  Some bird species are ecologically intolerant. An "intolerant"
species is one that has very narrow requirements and seems to be
unable to adapt to other ecological conditions. Two examples are
Kirtland's Warbler and the Everglade Kite. The breeding habitat

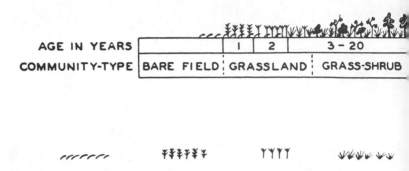

FIGURE 17. Schematic diagram of secondary ecological succession in the Piedmont region of Georgia. (By permission from *Fundamentals of Ecology*, by Eugene P. Odum, published by W. B. Saunders Company. Copyright, 1959.)

of the Kirtland's Warbler is limited to an area of about 60 by 100 miles in the jack pine plains of central Michigan (page 325). Here, however, it nests only where certain special conditions prevail. This semicolonial species seems to require a large breeding area in which the pines are suitable only from the time they are 3 to 5 feet high until they reach a height of about 18 feet. This situation exists in a given area for the short period of about 15 years. The usual ground cover during this period consists of aromatic wintergreen, blueberry, sheep laurel, and sweet fern. Although the birds nest in plantations of jack pines, they seem to prefer areas of natural growth where there are open spaces between clumps of trees. Complete fire control in the breeding range of the Kirtland's Warbler presumably would lead to its extinction. The Everglade Kite (Fig. 18), which breeds near Lake Okeechobee in Florida, lives almost exclusively on the fresh-water snail *Pomacea*. In this instance, destruction of the snails by altering their habitat adversely by human activities presumably would result in the extermination of the Florida population of this kite.

Other species are ecologically tolerant; they occupy many different habitats. The House Wren, Robin, Chipping Sparrow, and such introduced species as the House Sparrow and the Starling are good examples of tolerant species.

25 – 100	150 +
PINE FOREST	OAK-HICKORY FOREST CLIMAX

SHRUBS   PINE   HARDWOOD   OAK   HICKORY
UNDERSTORY

FIGURE 18. Male Everglade Kite on nest. (Courtesy of Samuel A. Grimes.)

TABLE 1

Distribution of Breeding Passerine Birds in a Secondary Upland Sere, Piedmont Region, Georgia

Plant Dominants Age in Years of Study Area Bird Species (with a Density of 5 or More in Some Stage)	Forbs 1–2	Grass 2–3	Grass-Shrub 15	 20	Pine Forest 25	 35	 60	 100	Oak-Hickory Climax 150–200
Grasshopper Sparrow	10	30	25						
Eastern Meadowlark	5	10	15	2					
Field Sparrow			35	48	25	8	3		
Yellowthroat			15	18					
Yellow-breasted Chat			5	16					
Cardinal			5	4	9	10	14	20	23
Rufous-sided Towhee			5	8	13	10	15	15	
Bachman's Sparrow				8	6	4			
Prairie Warbler				6	6				
White-eyed Vireo				8	16	4	5		
Pine Warbler					16	34	43	55	
Summer Tanager					6	13	13	15	
Carolina Wren						4	5	20	10
Carolina Chickadee						2	5	5	10
Blue-gray Gnatcatcher						2	13	5	5
Brown-headed Nuthatch							2	5	13
Eastern Wood Pewee							10	1	3
Ruby-throated Hummingbird							9	10	10

Species									
Tufted Titmouse							6	10	15
Yellow-throated Vireo							3	5	7
Hooded Warbler							3	30	11
Red-eyed Vireo							3	10	43
Hairy Woodpecker							1	3	5
Downy Woodpecker							1	2	5
Great Crested Flycatcher							1	10	6
Wood Thrush							1	5	23
Yellow-billed Cuckoo								1	9
Black-and-white Warbler									8
Kentucky Warbler									5
Acadian Flycatcher									5
Totals (including rare species not listed above)	15	40	110	136	87	93	158	239	228

Figures are occupied territories or estimated pairs per 100 acres.
By density, the "dominant" species for each stage are as follows:

1. Forb and grass stage: Grasshopper Sparrow and Eastern Meadowlark.
2. Grass-shrub stage: Field Sparrow, Yellowthroat, and Eastern Meadowlark.
3. Young pine forest (25–60 years): Pine Warbler, Rufous-sided Towhee, and Summer Tanager.
4. Old pine forest (with well-developed deciduous understory): Pine Warbler, Carolina Wren, Hooded Warbler, and Cardinal.
5. Oak-hickory climax: Red-eyed Vireo, Wood Thrush, and Cardinal.

Reproduced by permission of Eugene P. Odum, from *Fundamentals of Ecology*, W. B. Saunders Company, 1959.

There are differences, as well, in the distribution of birds within a given habitat, so that one may speak of the *ecological niches* selected by different species. In a mature deciduous forest, for example, the Cerulean Warbler confines most of its activities to the upper branches of the trees; the Acadian Flycatcher and Red-eyed Vireo, to intermediate heights; the Ovenbird, to the ground and understory. The Ovenbird is also an example of a species that occupies various habitats in different parts of its breeding range. Although it is one of the characteristic breeding birds of deciduous forests, it also is one of the common birds in coniferous forests in some areas (e.g., central and upper Michigan).

FOOD

Food, of course, is a critical biological factor in the environment of birds (Figs. 19, 20). Although most birds give only animal food to their young, adult birds eat all manner of vegetable and animal

FIGURE 19. A Chimney Swift feeding one of its nestlings. (Courtesy of Richard B. Fischer and the New York State Museum and Science Service.)

FIGURE 20.   A Broad-winged Hawk at its nest with a mole. (Courtesy of Samuel A. Grimes.)

material.   They secure this food from every available source: on the ground, in the ground, on water, under water, on tree trunks, in tree trunks, on branches, twigs, and leaves, and in the air.   Vultures, some gulls, and other birds regularly feed on carrion.   Table 2 summarizes the different feeding sites utilized by a large number of birds in the pine-oak habitats studied by Marshall.   (For a discussion of birds' feeding habits, see Lack, 1954, and Chapter 9 in Van Tyne and Berger, 1959.)

ANIMALS

Animals make up an important part of the ecological complex that forms a bird's habitat.   Some are related to birds as enemies, as parasites, or as benefactors (see Chapter 8).

TABLE 2
Feeding Sites of Birds in Pine-Oak Woodlands of Southern Arizona

Foliage and twigs (arthropods)
  Pines
    Mexican Chickadee
    Olive Warbler
    Grace's Warbler
  Pines and riparian trees
    Solitary Vireo
    Red-faced Warbler
  Oaks
    Plain Titmouse
    Bridled Titmouse
    Bushtit
    Hutton's Vireo
    Black-throated Gray Warbler
  Riparian trees
    Sulphur-bellied Flycatcher
    Wied's Crested Flycatcher
    Warbling Vireo
  Brush
    Bewick's Wren
    Virginia's Warbler
  Brush and fallen trees
    House Wren
Foliage and twigs (birds)
    Goshawk
    Cooper's Hawk
    Sharp-shinned Hawk
Branches and trunks (arthropods)
  Pines
    Hairy Woodpecker
    Pigmy Nuthatch
    Brown Creeper
  Oaks
    Arizona Woodpecker
  Pines, oaks, and riparian trees
    Whiskered Owl (also to ground)
    White-breasted Nuthatch
Foliage and air (arthropods)
  Pines
    Flammulated Owl
    Broad-tailed Hummingbird
    Audubon's Warbler

Oaks
    Elf Owl
    Ash-throated Flycatcher
  Riparian growth
    Blue-throated Hummingbird
    Black-chinned Hummingbird
  Brush
    Blue-gray Gnatcatcher
  Pines and oaks
    Whip-poor-will
    Painted Redstart
  Pines, oaks, and riparian growth
    Rivoli's Hummingbird
    Olivaceous Flycatcher
    Buff-breasted Flycatcher
Air (arthropods)
  In continuous flight
    Lesser Nighthawk
  From ground
    Poor-will
  From trees
    Cassin's Kingbird
    Thick-billed Kingbird
    Western Wood Pewee
    Coues' Flycatcher
Crown foliage (vegetable matter)
  Pines (pine seeds)
    Thick-billed Parrot
    Red Crossbill
  Oaks
    Band-tailed Pigeon (acorns)
  Pines, oaks, and riparian trees
    (arthropods also)
    Coppery-tailed Trogon
    Scott's Oriole
    Hepatic Tanager
    Black-headed Grosbeak
    Lesser Goldfinch
Ground, trees, and air (arthropods)
    Eastern Bluebird
    Western Bluebird

TABLE 2

(*continued*)

Ground (arthropods)	Curve-billed Thrasher (bulbs)
Sparrow Hawk	Rufous-sided Towhee
Screech Owl	Brown Towhee
Roadrunner (lizards also)	Rufous-crowned Sparrow
Pygmy Owl (lizards also)	Mexican Junco
Spotted Owl (mammals also)	Chipping Sparrow
Ground (seeds, vegetable matter,	Site general (food includes acorns)
arthropods)	Red-shafted Flicker
Harlequin (Mearns') Quail	Acorn Woodpecker
(bulbs)	Scrub Jay
Turkey	Mexican Jay
Mourning Dove	Steller's Jay

Reproduced by permission of Joe T. Marshall, Jr. (1957) and the Cooper Ornithological Society.

Within a given habitat, the relationships among different bird species are of two types: *interspecific* and *intraspecific*.

1. Interspecific relationships are illustrated by breeding parasitism (page 267), nesting associates (page 222), feeding parasitism, predation, and, presumably, by competition for food or nesting sites. Frigatebirds attack boobies and gulls in order to steal food from them, and Bald Eagles rob Ospreys of fish that they have captured. Brown Thrashers, Starlings, and House Sparrows sometimes steal earthworms that Robins have pulled from the ground. Birds that eat adults, young, or eggs of other birds are several hawks and owls, gulls, jaegers, skuas, crows, jays, some shrikes, and the House Wren.

2. Intraspecific relationships among individuals of the same species may be classified as competitive relationships, social relationships, sex relationships, and family relationships. These are discussed in Chapters 7 and 8.

Bird Populations

A *population* of birds is defined as the total number of individuals found in a given area, but one may speak also of the total population of a species throughout its entire range. Populations fluctuate in numbers of individuals from year to year. These fluctuations result from changes in climatic conditions, biotic community succession, predation, epidemics, and unknown factors. Populations possess characteristics which are peculiar to the population rather than to the individuals themselves: density, natality (birth rate), mortality (death rate), age distribution (see page 266), biotic potential, dispersion, growth form (Odum, 1959: 149). These form the basis for the advanced study of bird populations; they are treated incidentally in Chapter 8 (see also Pettingill, 1956: 298). One may wish also to study the combined population of all species inhabiting a given area.

The study of a population obviously involves some method of counting the individuals, i.e., determining the density of the population. Density is determined by taking a *census*. Three methods commonly used are: (1) census by direct counting; (2) census by sampling; (3) census by application of indices. The number of birds that actually occupy a unit of habitat that is suitable for the species constitutes the *ecological density* of the species; this number can be learned only by making a direct count. More often, however, students of bird populations present their results in terms of the number of individuals or pairs per 100 acres. Usually data obtained from a study of a small area (sample-plot census) are projected mathematically to the 100-acre unit (census by sampling); the total density obtained in this manner is referred to as *crude density*. For a strip census, another sampling technique, the birds are counted in a strip of measured width of representative habitat that transects a study area. Sample-plot censuses and strip censuses often are taken by students who walk through an area a few times and count the number of singing male birds. Censuses by application of indices, an equally unacceptable approach to the serious study of bird populations, involve a count of the number of birds seen or heard per time unit (e.g., per hour or per day) or a count of the number seen or heard per distance unit (e.g., per mile). Data on crude density provide a basis for comparison between different areas and by different authors (providing the authors' competence and techniques are equivalent), but the significance of such density figures often is problematical. In most instances, the figures represent the grossest sort of rough estimate despite the frequent application of statistical methods in an effort to give an air of respectability to the publication of inadequate data. The accurate determination of density in most habitats is extremely difficult, and all too often students attempt to take censuses before they have an adequate knowledge of habitats or of bird song and behavior. Time of day, time of season, climatological factors, and differences in species' behavior patterns affect the song pattern and general activity of birds, and, therefore, must be considered when studying bird populations (see, e.g., Klonglan, 1955; Mayfield, 1960).

Bird migration has been recognized as one of the marvels of the animal world since ancient times. Jeremiah spoke of the stork as knowing "her appointed times" and of cranes, doves, and swallows as observing "the time of their coming." Some insects (butterflies, dragonflies), fish (eels, salmon, smelt), and mammals (bats, bison, caribou) have also developed migratory habits, but it is the sudden appearance and disappearance of birds as the seasons change that has intrigued man throughout the ages.

SOME FACTS ABOUT MIGRATION

For birds as a group, migration is an adjustment to unfavorable conditions during part of the year in some area. Migration is perhaps more general among North American birds than people commonly realize. For example, of the 215 or so species that are known to breed in Michigan, less than 20 appear to be wholly nonmigratory there. These include several species of grouse, Greater Prairie Chicken, Bobwhite, several species of owls, Pileated Woodpecker, Red-bellied Woodpecker, Downy Woodpecker, Tufted Titmouse, White-breasted Nuthatch, Carolina Wren, and Cardinal. This

4
Migration

chapter deals primarily with Northern Hemisphere birds, but migration is also characteristic of Southern Hemisphere birds. Nearly a century ago William H. Hudson, the author of *Green Mansions,* described the migration of Argentine birds northward toward the equator at the onset of cold weather and back again at the beginning of the Argentine summer. Alexander Wetmore, in 1926, was one of the first to give a general account of bird migration in South America. A few years later, James P. Chapin described the migration of African birds.

Latitudinal Migration

Most species migrate from north to south in the fall and in the opposite direction the following spring. The distance traveled may be several thousand miles or it may be only a few hundred miles,

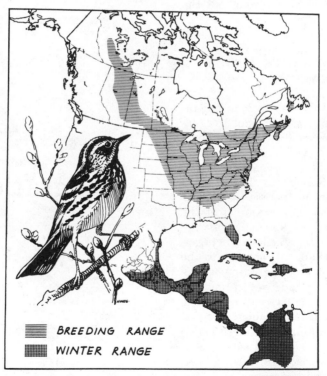

FIGURE 1. Summer and winter homes of the Black-and-white Warbler. (Courtesy of Frederick C. Lincoln and the U. S. Fish and Wildlife Service, from a drawing by Robert Hines.)

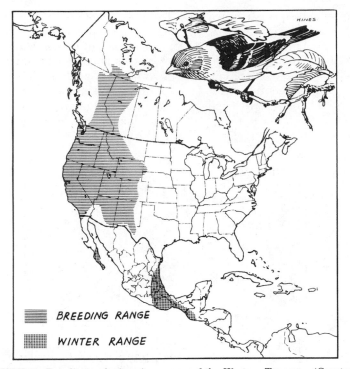

FIGURE 2. Breeding and wintering ranges of the Western Tanager. (Courtesy of Frederick C. Lincoln and the U. S. Fish and Wildlife Service, from a drawing by Robert Hines.)

as for American Goldfinches, Tree Sparrows, and Slate-colored Juncos that winter in northern states. House Wrens, Robins, Eastern Bluebirds, Hermit Thrushes, Chipping Sparrows, and many other species spend the winter in the southern part of the United States. Still others fly on to Central or South America (Figs. 1, 2). The longest migrations are performed by several species of shorebirds. After nesting in northern Alaska, Sanderlings (Fig. 3) fly to southern Argentina for the nonbreeding season. The maximum distance (about 11,000 miles) between the summer and winter homes of any species is that of the Arctic Tern. This species is unusual also because it crosses the Atlantic Ocean to and from the Old World during its migration flights (Fig. 4). Unlike most North American migratory species, Heermann's Gulls move northward to spend the winter.

Some of the intricacies of migration have come to light as a re-

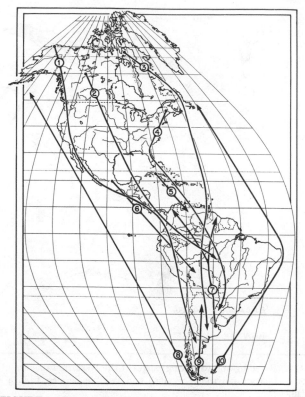

FIGURE 3. The postbreeding migrations of some American birds.
1. Sanderling. Northern Alaska to southern Argentina.
2. Red-eyed Vireo. Mackenzie to Mato Grosso.
3. American Golden Plover. Melville Peninsula to Argentina.
4. Bobolink. Maine to southern Brazil.
5. Gray Kingbird. Cuba to Venezuela.
6. Sulphur-bellied Flycatcher. Southern Mexico to Bolivia.
7. Brown-chested Martin. Argentina to British Guiana.
8. Sooty Shearwater. Magellanic Islands to Alaska coast.
9. Rufous-backed Ground-tyrant. Tierra del Fuego to northern Argentina.
10. Wilson's Petrel. Falkland Islands to Newfoundland.

(By permission from *Fundamentals of Ornithology* by Josselyn Van Tyne and Andrew J. Berger, published by John Wiley & Sons, Inc. Copyright, 1959.)

sult of marking birds with aluminum bands, placed around the bird's tarsus, so that precise identification of individual birds is possible. A migrating bird does not travel to just any area in the spring and the fall. It has been demonstrated many times that a bird often returns to the same small area each spring to carry out its nesting activities, and that it also tends to return to the same wintering area each year. Baldwin (1931) began to band birds near Cleveland, Ohio, in 1914, and at Thomasville, Georgia, during the following winter. He reported that many of the Ohio birds returned to the same area for nesting in successive years, and that such species as the White-throated and Chipping sparrows returned to the same wintering area in Georgia. Baldwin described his techniques in detail, and called attention to the types of data that

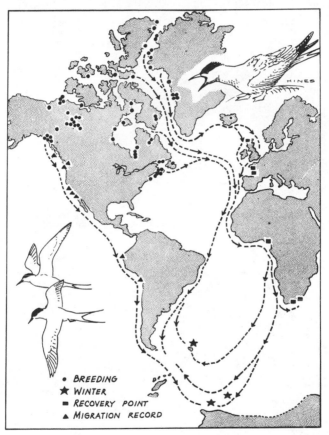

FIGURE 4. Distribution and migration of the Arctic Terns of eastern North America. Only the Arctic Tern and the Greenland race of the Wheatear are trans-atlantic migrants. The extreme summer and winter homes of the Arctic Tern are 11,000 miles apart, and, as the route taken is circuitous, these terns probably fly at least 25,000 miles during their annual migrations. (Courtesy of Frederick C. Lincoln and the U. S. Fish and Wildlife Service, from a drawing by Robert Hines.)

could be obtained from banding studies.   More recently, Paul B.
Dowling reported a return of 31.7 per cent of 103 banded Tree
Sparrows to a wintering ground in Missouri.   Josselyn Van Tyne
(1932) was apparently the first ornithologist to show that birds
also return to the same wintering areas in the tropics.   He banded
99 Indigo Buntings at Uaxactum, Guatemala, during March and
April, 1931.   Several of these birds were trapped in the same jungle
clearing the following year.

It seems reasonable to assume, therefore, that individual birds
probably follow the same migration route each year.   However, the

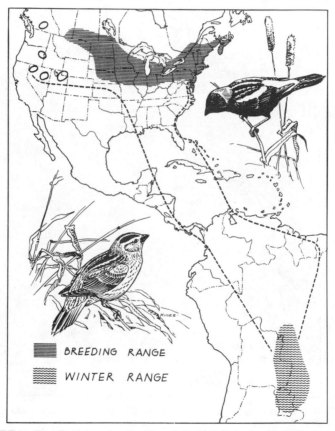

FIGURE 5. Distribution and migration of the Bobolink. It should be noted that
colonies have become established in western areas and that these birds show no tendency to take a short cut across Arizona, New Mexico, and Texas, but adhere to the
ancestral route of migration. (Courtesy of Frederick C. Lincoln and the U. S. Fish
and Wildlife Service, from a drawing by Robert Hines.)

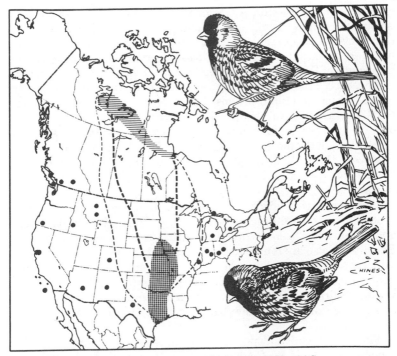

FIGURE 6. Breeding and winter ranges and migration of Harris' Sparrow, an example of a narrow migration route through the interior of the country. The heavy broken lines enclose the region traversed by the majority of the birds; the light broken lines enclose the country where they occur with more or less regularity; the heavy dots indicate records of accidental or sporadic occurrence. (Courtesy of Frederick C. Lincoln and the U. S. Fish and Wildlife Service, from a drawing by Robert Hines.)

breeding and wintering grounds of most species cover thousands of square miles, and the migration path of these species spreads over an area hundreds of miles in breadth (Figs. 5, 6). In contrast to the migration front of such species as the Bobolink, a few species have remarkably narrow routes. The Ipswich Sparrow, for example, migrates from Sable Island, Nova Scotia, to wintering grounds along the Atlantic coast from Massachusetts to Georgia. The entire route along the coast apparently is restricted to the shore line and may be only a few hundred yards across in some places.

Day migrants are influenced by major topographical features, such as mountains, rivers, large lakes, and seacoasts; in some localities the migration route may become very narrow. Two famous points of concentration for migrants are Pt. Pelee, Ontario, and Cape May, New Jersey. Soaring birds (hawks, ospreys, eagles, vultures) require rising air currents, and may follow mountain ridges even though they are not along the shortest route to the birds' destination (e.g., Hawk Mountain, Pennsylvania, where thousands of hawks are "funneled" along a relatively narrow route).

The early study of banding returns led to the concept of "flyways." Lincoln (1950) proposed that North American migratory birds, particularly waterfowl, "adhere with more or less fidelity" to one or another of four migration routes: Atlantic, Mississippi, Central, and Pacific flyways (Fig. 7). Further study has shown, however, that Mallards, American Widgeons, and other ducks banded on the same breeding ground may go south on all four flyways.

Most migrating birds fly at moderate heights, the majority probably below 3000 feet. Some strong-flying shorebirds, ducks, and geese have been recorded at altitudes of 5000 to 9000 feet. Exceptions also are found among birds that migrate through mountain passes. When flying in the face of strong wind over large bodies of water, migrating birds may fly within a few feet of the water. Baird et al. (1958) reported that several species of swallows along the Atlantic coast flew "from wave-top level" to about 10 feet above the water.

The rate at which a species moves northward in spring was first reported by Wells W. Cooke in 1915. He found, in general, that early migrants advance into the north more slowly than species that leave the wintering grounds later in the spring. The "species front" of the Black-and-white Warbler advances an average of 20 to 25 miles per day in its migration from Florida to Lake Superior. The Blackpoll Warbler, on the other hand, starts late in spring and advances at an ever-increasing rate, increasing from 30 to more than 200 miles per day (Fig. 8). The speed of northward movement of some species is thought to be related to the advance of isotherms (lines of equal temperature) in the spring. For many species, however, the relationship between isotherms and the advance of the species front remains obscure. Allan R. Phillips reported that the race of the Yellow Warbler that breeds in Arizona reaches Arizona in March and early April, that more northern forms arrive in late April, and that the race that nests in western Canada and Alaska does not reach Arizona until May. In speaking primarily of eastern races of the Yellow Warbler, Lincoln (1950) said that "the birds reach New Orleans about April 5, when the average temperature is 65° F. Traveling north much faster than does the season, they reach their breeding grounds in Manitoba the latter part of

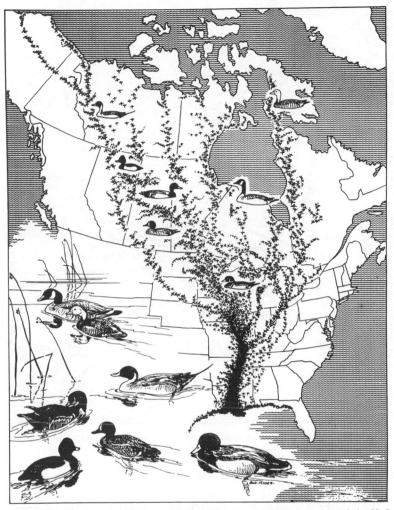

FIGURE 7. The Mississippi flyway. (Courtesy of Frederick C. Lincoln and the U. S. Fish and Wildlife Service, from a drawing by Robert Hines.)

May, when the average temperature is only 47°. Encountering progressively colder weather over their entire route, they cross a strip of country in the 15 days from May 11 to 25 that spring temperatures take 35 days to cross." Thus, a great deal remains to be learned about the rate of spring migration for different populations of a species. There is a wealth of data on the appearance

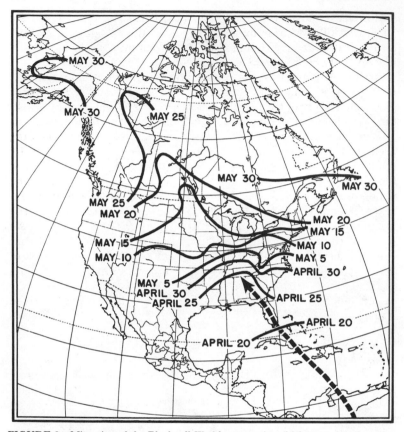

FIGURE 8. Migration of the Blackpoll Warbler, a species which starts late in spring and then migrates more and more rapidly as the season progresses. (By permission from *Fundamentals of Ornithology* by Josselyn Van Tyne and Andrew J. Berger, published by John Wiley & Sons, Inc. Copyright, 1959.)

of the first bird in spring for nearly all species, but little information on the arrival of the bulk of the population, or of the last arrivals. Even less is known about fall migration.

More intriguing, in many respects, than the advance of the species front is the speed at which individual birds migrate. This can be determined only by capturing (and banding) a bird just before its departure from the breeding grounds and capturing it again at the end of a migratory flight. These fortuitous circumstances have occurred only a few times despite the millions of birds that have been banded in the United States and Canada. A Lesser

Yellowlegs banded at Cape Cod, Massachusetts, on August 28, 1935, was killed at Martinique in the West Indies 6 days later; this bird averaged about 316 miles per day. Chimney Swifts have been known to fly 80 miles in 1 day and 600 miles in 4 days.

Arthur A. Allen was one of the first to point out that the first wave of spring migrants consists primarily of male birds. In his pioneering study of the breeding behavior of the Red-winged Blackbird (published in 1914), Allen reported that the first arrivals at Ithaca, New York, were adult males that were en route to breeding areas farther to the north. These were followed in succession by adult males that remained to breed (resident males); migrant females and immature males (those hatched the preceding year); resident adult females; resident immature males; and resident immature females. Several weeks sometimes elapsed between the arrival of the males and the arrival of the females. In her classic study of the Song Sparrow in Ohio, Margaret M. Nice found that the birds usually arrived in two main flights: an early migration of breeding males in late February or early March, and the main flight of breeding males and females, and also transients, the middle of March. Of 22 banded males she found that 5 birds arrived consistently early and 6 arrived consistently late. Female birds hatched the previous year sometimes came very late.

Some individuals of a species may stay on their breeding grounds throughout the winter, whereas others migrate, sometimes for a considerable distance. This "partial migration" occurs among Song Sparrows, Mockingbirds, and gulls. Blue Jays often migrate in large flocks but banding studies have shown that some breeding jays in Michigan and other northern states are permanent residents. The extent of the migratory journey may vary with age or sex. Among Herring Gulls, for example, first-year birds migrate farther than second-year birds, and older birds appear not to migrate at all. Female Tree Sparrows in the Middle West are said to move farther south than the males, and John T. Emlen reported that the two sexes of the White-crowned Sparrow tend to migrate to different wintering grounds in California, females predominating east of the Sierras, males west of the Sierras.

In some species the time of migration and/or the migration route of young birds hatched that year is not the same as the time or route of the adult birds. The adult Brown-headed Cowbird migrates earlier than the young, particularly in the northern parts of its breeding range. Adult American Golden Plovers migrate southward from Labrador over the Atlantic Ocean to South America. Young plovers, however, migrate southward through the interior of the

United States; in the spring, all of the birds move northward through the Mississippi valley.

Migratory birds have been classified according to their migration behavior as either "weather" migrants or "instinct" migrants. For certain species, these terms have been useful, but it should be realized, as Farner (1955) pointed out, that it is likely that these two categories represent the extremes of types of migratory behavior, and that many intermediate types lie between the extremes. The early spring "weather" migrants appear to be greatly influenced by the weather (particularly temperature), whereas the "instinct" migrants of late spring are little affected by weather.

Weather changes in the United States result from the mixing of air masses originating in the tropics (moist warm air) and the arctic (cold dry air). Weather by the day or week (as contrasted to seasonal changes) consists of a series of high and low pressure areas, each of which may cover as much as a third of the United States; these areas move across the country in a roughly easterly direction. A low-pressure area (low barometric reading) consists of a large mass of warm air which rises and flows counterclockwise toward its center as it moves forward. Rain, snow, and even tornadoes may occur in a low-pressure area, but the air is always calm at its center. A large mass of cold air, of greater density, exerts greater downward pressure (barometers rise), spirals outward clockwise as it moves forward, and is described as a high-pressure area. As a rule, it brings clear skies because moisture is not forced up to condense and form clouds. Each pressure area or large mass of air is preceded by a "front" which may be relatively sharp or wide. A "cold front," in which the cold air pushes under the warm air and displaces it, usually causes considerable disturbance and ushers in a high-pressure area or cooler weather. In a "warm front," which is more peaceful and follows a high-pressure area, the warm air overrides the cold air (slides up over it) as it displaces the cold air, and warmer weather follows.

Cooperative studies have suggested that the migratory movements of many passerine birds seem to be closely related to changes in air temperature and wind direction. Bagg et al. (1950) showed that spring migratory movements in the eastern United States begin at the onset of warm fronts, when barometric pressure is falling and a moist warm air mass from the Gulf of Mexico and the Caribbean Sea is moving northward. They distinguished two types of migration "waves": the *onrushing wave* and the *arrested wave*. Onrushing waves take place at times of low pressure, southerly winds, and a significant rise in temperature; thus, the birds move into or through a given region during the interval between the passage of a warm front through that region and the subsequent arrival of a cold front. Bagg and his collaborators explain the arrested wave simply by postulating that "cloudiness and rain are likely to be encountered by the onrushing wave as the cold front approaches from the west or northwest. If still in motion when overtaken by the cold front, the onrushing wave will be grounded and thus form an arrested wave until the meteorological cycle is complete and a further advance takes place." An excellent example of arrested waves is offered by the situation found along the Gulf Coast. Migrants are uncommon or absent there during fair weather, but they appear suddenly, regardless of time of day, with the arrival of bad weather.

Bagg (1955) presented a stimulating analysis of the influence of weather conditions on migration of the Indigo Bunting, in which he concluded that numbers of this species flew nonstop from Yucatan to points as far north as Maine and Nova Scotia on April 17–18, 1954. He proposed that these long flights were possible because of the unusually favorable strong tropical air flow (Figs. 9, 10). That many of the birds reached areas beyond their normal breeding range, as well as much earlier than expected on their breeding grounds, could be explained by the direction of air flow. The birds were deflected from the course they would have followed normally by the direction of the favorable winds, upon which their migration, in part, was based.

Williamson (1955) referred to such deflection as *migrational drift*. He believed that wind "is the migrant bird's greatest enemy, and this is especially true of the large number of species whose journeys (because they require the daytime for feeding) must be performed largely by night." With respect to the Indigo Buntings, it was estimated that extensive fat deposits, characteristic of migratory birds, would make it possible for these birds to remain air-borne for about 36 hours, long enough to make the flight from Yucatan to Maine. One sees in the vagaries of weather a partial explanation, at least, for the occurrence of birds far out of their normal range and of differences in time of spring arrival of species from year to year.

Lack (1960) reviewed the subject of migration of passerine birds and concluded that warm temperatures in spring and cold temperatures in the fall were the primary weather factors that influence migration. According to Lack, "migration is unaffected by the general weather situation as such or by barometric pressure, while the available evidence suggests that it is also unaffected by stable

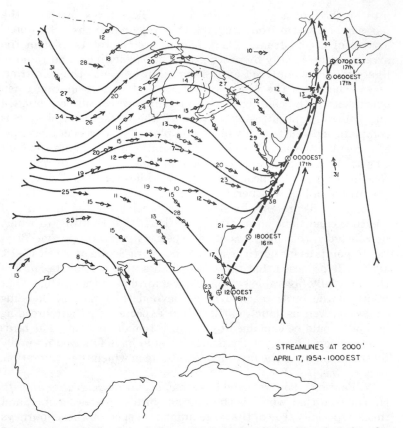

STREAMLINES AT 2000'
APRIL 17, 1954-1000 EST

FIGURE 9. Streamlines for 10:00 A.M. E.S.T. April 17, 1954. Hypothetical track, at 2000 feet, for an Indigo Bunting arriving in Washington County, Maine, is indicated by the dashed line. Positions of the bird at various times are indicated. (Courtesy of Aaron M. Bagg, from *Bird-Banding*, 39, 1955.)

air conditions, or by wind direction as such." Lack's summary of a considerable amount of contradictory evidence points to the need for more careful studies of migration patterns among birds.

Strong-flying small birds and most of the larger birds migrate during the daytime: hawks, pigeons, swifts, hummingbirds, swallows, crows, jays, pipits, waxwings, shrikes, most blackbirds, Eastern Kingbird, Horned Lark, Robin, Eastern Bluebird, Pine Grosbeak, and Snow Bunting. Large birds that are secretive in habit and most small birds migrate at night: rails, woodcock, cuckoos, woodpeckers, tyrant-flycatchers, titmice, nuthatches,

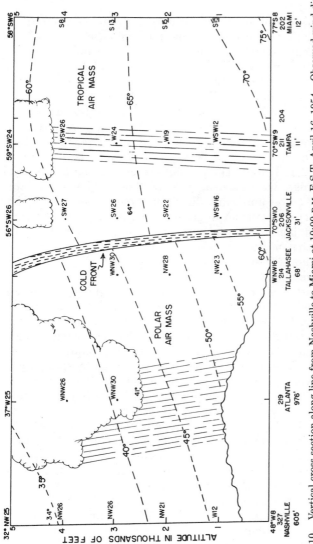

FIGURE 10. Vertical cross section along line from Nashville to Miami at 10:00 P.M. E.S.T. April 16, 1954. Observed wind directions, speeds in knots, and temperatures in degrees Fahrenheit are indicated above each reporting station. Lines of equal temperature (isotherms) for every 5° F. are shown as dashed lines and relative humidities aloft are reported by radiosone. The cold front at this time lies a short distance northwest of Jacksonville and is moving from left to right across the section. Scattered showers are falling in the tropical air ahead of the front, while rain is falling within the cold air some distance to the rear of the front. Data are given for levels from the surface to 5000 feet. (Courtesy of Aaron M. Bagg, from *Bird-Banding*, 39, 1955.)

creepers, wrens, most thrushes, kinglets, vireos, wood-warblers, meadowlarks, orioles, and the majority of sparrows (finches). However, nocturnal migrants may move along slowly while feeding during the day.

Attempts have been made to estimate the number of migrating birds by tabulating the call notes heard at night ("chip-counting"). This undoubtedly is a wholly unreliable technique for determining the total numbers of any species that migrates at night. Ornithologists also have studied nocturnal migration by pointing a telescope at the moon and counting silhouettes of birds crossing its face. Lowery (Lowery and Newman, 1955) refined this technique, pointed out its limitations, and analyzed the problems involved. Figures 11 and 12 illustrate the changing size of the effective field of observation as the moon moves across the night sky. Lowery and Newman believe that herons, geese, and shorebirds migrate in close formation at night but that nearly all small birds fly alone and that they are more or less uniformly distributed over large areas. They believe, also, that nocturnal migrants generally fly with the wind, whereas low-flying daytime migrants often must fly into the wind. They found that nocturnal migration is at its height during the hour before midnight and that the number of birds flying tapers off rapidly after midnight.

More recently, radar has been used in the study of migration. Preliminary radar studies indicate that nocturnal migration involves many more birds than daytime migration, that most birds fly at altitudes between 2000 and 3000 feet, and that the heaviest migration occurs when the sky is clear. Like other techniques, the radar method has its limitations; its use alone entails many speculations. It has the advantage that the radarscope can be used continuously for long periods, thus providing photographic film that later can be interpreted and correlated with information obtained by moonwatching and by daytime observations on the kinds of birds that have moved into an area. To be most effective, studies of nocturnal migration should include all three techniques.

Geese are well known for migrating in close-knit flocks, often in a V-shaped pattern. Some other birds also migrate in flocks containing a single species, e.g., Chimney Swifts, nighthawks, kingbirds, waxwings, crossbills, and crows. Mixed flocks, composed of several species of the same family, are characteristic of swallows, blackbirds, and wood-warblers. Flocks composed of a single sex or of one age group were mentioned previously. Some birds (e.g., grebes, kingfishers, shrikes) migrate alone rather than in groups.

It has been known for over a hundred years that birds increase in weight about the time of migration. In recent years premigratory

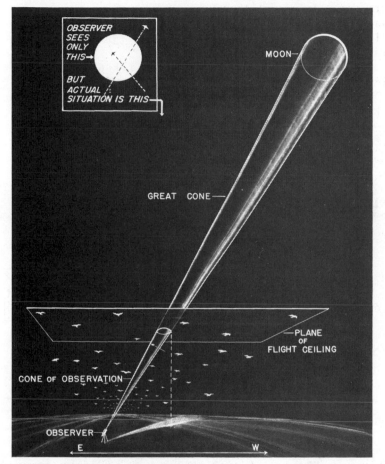

FIGURE 11. The field of observation, showing its two-dimensional aspect as it appears to the observer and its three-dimensional actuality. The *flight ceiling* is the highest level at which birds are flying; the *great cone* is the entire observation space between the telescope and the moon; the *cone of observation* is that part of the great cone lying beneath the flight ceiling. The breadth of the cone is greatly exaggerated in the illustration. (Courtesy of George H. Lowery, Jr., from "A Quantitative Study of the Nocturnal Migration of Birds," by permission University of Kansas Museum of Natural History.)

fat deposition has been studied in several species of birds (e.g., Oregon and Slate-colored juncos, White-crowned and White-throated sparrows), and it has been learned that fat deposition can be stimulated experimentally by exposing caged birds to increased environmental temperatures and increased periods of light (photoperiod). Similar experiments have shown that the phenomenon of

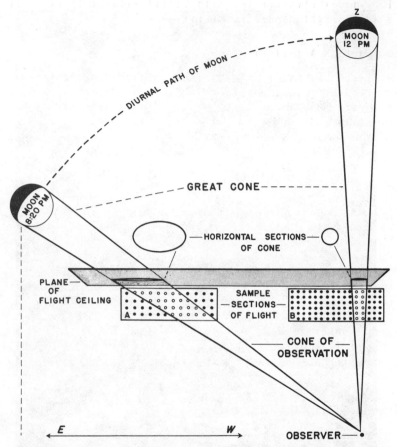

FIGURE 12. The changing size of the effective field of observation. The sample sections A and B represent the densities of flight at 8:20 and 12:00 P.M., respectively. With twice as many birds in the air at midnight, when the moon is at its zenith (Z), as there were at the earlier hour, only half as many are visible because of the decrease in the size of the cone of observation. Note that when the moon is overhead a horizontal section of the cone is circular, but when the cone is inclined this circle becomes elongated into an ellipse. (Courtesy of George H. Lowery, Jr., from "A Quantitative Study of the Nocturnal Migration of Birds," by permission University of Kansas Museum of Natural History.)

premigratory fat deposition does not occur in nonmigratory races of the same species, nor does it appear to occur in the Song Sparrow. It has been suggested, therefore, that there are physiological differences between different migratory species. Little comparative work has been done with strictly nonmigratory species. Female

Ring-necked Pheasants, Willow Ptarmigan, and Blue Grouse exhibit a spring weight increase but the males do not.

Altitudinal Migration

Species that live in mountains may adjust to changing seasons simply by moving downward to lower elevations, where food and cover are available during the winter. Throughout most of their breeding range, Slate-colored Juncos migrate southward but those inhabiting the Great Smoky Mountains of Tennessee are said to move only to lower elevations. Similarly, Mountain Quail, which nest at elevations up to 9500 feet in central California mountains, migrate downward on foot in single file to areas below 5000 feet in the fall.

A few species migrate to a higher elevation in winter. A good example is the Blue Grouse, which moves upward in the northern Rocky Mountains after the breeding season to winter in fir and pine forests. This upward movement seems to be correlated with food supply, and one study revealed that 99 per cent of the grouse's winter food in Idaho consisted of needles and buds of Douglas fir (*Pseudotsuga taxifolia*). Frederick V. Hebard suggested that certain species of passerine birds (e.g., White-winged Crossbill, Pine Siskin, Pine Grosbeak) wintering in the mountains of Colorado make daily movements to higher elevations in late winter and early spring, perhaps because of increased "feeding time and effective daylength" there.

Longitudinal Migration

A few species migrate east or west, rather than north or south, after the breeding season. M. J. McGee showed by banding that Evening Grosbeaks that nest in northern Michigan spend the winter in New England (Fig. 13). Similarly, California Gulls that breed in Utah migrate westward to winter on the Pacific coast. White-winged Scoters move from breeding grounds in central Canada almost due east and due west to winter on the Atlantic and Pacific coasts.

Postbreeding Northward Migration

Herons, egrets, and Bald Eagles are noted for large-scale movements northward at the end of the breeding season. These flights appear to consist largely of young birds of the year. Charles L.

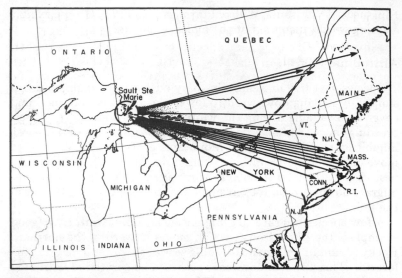

FIGURE 13. The east-west migrations of Evening Grosbeaks between their breeding
ground in Michigan and the New England wintering ground, as demonstrated by the
recovery of banded individuals. (By permission from *Fundamentals of Ornithology*
by Josselyn Van Tyne and Andrew J. Berger, published by John Wiley & Sons, Inc.
Copyright, 1959.)

Broley, who banded many nestling Bald Eagles in Florida, found
that the young move northward soon after leaving the nest, and
that some were recovered as far north as Maine by June (Fig. 14).
It has been suggested that the summer heat of Florida is too great
for the Bald Eagle, a northern species which has probably only
recently spread into Florida, and that it is able to profit during the
cooler season by the abundant food and plentiful nesting sites, but
that it is not adapted to the higher temperatures of the Florida
summer. Numbers of Common Egrets, Little Blue Herons, and
Snowy Egrets often move into northern United States and southern
Canada during July and August. Banding studies of young Black-
crowned Night Herons in Massachusetts revealed that as many as
79 per cent moved as far as 500 miles to the north.

Sporadic Irruptions

A number of species exhibit a pattern of erratic wandering in the
nonbreeding season. Among these are the crossbills, Pine Grosbeak,
Evening Grosbeak, and Purple Finch, which may feed largely on
conifer seeds. Large "flights" of other northern species tend to

occur fairly regularly in cycles of four or more years. The reason
for this is largely unknown, but a shortage of food in the north may
be involved. One of the best-documented examples is that of the
periodic southward movements of the Snowy Owl (Fig. 15). These
large white birds move into the northern United States (sometimes
as far south as Virginia) about every four years. Other northern
species occasionally move southward in large numbers but appar-

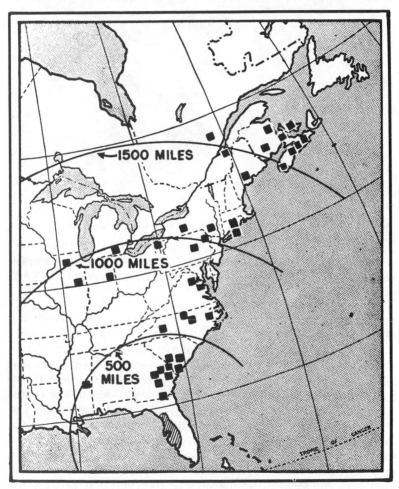

FIGURE 14. Records of young Bald Eagles banded in the nest in west Florida and
recovered in the north during their first year. (By permission from *Fundamentals of
Ornithology* by Josselyn Van Tyne and Andrew J. Berger, published by John Wiley &
Sons, Inc. Copyright, 1959.)

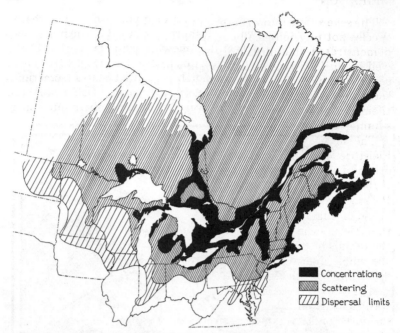

FIGURE 15. The great "flight" of the Snowy Owl into northern United States in 1941–1942. (Courtesy of L. L. Snyder.)

ently not with any degree of regularity. Some well-known examples are the Black-backed Three-toed Woodpecker, Great-horned Owl, and the Dovekie.

ORIGIN OF MIGRATORY BEHAVIOR

Many theories have been offered to account for bird migration, but the origin remains unknown. Many writers agree that migratory behavior may have evolved several times during the evolutionary history of birds. It was suggested at one time that the scarcity of food during northern winters was the explanation for most bird migration. To be sure, insectivorous birds are not adapted to life in northern winters, but many species leave their breeding grounds while there is an abundant food supply. Moreover, some predatory and seed-eating species migrate whereas closely related species remain throughout the year in the far north. Lack (1960) emphasized the importance of food supply in his review of passerine migration.

The severe cold of northern winters would be a limiting factor for species not physiologically adapted for life there, but it has been demonstrated that migratory seed-eating birds survive perfectly well in outdoor aviaries in Canada when given adequate food and cover, and individual birds of some primarily insect-eating species sometimes winter in the northern states. Many species also leave their breeding grounds in July and August before the heat of summer is over.

The many major and minor advances and recessions of the Pleistocene ice front once seemed a plausible explanation for the origin of the migratory habit among North Temperate Zone birds. It is now generally agreed, however, that whatever influence Pleistocene glaciation may have had it was not responsible for the origin of migratory behavior. Reginald Moreau (1951) concluded that Pleistocene climatic fluctuations did no more "than determine the details of the specific migrations" we now see, and added that the whole glaciation period occupied a time "less than one hundredth part of the age of the class Aves."

A few writers have postulated that the Southern Hemisphere was the original home of many species that now breed only in the far north and that these species return to their "ancestral home" after the nesting season. There is a great deal of evidence against this belief.

ANNUAL STIMULUS FOR MIGRATION

In considering the causes of migration, ornithologists have separated environmental factors into two groups. *Ultimate factors* are those which have exerted a positive selective evolutionary influence on those birds which developed migratory behavior, and a negative selective influence on birds which failed to develop migratory behavior (i.e., birds which did not develop this behavior did not survive). Ultimate factors, therefore, are those which have made migratory behavior advantageous to a species; they include such things as an abundant food supply, suitable nesting conditions, and optimum daylight hours for raising young. *Proximate factors* are those which stimulate a migratory state or condition in the individual bird and which lead to actual migration. The "migratory state" of the individual bird consists of physiological changes which include the deposition of subcutaneous and peritoneal fat (premigratory fat deposits) and a change in the secretion of hormones. In the spring, it also includes a great increase in the size and activity of the gonads. The proximate factor which has received the greatest amount of experimental attention is that of increasing day-length in the spring and its effect on migratory behavior and on the development of the gonads (see pages 203–206). Whether or not there exists an internal or innate rhythm of activity in the endocrine glands that is independent of environmental factors remains in debate.

Evidence obtained from experiments on several species of North Temperate Zone birds indicates that a number of interrelated annual cycles seem to be photoperiodically controlled but that the control does not necessarily operate in the same way for each species. Nor can it be stated with assurance that there is or is not an immediate causal relationship between the migratory and the gonadal cycles. Furthermore, Wolfson (1959) has pointed out that "gradually increasing day lengths (or an increase in day length) are not necessary to induce spring migration. The role of day length, once the birds are ready to respond, is the *regulation of the rate* at which the response proceeds." Premigratory fat deposition is characteristic of birds prior to the fall migration, as in the spring, but other physiological conditions appear to be different from what they are in the spring. Wolfson has summarized the situation by stating that "after the breeding season, the gonads regress, the birds molt, and subsequently, there is a physiological change, which precedes the onset of fall migration. Nothing is known about the factors which regulate this state. When the fall migration gets underway in September and October the day lengths have reached a value which is effective for the beginning of the preparatory phase of the next spring migration. And thus a new cycle begins." Although a great deal has been learned about the relationship of the change of day-lengths to the increase in gonad size in experimental birds, Wolfson has pointed out that "the relation between physiological changes induced by increasing day length and the actual release of migratory behavior are not known."

BIRD NAVIGATION

How does a bird manage to navigate so accurately that it can return to the same hedgerow each spring and to the same jungle clearing each fall? No one knows the answer. Many theories have been offered to explain bird navigation, and each new theory has its day, but sooner or later someone presents evidence to refute it.

Some simple and some very elaborate (and often very artificial) experiments have been devised in an effort to seek answers to the problem. The theories deserve only brief mention. None of the research has involved a study of the bird's anatomical and physiological mechanisms, and very few workers have even considered them seriously. Consequently, all sorts of special senses have been postulated without any basis in fact. We do not even know very much about the bird's ordinary senses.

Some of the more interesting experiments deal with the ability of birds to "home" when removed from their nests. These experiments, like all of the others, do not tell how the birds navigate; they prove simply that they are very good at it. Preliminary experiments to test the homing ability of nesting Purple Martins were conducted by William E. Southern at the University of Michigan Biological Station during the summer of 1958. He released 16 adult martins (14 females) at distances of 1.75 miles to 234 miles from their nests; all returned to their nests. The birds, carried in closed boxes, were transported to the release point by automobile. One female martin was released at Ann Arbor (234 miles south of the Biological Station) at 10:40 P.M., July 7; she had returned to her nest with young before 7:15 the following morning. Another female released at Ann Arbor at 6:50 A.M., July 8, had returned to her nest by 5:30 P.M. that day, and perhaps several hours earlier; this bird had been kept in a darkened container 23.8 hours. More remarkable in many respects is the case of the Manx Shearwater that Rosario Mazzeo took by airplane from Wales to Boston. This bird returned to its nesting burrow 3200 miles away in 12 days 12½ hours. It traveled at a rate of more than 250 miles per day from a point outside the species' range and on an east-west route at right angles to its normal migration path.

Donald R. Griffin (1952) outlined three types of homing in birds:

Type I is homing by reliance on visual landmarks within familiar territory and the use of wandering "exploration" when the bird is released in unfamiliar territory.

Type II depends on the bird's ability to maintain a certain direction even when crossing unfamiliar territory.

Type III depends on the additional ability which some birds exhibit, when released in unfamiliar territory, to choose approximately the correct direction to their destination. This is the type used by all birds that migrate long distances between limited summer and winter areas. Experiments with a few species have revealed that nonmigratory species have poor homing ability.

It has been suggested that a young bird may develop an awareness of its general breeding area through the process of imprinting
(which occurs within a few hours after hatching; see page 143),
but the evidence does not support this belief. For example, Robert
A. McCabe reported that Wood Ducks were taken from central
Illinois to Madison, Wisconsin, when three to five weeks old, and
were released there when about seven weeks old; these birds left
with the fall migration. Some of these banded birds were known
to have returned to Madison and to have nested there in subsequent
years. Other young Wood Ducks were taken from the same Illinois
hatchery to an area in Indiana 180 miles to the east. They made
that their breeding area. In neither instance did any of the young
return to their hatching place in Illinois.

Although the young of a few species (e.g., Brown-headed Cowbird) migrate in the fall after all adults have gone south, it might
seem reasonable to assume that the young of many species learn
their migration route by following older birds. There is no evidence
that this is the case, but there is evidence that some young birds
do not learn the migration route by following the adults. Frank
Bellrose trapped several hundred young Blue-winged Teal and kept
them in captivity until long after the teal migration had ended,
after which the birds of the year were released. Banding returns
indicated that these young birds followed the same migration path
used by the adult birds and that they spent the winter in the
same areas.

Bird Navigation and the Coriolis Force

In 1946 Gustav Ising proposed that bird navigation may depend
upon the mechanical effects which result from the rotation of the
earth (the Coriolis force). The Coriolis force is strongest at the
poles and is zero at the equator. Theoretically, therefore, a bird
might thus judge its latitude. However, the force is so small and
the confusing factors (such as variation in the speed of the bird,
effects of wind and air turbulence) are so great that the detection
and measurement of the extremely small changes which the theory
requires seem well outside the sensitivity of the bird's sense organs.
According to V. C. Wynne-Edwards, a change of speed from 40 to
39 miles per hour in a bird's flight speed could alter the Coriolis
effect by 2.5 per cent, the same change that would be registered by
a geographical displacement of about 150 miles.

Bird Navigation, Terrestrial Magnetism, and Coriolis Force

Henry L. Yeagley experimented with homing pigeons and postulated that birds sense their "latitude" by the effects of the Coriolis force and their "longitude" by the strength of the vertical component of the earth's magnetic field. In North America the variation in these two forces constitutes a grid, one set of lines being the parallels of latitude (lines of equal Coriolis force) and the other being arcs drawn about the North Magnetic Pole as a center. Yeagley trained pigeons to return to a home loft in Pennsylvania, and then released them in Nebraska near a point where the lines of the two forces intersect exactly as they do at the home loft in Pennsylvania. Only a very few pigeons reached even the vicinity of the Nebraska loft, but Yeagley presented evidence for what he considered to be a significant "tendency" to fly in that direction! Several authors have presented detailed criticisms of Yeagley's hypothesis.

Bird Navigation Related to Vision

Daytime migrants often follow rivers, coastlines, or mountain ridges, even when these carry the birds away from a direct flight line to their destination. Many studies have indicated that birds use such visual clues in modifying their migration routes according to the topography of the land. Such clues, however, do not explain the bird's ability to navigate on its first migratory flight, nor is there any evidence to suggest that a bird "learns" its migratory path. One might ask also: how does the bird know when it has reached its destination?

Experiments with homing pigeons, gulls, Starlings, and other birds have shown that their homing ability is considerably reduced when they are released during cloudy weather. It seemed logical to suggest, therefore, that birds orient themselves in relation to the sun. Gustav Kramer designed experiments to test the relationship of the sun to migratory movements of Starlings. He placed Starlings in hexagonal cages containing a series of windows and an "environment" which could be revolved about the cage. The birds oriented continuously toward a given compass direction regardless of the time of day, even when their view of the outdoors was limited to six square equally spaced windows, each subtending about 20° and revealing only a patch of sky well above the horizon. Kramer then taught Starlings to find food in closed containers placed in a fixed relation to the light source. When the light source was shifted 90° by the use of mirrors, the Starlings made a corresponding shift in their orientation. When artificial light was substituted, the birds continued to react in the same manner, seeking food in a direction relative to the artificial sun and correcting for the passage of time as they had for the real sun. A heavy cloud cover prevented sun orientation.

G. V. T. Matthews, after studying homing in pigeons, gulls, and shearwaters, proposed that birds use the sun arc for direction finding; the sun arc is simply the path followed by the sun across the sky. The theory requires that the bird have an accurate memory of the sun-arc characteristics at its home locality, an accurate internal clock-like mechanism, and an eye capable of measuring small angles. This seemed reasonable to Matthews because the stimulus for the onset of migration among North Temperate Zone species appeared to be changes in day-length, and these are governed by the rising and sinking of the sun arc. However, the bird must be able to measure the altitude of the sun above the horizon to within 1° of arc and to measure angles up to 90° with this degree of accuracy; the bird also must possess an "artificial horizon" to serve as a basis for the measurements. Kramer (1957) criticized Matthews' theory and remarked that he thought there was little justification for the sun-arc hypothesis. He added that "our present knowledge consists merely of fragmentary observations which so far allow no plausible interpretation."

A very large number of birds migrate by night, as mentioned above, and although some authors proposed that nocturnal migrants "took their bearings," so to speak, before the sun set, the idea was not generally accepted. The next "obvious" answer was that nocturnal migrants navigate with reference to the moon and stars. Sauer (1958, and earlier) conducted experiments with several species of Old-world warblers. The birds were placed in cages in a planetarium with a cupola 20 feet in diameter. Sauer's data (like most of those obtained in laboratory experiments with caged birds) consisted of "migratory restlessness" (*Zugunruhe*), the tendency of captive birds to become active at night during the normal migration period for the species. The warblers perched in their cages facing in the direction of the migratory path characteristic for their species. When the perches were rotated, the birds again turned toward the proper compass direction. The warblers failed to orient properly when the sky was cloudy. Kramer (1957) stated that the moon effects obtained by Sauer probably "are not genuine orientation responses, but correspond to similar positively phototactic behaviour of a shrike under conditions of diffuse light. In fact the warbler aims at the illuminated wall without relation to the due compass direction. . . . If determinate patterns of stars are involved, then—as in the case of sun orientation—mechanism to allow for the steady motion of the fixed stars must be part of night orientation." Sauer had concluded that Old-world warblers have a "remarkable hereditary mechanism for orienting themselves by the stars." In view of the fact that birds have been migrating by day and by night for many thousands of years, it seems reasonable to assume that they possess remarkable ability and that birds are aware of the sun and the stars. The experiments on sun and star navigation have "proved" this; they have not told us how the bird actually navigates, nor anything about the bird's internal mechanism which coordinates visual information gained from the sun, the moon, or the stars.

In brief, no one knows exactly what factors stimulate migratory behavior or how birds navigate.

5

Behavior

Behavior involves all of a bird's activities. The swift's pattern of flight, the phalarope's method of feeding, and the Henslow's Sparrow's nighttime singing are examples of types of behavior. The study of behavior is at once both simple and complex—simple because it is relatively easy to observe what a bird is doing; complex when one tries to understand the meaning and to explain the causes of the behavior. I have chosen, therefore, to divide this chapter into two main parts: theoretical aspects of bird behavior, and selected examples of common bird activities (Fig. 1). The following three chapters are devoted to major behavioral activities.

We should recognize two things at the outset. Psychology has been defined as "that branch of science which treats of the mind and mental operations, especially as they are shown in behavior." The study of bird behavior is an outgrowth of comparative psychology or the study of the "mental activity" of animals. When we attempt to interpret the actions of birds, we should not ascribe human emotions to them. "Little Jenny Wren" is not a "devoted mother" in the sense that many human mothers are; she is devoted because she has little or no control over physiological processes that take place within her body; we have no justifica-

FIGURE 1. Male Red-winged Blackbird attacking a stuffed crow. (Courtesy of Samuel A. Grimes.)

tion for ascribing to her such feelings as love or a sense of duty. We are dealing here with *ethology*, the objective study of behavior (Tinbergen). Secondly, a theory is a "working hypothesis." The widely accepted theories of bird behavior have been elaborated primarily by European biologists, who, I am sure, would be the first to acknowledge that, even though some bird activities seem to conform to certain theoretical concepts, we know virtually nothing about the actual neurophysiological or "mental" processes which really are the basis for a bird's behavior.

The study of bird behavior is still in its infancy. Despite some misuse of the concepts proposed to increase our understanding of bird behavior, the beginning student should not neglect this important subject. He needs to learn the behaviorist's special vocabulary in order to understand the literature and to record his own observations more effectively. Used with an awareness of their implications and limitations, these terms do enable one to develop a more meaningful insight into the intricacies of the bird's world. "The student of behavior should seek to explain behavior, and not to prove that it cannot be explained" (Tinbergen, 1952).

THE THEORETICAL FRAMEWORK

Instinctive Behavior

Although much criticized by some students of animal behavior, the concepts proposed by Konrad Lorenz and Niko Tinbergen have been accepted by many ornithologists. It seems proper, therefore, to place emphasis on the theories of Lorenz and Tinbergen in a book on bird study.

If behavior is what the bird does, it follows that any behavior pattern is the result of muscular activity which causes the movements of head, neck, wings, tail, etc. With the exception of heart muscle, however, muscles in general do not contract unless they are stimulated by nerves to do so. Such a nerve is called a *motor nerve;* the impulse it conducts stimulates a muscle to contract (to shorten). The motor nerve itself must receive some sort of a stimulus, either from the surface or from the interior of the body. If, for example, one touches a hot stove, one almost immediately jerks the hand away. *Sensory nerves* conduct impulses which, reaching consciousness, one interprets as "hotness"; almost before one is aware of the sensation, however, muscles of the limb contract so that the hand is withdrawn. In this overly simplified example, sensory nerves conduct impulses to motor nerves which, in turn, stimulate muscles to contract. In its simplest form any muscle action is the result of a *stimulus* (conducted by nerves) and a *response* (effected by muscle contraction).

However, birds perform complex and remarkable acts which cannot be explained as a simple stimulus-response relationship. Moreover, we have no basis for attributing to birds the thought processes characteristic of man. Herein lies much of the difficulty, for man is all too often wont to explain the world about him in terms of his own subjective feelings and emotions. It also is characteristic of man to give fancy names to phenomena that he cannot understand. Usually, therefore, the names really do not explain anything, but the implication is that the man who uses them knows what he is talking about—thus, we proceed.

Instinct

The word "instinct" has been used in many contexts by different writers to describe a large class of unexplained animal activities. A dictionary definition is: "natural and unreasoning prompting to action; as, the web-building *instinct* of spiders." Major "instincts" of birds are those related to reproduction, migration, feeding, fighting, social relations, and care of the exterior of the body. The instincts are inherited. They are set off or "triggered" by environmental stimuli (especially visual and auditory stimuli), and their expression often takes the form of rigid behavior patterns. The poorly understood neurophysiological processes that effect the behavior patterns are, for convenience, referred to as "drives" or "motivations." These drives may be activated or "motivated" by external and/or internal stimuli. Furthermore, the internal stimuli may be hormones or visceral sensory stimuli, or they may even arise "spontaneously" (i.e., without any apparent extrinsic stimulus) *within* the central nervous system (see page 289). What this means is that the ethologist does not understand these processes or how they effect the behavior that can be observed.

Consummatory Act and Appetitive Behavior

To Lorenz, Tinbergen, and others, instinct is innate behavior—behavior that has not been affected by learning processes. Such instinctive behavior, Lorenz proposed, is expressed by a series of *fixed-action patterns*. The final behavior resulting from the sequential development of a fixed-action pattern is called the *consummatory act*. It is essentially a simple and highly stereotyped activity; it is the last step in a chain of reactions related to some instinctive drive; its completion "satisfies" an internal drive. Tinbergen postulated a series of functional "centers" (neurophysiological "motivational" processes) within the central nervous system for the integration of the several fixed-action patterns of the major instincts. *Innate releasing mechanisms* at different levels, however, block the discharge of the component steps in an innate behavior pattern until *sign stimuli* (releasers) are received, whereupon the blocking or inhibitory action of the innate releasing mechanism is removed. The consummatory act cannot take place until appropriate releasers are present to counteract the inhibitory impulses existing at different levels. In the absence of the releasers, the motivational drive finds expression in *appetitive* (exploratory) *behavior*. Appetitive behavior has been defined as the "variable introductory phase" of an instinctive behavior pattern. The entire pattern is a hierarchical system: intrinsic motivational impulses arise from a "superordinated" center at the top; the many types of appetitive behavior occupy an intermediate position; and the consummatory acts and their constituent motor actions represent the bottom of the hierarchy. As a result of detailed studies of the Great Tit in England, Hinde (1953: 194) concluded that appetitive behavior and consummatory act differ only in degree: "consummatory acts could be regarded as forms of appetitive behaviour in which only one motor pattern is possible."

What does this mean in terms of bird behavior? The major motivational drive of a hungry bird is expressed in hunting or food-seeking behavior. The consummatory act for the bird is swallowing food, a relatively complex series of muscular actions. Everything leading up to swallowing is appetitive behavior. This may involve several variable actions and responses to sign stimuli, such as flying over a hunting territory, sighting one of several possible types of prey, which will determine the type of attack to be made, and then the attack itself. Another oft-cited example pertains to nest-building, one phase of the reproductive drive. The construction of the nest constitutes the consummatory act (or acts). Appetitive behavior, again, involves a series of variable actions and responses to sign stimuli: searching for a proper nest site; searching for suitable nest materials; finding the materials, picking them up; and flying to the nest site. Migration ("the first sign" of reproductive behavior) also has been considered as appetitive behavior: "in migratory Passerine birds spring migration continues until the sign stimuli indicative of a suitable habitat are encountered" (Hinde, 1953: 198).

"Derived" Activities

The bird, of course, is subject to many different drives or instincts, several of which find expression every day. In general, only one drive can be dominant at a particular time, however, and conflicts between drives arise. Moreover, the intensity of a given drive depends on many factors, both internal and external. Consequently, an instinctive behavior pattern may not find expression through its own consummatory act. Certain perplexing behavior patterns are called "derived" activities: *displacement activities* result from a surplus of drive, i.e., they are primarily the outcome of high-intensity motivation; *intention movements* result from low-intensity motivation; *redirection activities* result from relatively high motivation but do not involve "sparking over."

1. DISPLACEMENT ACTIVITIES

Tinbergen postulated that the fixed-action patterns build up a kind of "tension" (specific action potential) within the central nervous system, and that the "tension" becomes "dammed up" when appropriate sign stimuli are not present in the environment to release the behavior pattern or the consummatory act. The effect of this "tension" is to lower the threshold necessary for the release of a particular behavior pattern, with the result that the instinctive behavior occurs without external stimuli. In such *overflow* (or vacuum) *activity* the performance of the consummatory act does not correspond to the environmental situation or to the general behavior of the bird. The overflow activity may also express itself in displacement activities, in which the actual behavior is irrelevant to the initial fixed-action pattern. Thus, a displacement activity (an "allochthonous" activity) is an activity characteristic of one instinct but which is caused (because of lowered thresholds and a postulated process called *sparking over*) by the drive of another instinct. The activity takes the form of "irrelevant" movements. Conflicts between drives often occur. When two male birds are attempting to establish a territory, for example, a conflict may occur between the drives for fighting and for escape. The two drives are incompatible, so that neither can be discharged through its own consummatory act. The tension or energy of the drives may find release in irrelevant behavior: one or both birds may stop their chasing and begin to preen, to pick up nesting material, or to peck at the ground. Other examples that ethologists interpret as representing displacement activities *under certain circumstances* are shaking the plumage, wiping the bill, bathing, drinking, singing, grass-pulling, false-brooding, sleeping, and even copulating. These displacement activities are presumed to "use up" part of the specific action potential; they "are outlets through which the thwarted drives can express themselves in motion" (Tinbergen, 1952). It should be emphasized that an activity qualifies as a displacement activity only when it is irrelevant to the general behavior of the bird at the time it occurs.

2. INTENTION MOVEMENTS

Intention movements represent the initial phase of some appetitive behavior; they differ from displacement activities in that they are caused by the drive of their own behavior pattern (they are "autochthonous" activities). They are incomplete or incipient movements that result from the low activation of an instinctive behavior pattern, and they reveal to the observer what the bird "intends" to do.

In preparing to fly, a bird may bend its "legs," lower its head, lift its wings away from the body, and raise its tail. A bird about to hop from one branch to another may bend both the heel and the hip joint (so that the breast is lowered), retract the head and neck, partly extend the wings, and raise the tail. The first intention movement preceding walking or hopping often is a "bow," an action in which the head and breast are lowered and the rump and tail are elevated. During the second phase of the intention movement, the bird stretches itself, raises the head and breast, and lowers the rump and tail. By knowing the sequence of events in a locomotor pattern, one can identify the intention movements. This enables one (theoretically) to recognize the underlying drive and (in carefully studied or simple instances) to predict what the bird is going to do. The situation is complicated, however, because the intention movements may be incomplete or modified. A bird motivated to fly, for example, may just barely bend its heel joints, or it may not bend them at all before flying. It may exhibit but one of the steps in the usual sequence of events, and that one step may be so modified that it bears little or no resemblance to the "typical" pattern. Nevertheless, there seems to be little doubt in the mind of the ethologist that these (and other) modified or incomplete movements are anything else than intention movements of low intensity.

3. REDIRECTION ACTIVITIES

Moynihan (1955a) believes that the interpretation of many bird movements as displacement activities is "obviously unwarranted." He states that "of the many apparently irrelevant acts cited by Tinbergen (1952) . . . it is probable that no more than a third, at best, are really displacement activities in the conventional ethological sense" (i.e., in the sense outlined above). Therefore, he proposes a third type of derived activity, *redirection activities*. These do not require an elaborate sparking-over process in the central nervous system and they differ fundamentally from displacement activities in that they are caused by the drive of their own behavior pattern, and thus are similar to intention movements. According to Moynihan, "redirection movements can be defined as autochthonous activities of a drive directed toward an object or animal other than the one releasing and usually directing them (although the releasing object or animal remains available, or partly available, as a potential goal at the time)." To cite only one example, a passerine bird that stops fighting and begins to peck at the ground probably is not exhibiting displacement feeding but rather redirected attack pecking.

Ambivalence

When the motivation is strong, only one drive can be dominant at a time; the drives are mutually exclusive. When, however, the motivation is moderate, the animal may obey two drives simultaneously so that *ambivalent behavior* results. Depending upon the intensity of the drive, the ambivalent behavior involves intention movements or displacement activities from two drives, usually those of attack and escape. Tinbergen interprets the "upright threat posture" of the Herring Gull as "the simultaneous combination of the intention movements of attack and withdrawal."

Ritualization and Bird Display

All sorts of bird display patterns are presumed to be derived from intention movements, redirection activities, or displacement activities. These activities become *social signals* (social releasers) in that they serve as stimuli which evoke a response in other members of the same or another species. Their releaser function is a secondary adaptation resulting from an evolutionary process termed "ritualization." Hence, one may speak of the derived activities themselves (which do not have a releaser function) and the secondarily adapted derived activities (which have evolved into social releasers). During the process of ritualization, however, the derived activity may be greatly modified (by exaggeration, by simplification, or by a shift in the threshold of, or by a loss of coordination among, its component elements). In fact, "it may even be impossible to recognize a releaser as a displacement activity at all, until comparison with less specialized movements in closely related species reveals its origin" (Tinbergen, 1952: 23).

Young passerine birds perform begging movements when hungry. The birds crouch, raise the head, flutter the wings, and give food calls (Fig. 2). The movements are presumed to serve as releasers for the adult's feeding responses. It has been suggested that the begging movements are secondarily adapted locomotor intention movements. The wing fluttering or trembling "has something to do with flight." Some fledglings not only flutter the wings but also rapidly bob the head and breast up and down, which is "doubtless a symbol of hopping." The first intention movement (the bow) in walking or hopping in a secondarily adapted form becomes the crouching behavior of an alarmed Horned Lark according to the ethologist. The "freezing" behavior (with bill and head pointed

FIGURE 2.   Male Hooded Warbler at nest with young.   (Courtesy of Samuel A. Grimes.)

skyward) of the American Bittern represents the second phase of the walking intention movement; the first phase is omitted (Fig. 3). The behavior and the cryptic colors of both these birds aid in concealing them from predators and presumably evolved more or less together.

Most types of display are believed to have survival value for the species.   Displays serve as a means of communication among the members of a species; they may have both a "psychological" and a physiological effect on other birds (see Chapter 7).   Displays may stimulate the opposite sex (attract it or raise its sexual drive), strengthen and maintain the pair-bond, "tie" the partner to the nest site, serve as a threat (intimidation) to another bird, serve to effect reproductive isolation, or divert a predator (distraction behavior).   Fixed-action patterns once were thought to be so rigid, specific, and constant that they could be used easily in taxonomic studies. As more and more information has become available, however, it has become evident that behavioral data must be analyzed carefully if unwarranted conclusions are to be avoided (see page 341).

Hostile Behavior

It is not true, of course, that the expectant mothers of bird ethologists were frightened by an "aggressive" gull—it just seems that way because of their exaggerated emphasis on hostile behavior.

In his discussion of derived activities, Tinbergen (1952: 11) commented that "there are, mainly, two types of situations in which displacement activities occur: a hostile situation, and a purely sexual one." Many of the displays between the sexes also are considered hostile in nature. Moynihan (1955b) stated: "Among the commonest social behavior patterns in most birds are a great variety of hostile activities, i.e. behavior patterns produced by attack and/or escape motivation." Consequently, conflicts among

FIGURE 3. Young Least Bittern showing "freezing" behavior. (Courtesy of Walter P. Nickell.)

drives arise in many social situations. During the breeding season, for example, the first reaction of a male to a female is a mixture of sexual, aggressive, and escape responses. Neither sex must be too "aggressive" or too "timid" if courtship and subsequent copulation are to take place. Therefore there must be a balance or compromise among the drives. The effect of most hostile displays is to reduce the probability of actual physical combat between two male or two female birds (Fig. 4).

As long ago as 1941, David Lack commented that the considerable difficulties in the study of animal behavior had been complicated unnecessarily through problems of terminology. In the battle of terminology, hostile or aggressive behavior also has been called *agonistic behavior* ("any behavior appearing in conflict between animals, including fighting and escape behavior"). Moynihan (1955b) has classified hostile behavior as follows: threat, exemplary, appeasement, and deceptive displays, plus two unnamed categories of "somewhat anomalous" displays. He points out that "some hostile displays may subserve a hostile function during interspecific disputes; and others may have a non-hostile significance in certain particular intraspecific relationships at certain times. . . . The vari-

FIGURE 4. Male Painted Bunting attacking a stuffed male of the same species. (Courtesy of Samuel A. Grimes.)

FIGURE 5. Male Brown-headed Cowbird "bill-pointing," a type of hostile display.
(Courtesy of Arthur A. Allen.)

ous types of hostile display are neither absolutely incompatible nor
always clearly separated. Many birds may alternate several displays very rapidly, or combine two distinctly different displays
simultaneously (e.g. superimposing appeasement upon threat)."
(Fig. 5.)

These concepts are based on the theory that birds are primarily
hostile animals—they want to be alone. Not all ornithologists
accept this view, perhaps, in part, because they feel that the "hostile" nature of birds has been overemphasized. Fraser Darling
(1952) believed that fighting and singing often serve as a form of
social stimulation, and that an important function of bird territoriality is providing *periphery*, which he defined as "that kind of
edge where there is another bird of the same species occupying a
territory." In this concept, territories become units in a social
network. Fighting and singing may be as important for the *mutual
stimulation* of adjacent pairs of a species as it may be in reducing
interference between the pairs during the nesting season. The

social-stimulation school is less vociferous than the hostile-behavior
school, and there is a great need to study bird behavior in terms of
the possible "gregariousness" of birds. There is *no experimental
evidence* that "proves" that either is the overriding drive in bird
behavior.

Learning

Before a student accepts the Lorenz-Tinbergen theory of bird
behavior, he should study the paper by Lehrman (1953). The
essentially arbitrary distinction between "innate" behavior and
learned behavior stems from the old argument over the relative
importance of heredity and environment. Most investigators now
agree that it is virtually impossible to separate the two factors
even on theoretical grounds. We must believe at this time that all
behavior, whether "instinctive" or learned, is due to neurophysiological and/or neuroendocrine processes. Most ornithologists,
therefore, do not study the causes of behavior; they record bird
activities and "explain" them by using a "causal" vocabulary.

So little is known about learning processes, especially in birds,
that a discussion of the theories seems unjustified in an elementary
book. Dr. Frank A. Beach (1951) summed up the situation when
he remarked: "Current concepts of learning are too confused and
contradictory to be useful in interpreting much of the complex behavior that occurs under natural conditions." It will suffice to
point out that bird students have cited examples which illustrate
several proposed types of learning processes *in wild birds*.

Habituation

Habituation is an activity within the central nervous system
"whereby innate responses to mild and relatively simple stimuli,
especially those of potential value as warning of danger, wane as
the stimuli continue for a long period without unfavorable results."
A well-known example is man's ability to "tune out" constant
sounds in his environment. A young bird may have to learn that
large insects and some other animals (e.g., a frog or a chipmunk)
are not a source of danger. At the age of 14 to 21 days, Blue-
winged and Kirtland's warblers (Fig. 6) that I have raised typically
crouched or hopped away from a fluttering cabbage butterfly.
Within another week, the birds either ignored or captured and ate
such a butterfly. Similarly, a hand-raised domestic chick may be
greatly alarmed when a food utensil is changed, such as substitut-
ing a larger and deeper drinking cup, but soon adapts to the new
utensil.

FIGURE 6. An approximately 11-day-old Kirtland's Warbler hand-raised by A. J. Berger. (From a kodachrome transparency taken by Josselyn Van Tyne.)

Trial-and-Error Learning

As the name suggests, this is the process of selecting different responses until the one appropriate to the situation is achieved. Most examples pertain to feeding and drinking. It has been said that a dove's drinking movements are innate but that the bird "has no concept of water as being the stuff to drink." The young of some species may have to learn what is edible and what is inedible. I know of no experimental evidence, however, that indicates that the "billing" or "mouthing" of leaves, bark, and other "inedible" material, which is characteristic of young passerine birds, may not subserve some other function.

Imprinting

Lorenz believed that imprinting differed from learned behavior in that it can occur only during a very brief period immediately after the bird hatches, and that it is irreversible (i.e., the imprinted bird does not "forget"). Learning, on the other hand, is not re-

stricted to a limited period, and learned behavior may be forgotten
and relearned.   As a special phenomenon distinct from learning,
therefore, Lorenz felt that imprinting gave support to the theory
of instinctive behavior and sign stimuli: the innate behavior pattern
is released by a learned sign stimulus, which, in this instance, is the
first moving object the young bird sees.   Further study, however,
has revealed that imprinting is not always irreversible, nor is it
always dependent upon events that occur within the first few minutes after hatching.   Consequently, most people now view imprinting as differing only in degree from other learning processes.

Imprinting, as an interesting phenomenon, is well documented.
In the classical example, geese hatched from artificially incubated
eggs accepted Lorenz and followed him as they would have followed their own parents.   Imprinting has been demonstrated for
many ducks, gallinaceous birds, coots, doves, ravens, and other
birds (Fig. 7).   Incubator-hatched chicks, ducklings, and goslings
have become imprinted on such objects as a white box, a black box,

FIGURE 7.   An imprinted Canada Goose gosling following a box containing an alarm
clock.   (Courtesy of A. Ogden Ramsay; photograph by Leland A. Graham.)

a green box containing an alarm clock, a football, an orange ball, a red cage, as well as large and small canvas-covered frames of different colors. These objects had one thing in common during the experiments: all were seen in motion by the young birds. In a few instances birds have become imprinted to stationary models. Imprinted birds that have been studied typically direct sexual displays toward the animal, including man, on which they were first imprinted, but attachments to inanimate objects have been reported. Some examples of imprinting in relation to parent-young recognition are discussed in Chapter 8. It has been suggested without any definite evidence that imprinting may be important in other learning activities of birds, such as learning territory.

SOME BIRD ACTIVITIES

The student should not be discouraged because of the hypothetical nature of concepts pertaining to bird behavior. The literature on this subject does have a lighter side. Lorenz (1958) reports that courtship behavior in certain ducks consists of 10 motor patterns that are welded together in different combinations (Fig. 8). The basic patterns are these: (1) initial bill-shake; (2) head-flick; (3) tail-shake; (4) grunt-whistle; (5) head-up–tail-up; (6) turning toward the female; (7) nod-swimming; (8) turning the back of the head; (9) bridling; (10) down-up movement. These short characterizations of the motor patterns provide an excellent type of shorthand for recording field observations, especially if one refers to each step only by number. For example, a given observation might be recorded rapidly as 10, 4, 3, 2, 5, 6, 8. Translated, of course, this means that the bird went through the following motor movements: down-up, grunt-whistle, tail-shake, head-flick, head-up–tail-up, turning toward the female, turning back of the head. The full import of this sequence of events is best appreciated if one repeats the steps aloud in a rapid, rhythmic cadence.

Anting

Few of the minor bird activities have aroused as much interest as "anting," the application of ants and other foreign substances to the plumage and perhaps to the skin (Fig. 9). At least 24 species of ants and more than 40 substitute substances have been used in anting by over 150 different species of birds (Whitaker, 1957). The substitute materials include such items as fruits, raw

FIGURE 8. Courtship display patterns of the Mallard. (Courtesy of A. Ogden Ramsay and the editor of *The Wilson Bulletin;* drawing by E. Carey Kenney.)

FIGURE 9. Female Orchard Oriole anting. (Courtesy of Arthur A. Allen.)

onion, burning matches, grasshoppers, hair tonic, smoke, prepared
mustard, vinegar, hot chocolate, and moth balls. Despite its wide
occurrence and the promulgation of many theories, the real cause
or "objective" of anting remains unknown. In her masterful summary of the subject, however, Whitaker presented evidence suggesting that anting in her captive Orchard Oriole was stimulated
by the thermogenic property of certain ants, that is the "burning
or warming quality" of formic acid or other substances produced
by the ants.

Two general types of anting are distinguished: *active anting,* the
bird holds the ants in its bill and anoints the feathers; *passive anting,* the bird stands or sits among the ants, fluffs its feathers, and
allows the ants to crawl into the plumage. The primary areas
anointed in active anting are the under tail coverts (and perhaps
the skin surrounding the vent) and the base of the rectrices, but
the wing tips and the entire length of the rectrices frequently are
treated. In general, only the under parts are anointed. Passive
anting by birds ("seldom under 10 inches" in length) usually or
invariably is performed with species of ants that can spray repug-

natory fluids as a fine mist. So awkward are some of the postures
assumed as an anting bird turns its tail to one side or between its
feet that the bird may trip, fall, or turn a complete forward roll.

The Blue-winged Warbler is one of the few species of wood-warblers that has been observed anting, but I once saw one of my hand-
raised Kirtland's Warblers anting in an indoor aviary at 9:25 P.M.
The bird picked up one or more small black ants in its bill, turned
its tail about 90° from its normal position (first to one side, then
to the other side) and rubbed its bill in the under tail coverts
and/or base of the tail feathers. The bird anted for about two
minutes.

Bathing

Sun-bathing and water-bathing are common bird activities, and
some species take dust baths as well. The general pose of a *sun-
bathing* passerine bird is one in which the bird fluffs out its feathers,
leans to one side, opens the bill, spreads the tail feathers, and
either droops or extends one or both wings (Fig. 10). The bird
may face the sun but usually places one side toward the sun.
Kirtland's Warblers that I raised were first observed sun-bathing
at the age of 17 to 23 days. The birds usually bathed on the
ground, occasionally on a window sill. They placed either the right
or left side toward the sun, leaned away from the sun, fluffed out
the body feathers, spread the wing on the side toward the sun,
spread the tail, and pointed the head and open bill upward, the
eyes being wide open. The only wild Kirtland's Warbler (an adult
male) that I have seen sun-bathing alternated short periods (15 to
20 seconds) in the sun-bathing posture with short periods of preening or feeding on or within a foot of the ground. This bird crouched,
fluffed its feathers, raised its tail, spread both wings slightly, and
tipped its head backward. When one year old, a captive Yellow-
bellied Flycatcher took a "sun" bath under a floodlight (150 watts)
in an outdoor cage at 9:45 P.M. The bird was perched on the
nearest branch to the light (16 inches away); it leaned away from
the light, fluffed out its feathers, fanned its tail and its left wing
(the one closest to the light), and opened its bill. The temperature
was 79° F.; the entire day (July 7) had been cloudy; the relative
humidity was very high. After maintaining this pose for nearly
one-half hour, the bird fed by capturing insects attracted to the
light.

The cause of sun-bathing behavior remains obscure. It has been
suggested that the bird's eyes absorb ultraviolet rays; that the

FIGURE 10. Sun-bathing postures of some passerine birds, showing different levels of response to the sun. 1 and 2, White-throated Sparrow; 3, Cardinal; 4, Catbird; 5 and 6, Mockingbird; 7, Blue Jay. (Courtesy of Doris C. Hauser and the editor of *The Wilson Bulletin*.)

secretions of the oil gland, when applied to the feathers, provide a source of vitamin D when exposed to sunlight; that the behavior is the result of direct exposure to the sun's rays; and that it is motivated by increased heat.

Water-bathing is a common summer activity and some birds bathe during the winter as well. With the possible exception of some desert species, all birds probably take water baths, although the methods vary widely. Several species may congregate at shallow puddles or at bird baths, there to bathe simultaneously or by turns. Commonly, the bird hops into the shallow water, tips its throat and breast into the water, and flaps its wings, thus splashing water into the plumage. After the bird is thoroughly wet, it hops or flies to a perch and alternates preening activities with rapid fluttering of the wings and tail until the plumage is dry again.

Some species rarely follow this procedure, however. My personal experience is based primarily on certain species that I have raised in captivity. It seems likely, for example, that wild *Empidonax* flycatchers (and probably other genera) typically take a bath while perched on a branch when it is raining, or by flying into wet vegetation. Wild Scissor-tailed Flycatchers, kingbirds, and swallows have been observed to bathe during flight by swooping low over ponds and dipping into the water. The age at which I observed hand-raised flycatchers take their first water bath was: Acadian Flycatcher, 16 days; Yellow-bellied Flycatcher, 37 days; Traill's Flycatcher, 38–39 days. However, these ages probably are not very significant in some respects, particularly the early age for the Acadian Flycatcher. In this instance, the bird was perched on my desk, where it slept most of the time between short periods of activity. During one such period, the bird hopped into a small food dish, lowered its breast, and fluttered its wings as though it were taking a bath; no water was in sight. An hour later I placed the bird in a small dish of water, but it merely looked at the water, preened its feathers, and then flew to a perch. I put the bird in the water again, whereupon it immediately took a thorough bath.

A Yellow-bellied Flycatcher went through the motions of water-bathing when 28 days old. Two young Blue-winged Warblers were taking a bath at the same time in a pan of water on the aviary floor. The flycatcher flew up and alighted on the floor a few inches from the pan. The rapidly fluttering wings of the warblers splashed some water on the floor and on the flycatcher, which immediately went through typical bathing motions: head and breast were lowered toward the floor and the wings were fluttered rapidly. As soon as the warblers left the pan, the flycatcher hopped to its edge, took a drink, and looked at the water but did not enter it to bathe. The bird then flew to a branch and shook its wings as though it had taken a complete bath. Traill's and Yellow-bellied flycatchers took their first real baths when I was watering plants with a fine hose spray in an outdoor cage. Both birds flew to branches in line with the spray, fluttered their wings for a time, and then flew to branches out of the spray and shook their wings; they returned

to the spray several times. When the birds were older, they typically took baths by flying through the spray repeatedly. The birds
also took baths when it was raining, and sometimes they flew down
to wet grass and fluttered through it. The Yellow-bellied Flycatcher, especially, sometimes went through bathing motions
merely at the sight of rain or the hose spray. Several times I saw
it fly into water in a pan and, without hesitating, fly out of it to a
perch. Many birds do much preening and shaking of wings after
a bath, but the flycatchers preened very little. Their wings were
dried primarily by flapping them very rapidly; when very wet, the
wings were extended and drooped, only infrequently being flapped.

Captive Blue-winged Warblers took their first bath when 17
days old. The birds got so thoroughly soaked that they were unable
to fly. At this early age, the birds did not preen after a bath but
perched quietly with wings drooping; infrequently they shook
their wings. When older, the birds hopped from branch to branch
after a bath, shaking their wings and tails vigorously; they preened
primarily after the feathers were nearly dry. Dr. George M. Sutton
found that hand-raised Field Sparrows began to bathe at 20 days
of age.

There is rarely any standing water on the sandy jack pine plains
inhabited by the Kirtland's Warbler during the breeding season,
and wild birds apparently have never been observed to bathe in
puddles of water. The birds do so in captivity, although this is
not their preferred way of bathing. Captive birds often do take
baths in pans of water several times a day. I first observed bathing when the birds were 19 to 22 days old. Older birds took baths
in the rain and by flying on to the surface of a wet leaf (e.g., poin-
settia or elderberry), where they crouched down and went through
typical bathing movements. During the winter, when confined to
an indoor aviary, the birds often performed bathing movements at
the sight and sound of water dripping from plants on a shelf.
Occasionally, older birds flew down to wet grass and walked through
it, then flew to a branch to preen and shake their wings and tail.
A Slate-colored Junco has been observed to take a bath in this
manner, and there are reports of a few birds taking a bath in snow
(Downy Woodpecker, Horned Lark, Black-capped Chickadee,
Slate-colored Junco).

Dust-bathing is a common behavior pattern of many birds, but
very little seems to have been written about the subject. It is
practiced especially by quail, grouse, pheasants, and some hawks
and owls, but it also is characteristic of such passerine birds as
Horned Larks, Wrentits, House Sparrows, Vesper Sparrows, and

Field Sparrows. The bathing motions in general are similar to those used in taking a water bath. Gallinaceous birds have special dusting areas that they visit day after day. House Sparrows often engage in social dust-bathing in which a dozen or more sparrows bathe at the same time. Summer dust-bathing of Vesper Sparrows is a notable feature of this species' behavior. Dr. Sutton observed dust-bathing by a captive Vesper Sparrow when the bird was approximately three weeks old. Dust-bathing is presumed to be effective in reducing the number of external parasites found on birds, particularly bird lice (Mallophaga).

Behavioral Mimicry

Although found in a few other birds, behavioral mimicry is especially characteristic of titmice and chickadees. When disturbed on the nest, these hole-nesting birds typically do not leave the nesting cavity but emit hissing sounds accompanied by a display. With open bill and partially spread wings, the bird may sway slowly back and forth for several seconds, after which the bird jumps upward very suddenly, hisses, and slaps the sides of the cavity with its wings. Even when one is acquainted with this "snake display," its explosive performance is startling.

Distraction Behavior

Distraction behavior has been defined as any behavior pattern of an adult bird that tends to divert an intruder from the eggs or young (Figs. 11, 12). Ethologists have suggested that it results from the conflict between the drive to incubate (or brood) and the drive to flee from an enemy. E. A. Armstrong proposed that distraction display and displacement activities with a diversionary function (e.g., displacement brooding or feeding) be included under the term *diversionary display.* Distraction behavior has been reported in several hundred species of birds. Phylogenetically, it occurs in birds as widely separated as loons and finches. It is found among ground nesters, tree nesters, and some hole-nesting species.

The details of the behavior vary widely among these birds. A common pattern is aptly described by the words "injury-feigning" or "broken-wing display." Near the end of the incubation period especially, a Killdeer frightened from its nest typically runs off a short distance, falls to the ground, leans to one side, spreads its tail (thus displaying its cinnamon-colored rump), and rapidly flaps one or both wings, while giving alarm notes. The bird may then

FIGURE 11.   Distraction behavior of a Common Nighthawk.   (Courtesy of Samuel A. Grimes.)

stand up, run a few feet, and repeat the performance.   The distraction display of some species (e.g., Common Loon, Turkey) is similar to their courtship display, and it has been reported that the similarity is so close in Wilson's Plover that the male has been stimulated to attempt to copulate with a displaying female that

FIGURE 12.   Distraction behavior of a King Rail.   (Courtesy of Brooke Meanley.)

has been frightened from her nest. Another pattern has been called the "rodent-run" display. It has been described especially for certain shorebirds (American Golden Plover, Sanderling, Spotted, Pectoral, and Purple sandpipers), but also for the Green-tailed Towhee. When a towhee is flushed from its nest, it may drop nearly straight to the ground without using its wings, and then run along with its tail elevated, very much resembling a scampering chipmunk.

Dominance

Schjelderup-Ebbe first used the word *dominance* to describe the interrelationships among the members in flocks of certain birds. One bird is dominant over all others, but there also is a social hierarchy among the other members of the flock. Each bird is dominant over all birds below it in the hierarchy but subordinate to all birds above it. Among domestic chickens, for example, a relatively fixed *peck order* is established in each flock. The dominant bird (either cock or hen) has precedence in going to food or water supplies and can peck any other bird in the flock, usually without any retaliation from the subordinate members. This social order is less rigid in pigeons, canaries, and many wild birds, and the dominant and subordinate roles may vary seasonally. Birds subordinate in neutral or feeding grounds may be dominant in their nesting territories. Interspecific dominance can be observed readily among foraging winter flocks composed of several species of birds or at feeding trays. At a winter feeding tray, a Downy Woodpecker usually is dominant over other species; White-breasted Nuthatches are dominant over titmice and chickadees; and in a winter flock of titmice, one bird usually is dominant over the others.

Opening Milk Bottles

First reported in England in 1921, there were over 400 records of this interesting behavior by 1949. It also has been observed in Scotland, Ireland, Sweden, Denmark, Holland, France, and the United States. The behavior is more characteristic of several species of European titmice but there are records for such species as the House Sparrow, Starling, British Robin, Song-Thrush, Chaffinch, and the Great Spotted Woodpecker. There is at least one record of a Steller's Jay opening a milk bottle at Seattle, Washington.

When a milk bottle is capped by a thin metal foil, a bird usually punctures the cap by hammering it with its bill. The bird may then drink milk through the hole or first tear off most of the foil. Cardboard caps may be removed in one piece or successive layers may be stripped off until the bird can puncture the cap. Birds have been known to drink as much as 1½ to 2 inches of milk from a bottle they have opened.

Titmice are "curious" birds that investigate new and conspicuous objects they encounter. It has been suggested, therefore, that the birds first find the milk bottles in their appetitive behavior of food-seeking. Then (by trial-and-error learning) they learn to return to the bottles. Small groups of titmice have been observed following a milkman and flying to the bottles almost as soon as they have been put on a porch. Titmice are sedentary in habit, rarely moving more than a few miles from their place of hatching. Consequently, it would seem that many birds have learned to open milk bottles *de novo* in different parts of their range, but that some individuals have learned the behavior from other birds as they move about in groups during the nonbreeding season. It has been suggested that this "copying behavior" is due to the process called *local enhancement,* which modifies the appetitive behavior and initially is independent of the reward provided by the milk.

Paper-Tearing

Numerous reports from the British Isles tell of titmice entering houses and stripping pieces of wallpaper off the walls. In some instances, titmice chased from a house would persist in flying about and pecking at a closed window in an effort to return to a particular room. This peculiar behavior is more common in autumn when the rainfall is subnormal. The birds do not confine their efforts to tearing wallpaper but have directed their attacks against such things as covers of books, name cards on doors, lampshades, match boxes, clothing (indoors or on an outdoor line), leather, straw baskets, and oilcloth.

Roosting

Some species of birds sleep in groups containing hundreds or thousands of birds, particularly at the end of the breeding season. These roosting flocks may be composed of a single species (homogeneous aggregations) or of several species (heterogeneous

FIGURE 13. Method used by Brooke Meanley to band blackbirds at night roosts during February and March in Arkansas. In order of relative abundance, species occupying the roost were Red-winged Blackbird, Common Grackle, Brown-headed Cowbird, and Rusty Blackbird; 4000 birds were banded in 10 nights. (Courtesy of Brooke Meanley and Garner Allen, from *Bird-Banding,* 27, 1956, p. 171.)

aggregations). The enormous flocks of Starlings that roost on public buildings or in shade trees in towns in late summer have received much publicity because the birds are a nuisance. House Sparrows also roost in groups in barns, in haystacks, on ivy-covered walls, or in trees. Crows congregate by the hundreds to sleep together in wooded areas. The birds may be relatively quiet in the evening when they come from all directions by ones, twos, or in small groups, and suddenly drop from the sky to a favorite roosting tree. In the early morning before sunrise, however, the birds begin to call while still on their roosting perches; the loud raucous chorus that results drowns out all other sounds if one is close to the roost. Chimney

Swifts present an intriguing sight as they swarm through the summer sky and then in rapid succession dive head first into a chimney to roost. *Cock roosts* have been described for Common and Lesser nighthawks in the western United States. As many as 100 Common Nighthawks have been found roosting on horizontal branches of clumps of cottonwood and black locust trees in Idaho. Such daytime roosting flocks are thought to be composed almost entirely of adult males, most of which are breeding birds. After the breeding season Red-winged Blackbirds, Brown-headed Cowbirds, and Common Grackles gather in large and noisy flocks to roost together in trees and bushes, often in marshy areas (Fig. 13). Little study has been made of these heterogeneous flocks, or of those species which sleep alone, in pairs, or in small groups.

Alexander Skutch has described the sleeping habits of some Central American birds, among which are wrens that build "dormitories," nests that are used only for sleeping. Cactus Wrens use nests for roosting throughout the year; male and female wrens sometimes build roosting nests in the same cholla cactus (Fig. 14).

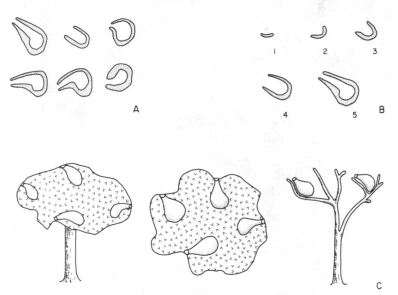

FIGURE 14.   A. Common variations in the shape of Cactus Wren nests.   B. Stages in the construction of a roosting nest.   Occupation usually begins at stage 3.   C. Common locations of roosting nests in cholla cacti: left, *Opuntia fulgida;* center, *O. fulgida,* top view; right, *O. spinosior.*   Nest entrance usually faces outward.   The number of nests in a cholla varies, there seldom being more than two usable nests.   (Courtesy of Anders H. and Anne Anderson and the editor of *The Condor.*)

Some species that excavate nesting burrows in the ground use these as dormitories during the nonbreeding season. Frazier and Nolan (1959) found from 5 to 14 Eastern Bluebirds roosting together in a bird house during the winter in Indiana: "The birds slept heads together and bodies pointed downward, forming an inverted cone." Communal winter roosting in cedar trees has been reported for Purple Finches, and Owen A. Knorr estimated that at least 150 Pigmy Nuthatches roosted together in the hollow trunk of a dead yellow pine. Gray-crowned Rosy Finches have been observed to spend winter nights in the retort-shaped mud nests of Cliff Swallows. The Ruffed Grouse is well known for its habit of diving from the wing into a snowdrift and spending the night there; a freezing rain during the night may form a crust over the snow so that the birds are unable to burrow out the next morning (Fig. 15). Coveys of Bobwhite roost together in a circle on the ground with

FIGURE 15. An Eastern Meadowlark that had been imprisoned under snow crust in Wake County, North Carolina. Jack Dermid heard the bird thrashing around under the snow and made a hole in the crust to release the bird. (Courtesy of Jack Dermid.)

FIGURE 16.   Winter roosting site of a male Downy Woodpecker at Ann Arbor, Michigan.

each bird having its head facing outward.   Brown Creepers are said to sleep while clinging vertically in a depression in a tree, and even to excavate their own roosting shelter.   Better known are the winter roosting cavities excavated by woodpeckers.   In October, 1959, a male Downy Woodpecker excavated such a roosting cavity in a large growth on a dead maple stub in our yard (Fig. 16). Several times during November the bird visited the cavity for a few minutes at midday and threw out chips of wood.   White-breasted Nuthatches, Tufted Titmice, and Black-capped Chickadees sometimes examined the cavity during the day.   The woodpecker typically flew out of the woods and directly into the roosting cavity in the evening.   In the morning the bird would stick its bill and head out of the hole, look around for a minute or more, and then withdraw its head for a short time, after which the bird would fly out of the hole to a nearby tree (Table 1).

Wing-Flashing

The term "wing-flashing" was coined to describe a peculiar behavior pattern of the Mockingbird (Fig. 17).   Performed most often when on the ground, wing-flashing involves extending the wings upward in "archangel fashion," thus displaying the large white

TABLE 1
Roosting Behavior of Male Downy Woodpecker at Ann Arbor, Mich.

	Left Cavity	Temperature	Entered Cavity	Temperature	Foraging Time	
					Hours	Minutes
November 26	7:42 A.M.	31° F.	4:33 P.M.	32° F.	8	51
November 27	7:52	30	4:49	34	8	57
December 22	8:26	14	4:21	27	7	55
December 23	8:18	24	4:35	29	8	17
December 24	8:24	29	4:24	34	8	00
December 25	8:19	35	4:12	39	7	53
December 26	8:17	40	4:22	47	8	05
January 19	8:18	24	4:50	32	8	32
January 20	8:08	22	4:55	27	8	47
January 21	8:10	19	4:46	26	8	36
January 22	8:16	19	4:58	26	8	42
January 23	8:10	22	4:33	29	8	23
February 14	7:47	18	5:15	22	9	28
February 15	7:45	21	4:56	33	9	11
February 16	7:43	32	5:06	40	9	23
February 17	7:41	38	5:16	38	9	35
February 18	7:46	30	5:14	32	9	28
March 20	6:37	22	5:40	32	11	03
March 21	6:50	19	5:43	29	10	53
March 22	7:02	28	5:38	32	10	36
March 23	6:58	19	5:49	32	10	51
March 24	6:40	26	5:30	27	10	50
April 18	6:15	37	6:35	50	12	20
April 19	5:45	32	6:24	56	12	39
April 20	5:52	43	7:07	63	13	15
April 21	5:41	58	7:03	63	13	22
April 22	5:35	45	7:01	74	13	26

wing patches. The distinguishing feature of this behavior is that the wings are extended by steps, the successive movements being separated by momentary pauses. As many as five such pauses may occur before the wings are fully extended. Often the wings are "flashed" in this manner after a short run along the ground. Sometimes the wing extension is incomplete. Several theories have been proposed to account for this behavior, e.g., that it is a means of flushing prey, or that it is performed as a displacement act when the bird is "frustrated" or "sexually excited." Much of the evidence presented, especially on young birds, suggests that this is an "instinctive" pattern that is released when the bird encounters something new in its environment. This behavior also has been re-

FIGURE 17. Adult Mockingbird flashing its wings. (Courtesy of George Miksch Sutton, from an original drawing first appearing in *The Wilson Bulletin*, 1946, Plate 8.)

ported in two species of mockingbirds that do not have wing patches, in the Brown Thrasher, and in feathered nestling and fledgling Mockingbirds. It is doubtful that the wing-flashing described for a few other species of birds is homologous to this behavior in the mockingbird family.

6

Song

The average person walks along city streets and country lanes oblivious of the wide variety of songs and calls of birds. Even after one becomes aware of bird songs, many surprises lie ahead. For bird sounds range from the raucous calls of crows and gulls to the insect-like notes of the Henslow's and Savannah sparrows, from the buzzy notes of the Blue-winged Warbler and Clay-colored Sparrow to the loud, penetrating whistle of the Cardinal, from the rollicking song of the Bobolink to the flute-like song of the Wood Thrush. Furthermore, some species have two totally dissimilar songs. The Blue-winged Warbler's common song is described as *beee-bzzz,* but the bird also has an alternative song (*chi-chi-chi-chi-chi-chi-chi-zeee*) which is both longer and different in quality. Moreover, the Golden-winged Warbler gives this same alternative song, in addition to its usual song (*beee-bz-bz-bz*). The male Grasshopper Sparrow has three distinct songs, all of which sound more like insect noises than bird songs.

A few birds sometimes sing from the ground, but, as a rule, they sing from an elevated perch. For the Horned Lark, the elevated perch may be merely a large stone or a fence post; for a Savannah Sparrow, it may be a tall weed; for an Indigo Bunting, it may be one of the upper branches of a tree. Both the Blue-winged and Golden-winged warblers are noted for singing from an exposed perch high in a tree. The males of most species have favorite *song perches* in different parts of their territory. Here they sing from one perch for a while, and then fly to another perch to sing again, using the same perches day after day. Such song perches often are used as a basis for determining the extent of territory defended by a given male, and they may give a rough approximation of territory size.

Many birds that inhabit open areas have a flight song, e.g., Upland Plover, Horned Lark, Sprague's Pipit, Wheatear, Bobolink, Cassin's Sparrow, Lapland Longspur, Snow Bunting. Some species that inhabit brushy or wooded areas have special flight songs that may be like or unlike the primary advertising song. Some of these species are Traill's and Acadian flycatchers, Western Meadowlark, Blue-winged and Golden-winged warblers, Ovenbird, Yellowthroat, Indigo Bunting, goldfinches, and Bachman's, Grasshopper, and Song sparrows (Fig. 1). Some of these species give their flight song primarily at twilight or dusk. The Ovenbird's flight song is given most often about sunset, but I once heard the song at 1:00 A.M.

THE SYRINX

The birds' "voice box" or *syrinx* is unique among animals. Man's voice box, the *larynx,* is located at the entrance to the windpipe

FIGURE 1. Bachman's Sparrow at nest with young. (Courtesy of Samuel A. Grimes.)

(*trachea*); the syrinx is found at the opposite end, where the trachea divides to form two *bronchi* (sing., bronchus). Birds have a larynx, too, but it is, so far as we know, not responsible for any of the songs or calls of birds. In most birds, both the trachea and the bronchi take part in the formation of the syrinx, so that we call it a *tracheobronchial* syrinx. In a few birds, the syrinx is located entirely in the trachea (*tracheal* syrinx) or in the bronchi (*bronchial* syrinx; Fig. 2). Turkey Vultures do not have a syrinx at all.

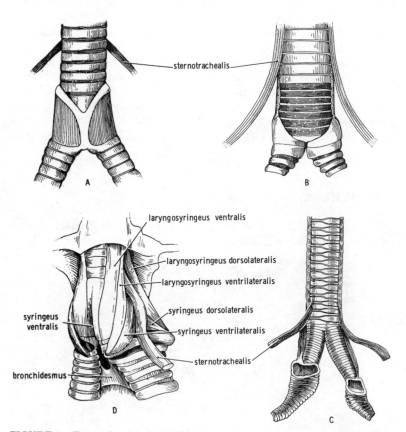

FIGURE 2. Types of syringes. A. Tracheobronchial syrinx of an asity, *Neodrepanis coruscans.* B. Tracheal syrinx of an antpipit, *Conopophaga aurita.* C. Bronchial syrinx of the oilbird *Steatornis caripensis.* D. Tracheobronchial syrinx of the sunbird *Arachnothera longirostris,* showing the large number of intrinsic muscles. (By permission from *Fundamentals of Ornithology* by Josselyn Van Tyne and Andrew J. Berger, published by John Wiley & Sons. Copyright, 1959.)

The trachea is supported by a series of cartilaginous or bony rings; the bronchi are supported partly by complete rings and partly by C-shaped semirings, the inner, open side of each being closed by a membrane. As a rule, the tracheal rings and bronchial semirings that form the syrinx are larger in diameter (and/or in width) than neighboring rings, so that the syrinx is a conspicuous dilation in the tracheobronchial tree. Inside the expanded chamber thus formed there is a *semilunar membrane,* supported by a bony bar (the *pessulus*). *Internal* and *external tympaniform* (drum-like) *membranes* span the spaces between the modified tracheal or bronchial rings. After studying the syrinx in several species, Miskimen (1951) concluded that sounds are produced by vibrations of the tympaniform membranes during expiration, and that no sound is produced during inspiration. The function of the semilunar membrane remains obscure. Miskimen removed this membrane from the syrinx of a Starling and could detect no modification of sounds when air was forced through the syrinx.

Intrinsic muscles—i.e., those which arise on the trachea and insert on some part of the syrinx—are found in almost all songbirds; from one to eight pairs have been described in various species. Miskimen concluded that there is a "direct correlation between the degree of development of the syrinx, with respect to muscles and attachments, and the quality (variety of notes) of the song." At the same time, a bird with a large number of muscles does not necessarily have a "musical" song or a wide variety of calls. The Common Crow, with its limited number of calls, has six pairs of intrinsic syringeal muscles. Among North American passerine birds, the tyrant-flycatchers have the fewest syringeal muscles.

Although usually a straight but flexible tube, the trachea of some birds is greatly elongated and forms loops within the thorax, between ventral musculature and the skin, or within the sternum (Fig. 3). Such tracheal loops, which add resonance to the bird's calls, may occur in both sexes or only in adult males. The tracheae of some male ducks contain either one or two dilatations between the larynx and the bronchi, in addition to a *tracheal bulla,* an enlargement at the tracheal bifurcation.

CLASSIFICATION OF SONG TYPES

Songs and call notes differ primarily in function and to some extent in length, but the distinction is not always sharp. Examples of call notes were given on page 46. Song, as one ordinarily

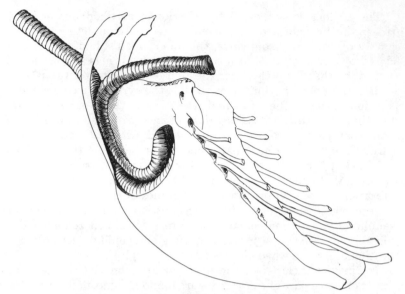

FIGURE 3.   Sternum and trachea of Sandhill Crane.

thinks of it, is primarily a characteristic of passerine birds (the "songbirds"), but not all songbirds sing and some nonpasserine birds do (e.g., Bobwhite, Mourning Dove, Upland Plover).   Song is typically the function of the male, but again there are many exceptions.   It is customary to classify songs according to their function, or presumed function.   In some instances, the same song is used for several purposes.   A flight song, for example, may be given as an advertising song, as a signal song, or for as yet undetermined reasons.

Primary Song

Advertising, or *territorial, song* serves to attract a mate and/or to repel other birds of the same sex.   For the most part, advertising song is given by the male in the establishment and defense of a breeding territory.   It functions as a warning or threat to other members of the species, especially of the same sex.   It is one of the important biological isolating mechanisms that reduces the chance of interspecific matings by attracting a female of the same species. Smith (1959) stated that the most familiar of the Grasshopper Sparrow's songs (*tip tup zeeeeeeeeeeeee*) is an advertising song, which may be sung as many as 220 times an hour when territories are being established.   The male alternates the song with a display.   While crouched on a perch with his head lowered between his shoulders, the bird raises and flutters one or both wings.   If a neighboring bird sings, the male then stands erect and sings, after which he again assumes the crouched position and flutters his wings (Figs. 4, 5).   Smith calls the longer song of the Grasshopper Sparrow the *sustained song* (*tip tup a zeeeeeeee zeee zeedle zeee zeedle zeedle zeeeee*).   The first part serves as a warning to other males but most of the song seems to function primarily to attract a female and, thereafter, as a signal song, to maintain the pair bond. The "drumming" of the Ruffed Grouse and of woodpeckers, as well as other mechanically produced sounds (such as those discussed on page 46), may properly be called advertising "songs" because they fulfill one or both of its assigned functions.

Signal song is any song that serves to coordinate the activities of birds, particularly of a mated pair.   The song itself may be the same as the territorial song, but it subserves some other purpose. Signal songs are used during the courtship period and, later, to call the incubating female off the nest, to stimulate gaping by the nestlings, or to maintain the bond between the pair.   The *trill,* the third of the male Grasshopper Sparrow's songs, "apparently serves

FIGURE 4.   Attitudes of male Grasshopper Sparrow during the grasshopper-song sequence.   A. Crouched position.   B. Wing-fluttering.   C. Delivering the song.   (Courtesy of Robert L. Smith and the editor of *The Wilson Bulletin.*)

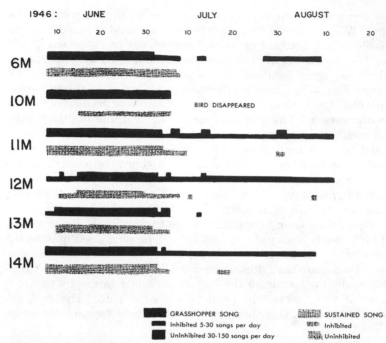

FIGURE 5. Frequency of song among male Grasshopper Sparrows during the summer of 1946 in Jefferson County, Pennsylvania. (Courtesy of Robert L. Smith and the editor of *The Wilson Bulletin.*)

as a bond to hold the pair together, and as a signal to both the female and the young that the male is approaching the nest" (Smith, 1959). Duetting and antiphonal singing probably function in coordinating activities of a pair and in maintaining the pair-bond.

Emotional song, a term used for want of a better one, encompasses a variety of songs that cannot be associated directly with securing a mate and defending a territory. In general, one can say that neither the cause nor the function of emotional song is known. To say that it is an outlet for "excess energy" is merely to beg the issue. Twilight, postbreeding, and some winter and flight songs may be included under this category.

Female song is less common among North American birds than among those in some parts of the world. Female Mockingbirds have a territorial song that is given primarily in the nonbreeding season. Songs of female Mockingbirds, Gray-cheeked Thrushes, Cardinals, and Rose-breasted and Black-headed grosbeaks are nearly as elaborate as those of the male. Female Wood Thrushes and Black-headed Grosbeaks sing while incubating. Some sing occasionally or under special conditions, e.g., Cactus Wren, Loggerhead Shrike, Wrentit, Bullock's Oriole, Summer Tanager, Indigo Bunting, Rufous-sided Towhee, and White-crowned, Grasshopper, and Song sparrows. Among species in which both sexes sing, they may sing the same or a different song and either simultaneously (*duetting*) or alternately (*antiphonal singing*). Examples among North American species are these: California Thrasher, Carolina Wren, Gray-cheeked Thrush, and Cardinal.

Secondary Song

Very little has been written about secondary song in American birds but it may be useful, for purposes of description, to name two types of songs that may be classified as secondary song.

Whisper song has been defined as the soft inward rendering of the primary advertising song, with or without slight variations. It has no territorial or signal implication and it may be sung by either sex. Whisper songs may be given during any part of the year.

Subsong differs from whisper song in that it is unlike the primary advertising song. Most of the first song attempts of juvenile birds are subsongs.

DEVELOPMENT OF SONG

The first song is generally an indefinite warble, nonspecific in character; it may be given by nestlings. Margaret M. Nice (1943) reported that the first warbling songs of four hand-raised Song Sparrows were given between the ages of 13 and 20 days; two birds had "adult songs of definite form" at 159 and 192 days of age, respectively. Amelia Laskey found that two hand-raised female Cardinals first gave soft warbling songs, totally unlike the adult song, at ages of three and four weeks. I first heard one of my hand-raised male Kirtland's Warblers sing when it was about 38 days old. It gave a very low, hoarse warble, resembling somewhat the song of the Purple Finch.

Little is known about song learning in North American birds. Careful experiments with European birds suggest that the songs and call notes of some species are entirely inherited, that the songs of some are almost wholly learned from older birds (e.g., Skylark, Linnet), and that among other species the juvenile song is "innate" but the adult song is learned (e.g., European Robin, European

Blackbird, Chaffinch). In her study of the Song Sparrow, Mrs. Nice found "no case of a male having the song of his father or grandfather," and further that two males from the same nest "had no song in common."

Adult birds, as well, may imitate the songs or calls of other birds. Such *vocal mimicry* is developed to a high degree in many Old-world birds. Its significance is poorly understood. Over 50 Australian species have been classified as "master," "minor," and "casual" mimics. The best mimics inhabit wooded country and are strongly territorial. In writing of these Australian birds, A. J. Marshall (1950) suggested that "lack of visibility places a premium on sound and that it is biologically advantageous for individuals to make more and more sound in order that territorial rivals and members of the opposite sex will be constantly aware of their presence." These birds could, of course, make just as much noise by singing *their own songs,* so that we really have no explanation for the prevalence of vocal mimicry among Australian species or any others. Marshall did demonstrate for some species, however, that there is a correlation between vocal mimicry and seasonal changes in the gonads. The best known mimics among American birds are the Mockingbird and the Starling (an introduced species). The "pewee" and "bobwhite" calls of the Starling often fool beginning students. Parrots, magpies, crows, and ravens apparently mimic only in captivity.

SONG CYCLES

The seasonal song cycle begins in the spring for most birds of the Northern Hemisphere. Singing is most pronounced during the nesting season, and most birds sing very little at other times of the year. Mockingbirds, Wrentits, and Cactus Wrens, which tend to defend a territory throughout the year, sing during the winter but not as persistently as in the breeding season. Titmice, Starlings, and Cardinals often sing on clear, cold February days in northern states. Most wood-warblers and sparrows sing during migration.

Song behavior during the nesting season varies widely among different species. Among many nonpasserine species, display and accompanying sounds are discontinued after pairing is accomplished. Unlike their behavior at other times of the year, Blue Jays become very quiet and inconspicuous while nesting. There is a marked decrease in song by Grasshopper Sparrows and Song Sparrows after the male secures a mate, but he begins to sing again when the female starts to build a nest. Nearly all male tyrant-flycatchers, wrens, thrushes, vireos, wood-warblers, and sparrows sing throughout the incubation and nestling periods. Male Warbling Vireos and Rose-breasted and Black-headed grosbeaks sing while incubating. Male wood-warblers, especially, are noted for singing while carrying a billful of food for the young. Birds rarely sing while undergoing the annual molt at the end of the breeding season, but many species have a short song period (postbreeding) after the molt has been completed.

There is a daily song cycle as well. Most species sing less during the middle of the day than in early morning or late afternoon. A midday slackening of song often is correlated with high heat and wind or humidity. Midday singing does occur on cloudy days, and many birds sing during a light rain. The Red-eyed Vireo sings more or less continuously throughout the day, with little regard for weather or season.

Few people have had the patience to count the number of songs given by a particular bird during one entire day, but Louise deKiriline Lawrence reported that a male Red-eyed Vireo sang 22,197 songs in one day. Harold Mayfield made observations from a blind at a Kirtland's Warbler nest on June 21, 1956, the day before the first egg hatched. The male sang 2212 songs between 4:57 A.M. (first song) and 7:56 P.M. (last song); sunset was about 8:25 P.M. E.S.T. The temperature during this period ranged from 56° to 88° F. The number of songs for each hour ending as indicated was:

5:00 A.M.	21	1:00 P.M.	122
6:00	87	2:00	121
7:00	282	3:00	72
8:00	305	4:00	168
9:00	246	5:00	90
10:00	238	6:00	15
11:00	200	7:00	10
12:00 noon	157	8:00	78

The time of the first morning song varies among different species and among individuals of the same species. It varies also with locality and with the season. Within a given locality, however, certain species begin their morning song period earlier than others. Five days after Mayfield made his observations, I arrived at the Kirtland's Warbler study area at 3:30 A.M. A bright moon and a few high scattered clouds were in the predawn sky. Seven or eight Common Nighthawks could be heard calling at one time. Of daytime birds, I heard the first (a Robin) at 3:50 A.M. The following species began to sing within the next five minutes: Field Sparrow, Rufous-sided Towhee, Vesper Sparrow, Eastern Bluebird, and Eastern Kingbird. A Clay-colored Sparrow began to sing at 4:00 A.M.; Mourning Dove, 4:11; Chipping Sparrow, 4:12; Brown Thrasher, 4:16; Kirtland's Warbler, 4:23.

Some birds (e.g., Eastern Wood Pewee, Great Crested, Scissor-tailed, Traill's, Acadian, and Least flycatchers) have special morning twilight (or dawn) and evening songs, which seem to be correlated with changing light intensities, and which seem not to be related to territorial defense. The thrushes are noted for evening singing. Many daytime-singing birds, often or occasionally, sing at night. Some examples are the Black-billed and Yellow-billed cuckoos, marsh wrens, Mockingbird, Ovenbird, Yellow-breasted Chat, and Field, Henslow's, and Grasshopper sparrows.

VARIATION IN SONGS

The songs of different individuals of a species often vary considerably in pitch and pattern. These variations are readily apparent to one who is attuned to bird songs. A. A. Saunders reported that no two Song Sparrows sing songs that are exactly alike, and that each Song Sparrow has from 7 or 8 to 20 or more different songs. This situation often is confusing to the beginning student, especially until he realizes that each bird species has a basic song pattern. After one learns this basic pattern, one usually recognizes the species immediately, and then, more or less as an afterthought, may observe that the song is not "typical" for the species. One does hear atypical songs from time to time, so that the bird has to be seen to be identified. I found a male Song Sparrow whose song began with two or three loud, Cardinal-like whistles followed by a normal song. Borror (1961) reported instances of a Chipping Sparrow singing the song of a Clay-colored Sparrow, of a Rufous-sided Towhee and a Bachman's Sparrow singing Field Sparrow songs, of a Field Sparrow singing a song similar to that of a Prairie Warbler, and of a Red-eyed Vireo that had towhee-like songs.

The application of sound-analyzing equipment to recordings of bird songs has given us a much better understanding of the nature of bird song and its variation than have all of the subjective methods used in the past (page 45). This equipment makes graphs (audiospectrographs) which show all of the frequencies present, give minute details of the rhythm, and give some data on the loudness of the songs. One can learn to "read" the graphs just as a musician "hears" a musical score as he reads it. Audiospectrographs of the songs of five different Yellowthroats, six Vesper Sparrows, and eight Chipping Sparrows are shown in Figs. 6, 7, and 8. Dr. Donald J. Borror (Fig. 9), one of the leading students of bird-song analysis, reported that the maximum number of song patterns in recordings of a single individual is 8 for a Rufous-sided Towhee, 11 for a Cardinal, 13 for a Song Sparrow, 18 for a Wood Thrush, 22 for a Carolina Wren, 37 for a Bachman's Sparrow, and 58 for a Lark Sparrow. These numbers refer to song *patterns* only; the songs of a particular pattern may vary in number of phrases, in the presence or absence of some phrases or notes, in the types of phrases at the beginning or ending of a song, etc. Thus, of 462 recorded songs of one Maine Song Sparrow, which had 13 distinct song patterns, there were 187 different songs. In recordings of songs of the Wood Thrush, Hermit Thrush, Indigo Bunting, Vesper Sparrow, and Lark Sparrow, Borror found no instances of two different birds singing songs of the same pattern. There is less variation in the songs of the Field Sparrow than in many other birds, but even in this species few individuals have songs with exactly the same pattern.

Songs may vary in different parts of a species' range. The populations having different songs are called *song races;* the songs are called *song dialects.* Such geographic variation in song occurs in a number of species: White-breasted Nuthatch, Ruby-crowned Kinglet, Carolina Wren, Western Meadowlark, Red-winged Blackbird, Cardinal, Rufous-sided Towhee, Bachman's, Chipping, and Song sparrows, and Snow Bunting. Variation may occur also within local populations (*local song dialects*), as in the White-crowned Sparrow of the western United States.

The significance of the large amount of variation in the songs of an individual and among different individuals of a species remains largely conjectural. It seems likely that birds distinguish differences in songs better than man can, and that both species and mate recognition depend in part on songs and call notes. Borror reported that the advertising songs of each Ovenbird consist of a single pattern (or phrase type), which differs only in the number of phrases given in different songs. In their study of the same species, Weeden and Falls (1959) concluded that male Ovenbirds apparently "can distinguish between songs of different individuals of their species and can recognize songs of particular individuals (their neighbors)," and that "they react more strongly to songs of non-adjacent birds than to songs of their neighbors." In his study of several species of thrushes, Dilger (1956) concluded that the

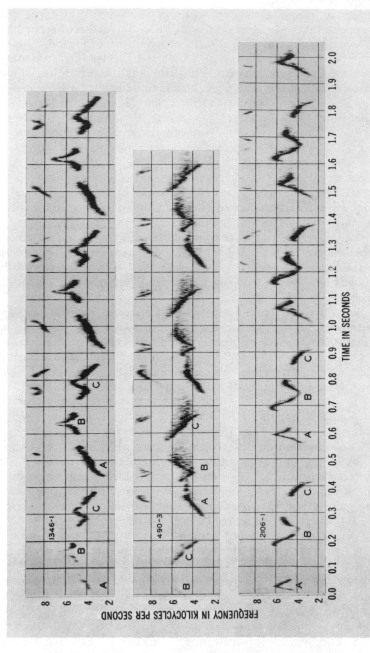

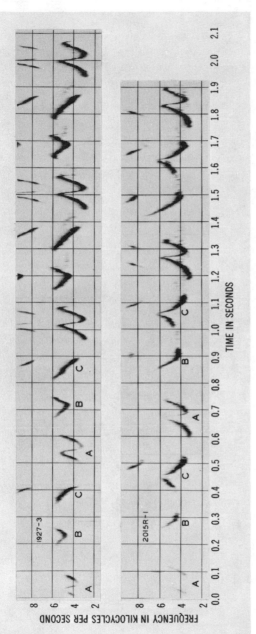

FIGURE 6. Audiospectrographs of songs of five male Yellowthroats. All recordings were made with a Magnemite recorder, Model 610-B; the graphs were made with a Vibralyzer. The letters on the graphs are the notes of a phrase. (Courtesy of Donald J. Borror.)
1346-1: Urbana, Ohio, April 30, 1955.
490-3: Columbus, Ohio, May 2, 1953.
2106-1: Lincoln County, Maine, July 1, 1956.
1927-3: Columbus, Ohio, May 25, 1956.
2015R-1: Hocking County, Ohio, June 3, 1956.

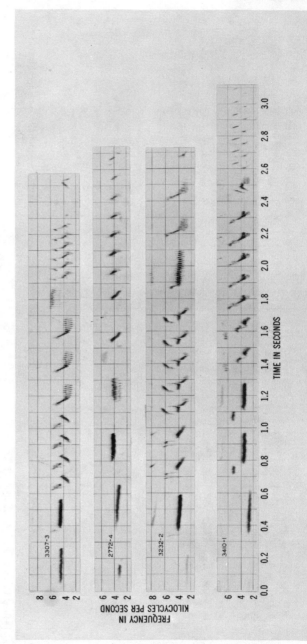

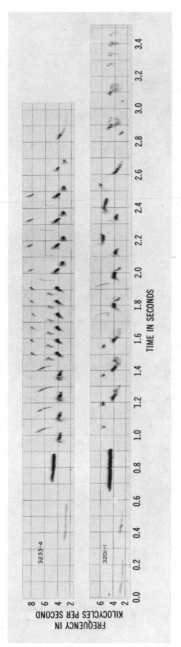

FIGURE 7. Audiospectrographs of songs of six male Vesper Sparrows. The number before the hyphen is the number of the recording, and the number after the hyphen is the number of the song in the recording. (Courtesy of Donald J. Borror.)

3307-3: Reynoldsburg, Ohio, May 1, 1958.
2772-4: Oscoda County, Michigan, May 31, 1957.
3232-2: Franklin County, Ohio, April 19, 1958.
3410-1: Delaware County, Ohio, May 17, 1958.
3233-4: Franklin County, Ohio, April 19, 1958.
3201-1: Reynoldsburg, Ohio, April 13, 1958.

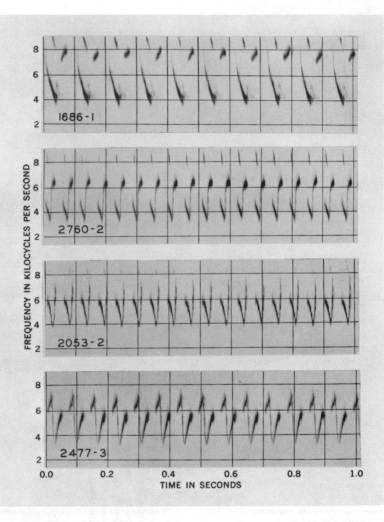

FIGURE 8. Audiospectrographs of songs of eight male Chipping Sparrows. (Courtesy of Donald J. Borror.)
   1686-1: Franklin County, Ohio, April 13, 1956.
   2760-2: Oscoda County, Michigan, May 30, 1957.
   2053-2: Lincoln County, Maine, June 20, 1956.
   2477-3: Franklin County, Ohio, April 27, 1957.

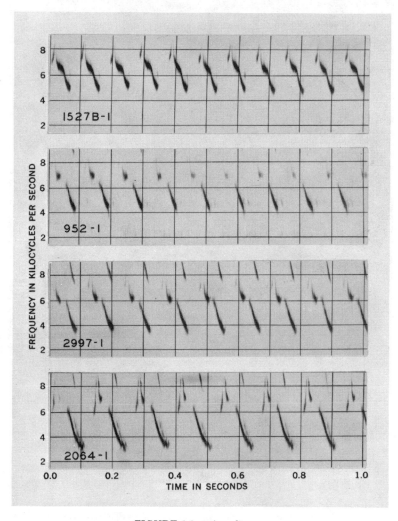

FIGURE 8 (*continued*)
1527B-1: Lincoln County, Maine, July 7, 1955.
952-1: Franklin County, Ohio, May 2, 1954.
2997-1: Lincoln County, Maine, July 14, 1957.
2064-1: Lincoln County, Maine, June 20, 1956.

FIGURE 9.   Dr. Donald J. Borror with his equipment for recording bird songs in the field.   (Courtesy of Donald J. Borror and the Department of Photography of Ohio State University.)

principal reproductive isolating mechanisms, which prevent mixed pairings among the species, "are the species specific vocalizations of the males (advertising songs) acting as sign stimuli to the corresponding specific releasing mechanism of the females."

A great deal has been written about two main types of songs (*fee-bee-o* and *fitz-beu*) given by Traill's Flycatchers in the eastern United States, and Kellogg and Stein (1953) published audiospectrographs of the two types. Only one song-type is given in most parts of the range, but in central New York birds singing either one type or the other are sometimes found in the same area. Stein (1958) proposed that "the two song-types represent distinct species in the Ithaca area at least; that these two breed within hearing range of one another, and that although interbreeding is possible, it apparently does not occur." It is my opinion that Stein's data are much too meager to justify these conclusions.

Some of the problems encountered in trying to interpret the meaning of a bird's reactions to recordings of bird calls are demonstrated by the work of Hubert and Mable Frings (1959), who studied the reactions of Herring Gulls and Common Crows to recorded call notes. They found that French populations of Herring Gulls ignored recordings of certain calls of American Herring Gulls,

FIGURE 10. Fledgling Fish Crows calling for food. (Courtesy of Samuel A. Grimes.)

which they cite as an example of different dialects in the calls within a species. They also found that crows living in Pennsylvania during the breeding season responded to recordings of the distress call of French Jackdaws but that wintering Pennsylvania crows did not, nor did crows that nested in Maine. This puzzling difference in reaction to strange calls they explained as follows. The breeding crows of Maine winter in Pennsylvania and at no time associate with other species of crows. Therefore, they respond only to their own call notes. The breeding crows of Pennsylvania, however, winter in the southern states where the Fish Crow (Fig. 10) is found. By hearing the calls of the Fish Crow, the Common Crows apparently learned to respond to the general features of crow calls as well as to their own species' calls. Consequently, they also responded to the call of the Jackdaw. Similarly, René-Guy Busnel in France found that the Jackdaw, Rook, and Carrion Crow, which feed and roost together, responded to each other's calls and to the "assembly call" of the Common Crow, but they did not respond to the Common Crow's alarm call.

The breeding season is the focal point of a bird's life. The life expectancy of most wild birds is relatively short, and an annual nesting cycle appears necessary for the continuance of the species. Although no other class of animals has attracted the interest of so many students, both amateur and professional, there are great gaps in our knowledge of the breeding activities of even the common species.

The accumulation of accurate information depends on the use of certain techniques and, of equal importance, on an objective approach to bird study. One cannot rely on memory, and it is imperative that the student acquire the habit of making a written record at the time that observations are made. Birds must be marked individually in order to obtain positive information on such points as second broods, change of mates during the breeding season, and age at sexual maturity. Most small birds can be marked satisfactorily with colored leg bands but these often are unsatisfactory for species that have very short tarsi or for those which spend most of their time in the air. Colored skin tags and plastic collars have been used for marking adult game birds, and some precocial species have been marked by injecting the eggs with dyes so that the young are already color-marked

7

Courtship and Nest Building

at hatching.   Two other methods are useful until the annual molt:
painting wing or tail feathers with dyes or airplane dope (Fig. 1),
and attaching strikingly colored feathers to those of the bird.

DISPLAY AND THE BREEDING CYCLE

Most display patterns serve as social signals and they are presumed
to have evolved from derived activities (page 134) through the
process of ritualization.   In other words, derived movements
which originally were outlets of "surplus excitation" have secondarily acquired a releaser function.   The new motor patterns of the
displays become "emancipated" from the derived movements in
that they are more or less independent of the original fixed-action
patterns in the central nervous system.   Ritualization is thus a
type of adaptive evolution.

FIGURE 1.   Adult Chimney Swift with wing feathers marked with model airplane
dope.   (Courtesy of Richard B. Fischer and the New York State Museum and Science
Service.)

There is ample evidence to demonstrate that brightly colored areas (on the wings, head, rump, tail, etc.) are used in display. It is generally agreed that the colored areas and the display patterns evolved more or less together until, eventually, they acquired a releaser function. Male birds usually are the more brightly colored sex, and it is assumed that sexual dimorphism in birds resulted from the process of *sexual selection*. That is to say, it is advantageous to a species if plumage colors and display patterns are so specific in nature that only males and females of the same species will react to each other's sign stimuli. This assumes, of course, that the evolution of color and display in the male has been accompanied by an evolution of the female's "innate perceptory pattern," so that she is attracted to (and stimulated to sexual activities with) the male. Among those species that do not exhibit sexual dimorphism, visual and auditory sign stimuli must have evolved in order to insure a successful breeding cycle and, thus, the survival of the species.

The majority of bird displays are performed during some phase of the nesting cycle. The cycle itself can be separated into several stages: establishment of territory, acquiring a mate, copulation, nest-building, egg-laying, incubation, and caring for the young. A particular display or ceremony (sometimes in modified form) may function during more than one of the stages: the display may be the same, but it may elicit a different response in the mate. This difference in response has led to the following classification based on functions of the displays.

1. *Antaposematic display* is threat display (intimidation) between rivals, specifically between rival males of the same species. The object of antaposematic display and fighting between rivals is the acquisition and maintenance of a territory.

2. *Gamosematic display* brings the sexes together and results in pair formation (mating). The female may locate the male either by visual or by auditory signals: color and special behavior patterns, song, and song flight.

3. *Epigamic display* synchronizes the mated pair for copulation. The term is used also in a broader sense to include all types of display that bring the sexes together and lead to copulation (i.e., both gamosematic and epigamic display), and, then, is synonymous with "courtship."

4. *Postnuptial display* includes all displays and ceremonies that take place between the pair after copulation has ceased and incubation has begun. It includes many forms of greeting and nest-

relief ceremonies, which presumably hold the pair together. It is characteristic of gannets, storks, and other birds that spend a long time in incubating and taking care of the young.

So varied are the display and nesting patterns exhibited by birds, however, that it is virtually impossible to summarize them in a short chapter within the framework of any arbitrary system of classification (see Armstrong, 1947). Such a system is useful for purposes of description and reporting observations, but for a mated pair the nesting cycle is a continuum of mutually stimulating behavior patterns. Therefore, we have selected for presentation several important activities, all of which include some type of display.

Functions of Courtship

Courtship may be defined as any behavior pattern (including song) that brings the sexes together and leads to copulation. It may consist of elaborate displays that continue for several weeks or months. It has been suggested that prolonged courtship may be necessary to stimulate internal physiological processes (in the gonads and other endocrine glands), and that it "serves not only to release sexual behavior in the partner but also to suppress . . . the tendencies to aggression or escape" (Tinbergen, 1954b). Tinbergen and others believe (see page 139) that aggression and flight in many animals "are just as important elements in reproductive behavior as the physical union itself." Four main attributes of courtship display have been outlined by Tinbergen (1954a):

1. Song, song flights, and other special displays serve an orientation function: they attract a female to the male's territory or to a nest site.

2. Courtship displays serve to suppress nonsexual responses (i.e., aggressive and escape drives) in the mate.

3. Displays serve to synchronize the sexes. For birds of the Temperate Zone, there is a relationship between increasing daylength and the development of the gonads so that a "gross synchronization" of the sexes results. A finer synchronization, leading to copulation, is effected by the signal function of display. That visual stimuli can effect physiological changes has been shown for the pigeon: ovulation is induced by the sight of the displaying male, and the sight of the incubating female induces changes in the male's crop glands, which secrete "pigeon's milk" for the young.

4. Because courtship displays are specific, they serve as *biological isolating mechanisms*, i.e., they tend to insure that pair-bonds

and copulation will occur only between individuals of the same species. If this is so, a bird must be able to "identify" other members of the species and their sex. There has been much debate over the terms "species recognition" and "sex recognition," however, primarily because of the implications of the word "recognition." Again relying on the Lorenz-Tinbergen theories of fixed-action patterns and social signals, ornithologists conclude that the majority of relationships between the members of a species and of the mated pair result from the interplay of social signals; the birds do not form concepts of species or sex. The interaction between the sexes can be illustrated by presenting information obtained by Margaret M. Nice (1943) in her pioneering studies of the Song Sparrow. The first reaction of a male Song Sparrow (the *actor*) in breeding condition is to fly at any intruder on its territory. If the intruder (the *reactor*) is another male Song Sparrow in breeding condition, the reactor displays and the actor then exhibits its second reaction by fighting the intruder (by song, display, or actual attack). If, however, the intruder is a female Song Sparrow in breeding condition, she remains on the territory and gives special call notes, in which event the second reaction of the male is to court her. "The actor's signals are his display: his evident possession of a territory in many cases, his song, bright colors, and special gestures. These serve as a warning to other members of the same sex and an invitation to a mate. The reactor, according to its sex or condition, shows its signals—challenge, avoidance, or approach." The student should note again that the behavior of a bird depends on internal conditions (both physiological and "psychological") and on external situations (such as social signals). Among North American thrushes, in which the sexes are alike in plumage pattern, it has been suggested that the primary sign stimuli that prevent interspecific mating are the advertising songs of the males (Dilger, 1956).

Pair Formation

The majority of birds are monogamous in that copulation takes place only between the members of a mated pair during a particular nesting cycle. The pair remains together during that nesting cycle (or longer), and we say that a pair-bond is formed between the male and the female. The time required to form a pair-bond varies from a matter of hours (e.g., Budgerigars) to several months (many ducks). Dilger found that three or four days are required to form the pair-bond in several species of thrushes. The length of the pair-bond formed likewise varies considerably among birds. Although several types of pair-bond have been described, it should be emphasized that many intermediate patterns are found and that detailed information of pair formation is lacking for the majority of birds.

1. The sexes meet only at the time of copulation, as in most grouse (page 198). A pair-bond, if formed at all, is of very short duration, and, in some instances, more than one male may copulate with a given female.

2. The sexes remain together only for a few days or until the eggs are laid and incubation begins. A familiar example is the Ruby-throated Hummingbird: the female constructs the nest, incubates the eggs, and takes care of the young by herself. There are a few instances (e.g., Northern Phalarope) in which the male incubates and takes care of the young; the female leaves after she has laid the eggs.

3. Most ducks form a pair-bond during the fall, winter, or early spring. Many have elaborate courtship displays and form a strong pair-bond, which, however, ends when the female begins to incubate the eggs.

4. The sexes of most species remain together throughout the breeding season, usually until the young have been raised. The pair-bond typically is formed after the male has established a territory, but in a few species (e.g., auks, gulls, Cedar Waxwing, Lesser and Lawrence's goldfinches) this happens while the birds are still in winter flocks. Much variation in the relations between the sexes is shown by the species in this category, and not all individuals of a given species behave in the same way. Such multiple-brooded species as Barn Swallows, House Wrens, Catbirds, and Eastern Bluebirds often change mates for a second brood, but not all individuals do so. Among migratory passerine species, the males often return earlier than the females, and both males and females tend to return to the same territory (or to one nearby) in succeeding years. A pair may remate for several years. We do not know if there is any carry-over in the pair-bond between such a pair. The remating in successive years may be due solely to the tendency to return to the same general area. A color-banded female Song Sparrow that I studied had the same color-banded mate (and territory) in 1948 and for four nests in 1949. For her fifth nest in 1949 she had an unbanded mate; I was unable to find the banded male again. The nesting area was destroyed during the winter of 1949–1950, and the female returned to a nesting area about a

quarter of a mile away. The pair of Robins that nests in your yard "throughout the summer" may not be the same pair at all. Howard Young found that 23 out of 39 pairs of color-marked Robins moved to new territories to raise a second brood. For cavity-nesting species, as well, it cannot be assumed that the same pair uses a particular nesting site throughout the season. Several workers have shown that a new pair of House Sparrows may move into a bird house almost as soon as the young of another pair have left the nest.

5. The sexes pair for life and remain together throughout the year. Little accurate information is available on such species but some evidence suggests that swans, geese, Common Terns, Ravens, some species of crows, Wrentits, White-breasted and Pigmy nuthatches, and Brown Creepers may form a permanent pair-bond.

Although the majority of birds are monogamous, two types of polygamy occur. Ring-necked Pheasants, Red-winged, Tricolored, and Yellow-headed blackbirds, hummingbirds, and most grouse, for example, are *polygynous:* one male fertilizes the eggs of several females. Some tinamous and phalaropes are said to be *polyandrous:* the females copulate with two or more males. *Promiscuity,* the more or less indiscriminate copulation without the formation of any pair-bond, has been ascribed to a few species (e.g., Boat-tailed Grackle). It has been stated that the European Oystercatcher tends to be promiscuous early in the nesting season. However, in a study of 110 adults banded at the nest, Wolfgang Jungfer later found that 24 pairs were mated for two years, 10 pairs for three years, 3 pairs for four years, 2 pairs for five years, and 1 pair for six years. Variation in behavior, as well as in structure, is a common occurrence in nature, and deviation from normal monogamous relationships has been reported for such birds as swans, hawks, and several passerine species (e.g., Tree Swallow, Mockingbird, Eastern Bluebird, Robin, Starling, Ovenbird, Kirtland's Warbler, House Sparrow, Cardinal, Song Sparrow). This disruption of normal monogamous relations sometimes results when one member of a pair is killed during the nesting cycle.

Copulation

Copulation is the act of transferring sperm from the male to the cloaca of the female (see page 298). The transfer is accomplished as the male balances on the female's back and presses the edges of the two cloacae together; a cloacal penis assists the process in ducks, gallinaceous birds, and a few others. Copulation may take place on the ground, in water, in bushes and trees, on telephone wires or fences, on nests or nest boxes, or in the air (some swifts). The primary object of copulation is fertilization of the eggs, but in some species it must serve also to stimulate both sexes and to maintain the pair-bond. House Sparrows and Red-bellied Wood-peckers, for example, may copulate as early as two months before the eggs are laid; in the sparrow copulation may continue through-out the incubation period. Black-headed Gulls and Common Terns are said to copulate even after the eggs hatch, and copulation of Starlings has been observed in nearly every month of the year. Copulatory behavior in many passerine species, however, is limited to the nest-building and egg-laying period, sometimes for a period of a week to 10 days before the nest is started. The Cedar Wax-wing, American Goldfinch, and some other double-brooded species start copulation again a few days before the young of the first brood leave the nest.

Copulatory behavior is induced by a series of displays between the sexes; it may be initiated by the male or the female. The precopulatory display may be simple or elaborate. A male Starling may omit all display but will mount a female after she pecks the feathers of his neck or shoulder. A female Song Sparrow indicates readiness for copulation by raising her head and tail and by spread-ing and quivering her wings. Great Blue Herons usually copulate in the nest following the performance of one or more of the numer-ous courtship rituals, as in this example: a male heron greets his mate by posturing and "howling"; both birds clap their mandibles and walk around each other in the nest; the male then strokes the female's head and back with his bill, after which the female crouches and the male steps on her back to copulate (Fig. 2). The females of some species (e.g., Red-bellied Woodpecker, Starling) may mount the male (*reverse mounting*) and flutter on his back as a preliminary step to copulation.

Copulation is completed in about 1 second in Song Sparrows but may continue for 12 to 15 seconds in the Great Blue Heron. Star-lings rarely copulate more than once after a given precopulatory display; male Song Sparrows may mount the female 2 to 4 times in rapid succession. I have seen a male House Sparrow mount a female 14 times in succession, pecking the female's head during each act; after he dismounted momentarily, the female crouched lower, opened her bill, and fluttered her wings. Some birds ignore each other after copulation and return to routine activities, but some species exhibit a postcopulatory display (Figs. 3, 4). A female

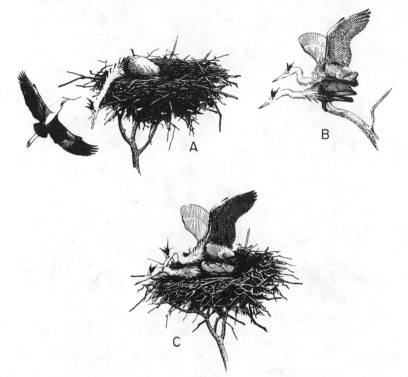

FIGURE 2. Copulatory behavior of the Great Blue Heron. A. Bird in nest drooping head and neck over side and shaking bill slowly from side to side; mate arriving with stick. B and C. Copulation on branch and in nest. (Courtesy of W. Powell and Betty D. Cottrille, from *Miscellaneous Publication No. 102,* University of Michigan Museum of Zoology.)

Song Sparrow gives a special call note. A male Bufflehead dismounts after copulation but holds onto the female's head with his bill, and the birds rotate around each other once or twice. After releasing his hold on the female, the male dips his head and breast into the water while shaking his wings as though bathing. Other species may preen, shake their feathers, exchange nesting material, or the pair may perch side by side and perform a mutual display.

In the discussion of "Functions of Courtship," we mentioned that the terms "species recognition" and "sex recognition" are in bad repute unless used in a restricted sense. David Lack pointed out some 20 years ago, however, that after the pair-bond has been formed, sex recognition is a matter of "distinguishing the mate individually from all others of her species." Such individual recog-

FIGURE 3. A. Postcopulatory shaking and preening of Great Blue Herons. B. A male
heron arriving at a second nest immediately after copulating with female in nest on
right. C. Postcopulatory quiescence. D. Neck-crossing ceremony; repeated a few seconds after the birds had righted themselves. E. Stick transfer ceremony. (Courtesy
of W. Powell and Betty D. Cottrille, from *Miscellaneous Publication No. 102,* University of Michigan Museum of Zoology.)

nition of a mate, either by sight or sound, has been proved for
several species (e.g., Black-headed Gull, Herring Gull, Black-
crowned Night Heron, Yellow-shafted Flicker, Song Sparrow). One
can cite experimental data that either support or counter the
instinct behaviorist's belief that birds do not respond to the total
environment but only to narrow and specific sign stimuli. Some of
these data are pertinent to the discussion of sex or mate recognition and copulation. It has been learned, for example, that adult
males of many species will attack mounted skins of males (or even
a small tuft of brightly colored feathers), and that they will mount
and attempt to copulate with mounted females (or models composed
of various materials) of their own species. One-year-old Red-winged
Blackbirds, however, copulated "indiscriminately" with mounts of
such totally dissimilar species as the Blue Jay, Cardinal, Eastern
Meadowlark, and Wood Thrush. A male wren may challenge a
mounted specimen by singing, but, receiving no response, will then

mount it. Some male birds (e.g., Common Tern, Yellow-shafted Flicker, Song Sparrow), however, are not stimulated to copulate with mounted female specimens. For male Song Sparrows, Mrs. Nice found that "special notes are necessary before a bird will have the meaning of a female."

FIGURE 4. Postcopulatory display of the Fulvous Tree Duck. (Courtesy of Brooke Meanley.)

One of the implications of imprinting is that "species recognition" (specifically as it involves sexual behavior in the adult) is imprinted on the young bird soon after it hatches. Rarely is it mentioned, however, that among shorebirds the species releasers seem to be "predominantly inherited," and that it is very difficult for a human to become a foster parent for these birds. Another puzzling problem is offered by such parasitic species as the Brown-headed Cowbird. The young Cowbird may be hatched in the nest of any one of about 200 species of birds, and, in those instances where the bird hatches after the adult Cowbirds have migrated, it may not see an adult until it reaches the wintering grounds. Even though a young Cowbird may never have seen another Cowbird, the immature birds gather in premigratory flocks; and they mate and copulate with their own kind the following spring.

Symbolic Display

"Courtship" feeding is the name given to a behavior pattern in which the male offers food to the female; the female's posture often simulates that of a young bird begging for food. It may occur as a part of the courtship period, during incubation (Fig. 5), or even when there are young in the nest. It has been observed just before or during copulation in some bitterns, Laughing Gull, Herring Gull, Rock Dove, Yellow-billed Cuckoo, Roadrunner, and some species of nuthatches, shrikes, and Galápagos finches. Because the main function seems not to be the food that is exchanged, courtship feeding is considered a type of symbolic display, and, as such, aids in maintaining the pair-bond. It occurs primarily in species in which the sexes remain together throughout the breeding season. The manner of presenting the food varies: there is usually a simple transfer from male to female in passerine birds, but waxwings may pass the food back and forth, and male cardueline weaverbirds are said to regurgitate the food to the female; males of some birds of prey pass food to the female in mid-air; the male Herring Gull regurgitates food on the ground in front of the female. Some species engage in *mock feeding,* in which no food is exchanged but the behavior pattern resembles actual courtship feeding.

Incipient courtship feeding consists of various forms of mutual "billing," "fencing," and "bill-sparring." These activities are considered to be closely related to the actual transfer of food. Grebes, herons, puffins, guillemots, pigeons, kingfishers, woodpeckers, waxwings, thrushes, corvids, and fringillids may engage in some form of mutual bill stimulation during the courtship period or even

FIGURE 5. A male Swainson's Warbler feeding the female on the nest. (Courtesy of Samuel A. Grimes.)

throughout the entire breeding season (rarely during the winter).

Symbolic nest-building, during the courtship period, is practiced by some birds (e.g., grebes, cormorants, Mockingbirds, Red-winged Blackbirds, Song Sparrows). Either one or both sexes may pick up, manipulate, or carry nesting materials for a short time.

TERRITORIALITY

The concept of bird territoriality was developed in Germany by Bernard Altum in 1868, and independently in England by Eliot Howard during the period from 1907 to 1920. The theory received widespread acceptance after 1920 as ornithologists found ample supporting evidence for it in their field work with some species of birds. Others minimized the significance of the theory because it did not, apparently, apply to all birds. With the initial enthusiasm characteristically aroused by a new theory, ornithologists tried to find a simple explanation for the function of territorial behavior, and many insisted that territory was necessary in order to insure an adequate food supply for a pair of birds and their young. It is doubtful that this is ever the sole function, particularly for passerine birds. It has been suggested that territories disperse birds so that epidemics are prevented, and that they may reduce the loss of birds to predators because a bird is thoroughly familiar with its own territory, but there is little factual support for these interpretations. Territorial behavior undoubtedly does aid in maintaining the pair-bond, in reducing interference by other members of a species during the breeding season, and in regulating the density of a species in a favorable habitat.

The theories of bird behavior elaborated by Lorenz and Tinbergen constitute a second important stimulus to bird study during the present century. We agree with Fraser Darling, James Fisher, and others, however, that the concept of the hostile or aggressive nature of birds has been overemphasized. Other important facets of the interrelationships among birds during the breeding season may be neglected because of the exploitation of this one theme. As pointed out on page 141, an important function of territory and territorial behavior may be one of mutual stimulation for the birds whose territories are units in a social network. It is possible also, especially for colonial species, that the displays of one species may serve to stimulate physiological or other development in another species.

Types of Territory

It is a fact that nearly all bird species exhibit territorial behavior (threat or intimidation display, song, etc.) during the breeding season (Fig. 6). As a general rule, a bird is dominant in its own territory, which it defends especially against members of its own species and sex. Song and various types of display presumably enable a bird to defend its territory without actually engaging in physical contact with an intruding bird. When threat displays are not effective in causing an intruder to leave the territory, fighting does occur, but it usually results in little damage to either bird; rarely is a bird killed.

Territory can be defined most satisfactorily by stating that it *is any defended area*. Four main types of breeding territories have been recognized, but in addition to these a bird may defend its mate, its young, a covey, a song or lookout post, or a food supply. For example, Norman French concluded that the male Black Rosy Finch defends the female, rather than a specific territory per se. The feeding area and the nest site may be widely separated in this

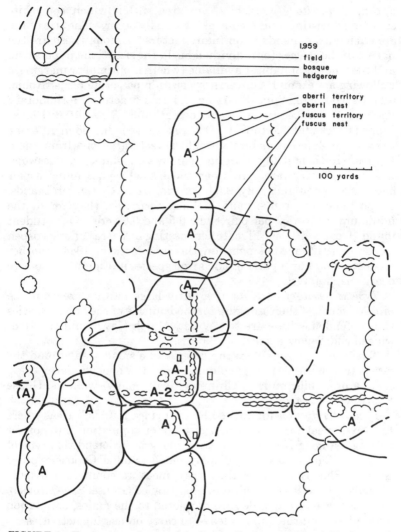

1,959
field
bosque
hedgerow

aberti territory
aberti nest
fuscus territory
fuscus nest

100 yards

FIGURE 6. Territories and nests of the Brown Towhee and Abert's Towhee on the San Xavier Reservation near Tucson, Arizona, in 1959. (Courtesy of Joe T. Marshall, Jr., and the editor of *The Condor*.)

species; when the female leaves the nest, the male follows her (leaving the nest unprotected) and drives off other males that approach too closely. Some birds also defend nonbreeding territories: feeding, roosting, or winter territories.

Type A territory consists of an area within which courtship, copulation, nesting, and food-seeking usually occur. The size of the area defended depends upon many factors. Among these are the nature of the species (or individual bird), the size of the population, and the amount of habitat available (whether optimal or marginal). Following are examples of territory sizes in passerine birds: Robin, 0.11 to 0.60 acre; Song Sparrow, 0.5 to 1.5 acres; Prothonotary Warbler, 1.9 to 6.4; Brown-headed Nuthatch, 5.2 to 10.6; Black-capped Chickadee, 8.4 to 17.1. Other studies conducted in different years or in different habitats would reveal variations from these figures. In their study of Song Sparrows on islands in Basswood Lake, Minnesota, James R. Beer and his colleagues found a pair nesting on an island only 0.04 acre in size. On larger islands, supporting four or five pairs of Song Sparrows, they found the minimum territories per pair to be 0.5 and 0.6 acre. One student found 19 pairs of Least Flycatchers nesting in 7 acres of open aspen woods in 1942, and 14 pairs on the same area in 1944; another student found but 9 pairs of the same species nesting in a 160-acre beech-maple forest.

Type B territory consists of a fairly large nesting area but the birds do much of their foraging for food outside of the area. Species that defend this type are the Willet, Marsh Hawk, and the Red-winged and Yellow-headed blackbirds.

Type C territory involves the defense of a small area around the nest. It is characteristic of colonial, and a few noncolonial, species, e.g., herons, gulls, murres, Chimney Swift, many swallows, House Sparrow.

Type D territory is illustrated by "dancing grounds," areas where the sexes meet for pair formation and/or copulation but not for nesting. Among North American birds, grouse defend this type of territory. The males may display alone (Ruffed Grouse, Spruce Grouse, Blue Grouse) or they may meet at communal display grounds or *leks* (Prairie Chicken, Sharp-tailed Grouse, Sage Grouse). In either case, the females are attracted to the males, copulation takes place, and the females leave to carry on nesting activities.

Cooperative Nesting

The South American Gray-breasted Parakeet and some species of African weaverbirds build cooperative nests. According to Friedmann (1950), large flocks of the Sociable Weaver may build a nest "as much as 25 feet long and 15 feet wide at the base and from 5 to 10 feet in height!" Each pair of birds has its own nesting compartment within the structure and takes care of its own young. Little is known about territorial manifestations in this species (Fig. 7).

Communal Nesting

This rare form of social nesting is practiced by two genera of cuckoos (*Crotophaga* and *Guira*) that live primarily south of the United States. The Groove-billed Ani nests in the Rio Grande Valley of Texas, and the Smooth-billed Ani has become established as a breeding bird in parts of Florida. Several adult anis build a communal nest, in which two or more females lay their eggs; all of the adults may share in incubation and in feeding the nestlings; less commonly, a single pair nests by itself. Present evidence suggests that the Groove-billed Ani usually is monogamous and that the Smooth-billed Ani may be monogamous, polygynous, and polyandrous "all in the same neighborhood," but this certainly needs verification. In speaking of the Groove-billed Ani, Alexander

FIGURE 7. A large cooperative nest of the Sociable Weaver of South Africa; parts of this old nest had fallen down owing to their own weight. (Courtesy of Herbert Friedmann and the Smithsonian Institution.)

Skutch remarked that they seemed to be equipped with no aggressive or defensive displays, and that he had never seen one bird fight or chase another. The members of one flock of Smooth-billed Anis, however, may exhibit strong territorial defense against a member of a strange flock. It is possible that the Acorn Woodpecker of the western United States engages in communal nesting but more information is needed.

LENGTH OF BREEDING SEASON

The phrase "length of breeding season" means several things. One may speak of the number of weeks or months in the year when one may find the nest (or dependent young) of a particular species, or of an individual member of that species, or of any species that nests in a given locality (Fig. 8). In southern Michigan, for example, active nests may be found in each of nine months but no single species is known to breed throughout that entire period. The nesting span of selected species is given in Table 1. Many species in the northern part of the United States carry on their nesting activities

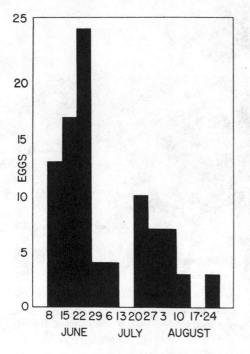

FIGURE 8. Number of first eggs found per week in nests of the Cedar Waxwing on South Bass Island in Lake Erie. (Courtesy of Loren S. Putnam and the editor of *The Wilson Bulletin*.)

TABLE 1
Southern Michigan Nesting Calendar

Species	Feb.	Mar.	Apr.	May	June	July	Aug.	Sept.	Oct.	Nov.
Great-horned Owl	—	—	—							
Horned Lark		—	—	—	—					
Mourning Dove		—	—	—	—	—	—	—	—	
Eastern Bluebird			—	—	—	—				
Robin			—	—	—	—				
Eastern Phoebe			—	—	—	—				
Song Sparrow			—	—	—	—	—			
Vesper Sparrow			—	—	—	—	—			
Cardinal			—	—	—	—	—			
Blue Jay			—	—	—					
Field Sparrow				—	—	—	—			
Catbird				—	—	—				
Sora Rail				—	—	—				
Rufous-sided Towhee				—	—	—	—			
Yellow Warbler				—	—	—				
Chipping Sparrow				—	—	—	—			
Red-winged Blackbird			—	—	—	—	—			
Scarlet Tanager				—	—					
Common Nighthawk				—	—					
Indigo Bunting				—	—	—				
Eastern Wood Pewee				—	—	—	—			
Traill's Flycatcher				—	—	—				
Cedar Waxwing					—	—	—			
American Goldfinch					—	—	—			

in May and June. These same species may nest earlier farther to the south, or later in Canada. Young Bald Eagles are found from May to July in Michigan; Charles L. Broley wrote that some young eagles leave the nest early in January in Florida.

Some species of birds attempt to raise only one brood of young each year—these are *single-brooded* species. Such species do not renest if they are successful in raising one brood of young birds. A *multiple-brooded* species is one that raises *to an independent stage* more than one brood during one breeding season. Birds are persistent during the span of their breeding activity, and both single-brooded and multiple-brooded species will renest repeatedly if a nest is destroyed. Even so, there are times (because of high nest mortality) when a pair of birds may be unsuccessful in raising any young during a particular nesting season. Some pairs of Song Sparrows may raise three broods, whereas other pairs may have an equally long breeding season without raising any young. A color-

banded female Song Sparrow in Michigan built five nests during the
period from April 24 to August 4, but in only two of the nests were
young fledged.

Within the normal time span of the breeding season, the number
of broods that can be raised by a multiple-brooded species depends
on the time required to raise a brood, the stage at which a nest is
destroyed, the interval between the destruction of a nest and a
renesting, and the interval between the fledging of one brood and
the start of another nest. The Cedar Waxwing may lay the first
egg in a second nest the day before the young leave the first
nest; two broods can be raised in an average period of about 65 days.
The interval between nest-leaving and the laying of the first egg in
the second nest varies from 3 to 10 days in the American Goldfinch, from 6 to 19 days in the Song Sparrow. The interval between
the destruction of a nest and the first egg in the new nest varies from
4 to 7 days for the Prothonotary Warbler, 5 to 7 for the Song
Sparrow, 5 to 15 for the House Sparrow, and 4 to 21 for the
American Goldfinch.

A species may be single-brooded in one part of its range but
double-brooded in another part (e.g., Prothonotary Warbler). The
individuals of some typically single-brooded species may raise two
broods (or attempt to) during certain years. We know little about
this for American birds, but the Kirtland's Warbler and American
Goldfinch (which actually may be typically double-brooded) are two
examples. Annual variation in the number of broods (one or two
broods) has been reported for the Great Tit in Holland. Moreover,
a higher percentage (68 per cent) of the tits nesting in coniferous
woods raised second broods than did those nesting in broad-leaved
woods (36 per cent).

The duration of the breeding season for a species must depend
on the physiological condition of the gonads and other endocrine
organs. Virtually nothing is known about the possible influence (if
any) of external factors on these organs near the end of a species'
breeding cycle. Evidence suggests that a bird will not renest, or
may even desert a nest containing eggs or young, after a certain
period because of a decrease in the internal stimuli responsible for
incubation and feeding behavior. Traill's Flycatchers in southern
Michigan probably do not renest if their nest is destroyed after the
third week in July. September nests of American Goldfinches
sometimes are deserted for no apparent reason even when they
contain young. In these two examples, only the females incubate
but both sexes feed the young. It seems unlikely that desertion of
nests with young is always due to the death of the female.

Almost all birds have one breeding season each year, but there are a few curious exceptions. Sooty Terns that nest on Ascension Island in the Atlantic Ocean appear to breed on a cycle that corresponds to a period of 10 lunar months (295.3 days), and the birds nest twice in some years. The nestling period of the Royal Albatross is so long that a female normally lays a single egg every other year; if a nest is destroyed early enough in the cycle, nesting may occur the following year. South Georgia King Penguins are reported to have a 14- to 18-month breeding cycle.

INITIATION OF BREEDING SEASON

One of the intriguing physiological phenomena in birds is the tremendous difference in size of the gonads between the breeding and nonbreeding seasons (Figs. 9, 10). In many Temperate Zone species, the testes of a breeding male may be from several hundred to 2000 times the sizes of those in a nonbreeding male. These seasonal changes in the gonads are controlled by two or more hormones secreted by the anterior pituitary gland, a small but essential gland suspended from the floor of the hypothalamus. Among the many functions of the hypothalamus is that of the control and integration of the gonadotropic activities of the anterior pituitary. In this respect it must be borne in mind that the hypothalamus through relatively direct connection receives information from both internal and external receptors. Therefore, the reproductive activity of birds may be controlled, or affected by, a variety of external stimuli. Of the external stimuli which may have an effect on the development of reproductive activity, the stimulus that has received the greatest amount of attention is the duration of the daily photoperiod. Much experimental evidence has been accumulated to demonstrate that the duration of the daily photoperiod may serve as an effective biological calendar in many species of birds. This appears to be the case particularly in many Temperate Zone migratory species. In these species, of all the locally available environmental changes in the wintering area, the change in daily photoperiod is the most reliable indicator that the time favorable for reproductive activity in the breeding area is approaching. The mechanism involved in these photoperiodic responses appears to include sensory cells (receptors) in the retina and possibly on the surface of the hypothalamus itself, which, when stimulated, result in a transfer of the stimulatory substance from neurosecretory cells in the hypothalamus to the anterior pituitary gland via a special

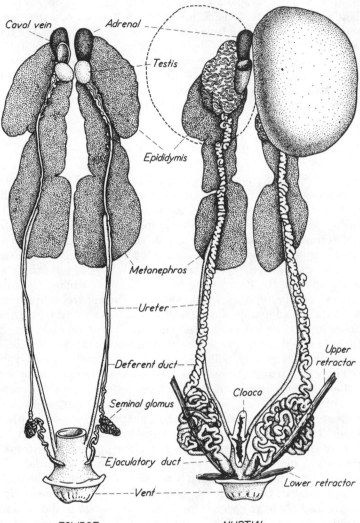

FIGURE 9. Urogenital organs of a male House Sparrow in eclipse and in nuptial condition; the latter was induced out of season by 17 daily injections of 0.1 cc. of pregnant mare serum. The retractor muscles are not shown in the left figure. (By permission of Emil Witschi, from *Biology and Comparative Physiology of Birds,* Vol. 2, published by Academic Press, Inc. Copyright, 1961.)

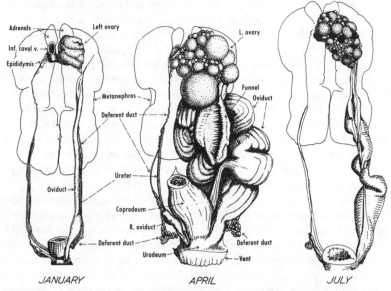

FIGURE 10. Urogenital organs of a female House Sparrow. January: eclipse condition. April: early nuptial condition; note enlargement of deferent ducts and right oviduct. July: incubating female taken from nest on July 27; regression stage; ovary contains several empty follicles and degenerating eggs. (By permission of Emil Witschi, from *Biology and Comparative Physiology of Birds,* Vol. 2, published by Academic Press, Inc. Copyright, 1961.)

portal system. The humoral material thus transferred stimulates the anterior pituitary to release additional quantities of gonadotropic hormones which in turn stimulate the development of the gonads. The gonads themselves secrete a sex hormone which causes the development of sexual behavior. It is possible that eventually the secretions from the gonads cause the hypothalamus to become insensitive to long daily photoperiods. Since the hypothalamus receives sensory information from many kinds of receptors, a number of factors have a modifying effect on the photoperiodically controlled development of the gonads. In the photoperiodically controlled birds, each period of gonadal development is followed by a refractory period in which the mechanism cannot be stimulated by long daily photoperiods. The refractory period is naturally eliminated by the shorter days of late autumn and early winter.

It seems probable that photoperiodic control mechanisms have been evolved independently many times in birds. Consequently, it should not be surprising to discover that they function somewhat differently in different species and that there may be varying degrees to which they are modified by other environmental factors. It should be emphasized also that photoperiodic control of the development of reproductive activity represents only one way in which this phenomenon can be controlled environmentally. Obviously, other schemes must be involved in equatorial and near-equatorial species where the annual change in day-length is relatively slight. Furthermore, it seems obvious that the irregular breeding periods of many desert and arid-zone species must be controlled on another basis. Much research is needed in order to understand such non-photoperiodic control systems.

It seems axiomatic that in the course of evolution species have developed mechanisms which assure that reproductive activity will occur at the time of the year when conditions are most favorable for survival of the young. It must be borne in mind, however, that the physiological preparation for reproduction requires a considerable period of time, usually several weeks to several months. It then follows that we must clearly recognize two groups of environmental factors with respect to control of the reproductive cycle. The first group has been designated as the *ultimate factors*. These are the environmental factors that have imposed a selective influence in evolution in favor of individuals with mechanisms that assure reproductive activity at the most favorable time of the year. Among the obvious ultimate factors are those of food supply and suitable nesting sites and materials. The *proximate factors* are those that operate on the individual bird giving it, in a sense, the necessary information to begin physiological preparation for reproduction so that the young will be produced at the most favorable time of the year. As indicated above, the proximate factor that has received the greatest amount of experimental attention is the increasing daily photoperiod in spring. Unquestionably there must be many species with proximate factors other than changing photoperiod. In the photoperiodically controlled species, there are certainly modifying or *secondary proximate factors* which cannot alone cause development of the gonadal cycle but which can modify the rate of development. In the females of most photoperiodic species the gonadal cycle is basically photoperiodically timed but complete development and oviposition require *essential secondary proximate factors* (such as courtship and display of the males).

AGE AT SEXUAL MATURITY

Certain generalizations have been made regarding the age at which birds first engage in nesting activities. Ducks, many gallinaceous birds, pigeons, some owls, and most passerine birds breed the year after they hatch; in most instances they are less than 12 months old. It has been postulated (on the basis of testis development in collected specimens) that some tropical passerine species are able to breed when only four to six months old. Geese, many hawks and owls, most gulls, swifts, and a few passerine birds breed when two years old; large birds of prey and storks, when four to six years old; and the Royal Albatross probably does not breed until it is at least eight years old. Age may also affect the time at which species nest within a given season. Tree Swallows, Starlings, and Eastern Bluebirds begin to lay eggs a little later during their first breeding season than do older birds. Among Eastern Bluebirds hatched during the same year, however, Amelia Laskey found that those hatched late (in August) laid as early (or even earlier) the following year as their contemporaries who had hatched early (in April).

NESTS

It is well in any field of study for the student to be aware of his heritage, to know the devoted students of the past who laid the groundwork for what is known today. Among those who studied the living bird are John J. Audubon, Alexander Wilson, Thomas M. Brewer, Spencer F. Baird, Charles E. Bendire, William Brewster, Francis H. Herrick, Arthur C. Bent, Lynds Jones, Thomas S. Roberts, and Arthur A. Allen. In no way can these keen field naturalists be criticized for the little we know about some aspects of the breeding biology of American birds. In the opening sentences of his *Key to North American Birds,* Elliott Coues stated boldly in 1903: "Field Ornithology must lead the way to Systematic and Descriptive Ornithology. The study of Birds in the field is an indispensable prerequisite to their study in the library and the museum." A long period followed, however, during which the naturalist was viewed as a "mere amateur," and there were those who asserted that the field study of birds (especially of their nests and eggs) was not to be considered a part of "scientific ornithology" at all. To those people, one had to be a taxonomist to be considered an ornithologist.

The chief contributing factor to the development of this attitude undoubtedly was the acceptance of the concept of the subspecies (page 334). Robert M. Mengel (1957), in his typically penetrating style, described this period as follows:

> By 1900 undescribed species were becoming very rare; besides providing new insight into the nature and variation of species, the "discovery" of the subspecies gave life to those whose chief goal was naming new kinds of animals. Unfortunately some of the devotees of this sport have lacked discrimination and conservatism and have not always been immune to the charge of undue haste. Whether or not done wisely, the naming of many subspecies (sometimes these were still described, hopefully, as "full" species) caused great proliferation of nomenclature and considerable confusion, and it became the task of "reviewers" (who themselves frequently described still further forms) to make order of the chaos. . . . A large school of ornithologists devoted themselves to this activity. . . .

The return to field studies of birds as an accepted part of ornithology in the United States received some impetus with the publication of Harry W. Hann's study of the Ovenbird (1937) and Margaret M. Nice's two monographs on the Song Sparrow (1937, 1943). As recently as 1951, however, Ernst Mayr was prompted to write that "instead of expending their energy on the describing and naming of trifling subspecies, bird taxonomists might well devote more attention to the evaluation of trends in variation," thus pointing out that the subspecies mania in its narrow concepts still persisted.

In a sense, however, field ornithologists are born and not made. Partly owing to the influence of Arthur C. Bent and Arthur A. Allen, "nest hunters" continued their activities, and a large book could be written about nests. Birds' nests vary in diameter from less than an inch (hummingbirds) to nine feet or more. Charles Broley mentioned a Florida nest of the Bald Eagle that was 20 feet deep and 9½ feet wide! Nests are constructed of all manner of plant materials, feathers, hair, spider webs, snakeskin, mud, paper, string, and many other items that man strews over the countryside. The Chimney Swift (Figs. 11, 12) and its relatives use saliva to hold together small twigs, plant fragments, moss, and other materials used in the nest; the nests of some species of the swiftlet genus *Collocalia* are composed almost entirely of hardened saliva and are used to make bird's-nest soup. The Palm-swift of Africa uses saliva to attach plant floss and feathers of other birds

FIGURE 11. Nest and eggs of the Chimney Swift. (Courtesy of Richard B. Fischer and the New York State Museum and Science Service.)

to the vertical surface of a palm frond. A flange at the bottom of the nest pad is narrower than the long axis of the eggs, and the two eggs are placed on their small ends and glued to the nest with saliva; the adults incubate in a vertical position. Some birds build no nest at all but lay their eggs on the ground (Fig. 13) or on rock ledges; King Penguins hold a single egg on top of their feet and incubate it there. Where trees are available, the Fairy Tern lays its single egg in a slight depression on a bare horizontal branch.

Richard Headstrom (1949, 1951) wrote two books that contain keys to the identification of the nests of most species of birds found in the United States. It is true, as he states, that the "best way of identifying a nest is when it is still occupied by the maker,"

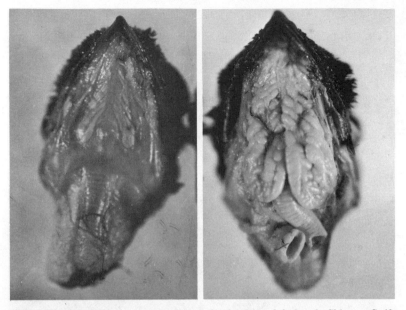

FIGURE 12. Left: Undeveloped salivary glands of an adult female Chimney Swift taken on April 30, 1955, near Sandersville, Georgia. Right: Fully developed salivary glands from an adult female Chimney Swift taken on May 30, 1956, at Macon, Georgia. (Courtesy of David W. Johnston and the editor of *The Condor*.)

but such keys offer the beginning student an excellent means of learning much about the general structure and location of nests. Just as it is necessary to learn where to look for birds, so is it necessary to learn where to look for their nests. There are birds that build their nests on the ground, in burrows in the ground, on floating vegetation in water, in swamp or marsh vegetation, in shrubs and trees, in cavities in trees (either natural or excavated by some bird), in hollow logs on the ground, on cliffs, in caves, in chimneys, in bird houses, and in or on buildings. I have often found the nests of Great Crested Flycatchers, House Wrens, and Eastern Bluebirds in metal newspaper tubes in rural areas; these species and the House Sparrow may also nest in rural mailboxes. The House Wren and Carolina Wren are noted for building in all manner of odd places. In writing of the Carolina Wren in Tennessee, Amelia Laskey (1948) reported: "Among my 37 nesting records, 17 nests were built in bird boxes, either stationary or swinging; nine on shelves or various ledges inside of a building; four among growing plants in window boxes; two within a sack of old clothes hanging in a hen coop; one each in several odd places such as within a paper sack of seeds, an outdoor cupboard, a crevice between a house wall and a down spout, a fold of quilt hanging in a garage, a wall basket (size of a paper cup) hanging at the front entrance of a house, a tin newspaper cylinder, and a mail box (both of these at the roadside)." She also reported an unsuccessful nesting of the Tufted Titmouse in a newspaper cylinder.

The Chimney Swift, as the name implies, usually glues its nest to a chimney, having forsaken the hollow trees that it once used, although P. B. Hofslund found a nest in the abandoned nesting cavity of a Pileated Woodpecker. Barn Swallows and Cliff Swallows often place their mud nests in or on buildings or under bridges. J. J. Hickey found a Barn Swallow's nest in an observation tower 107 feet above ground. The Common Nighthawk lays its eggs on

FIGURE 13. Black Skimmer at nest on ground with two eggs and one recently hatched young. (Courtesy of Samuel A. Grimes.)

FIGURE 14.   Eggs of Killdeer on the gravel roof of a schcol building at Bloomfield Hills, Michigan.   (Courtesy of Walter P. Nickell.)

the ground in wilderness areas, but on flat roofs of buildings in towns and cities.   There are several records of Killdeer laying their eggs on the gravel roof of buildings (Fig. 14).   Grebes, the Black Tern, Forster's Tern, and the Common Tern sometimes build nests on floating vegetation (Fig. 15).   Most woodpeckers excavate a nest cavity in dead trees, but some use living trees; the Gilded Flicker and the Gila Woodpecker often use a giant saguaro cactus; the Red-shafted Flicker has been known to excavate into the side of a haystack, a building, and a dirt bank.   Abandoned nesting cavities of woodpeckers are adopted by many other hole-nesting species that do not excavate their own cavities, e.g., Elf (Fig. 16), Flammulated, Pygmy, Saw-whet, Screech, and Whiskered owls; Great Crested, Wied's Crested, and Ash-throated flycatchers; Violet-green and Tree swallows; Prothonotary and Lucy's warblers; titmice, starlings, and bluebirds.   Chickadees and nuthatches use abandoned woodpecker holes but may also excavate their own nesting cavities.

The beginning bird student most often sees birds foraging in trees or flying over the treetops.   Even after he becomes fairly proficient in field identification he may have little idea where most birds build their nests—usually he assumes that they are high in a tree. Actually, relatively few birds nest in the upper branches of tall trees. Apparently no one has prepared a tabulation to show what percentage of the birds of North America build at different heights above the ground but F. W. Preston and R. T. Norris analyzed the nesting heights of the birds of a 90-acre tract in Pennsylvania. The area contained about 43 acres of woodland, 27 of bush-grown fields, 12 of grassland, and the remainder of lawns, roads, fence rows, buildings, etc. During the two years of the study, 741 nests of 36 different species were found in the area; it is to be emphasized that there were no low-nesting colonial species such as the Red-winged Blackbird. About half of the nests were no higher than three feet above the ground and about 45 per cent were located from two feet above to ground level; less than one-third of the nests were above six feet. Moreover, only 48 (6.5 per cent) of the 741 nests were placed at heights above 22 feet and the

FIGURE 15.   Nest of Common Tern on a muskrat house; Pt. Pelee, Ontario. (Courtesy of Walter P. Nickell.)

FIGURE 16.   An Elf Owl at the entrance to its nesting cavity in a saguaro cactus.
(Courtesy of Lewis W. Walker.)

number decreased rapidly above that level (only 1.5 per cent
were placed above 37 feet).   It seems likely that a similar pattern
of nesting heights holds true throughout North America and that
there is an even higher percentage of low-nesting species in those
areas where trees are rare or absent or where colonial species nest
(e.g., prairie, desert, tundra, and sea coast).

Nesting sites may vary considerably within a family, as illustrated
by North American species of wood-warblers.   Prothonotary and
Lucy's warblers nest in tree cavities (natural or woodpecker holes),
as well as in bird houses, and Lucy's Warblers sometimes adopt an
old nest of the Verdin.   "Always" is a dangerous word when writing about birds but some of the following species always (others,
virtually always) build their nests on the ground: Black-and-white,
Worm-eating, Tennessee, Nashville, Virginia's, Kirtland's, Palm,
Connecticut, Wilson's, and Red-faced warblers, the Ovenbird, and
Painted Redstart.   Golden-winged, Blue-winged, Orange-crowned,
Black-throated Blue, Kentucky, Mourning, and Canada warblers
typically build on the ground or within a few feet of it.   The water-
thrushes may build their nests in cavities on sloping ground or
among the upturned roots of a fallen tree, as well as on the ground.
Swainson's, Bachman's, Yellow, Magnolia, Myrtle, Chestnut-sided,

Blackpoll, Prairie, and Hooded warblers and the chats typically nest at low or moderate heights in shrubs and trees. High-nesting species (40 to over 100 feet) include the Parula, Cape May, Audubon's, Black-throated Gray, Cerulean, Blackburnian, Yellow-throated, Pine, Olive, and Hermit warblers, although nests of some of these species have also been found as low as three feet above the ground.

Generalizations are both helpful and misleading. It may be helpful to tell the beginning student that Traill's Flycatchers and Yellow Warblers nest in shrubs in wet areas or that the Hepatic Tanager builds its nests on horizontal branches of oak trees, but it may be doubted that such information will be of much assistance to one interested in finding nests. Such statements, too, often create the impression that birds in general always follow the same nesting pattern, which is far from true. Yellow Warblers frequently do nest in various species of moisture-loving shrubs but they also nest in dooryards, in *Crataegus* bushes on dry hillsides, and even at a height of 40 to 60 feet in cottonwood trees in the prairie region of Minnesota. Douglas S. Middleton reported a Yellow Warbler nest 39 feet from the ground in a climax beech-maple forest at Rondeau Park in southern Ontario; 24 other nests were built at heights ranging from 21 inches to 12 feet.

More needs to be learned about individual, seasonal, ecological, and geographical differences in nest sites selected by different birds. Some species (e.g., quail, pheasants, American Woodcock (Fig. 17), Whip-poor-will and most of its relatives, Horned Lark, Vesper Sparrow) apparently always build their nests, or lay their eggs, on the ground. The Rufous-sided Towhee, Field Sparrow, and Song Sparrow typically build early nests on the ground and later ones in bushes. Some species that usually nest in trees (sometimes at great heights) may nest on the ground in remote areas or on islands, e.g., Golden Eagle, Osprey, Great Blue Heron, Common Crow. Chipping Sparrows almost always nest in bushes or trees but once I found a nest on the ground in Crawford County, Michigan. Mourning Doves build at low to medium heights in shrubs and trees throughout much of the range of the species, but they nest on the ground in certain areas. They often build on the old nests of other species; Walter P. Nickell reported a dove's nest in a nest of the Black-crowned Night Heron located 25 inches above the water, and another nest 48¾ feet above ground in an abandoned Robin's nest.

The American Goldfinch is a good example of a species that exhibits considerable variation in nest sites; its nests have been found

FIGURE 17. Nest and eggs of the American Woodcock.

in at least 80 different species of trees and shrubs. In a marsh area near Madison, Wisconsin, Allen W. Stokes found that 68 per cent of 230 nests were built in elderberry (*Sambucus canadensis*), which was the most abundant shrub in the area. Hubert Lewis found 591 active goldfinch nests in thistles (mostly *Cirsium altissimum*) at St. Paul, Minnesota, during a four-year period; here thistles were the dominant plant. Of 243 nests in the vicinity of Bloomfield Hills, Michigan, reported by Walter P. Nickell, 26 per cent were in gray dogwood (*Cornus racemosa*), 18 per cent in hawthorn (*Crataegus* sp.), 10 per cent in red osier dogwood (*Cornus stolonifera*), 9 per cent in American and slippery elm (*Ulmus americana* and *fulva*); the remaining 90 nests were placed in 28 species of trees, shrubs, vines, and herbaceous plants. In marshy areas near Ann Arbor, Michigan, I have found most goldfinch nests in gray dogwood, ninebark (*Physocarpus opulifolius*), red osier dogwood, and shrub willows (*Salix* spp.). By concentrating on areas in which *Crataegus* was the predominant shrubby plant, however, I found 501 active goldfinch nests in *Crataegus* during the four-year period of 1955–1958. The goldfinch also nests in shade trees in towns and sometimes at a height of 45 feet or more along the edges of mature hardwood forests.

Although birds often select a nest site in the predominant plant in the habitat, as illustrated above, there are certain trees and shrubs that are rarely used as nest sites; some of these are smooth, poison, and staghorn sumac, quaking aspen, paper birch, weeping willow, black locust, shagbark hickory, tamarack, and arborvitae. Few birds nest in large elm trees but they are a favorite site for the Baltimore Oriole; Traill's Flycatchers, Catbirds, and goldfinches sometimes nest in sapling elms.

After analyzing the location and structure of thousands of nests of common Michigan birds, Walter P. Nickell (1958) concluded that three aspects of the vegetation in a particular habitat are important in providing nest sites and nesting materials: (1) the branching habits and other characters of individual plant species; (2) abundance, distribution, and growth stages; (3) availability of plants with bark, fibers, twigs, rootlets, leaves, and downs suitable for nest construction. Following are examples of these three points. The upright branching pattern of gray dogwood furnishes a vertical crotch with an average of four points of attachment for the attached-statant* nests of Traill's Flycatcher, Yellow Warbler, and American Goldfinch (Fig. 18). Shrub willows provide a similar type of vertical nest crotch. In his study of the goldfinch in Minnesota, Lewis found that the nests were placed in a three- or four-pronged crotch of thistles. The dense branching pattern, with both upright and horizontal growth, of hawthorns provides horizontal nest sites (often favored by Traill's Flycatchers) and vertical crotches (favored by Catbirds and goldfinches). Ninebark also provides both horizontal and vertical crotches. The common birds discussed in this paragraph show a wide tolerance for different habitats; in each they find shrubs that provide the optimal type of nest site. Ninebark is a swamp-inhabiting shrub; hawthorn typically grows on well-drained soil; gray dogwood is more tolerant and grows in both wet and dry situations. Nickell emphasized the importance of swamp milkweed (*Asclepias incarnata*) for the nest of the Baltimore Oriole. This species builds a pendulous† nest

---

* A *statant* nest is one which rests in its position (on the ground, in cattails, in a shrub or tree), either with or without surrounding supports, by virtue of the weight or bulk of the nest. It is not attached to any supports. Examples are the nests of the Pied-billed Grebe, Mourning Dove, Horned Lark, Catbird, Brown Thrasher, Blue Jay, and Vesper Sparrow. An *attached-statant* nest is one in which the materials of the sides of the nest are wrapped around one or more supports (usually vertical), as the nests of the Red-winged Blackbird, Indigo Bunting, and those shown in Fig. 18.

† A *pendulous* nest is suspended at the top rim of the nest; the bottom is unsupported so that the nest swings freely. A *pensile* nest is a hanging nest that is unsupported at the bottom but is attached so rigidly at its rim that the nest does not move in its supports.

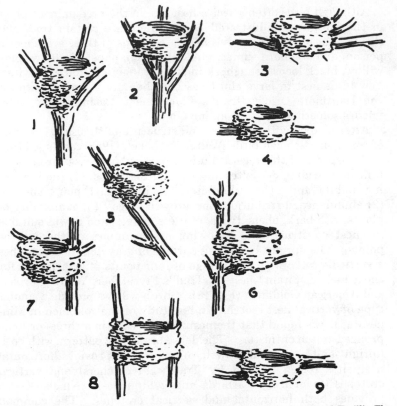

FIGURE 18.   Variation in placement of the attached-statant nests of Traill's Flycatcher, Yellow Warbler, and American Goldfinch in Michigan. (Courtesy of Walter P.
Nickell, from *Butler University Botanical Studies No. 13*, 1958.)

which is suspended from drooping branches above and typically
swings freely below (Fig. 19).   The birds collect the outer bark fibers
of the milkweed for building the framework of the nest; yarn, cot-
ton twine, and similar strong flexible materials are often used as a
substitute for milkweed fibers.   Nickell found that other species
regularly use milkweed bark in their nests: Traill's Flycatcher,
Eastern Kingbird, Cedar Waxwing, Yellow Warbler, American Redstart, Red-winged Blackbird, American Goldfinch.   Yellow Warblers and goldfinches are noted for dismantling abandoned nests
and reusing the material, perhaps because it is readily available.
Some species have been observed taking materials from a nest
being built by another species.

Nest Site Selection

Some of the larger birds of prey use the same nest for years, adding new material annually. A few species use the same nest for successive broods in a single breeding season, but the majority of multiple-brooded species build a new nest for each clutch of eggs. The location for the nest may be selected by the female, by the male, or by both sexes together. The female alone selects the nest site in those species that meet only for copulation and in those in which the males leave before incubation begins. The male apparently selects the site in the House Wren, Phainopepla, House Sparrow, Prothonotary Warbler, and perhaps in most hole-nesting species. Among the doves, crows, jays, waxwings, and crossbills,

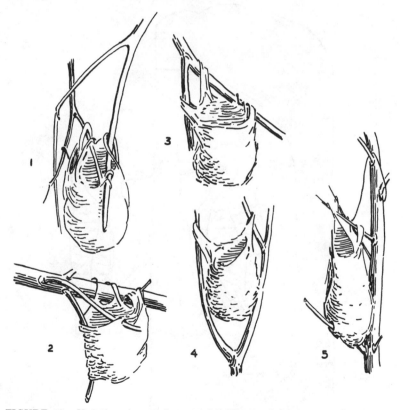

FIGURE 19. Variations in attachment of Baltimore Oriole nests. (Courtesy of Walter P. Nickell, from *Butler University Botanical Studies No. 13,* 1958.)

the male and female select the site together. It is not certain for many species of titmice and chickadees whether the sexes select the nest site together or whether the females are attracted to cavities already defended by the males. Lawrence Kilham (1958) described a ceremony in Red-bellied and Red-headed woodpeckers which he called "mutual-tapping." Tapping differs from the drumming of woodpeckers in that the bird pounds the wood at a much slower rate (about three times per second). Males attract females to an excavation or a potential nest site by calling "kwirr," by drumming, and by tapping. When the female arrives she alights near the male and both birds begin tapping. Mutual tapping may take place early in the morning before the male has left his roosting cavity, so that he taps on the inside and the female taps on the

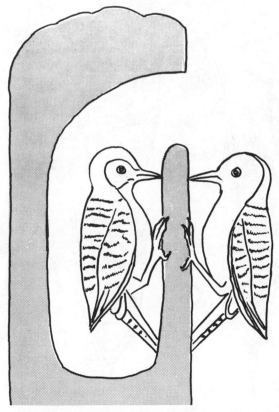

FIGURE 20. Mutual tapping of Red-bellied Woodpeckers. The male starts to tap on the inside of the cavity as his mate alights and joins in the tapping. (Courtesy of Lawrence Kilham and the editor of *The Auk.*)

outside of the cavity (Fig. 20). Mutual tapping probably serves to maintain the pair-bond and to "inform the male as to whether his choice of an excavation site is acceptable to his mate."

Role of Sexes in Building

Among species in which the sexes remain together throughout most of the breeding season, the male, female, or both may build the nest, as shown by the following summary.

1. Both sexes build the nest.
   a. Male and female share more or less equally in nest construction (or excavation): kingfishers, woodpeckers, waxwings, many swallows. (Kingfishers and woodpeckers do not build nests in their dirt tunnels or tree cavities.)
   b. Male builds "dummy" or "cock" nests: many wrens.
2. The female builds but the male provides the material: Mourning Dove, Ground Dove.
3. The female builds without help from the male: Red-eyed Vireo, Ovenbird.
4. The female builds but both sexes gather the material: Common Raven.
5. The male builds but the female provides the material: frigatebirds.
6. The male alone builds the nest: some shrikes, the Philippine Weaverbird; the male Phainopepla builds most of the nest.
7. No nest is built:* tropicbirds, most shorebirds, skimmers, auks, nighthawks, Whip-poor-will, Chuck-will's-widow, Poor-will.

Time Required to Build

A species which lays its eggs on the ground may spend no time in preparing the site, whereas some species work on a nest for weeks. Frank M. Chapman reported that the female Wagler's Oropendola, a relative of the blackbirds, spends from three to four weeks in constructing a bag-like nest that may be over three feet long. A pair of Kiskadee Flycatchers observed by Pettingill (1942) in Mexico took 24 days to build a nest. Most of the small passerine

---

* A nest is defined as the receptacle or structure prepared by a bird for its eggs or young. These species do not prepare or construct a nest but lay their eggs on the ground, on bare rock, or on the flat roof of a building. However, one commonly speaks of finding a nighthawk's nest, for example, even though the nest cannot be identified until the eggs have been laid. The place chosen for the deposition of eggs is spoken of as the nest. Because no formal construction is involved, one might say that these species have a nest without any definite structure.

species, however, build their nests in less than a week. The average number of days spent in nest construction by three species is: Prothonotary Warbler, 3.3 days; Cedar Waxwing, 5.6 days; American Goldfinch, 9 days early in the season but 5.6 days later on. A mated pair of Bank Swallows excavate a tunnel in a dirt bank two to three feet deep at the rate of about five inches per day, after which they construct a nesting pad in the enlarged nesting chamber.

Nesting Associates

Even species that defend Type A breeding territories sometimes exhibit considerable tolerance of other species and several species of birds may build their nests close together. Birds also nest in close association with a number of kinds of insects. The following classification summarizes these relationships:

1. Nesting associations among different species of birds.
   a. *Mixed colonies.* These are of two types. In one type large numbers of two or more species nest together: gull and tern colonies; herons, ibises, and anhingas nest in "heronries." In the other type, one or a few pairs of one species build nests in the midst of a large colony of some other species: a pair of terns nest in a colony of gulls; turnstones often nest in large colonies of terns and Black-headed Gulls.
   b. *"Protective" nesting.* A number of small birds have been found nesting in close association with larger birds, often birds of prey. Common Grackles, Starlings, House Wrens, and House Sparrows not uncommonly nest in the sides of Osprey nests, and Cliff Swallows nest near Prairie Falcon nests. Frederick V. Hebard reported the nesting of a Red-bellied Woodpecker and a Red-tailed Hawk in the same tree, and a Yellow-shafted Flicker nesting in the same tree with a Sparrow Hawk. Sutton and Pettingill (1942) found that each of 12 nests of the Social Flycatcher was built near the nest of some other species (Rose-throated Becard, Kiskadee Flycatcher, Boat-billed Flycatcher, Lichtenstein's Oriole).
   c. *Proximity nesting.* There are many reports of different kinds of birds building their nests unusually close together. Hubert Lewis said that Chipping, Clay-colored, and Song sparrows sometimes nest within a few feet of goldfinches

FIGURE 21. Nesting place of the Blue-winged Kookaburra in a terrestrial termites' mound, Northern Territory, Australia, showing old nesting hollows and an occupied nest site (indicated by arrow) drilled completely through a flange of the mound. (Courtesy of K. A. Hindwood and the editor of *The Emu*.)

and that a goldfinch and an Indigo Bunting reared broods in the same thistle. There is one record of a Pileated Woodpecker and a Yellow-shafted Flicker nesting in the same stump. A. L. Rand wrote of a Common Grackle nest that was built on the top of an active House Sparrow nest in Indiana.

2. Nesting associations between birds and invertebrate animals.
   a. *Birds nesting in termitaria.* Several species of Australian parrots and kingfishers excavate nesting cavities in termites' nests (Figs. 21, 22), and Fr. Haverschmidt reported the nesting of jacamars (family Galbulidae), woodhewers (Dendrocolaptidae), the Gray-breasted Martin, the Guiana House Wren (also called the Southern House Wren), and the Brown-throated Parakeet in termite nests in South America.
   b. *Birds building near the nests of ants, wasps, and bees.* This behavior has been noted especially in a number of Old-world birds (Fig. 23). The Black-throated Warbler

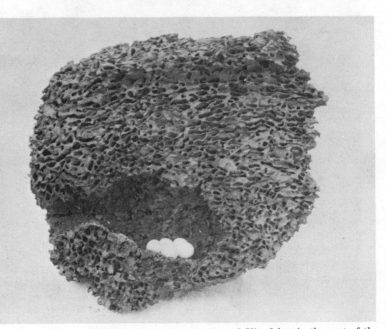

FIGURE 22. Vertical section of nest site of a Sacred Kingfisher in the nest of the termite *Nasutitermes walkeri,* near Sydney, Australia. (Courtesy of K. A. Hindwood and the editor of *The Emu.*)

FIGURE 23. Banded Finch and wasp nesting association in prickly-beard spider-flower shrub in Australia. Nest on right was in use by the finches; nest on left was used as a roost after the young fledged. (Courtesy of K. A. Hindwood and the editor of *The Emu*.)

(family Sylviidae) of Australia so often nests near hornet nests that it is called the "Hornet-nest bird." Pettingill (1942) described the interesting relations between ants and a bull's horn acacia, in which thorny shrub pairs of Kiskadee Flycatchers and Social Flycatchers nested simultaneously.

  c. *Inhabitants of birds' nests.*

    (1) *Parasites on nestlings or adults.* The bloodsucking larvae of several genera of insects have been found on the nestlings of many species of birds. At least 54

species of birds are known to be parasitized by the blowfly *Protocalliphora metallica.* Adult flies lay their eggs in birds' nests; the larvae feed intermittently, usually at night, by attacking various parts of the head and body or the bases of primary feathers, especially of nestling birds. Biting lice (Mallophaga), fleas (Siphonaptera), and hippoboscid flies (Hippoboscidae), as well as various species of ticks and mites, also are parasitic on birds.

(2) *Nest-cleaning insects.* This has been reported especially for some Old-world species, but a number of insects inhabiting nests are scavengers and may eat feces and other debris in the nest.

(3) *Miscellaneous inhabitants.* Over 400 insects, representing 8 species, have been taken from a single nest. Val Nolan has found 2 kinds of snails, 2 of spiders, 11 of mites, and 25 of insects from nests of the Prairie Warbler alone.

3. *Secondary uses of birds' nests.* Abandoned nests frequently are taken over by White-footed Mice (*Peromyscus*) and remodeled for their use; they are used as storage places and feeding platforms by small mammals (mice, chipmunks, Red Squirrels), and as roosting shelters by birds.

The word "egg" has two meanings. Everyone is familiar with the hard-shelled chicken's egg, which has within it the "white" (albumen) and the "yellow" (yolk). When we use the Latin word *ovum* (pl., ova) for egg, however, we mean specifically the reproductive cell produced by the female gonad. The life of the bird begins with the union (fertilization) of two reproductive cells (or gametes): the male sperm cell and the female ovum. The sperm cells (spermatozoa) are produced in the two testes; the ova develop in the ovary. Female birds typically have a single functional (left) ovary, the right ovary being rudimentary (undeveloped); in this they differ from other animals. However, hawks of the genera *Accipiter, Circus,* and *Falco,* and a few other birds, often have two well-developed ovaries.

THE EGG BEFORE LAYING

The "yolk" actually is the ovum or female sex cell. The tremendous size of this single cell is due to the food materials (deutoplasm) stored in it. The yolk of a domestic hen's egg occupies about 32 per cent of the total egg; a similar high percentage of yolk is found in other precocial species, and the yolk in some duck eggs is said to equal 50 per cent of the egg;

8

Eggs and Young

the egg of a passerine bird contains about 20 per cent yolk. The mature ovum of a leghorn chicken averages about 32 mm. in diameter; larger ova are produced by some birds and reptiles. By contrast, the diameter of a human ovum is about 0.14 mm., or just large enough to be visible to the unaided eye as a tiny speck. The ova of most mammals are equally small and some are only 0.07 mm. in diameter. It follows that the amount of deutoplasm in most mammalian ova is minimal; it is not needed because the fertilized eggs become attached to the inner wall of the uterus, where the embryos receive their nutrients from the female's blood stream (exceptions are the egg-laying mammals mentioned in Chapter 1). The embryo bird, on the other hand, is dependent solely on the food materials in the yolk and the albumen (which is mostly water).

The yolk in a chicken egg is composed largely of alternating bands of white yolk and yellow yolk (Fig. 1). The wider bands of yellow yolk are deposited during the daytime, the color being due to yellow pigments (carotenoids) present in the food; the white yolk is deposited late at night and during early morning hours. It is known that the color of the yolk of chicken eggs is influenced by diet, and olive-colored and orange-red yolks can be produced by including certain plant materials in the food. The general color of the yolk in most bird eggs is some shade of yellow; but the color is salmon red in the Gentoo Penguin; deep red to scarlet in the Sooty Tern, Common Tern, Arctic Tern, and Black-headed Gull; orange in the Common Loon, Brown Pelican, European Oystercatcher, and Great Black-backed Gull.

Only a small percentage of the ovocytes (undeveloped ova) present in the ovary of a female bird at hatching time ever mature. Emil Witschi (1956) reported that the ovary of a 13-day-old Red-winged Blackbird or Starling contains about 100,000 ovocytes; only about 50 of these will grow and be released from the ovary during the life of the bird. There is a very slow (microscopic) growth of 100 or more ovocytes during the winter and early spring in Starlings. Although most of these ovocytes are resorbed, a series of ova begins to accumulate yolk rapidly. As the amount of yolk increases, the ova move toward the surface of the ovary and finally protrude from it (Fig. 2). The final growth to form mature ova takes place in four to seven days. Each protruding mature ovum and its thin covering of ovarian tissue is called an *ovarian follicle*. *Ovulation* consists of the rupture of the mature follicle and the release of the ovum into the body cavity, as in mammals. The ovum then enters the funnel-like free end of the left oviduct. Fertilization occurs

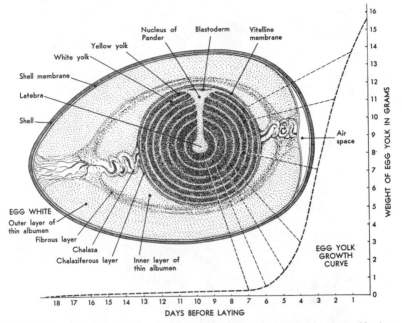

FIGURE 1.   Diagram showing the structure of the hen's egg at the time of laying. The graph indicates the rate of growth of the egg during the 18 days preceding its laying. The lines leading from the various layers of the yolk to the growth curve emphasize the time at which these layers were formed. (By permission of Bradley M. Patten, from *Foundations of Embryology,* McGraw-Hill Book Co., Inc. Copyright, 1958. And by permission of Emil Witschi, from *Development of Vertebrates,* W. B. Saunders Company. Copyright, 1956.)

while the ovum is in the body cavity or just after it enters the oviduct.

Normally only one ovum is released at a time, so that the ovary of a laying bird has a series of developing ova of different sizes. Double-yolked eggs are produced occasionally (triple-yolked eggs rarely); in most instances they are believed to result from the simultaneous development and release of two ova. If the ova are fertilized, the successful incubation of a double-yolked egg produces fraternal twins; twins from single-yolked eggs are very rare in birds but they have been reported in pigeons. In addition to pigeons and chickens, twins have been reported for the Brown Thrasher, American Goldfinch, and Song Sparrow; it is not known whether the eggs were single-yolked or double-yolked.

Little is known about the passage of the ovum through the oviduct in wild birds so that we must infer that the process is

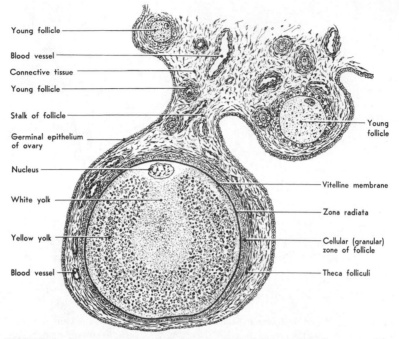

Young follicle

Blood vessel

Connective tissue

Young follicle

Stalk of follicle

Germinal epithelium of ovary

Nucleus

White yolk

Yellow yolk

Blood vessel

Young follicle

Vitelline membrane

Zona radiata

Cellular (granular) zone of follicle

Theca folliculi

FIGURE 2.   Diagram showing the structure of a bird ovum still in the ovary.   The section shows a follicle containing a nearly mature ovum, and a small area of the adjacent ovarian tissue.   (By permission of Bradley M. Patten, from *Foundations of Embryology,* McGraw-Hill Book Co., Inc.   Copyright, 1958.)

similar to that in the chicken (Romanoff and Romanoff, 1949). Ovulation of a new ovum occurs within a half hour after an egg is laid.   The new ovum reaches and passes through the short infundibulum of the oviduct in about 20 minutes (Fig. 3).   About three hours are required for the secretion of albumen around the yolk as it passes through some 60 per cent of the length of the oviduct.   The shell membranes (an inner and an outer membrane) are secreted by the isthmus in approximately one hour.   The egg then enters the uterine portion of the oviduct, where the volume is doubled as the albumen absorbs water secreted by the "uterus."   The egg remains in the uterus for about 19 hours, while the hard shell is deposited. Thus, in a sense, we can say that an egg—yolk, albumen, and shell —is "made" in five to eight days: four to seven days for the maturation and release of the ovum and one day for its passage through the oviduct.

Significance of Fertilization

An essential part of each cell in the bird's body is the nucleus. The *chromosomes* constitute an important part of the nucleus, and the chromosomes contain the *genes,* which are the basis for the

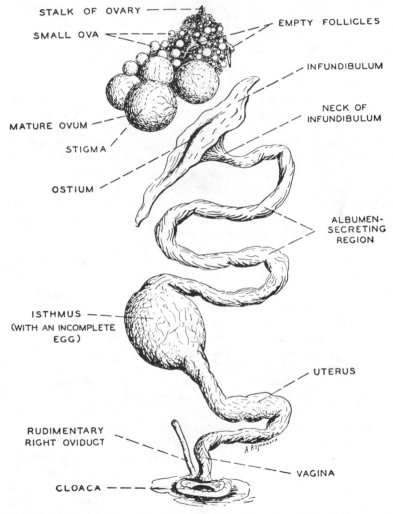

FIGURE 3.   Reproductive organs of the hen.   (By permission of Alexis L. Romanoff, from *The Avian Egg,* John Wiley & Sons, Inc.   Copyright, 1949.)

transmission of hereditary traits from one generation to the next. The cells of birds have a large number of chromosomes so that an exact count is difficult. Some species of thrushes are said to have 84 chromosomes in each cell nucleus. However, there are not 84 different kinds of chromosomes but rather 42 kinds, because the chromosomes occur in homologous pairs. One member of each pair is derived from the sperm cell; the other member of the pair is derived from the ovum. In general, the members of a given pair are similar in size and shape, but there is one notable exception. One pair of chromosomes (traditionally called the X and Y chromosomes) is primarily responsible for determining the sex of the individual, and members of a pair of sex chromosomes characteristically differ in size and shape. The sperm cells of most animals contain either an X or a Y chromosome; all eggs contain an X chromosome. Fertilization of an egg by an X-bearing sperm produces a female; fertilization by a Y-bearing sperm produces a male. The situation is different in birds, moths, and a few other animals. In birds all sperm cells contain an X chromosome. There is some difference of opinion about the sex chromosomes in female birds and not all birds may be alike in this regard, but two types of eggs are produced. One type has an X chromosome; the other type has either a Y chromosome or no sex chromosome at all—i.e., the female has a single sex chromosome rather than a pair. At any rate, fertilization of an X-bearing ovum by an X-bearing sperm produces a male, which is opposite to the situation found in mammals. For this reason, the sex chromosomes of birds sometimes are referred to as Z and W rather than X and Y.

To prevent doubling of the numbers of chromosomes with fertilization in each succeeding generation, the maturation of the reproductive cells involves a process called *meiosis,* in which the number of chromosomes is reduced by one-half (the haploid number of chromosomes). Each mature germ cell contains only one member of each pair of chromosomes; if the female cells have an unpaired sex chromosome, half of the eggs will have one more chromosome than the other half. Meiosis takes place in two steps. Only one of these steps has occurred in the ovum at the time of ovulation. The entrance of a sperm cell into the ovum stimulates it to complete the second step. The process is completed within a half hour, during which time the sperm moves toward the chromosomes of the ovum. Fertilization occurs when the two haploid sets of chromosomes come together. Fertilization not only restores the full species number of chromosomes (the diploid number; e.g., 84 in the thrushes mentioned above) to the fertilized egg (zygote) but it brings together maternal and paternal chromosomes, whose total gene complement determines the development of the individual. The inheritance of variations has far-reaching implications that involve survival and speciation.

Fertilization in birds is followed almost at once by cell division and growth of the zygote, which continue as the yolk passes down the oviduct. Development stops after the egg is laid; further growth does not take place unless the egg is incubated.

THE EGG AFTER LAYING

The yolk and albumen fill the eggshell completely at the time the egg is laid. Within an hour (depending on air temperature and humidity), an *air chamber* forms between the inner and outer shell membranes at the blunt end of the egg. The air chamber is thought to result from the differential contraction of the shell and its contents as the temperature of the newly laid egg decreases. The head of the developing embryo lies in the blunt end of the egg, and when the embryo is ready to hatch it gets its first air from the air chamber. When the chamber develops abnormally in some other part of the egg, the fully developed embryo may suffocate. The size of the air chamber increases as water evaporates from the egg during incubation. Lawrence H. Walkinshaw found that the air chamber in six eggs of the American Goldfinch averaged 3.4 mm. the day the eggs were laid and 10 mm. on the fifth day; the size of the chamber increased slowly to 11 or 12 mm. at the end of incubation. The approximate stage of incubation can be estimated by "candling" eggs that are not too heavily pigmented. By holding the eggs in front of a strong light, one can note the size of the air chamber and the stage of development of the embryo (see Fig. 4, and Hanson and Kossack, 1957).

Egg-Laying

Some birds begin to lay the day following completion of the nest; others wait two or three days; the American Goldfinch may wait a week or more before laying eggs.

Many birds lay their eggs on successive days, but not all do so. For example, some gulls, hawks, owls, and the Smooth-billed Ani lay on alternate days; the Groove-billed Ani, at two- to four-day intervals; and some Old-world birds lay their eggs a week or more apart. For such species we do not know whether the rate of

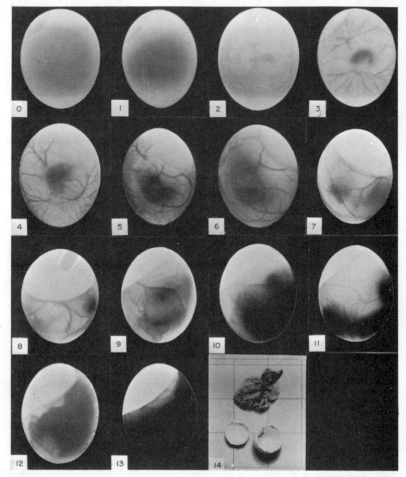

FIGURE 4. Incubation stages of Mourning Dove eggs as seen by candling. Days of incubation designated by numerals. (Courtesy of Harold C. Hanson and the editor of *The Wilson Bulletin*.)

passage through the oviduct is similar to that described above for the chicken, but one would assume that it is and that the interval between eggs reflects the difference in interval between successive ovulations. Some species, either typically or occasionally, lay at intervals of 25 or 26 hours rather than every 24 hours; for species that lay large clutches (e.g., Bobwhite, grouse), the time of laying becomes progressively later each day and an "evening" egg may be retained in the uterus overnight, so that a day in the laying sequence is skipped. Munir K. Bunni reported an increase in the interval between eggs in a clutch of the Killdeer so that eggs were laid both in the morning and afternoon. Minor variations in the laying interval between successive eggs in the clutch of an individual bird (or among different individuals of a species) probably depend on the number of hours the egg is retained in the uterus (Romanoff and Romanoff, 1949).

Most of the small birds of the United States lay their eggs early in the morning; nocturnal species such as the Common Nighthawk may not lay until late in the morning; the American Coot is said to lay just after midnight during the first part of the laying period; on two occasions a captive Mourning Dove laid an egg between 5:30 and 7:00 P.M.

The domestic hen and pigeon will lay eggs even when no male is present; hence, courtship and copulation (with subsequent fertilization) are not necessary stimuli for ovulation and egg-laying in these birds. For wild birds in general, however, the stimulating effects of courtship behavior with a male seem to be necessary for final development and release of ova. That environmental factors also play a part is evidenced by the difficulties encountered in trying to get birds (especially passerines) to breed in captivity. Lawrence Kilham's (1959) interesting and significant discussion of the nesting activities of a pair of captive Yellow-shafted Flickers will give the student an insight into some of the many interacting factors that play a part in the breeding cycle. Frank A. Hartman described the nesting activities of captive Sparrow Hawks over a period of several years; none was successful although some fertilized eggs were laid. L. S. Putnam and C. E. Knoder reported on five nestings in one year of a pair of captive Mourning Doves at Ohio State University; young were raised in four of the nests.

Size, Shape, and Color

The smallest eggs are laid by hummingbirds; those of most North American species of hummingbirds average about ½ inch in length and about ⅓ inch in maximum width. Examples of birds that lay large eggs are: Ostrich, 6.8 by 5.4 inches; Mute Swan, 4.5 by 2.9; California Condor, 4.3 by 2.6; Trumpeter Swan, 4.3 by 2.8; Common Loon and White Pelican, 3.5 by 2.2; Common Murre, 3.2 by 2.0; Razorbill, 3.0 by 1.9. In general, small birds lay relatively larger eggs than do most large birds, but precocial species lay larger eggs than altricial species of a similar weight. The Spotted Sandpiper and the Catbird are similar in size but the sandpiper's eggs are about twice the size of those of the Catbird; a similar relationship between size of bird and egg size is shown by the Upland Plover and the meadowlarks. There are some curious differences in relative egg size among both precocial and altricial species. The Canvasback and the Ruddy Duck lay eggs approximately the same size, yet the Ruddy Duck is only about a third as large as the Canvasback. The Yellow-billed and Black-billed cuckoos are considerably smaller than the European Cuckoo but they lay much larger eggs; in this instance the smaller egg of the European Cuckoo seems to be an adaptation to its parasitic breeding habits.

The egg sizes cited above represent average measurements of a number of eggs. The eggs of different individuals of a species vary in size as do those laid by a particular bird. A. C. Bent, for example, stated that 50 eggs of Traill's Flycatcher averaged 18.5 by 13.5 mm.; among these eggs, however, one measured 19.3 by 14.5 mm. and another 19.8 by 12.6 mm. Occasionally a bird lays a "runt" egg, one that is considerably smaller than the normal minimal size. One such egg, measuring 13.7 by 11.0 mm., I found in the nest of a Traill's Flycatcher. I have also found a runt egg and an abnormally shaped egg in nests of the American Goldfinch; these two eggs measured 12.9 by 9.7 mm. and 18.2 by 11.5 mm.; Lawrence H. Walkinshaw gave the average measurements for 93 goldfinch eggs as 16.5 by 12.4 mm. These abnormal eggs failed to hatch, but in one instance I know that an unusually long (29.0 mm.) Horned Lark egg did hatch successfully. Runt eggs probably are laid by all species at one time or another; they have been reported for such species as the Eared Grebe, Swainson's Thrush, Yellow-breasted Chat, and House Finch. Shell-less or soft-shelled eggs are laid frequently by domestic birds but they appear to be rare among wild birds; I once found a shell-less egg in the nest of Traill's Flycatcher.

F. W. Preston pointed out that reference to the "average" size of a species' eggs tells only part of the story. A small amount of information suggests that young birds and old birds lay smaller eggs than do birds in the prime of their breeding life. He also reported that there is more variation in the length than in the breadth of eggs.

The majority of birds' eggs are oval-shaped. Owls and toucans lay round (spherical) eggs. Swifts, hummingbirds, swallows, and some other birds lay elliptical or long elliptical eggs. Murres, auks, and shorebirds lay pear-shaped (pyriform) eggs; for those species that lay a single egg on rock ledges, this shape seems to be an adaptation which reduces the chances of the egg rolling off the ledge. Among shorebirds that lay a clutch of four eggs, the pyriform shape is advantageous because the pointed ends fit together so that the eggs form a compact group.

Plain white eggs are characteristic of some groups of birds, e.g., albatrosses, shearwaters, diving-petrels, pelicans, storks, flamingos, most pigeons and doves, parrots, owls, swifts, hummingbirds, kingfishers, and woodpeckers. Most bird species, however, lay colored eggs. We speak of an egg as being *immaculate* if the shell is a solid color, such as white eggs, or the pale blue eggs of the Dickcissel, Indigo Bunting, and bluebirds, and the bluish-green eggs of the Catbird and several American thrushes. Unlike the yolk, the color of the shell cannot be changed by altering the diet of domestic chickens; the shell color, produced by physiological processes, is inherited. This has been demonstrated clearly by studies of the Araucana or Easter Egg Chicken (Vosburgh, 1948). This breed, of uncertain origin, was discovered in Chile about 1914; the birds are now raised throughout the United States, in Canada, and several European countries. Each hen lays eggs of one color, but different birds lay blue, green, pink, gray, and olive-drab eggs in several shades; a chick hatching from an egg of one color may lay eggs of another color. Wild birds that normally lay immaculate eggs sometimes lay spotted eggs; the spotting may occur on a single egg or on all the eggs in a clutch. Such spotted eggs have been reported for the Eastern Phoebe, Lazuli Bunting, Indigo Bunting, Lesser Goldfinch, and American Goldfinch.

Most colored eggs are not immaculate, but are marked with spots, blotches, or irregular lines of various shades of brown, red, purple, or black (Figs. 5, 6). The darker pigment often is concentrated at the blunt end of the egg. Variation in the amount of pigmentation and in the pattern probably is the rule among the eggs of different members of a species and among the eggs laid by any given bird (Fig. 7).

Species that normally lay spotted eggs rarely lay unmarked eggs. John W. Aldrich, writing on the Long-billed Marsh Wren, said that 4 out of 107 sets of eggs in the U. S. National Museum contained from one to five white eggs. He also mentioned a colony of wrens in Ohio where he found sets of white eggs (one of six eggs) in two successive years. I once found a nest of Traill's Flycatcher with four unmarked white eggs.

Although birds' eggs exhibit a wide variety of color and marking, many species do lay eggs that have similar patterns, and it has been suggested that the color and pattern of eggs might be useful in

FIGURE 5. Eastern Wood Pewee nest and eggs, northern Florida. (Courtesy of
Samuel A. Grimes.)

determining relationships among birds. As an approach to this
problem, David Lack (1958) analyzed the eggs of 151 species of the
large thrush family (about 300 species). He noted that the colors
of eggs "tend to be associated with certain types of nesting site;
species nesting in deep holes tend to have immaculate white eggs;
those in shallower holes and niches speckled white, immaculate
blue or speckled blue eggs; those on the ground, amid herbage or
on ledges obscured brown, gray or olive eggs; those in forks in
bushes or trees blotched eggs, often with shadow-marks, on a
whitish or blue ground; those building domed nests immaculate or
speckled, white or blue, eggs." He concluded that egg color is
useless as a guide to classification of thrushes. It should be noted
also that Lack used the phrase "tend to be associated" and that the
eggs of such American thrushes as the Robin, Wood Thrush,
Hermit Thrush, and Veery do not fit into his generalized grouping.

Clutch Size

By "clutch" we mean the total number of eggs laid by one female
for a single nesting. Among the many species of birds, the clutch
varies from 1 to about 20. There is some uncertainty about the

larger clutches because two or more females sometimes lay in the same nest (e.g., ducks, pheasants, quail). A single egg is laid by most penguins, albatrosses, shearwaters, petrels, tropicbirds, some auks, some nightjars, and a number of Old-world species. Two eggs form the clutch of some penguins, loons, boobies, gannets, most pigeons, nightjars, hummingbirds, and many tropical passerine species. Many plovers, sandpipers, avocets, phalaropes, gulls, and terns lay a clutch of 3 or 4 eggs. Most passerine species in the Temperate Zone lay 4 to 6 eggs in a clutch, but wrens, chickadees, titmice, and nuthatches often lay from 6 to 13 eggs. Most ducks and gallinaceous birds lay from 6 to 15 or more eggs.

A few species (generally those with a clutch of one to three) invariably lay the same number of eggs, but for many birds geographical, seasonal, and annual variations in clutch size occur. Many tropical species lay smaller clutches than do Temperate Zone species; for example, the House Finch usually lays a clutch of two eggs in Mexico but four to seven in the United States. Seasonal decrease in average clutch size has been reported for a number of American species. Annual differences in average clutch size have been shown for some birds of prey, in which the clutch seems to vary with the relative abundance of the rodents that serve as food. My data on the American Goldfinch suggest that the number of six-egg

FIGURE 6. Brown-headed Nuthatch nest and eggs. (Courtesy of Samuel A. Grimes.)

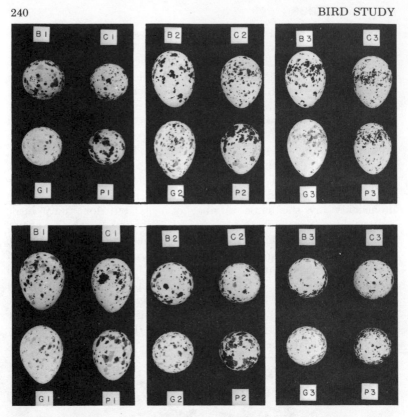

FIGURE 7. Eggs of the Common Tern to show variation in pigmentation within the eggs in a clutch. Left: Paraxial (above) and profile (below) views of the first egg in clutches B, C, G, and P. Center: Similar views of the second eggs of the same clutches. Right: Paraxial and profile views of the third (last) eggs of the same clutches. (Courtesy of F. W. Preston and the editor of *The Auk*.)

clutches varies from year to year. Clutch size also may vary with the age of the individual; in general, the average is smaller for birds laying for the first time and for very old birds.

Several theories—none of them adequate—have been proposed to explain differences in clutch size among birds, but there are puzzling exceptions to all of the generalizations proposed. It seems probable that clutch size, in general, is determined genetically but that it may be influenced by the physiological condition of the female and by environmental factors. These and other aspects of the problem are discussed in papers by Skutch (1949), Lack (1954), and Wagner (1957).

Indeterminate and Determinate Layers

We pointed out in Chapter 7 that both single-brooded and double-brooded species typically renest when a nest is destroyed (procellariiform birds appear to be exceptions). In such instances, broodiness behavior is inhibited temporarily, the female builds another nest, and then lays a new clutch of eggs. We do not know what controls these abrupt changes in the physiology of the female but they occur when the destroyed nest contains either eggs or young. A closely related problem is that found among species that have been called *indeterminate layers*. By removing an egg each day from the nest of a Yellow-shafted Flicker, Charles L. Phillips found that the bird did not stop laying after the typical clutch had been completed but laid 71 eggs in a 73-day period. It is assumed that ovulation in such species is influenced by sensory stimuli (either visual or tactile) received from the eggs and that ovulation continues until there are a definite number of eggs in the nest. Similar experiments have revealed other indeterminate layers: European wryneck, House Wren, House Sparrow, as well as domesticated birds (chickens, turkeys, guineafowl, ducks, geese) and their wild relatives. A *determinate layer* is one whose clutch size cannot be altered by adding or removing eggs from the nest during the egg-laying period. Among the few species tested (not all critically), pigeons, doves, Herring Gull, Ringed Plover, Black-billed Magpie, Barn Swallow, Eastern Bluebird, and Tricolored Blackbird appear to be determinate layers.

Much of the information in the literature probably is unreliable because pertinent details are lacking about the experiments, which often were conducted at only two or three nests. In reviewing this subject, Davis (1955) proposed that a species "may be considered an indeterminate layer if the addition of eggs to the nest at the start of laying results in a reduction of clutch size and if the daily removal of eggs results in an increase." He suggested that this definition may be too rigid, specifically as it includes the addition of eggs, and we agree that it is too rigid. We also support Davis' implication that the entire subject should be reinvestigated by using precise techniques on a large number of nests of each species.

Egg Recognition by Adults

In view of the wide range in color and markings of birds' eggs, one might assume that birds have a well-developed discriminatory ability with regard to their own eggs. Experiments show that this is not the case. It must be stated, however, that most of the careful experiments have been limited to a few species. Reactions to foreign eggs may vary between two closely related species or even among individuals of the same species. Some of the variations reported may have resulted from differences in the strength of the incubation drive at the time the experiments were conducted, although the evidence suggests that distinct species differences do exist. Moreover, a distinction needs to be made between the behavior of ground-nesting species and bush- or tree-nesting species.

Extensive experiments on the Laughing Gull (Noble and Lehrman, 1940) and the Herring Gull (Tinbergen, 1953) included such techniques as removing the eggs and placing them a short distance from the nest, moving the nests but leaving the eggs at the nest site, and putting painted or artificial eggs (made in natural and unnatural shapes) in the nests (Fig. 8). Tinbergen found that most Herring Gulls were more attracted to the nest site than to their eggs and would incubate on an empty nest while their eggs were in sight a short distance away. Not only would a gull accept the eggs of some other gull, no matter how different in color and pattern, but it would incubate wooden eggs painted blue or yellow. The importance of tactile stimulation in egg "recognition" is shown by Tinbergen's findings that Herring Gulls returned to nests containing wooden "eggs" of various shapes (rectangle, cylinder, prism) but that the birds would not incubate them if they had sharp edges. As Tinbergen remarked: "For when the birds made their choice and went to the rectangular blocks, they could truly be said to 'recognize' them as eggs. But when, after touching them, they left them,

FIGURE 8. Examples of wooden eggs used by Prof. Gerard P. Baerends of Holland in his experiments with Herring Gulls. (Courtesy of G. P. Baerends.)

one could with as much justification say that now they did not 'recognize' them as eggs." Noble and Lehrman found that Laughing Gulls were attracted first to the eggs and secondly to the nest site, and that they exhibited no discriminatory ability toward their own eggs, but did discriminate between natural and artificial eggs. Although the gulls sometimes accepted eggs painted blue or yellow, their behavior was disturbed by the abnormal colors. Both species of gulls typically rejected eggs painted red. Noble and Lehrman noted that the behavior of the Noddy Tern, which builds nests in bushes, is changed very little by adding colored eggs to the nest. As long ago as 1911, A. D. Du Bois substituted two Mourning Dove eggs for those of a Whip-poor-will and found the bird incubating the dove eggs the following day; apparently he did not follow the nest further.

Tinbergen uses the term "supernormal stimuli" in describing certain behavior reactions. The Ringed Plover, for example, "is more strongly stimulated by a white egg with large black dots than by its own eggs, which are buff with small brownish dots." When given a choice between a real egg and a giant artificial egg, Herring Gulls try to incubate the artificial egg even when its volume is 8 to 20 times that of the normal egg (Fig. 9). The European Oystercatcher also is known for its preference for giant eggs, and when given a choice between a clutch of three eggs (the usual clutch) and five eggs, it selects the five-egg clutch even though the birds apparently never lay more than four eggs in a nest.

"Egg-retrieving" is a behavior pattern found among ground-nesting species that have been studied, e.g., Gray Lag-Goose, Ringed Plover, Oystercatcher, Herring, Laughing, and Black-headed gulls, Sooty Tern, European Nightjar, and Common Nighthawk (Fig. 10). Details of the behavior vary with several factors. The Black-headed Gull will return to incubate in a nest from which all eggs have been removed and will then roll eggs back into the nest from a distance of about three feet (in one series of experiments). When some eggs are left in the nest, however, the gull will roll in some of the eggs only if they are placed less than a foot from the nest. A Herring Gull, on the other hand, may return to an empty nest and ignore the displaced eggs, may roll the eggs back into the nest, or may build a new nest around the displaced eggs. Noble and Lehrman concluded that "it is apparent that gulls and terns building shallow nests roll their displaced eggs more than do birds building deeper nests." Ground-nesting passerine species apparently never roll eggs back into the nest even when they are located only an inch or so from the nest rim.

FIGURE 9. Herring Gull rolling a giant wooden egg into its nest. (Courtesy of G. P. Baerends.)

Few experiments have been conducted with tree-nesting species, either passerine or nonpasserine. W. B. Savary used water colors to paint brown spots on three Eastern Bluebird eggs and then put them into a Song Sparrow nest; he put three of the Song Sparrow eggs in the bluebird's nest. All eggs were incubated until they hatched, but the Song Sparrow nest was destroyed soon after. The adult bluebirds fed the young birds and fledged one bluebird and three Song Sparrows from the nest.

That some passerine birds do discriminate differences in eggs there can be no doubt. There is, however, no evidence to suggest that they "recognize" their own eggs. The European ornithologist Bernard Rensch shifted eggs between nests of two species of Old-world warblers (Sylviidae). He placed eggs of the Lesser White-throat in the nest of a Garden-warbler. The eggs were accepted, but when the Garden-warbler then laid an egg, it was rejected, presumably because it differed from the majority of eggs in the nest. He also found that if all the eggs in a nest were painted red they were accepted more often than if a single egg was painted red.

The survival, as species, of the Brown-headed Cowbird and the Bronzed Cowbird depends on the acceptance of their eggs by the host species. Among the few species that typically eject cowbird eggs from the nest are the Catbird and the Robin, both of which lay bluish eggs wholly unlike those of the cowbird; other species of thrushes that lay blue eggs, however, apparently do not remove cowbird eggs from their nests. A few species (e.g., Cardinal), whose eggs are similar in size and color pattern to those of the cowbird, are prone to desert parasitized nests, but most of the host species do accept cowbird eggs. The discrepancy in size between cowbird eggs and those of many host species may be an advantage in terms of Tinbergen's supernormal stimuli.

INCUBATION

To incubate is to apply heat to eggs. Physiological processes during the nesting season induce incubation or broodiness behavior in one or both members of a mated pair. The incubating bird spends much time sitting on the nest with its abdomen pressed against the eggs. The development of *incubation patches* in the skin of the abdomen facilitates the heat transfer from the abdominal wall to the eggs. These patches, which are present only during the breeding season, are formed by the loss of some abdominal feathers and/or simply by an increase in the number of small blood vessels in the skin. Incubation patches, in general, occur only in the sex which incubates, but there are exceptions, and some groups of birds are said not to develop incubation patches at all (e.g., ratites and pelicaniform birds). The incubation patch in ducks and geese is

FIGURE 10. Female Common Nighthawk poking a displaced egg under her. (Courtesy of Milton W. Weller and the editor of *The Auk*.)

formed when the female plucks breast feathers to line her nest. Feather-plucking behavior is presumed to depend on hormonal stimulation. Hanson (1959) reported that feather plucking by a female Canada Goose occurs chiefly near the end of the egg-laying period and during the first part of the incubation period. New feathers (which differ in color from the old feathers) begin to appear on the denuded area about the time that the eggs hatch.

The *incubation period* is defined as the interval between the laying of the last egg in a clutch and the hatching of that egg when all of the eggs hatch. The incubation period varies among different families of birds from a minimum of 11 days to almost 12 weeks: Brown-headed Cowbird, 11–12 days; Eastern Meadowlark, 13–14; Ruby-throated Hummingbird, 16; Belted Kingfisher, 23–24; American Coot, 23–24; Canada Goose, 28–29; Sharp-shinned Hawk, 34–35; Royal Albatross, 77½–81 (see Nice, 1954). Statements in the literature which give an incubation period of 10 days are unreliable (Nice, 1953). The length of the incubation period for each species is a function of the inherent rate of development of the embryo, which is determined genetically. Although a slight increase in growth rate has been reported in artificially incubated eggs of some gallinaceous birds at a temperature of 38.9° C., it seems true, in general, that an increase over the normal incubation temperature does not speed up the inherent rate of development (without affecting the embryos adversely). Prolonged exposure at high temperatures kills the embryos. Experiments conducted by S. P. Baldwin and S. C. Kendeigh revealed that House Wren eggs showed a greater resistance to low than to high temperatures. The embryos survived moderately lowered temperatures for short intervals, but development was slowed and hatching was, in some instances, delayed as much as 36 hours over the expected hatching time. Similarly, Breckenridge (1956) found that incubation in three Wood Duck nests near Minneapolis ranged from 25 to about 31 days (Figs. 11, 12). The longest incubation period occurred at a nest in which disturbances caused the female to be off the nest for two unusually long periods (about 13½ and 9½ hours) at times when air temperatures dropped to 42° and 41° F., respectively. The inherent rate of development for each species requires a minimum incubation time at an optimal temperature. Therefore, Breckenridge suggested that "the shortest incubation period for any species approaches most nearly the period characteristic of the species since any temperature rise above normal will not shorten the period, but severe chilling can greatly increase the incubation period." For this reason, he proposed that emphasis should be

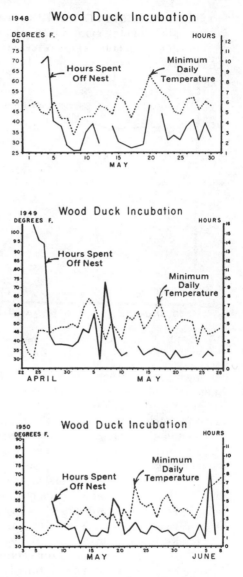

FIGURE 11. Recorded periods that female Wood Ducks spent off the nest correlated with minimum daily temperatures. (Courtesy of W. J. Breckenridge, from *Jour. Wildl. Manag.*, 20, 1956.)

placed on the shortest incubation time for a species rather than on the range of recorded periods. The eggs of the Common Swift seem to be affected less by lowered temperatures. In their study of this species in England, David and Elizabeth Lack (1954) found that the eggs hatched on schedule even though they often were

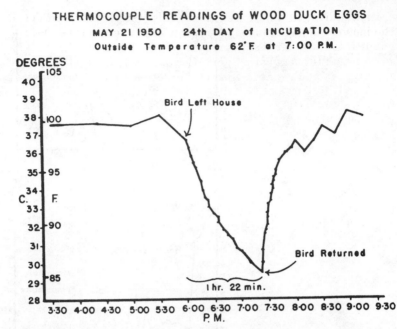

THERMOCOUPLE READINGS of WOOD DUCK EGGS
MAY 21 1950   24th DAY of INCUBATION
Outside Temperature 62°F. at 7:00 P.M.

FIGURE 12. Thermocouple recordings of heat loss in a down-covered Wood Duck nest. (Courtesy of W. J. Breckenridge, from *Jour. Wildl. Manag.*, 20, 1956.)

left uncovered for periods of several hours during cold weather, when both adults were searching for food. They remarked that "no other bird which nests in cool regions leaves its eggs unincubated for such long periods without harm."

Depending on the size of the species, the optimal incubation temperature is from 2 to 4° lower than the body temperature of the incubating bird (Witschi, 1956). In their study of seven nesting species at Anaktuvuk, Alaska, Irving and Krog (1956) reported that 74 per cent of their records of nest temperatures during incubation were between 33° and 37° C. (Fig. 13). This was very close to an earlier study made at Cleveland, Ohio, by R. A. Huggins, who found the mean incubation temperatures in nests of 37 species to be 34° ± 2.38° C. Therefore, Irving and Krog concluded that air temperature cannot modify the duration of embryonic development because the incubation behavior of the adults maintains nest temperatures "as uniform among the species as are the body temperatures" of the adults. This conclusion recognizes that the normal incubation pattern of the adult, rather than air temperature per se, is the critical factor, but it does not take into consid-

eration individual differences in incubation rhythm, variations in
the incubation pattern among tropical species, or unusual climatic
conditions for a particular species.   Thus, Lawrence H. Walkinshaw found the incubation period of the Chipping Sparrow to be
11 days when the mean average air temperature was between
66.2° and 76.0° F., but 13 to 14 days when the mean average temperature was between 48.7° and 53.2° F.   Nest temperatures were
not recorded, but this difference in incubation time, as Walkinshaw

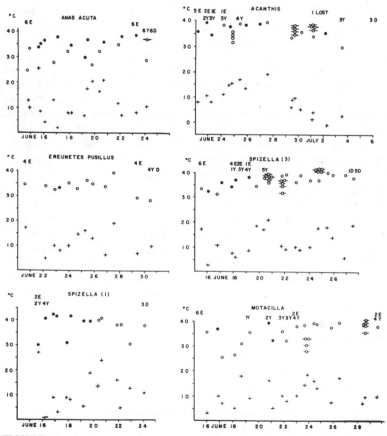

FIGURE 13.   Temperatures among eggs and nestling birds in arctic nests.   Solid
circles: adult bird on nest; open circles: bird off nest; circle with line: thermometer in
gullet of nestling; cross: air temperature.   Species: *Anas acuta,* Pintail; *Ereunetes
pusillus,* Semipalmated Sandpiper; *Motacilla flava,* Yellow Wagtail; *Acanthis* sp.,
Redpoll; *Spizella arborea,* Tree Sparrow.   (Courtesy of Laurence Irving, from *Physiol.
Zoöl.,* 29, 1956.)

suggested, might have resulted because an optimal incubation temperature could not be maintained in the loosely constructed nest of the Chipping Sparrow during long periods of cold weather.

The time that an incubating bird spends on the eggs is called the *attentive period;* the time off the eggs is the *inattentive period.* The rhythm of attentiveness varies widely among different species of birds. Hornbills (Bucerotidae) nest in tree cavities, and have the strange habit of reducing the size of the entrance by plastering it with mud and other substances, with the result that the female is imprisoned in the nesting cavity. Here she remains throughout the incubation period, as well as throughout the nestling period in most species. Hence, the eggs are covered essentially 100 per cent of the time. This is basically true also among species in which both sexes incubate. In some instances, this behavior is correlated with air temperatures during the nesting period. In his study of Clark's Nutcracker, L. Richard Mewaldt (1956) found that the adults were attentive 99.5 per cent of the time during 20 hours of daylight observation. He pointed out that this high percentage of attentiveness "has positive survival value when freezing and near-freezing temperatures are the rule, rather than the exception, during the February to April nesting season." A similar incubation pattern is essential for any species that nests in February, March, or April in northern parts of the United States (e.g., some hawks, owls, Killdeer, Mourning Dove, Horned Lark, Vesper Sparrow, Song Sparrow). Some tropical species are said to incubate less than 50 per cent of the total incubation period. Although such reports are based on the regrettable practice of using so-called "representative" time spans of observation during the incubation period, it seems likely that there is a positive correlation between long inattentive periods of some tropical species and relatively high air temperatures (and humidity), as well as with minimal daily fluctuations in air temperature.

The pattern of attentive behavior varies widely. For many small passerine species, diurnal attentive periods of from 15 to 30 minutes are alternated with inattentive periods lasting 6 to 10 minutes. Such patterns, however, often vary geographically, seasonally, with time of day, with changes in weather, with the stage of incubation, and among different individuals. Putnam (1949) spent an average of 11 hours per day for 17 days during egg-laying, incubation, and hatching at each of two nests of the Cedar Waxwing. He found the attentiveness of the two females to be: "28% and 42% on the day of the first egg, 40% and 61% on the second, 65% and 70% the third, 77% and 78% the fourth, and 87% and 88% on the fifth

when the clutches were complete. For the next 3 days the attentiveness increased gradually to 95%, and for the following 9 days
varied only from 93% to 97%. The highest percentage of attention
noted was 97.3, shortly before hatching." Long attentive periods
also are found among passerine species in which both sexes incubate
and among those in which the male feeds the female on the nest
(e.g., Kirtland's Warbler, American Goldfinch). Attentive periods
tend to be especially long among large birds; the longest are found
among albatrosses and penguins. L. E. Richdale reported that
Royal Albatrosses incubate continually for periods of 9 to 14 days;
the Emperor Penguin is said to incubate continually for 60 days.

Only the female incubates in many North American families, but
both sexes share in incubation in about half of the families of world
birds. Examples of passerine species in which the male assists in
incubation are the Blue Jay, Clark's Nutcracker, Warbling Vireo,
Rose-breasted and Black-headed grosbeaks.

Egg-turning during the incubation period is practiced by most
birds. The incubating bird periodically changes the position of the
eggs, usually by turning them with its bill. The yolk rotates each
time that the egg is turned, so that (normally) the developing
embryo always lies uppermost in the shell. Putnam reported that
a female Cedar Waxwing turned her eggs 12 times in 65 minutes,
noting that this frequency was not uncommon. As a result of his
extensive studies of the Herring Gull, Tinbergen concluded that
egg-turning behavior stops after the egg is pipped, presumably as a
response to movements or call notes of the fetus, which "cause the
parent to treat the pipped egg as a chick."

Two groups of birds do not exhibit broodiness behavior at all.
The megapodes of Australia, the Philippines, and intervening areas
bury their eggs in sand or piles of decaying vegetation. These
"nests" serve as natural incubators, and the adults of some species
pay no further attention to them after the eggs are laid. Females
of parasitic species lay their eggs in the nest of some other bird and
never incubate.

THE YOUNG AND PARENTAL CARE

The fully developed fetus cuts the eggshell with the egg-tooth on
its upper mandible; during this activity, the egg is said to be
"pipped." From 10 to 20 hours are required for the young of many
small species to break open the eggshell, but the egg of the Royal
Albatross may be pipped for over four days before the chick

emerges. The time span over which the eggs hatch depends on the
interval between the laying of successive eggs and whether incubation begins with the laying of the first or the last (sometimes,
penultimate) egg in the clutch. For precocial species, in general, all
the eggs hatch in a relatively short period, but for altricial species
they usually hatch over a period of two or three days. David F.
Parmelee reported that the hatching period of three- and four-egg
clutches of the Painted Bunting varied from about 4.5 hours to at
least 40 hours. The young hatch over a long period among species
that lay eggs on alternate days (or longer intervals) and that begin
to incubate with the laying of the first egg (e.g., hawks, owls,
American cuckoos).

Based on their relative development at the time of hatching,
birds are said to be *precocial* or *altricial.* The young of precocial
species are fully covered with down at hatching and are able to run
about (or swim) a short time after breaking out of the egg (e.g.,
ducks, geese, quail, pheasants, grouse, rails, shorebirds). The
young of many precocial species are never fed by the adults,
although they may lead the young to food. Altricial young are
helpless when hatched. They may be downy (herons, bitterns,
ibises, vultures, hawks, owls, etc.), have a scant covering of hair-like
down on the crown and back, or they may be naked (without any
down). Parental care among altricial species ranges from about one
to nearly eight months. The young of most precocial species leave
the nest within 48 hours after hatching, and the adults generally
leave the eggshells in the nest (but see Fig. 14). A few altricial
species (e.g., cuckoos) also leave the shells in the nest, but most
altricial species either eat the shells or carry them away.

Eggs are incubated; nestlings are brooded. Brooding behavior is
a continuation of incubation behavior. The rhythm for brooding
of very young nestlings is much the same as the incubation rhythm
during the last part of the incubation period. The ratio of attentive
to inattentive periods varies with the age of nestlings, weather,
time of day, sex, and species. In the March and April nests of
Clark's Nutcracker studied by Mewaldt, attentiveness by the two
adults was nearly 100 per cent through the first 9 days of the
approximately 20-day nestling period. Loren S. Putnam found that
female Cedar Waxwings brooded most of the time for the first
3 days of a 16-day nestling period in June to August nests (Fig. 15).
Many species continue to brood the young at night after daytime
brooding has ceased. Species that build open nests usually brood
nestlings of all ages during heavy rainstorms, and they may shield
them from the sun in hot weather (Fig. 16).

FIGURE 14.   Female Redhead eating eggshell of a newly hatched duckling.   (Courtesy of Milton W. Weller, from *Ecol. Monog.*, 29, 1959.)

Temperature Control

In view of the preceding discussion, one might conclude justifiably that newly hatched birds, as well as eggs, need protection from extreme temperature fluctuations, and this is, indeed, the case.   As long ago as 1824, W. F. Edwards pointed out that birds hatched without a covering of down are essentially cold-blooded animals in that their body temperature fluctuates considerably with changes in air temperature.   It often has been implied that temperature regulation is fully developed in newly hatched precocial birds.   The efficiency of the temperature control system has been studied in only a few species, but available information suggests that few, if any, bird species at hatching are as homoiothermic as the adults.

It should be pointed out that the body temperature of an adult bird when asleep may be as much as 6° C. lower than when the bird is engaged in vigorous activity (Irving and Krog, 1956).   Irving reported, in an earlier paper, that changes in body temperature in adults of Alaskan species "bore no relation" to air temperature; the changes were directly correlated with the degree of activity of the bird. By contrast, body temperatures of young birds fluctuate with changes in air temperature. Inadequate temperature control in the young bird is compensated for by the adults' brooding behavior.

The development of temperature control in young birds is related to several factors: the decrease in proportion of body surface to bulk; increase in nervous and hormonal control and in heat production; development of functioning air sacs and the growth of down or feathers. The rate at which this control develops varies considerably among different families. A precocial bird is more highly developed than an altricial bird at hatching but its temperature control mechanism is far from being perfected. In his excellent study of the Killdeer, Munir K. Bunni found that newly hatched young of this precocial species were able to maintain body temperatures at air temperatures of 23° to 40° C., but not at lower temperatures. The cloacal temperature of birds one hour to two days old dropped from 36.7° C. ($\pm$3.7°) to an average of 17.7° C. after

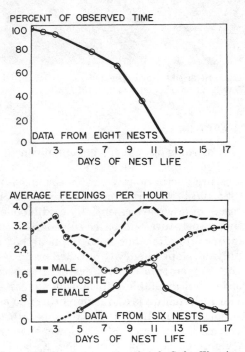

FIGURE 15. Upper: Relation between time female Cedar Waxwings spend brooding (during daylight) and the age of the young. Lower: Relation of average feedings per hour and day of nest life. (Courtesy of Loren S. Putnam and the editor of *The Wilson Bulletin*.)

FIGURE 16. Female Red-winged Blackbird shielding young from the sun. (Courtesy of Samuel A. Grimes.)

they were exposed one hour to an air temperature of 13° C., a temperature often encountered by the young of early nests. Efficiency of temperaturé control increased rapidly during the first 10 days, but not until the young were about 27 days old did the regulating system approach that of the adults. The young were brooded at night, as well as during the day in cold weather, until they were at least 10 days old; older young were brooded at times. During the first two days of life especially, this precocial species seems to have no more control over body temperature at low air temperatures than do other species studied, including passerine birds. Dawson and Evans (1957) reported that one- and two-day-old Field and Chipping sparrows were unable to maintain a body temperature warmer than the environment at air temperatures between 15° and 38° C. Both species were able to maintain body temperatures when seven days old.

Temperature regulation has been studied in several nidicolous*
(White and Brown pelicans, Great Blue Heron, Common Nighthawk) and seminidicolous species (Least Tern, several gulls). All
except the pelicans are downy at hatching. None has an adult-like
temperature control mechanism at hatching. Different techniques
used by the several investigators make direct comparisons difficult,
but it can be said that the body temperatures of the pelicans fluctuated the most (diurnal range of Brown Pelicans was 21.4 to
43.7° C.); that of the gulls fluctuated the least (Bartholomew and
Dawson, 1954). It seems evident from available data that we are
not dealing with pure cold-bloodedness or warm-bloodedness at
time of hatching but rather with varying degrees of efficiency in
temperature control among the families of birds. Therefore, we
question the wisdom of adding the temperature control factor to
the long-accepted definitions of altricial and precocial, as has been
suggested by some writers.

The behavior of both adults and young aids in compensating for
poorly developed temperature control mechanisms of the young.
The chief problem faced may be one of constantly low temperatures,
of constantly high temperatures, or of extreme daily fluctuations
in air temperature, depending on time and place of nesting. In
addition to brooding by the adult during cold weather, young birds
may increase heat production by shivering, or, in the case of the
Killdeer, by intermittent periods of running about in search of
food. Young (and adult) birds faced with unusually high temperatures resort to panting and/or fluttering their gular area (e.g.,
Screech Owls, Great Blue Herons, cormorants, nighthawks). Because of their large gular pouches, gular fluttering by pelicans is an
important mechanism for increasing heat loss. In their study of
White Pelican colonies in the Salton Sea, Bartholomew et al. (1953)
noted that, because the nesting area is entirely unshaded by vegetation, "the primary problems of temperature regulation, both
before and after hatching, relate to the prevention of over-heating,
rather than the prevention of cooling." Instead of incubating the
eggs or brooding the young, therefore, the adults often have to
shield them from the intense solar radiation. Older young often
move into shallow water during the heat of the day. Bartholomew
and his co-workers found that the mean body temperature of
swimming young was more than 3° C. lower than that of "dry
young" of a similar size.

* Nidicolous species are those whose young stay in the nest for some time after hatching; the young may be naked or covered with down at hatching. Seminidicolous species
are those whose young remain in the nest for some time after hatching but which leave
it long before they are able to fly; the term is not defined precisely.

Feeding and Nest Sanitation

The speed with which adults can change their behavior at the time the eggs hatch is demonstrated by some experiments conducted by Graber (1955), who used young from incubator-hatched eggs. He removed the eggs from a Bell's Vireo nest shortly after the last egg of the clutch was laid and then put a young Cardinal in the nest. He reported that the vireos brought larvae to the nest less than one minute later. In another instance, Graber put two hatchling Painted Buntings and a Cardinal in a Painted Bunting nest from which he then removed the eggs. The three young birds were fed by the foster parents and were fledged from the nest.

"Anticipatory food-bringing" needs to be mentioned because the phrase is a relatively new one in ornithological literature. The males of some species (e.g., wood-warblers; Nolan, 1958) bring food to the nest during the incubation period. The female may or may not be on the nest at the time of the male's visit, and, if she is present, she may or may not accept the food. It has been suggested that the male "anticipates" the hatching of the eggs and that the behavior is the expression of overflow or vacuum activity (page 135). The concept of anticipatory food-bringing undoubtedly arose from anthropomorphic thinking. We see no reason, at this time, to view the concept as anything else than a part of the broader behavior pattern of courtship feeding and feeding the incubating female, both of which have been inadequately studied.

Published data on the frequency with which adult passerine species feed their young reveal that the number of feedings per nestling per hour ranges from 0.8 to 8.4, with an average of about 4 feedings per hour. I watched a Great Crested Flycatcher nest on the day the young fledged, at which time the nest was attended by one adult. The adult fed the five nestlings 91 times between 5:12 A.M. (the first feeding of the day) and 12:10 P.M., when the first nestling flew from the nestbox. The adult fed the remaining nestlings 27 times between 12:10 and 7:05 P.M., when the last bird left the nest (the other nestlings left the nest at 12:42, 6:00, and 6:30 P.M.). During the afternoon, the adult spent more time feeding the two fledglings than the three nestlings. In contrast to passerine species, L. E. Richdale reported that an albatross chick is fed daily for about three weeks, after which it may be fed only twice a week. Feeding rate varies not only among species and with the age of the young but also with length of the nestling period, with weather conditions, and, sometimes, with number of young to be fed and the number of adults attending them. There are a few recorded instances (e.g., Chimney Swift, Pigmy Nuthatch) of

extraparental care, in which three or four adults fed the young in
a single nest. Among some multibrooded species (e.g., Barn Swallow, Long-tailed Tit, Wheatear, Eastern Bluebird) the young of an
early brood may sometimes help feed the young of a later brood,
and thus act as *juvenile helpers at the nest.*

The mouth lining in young birds usually is brightly colored, and
some nestlings (e.g., cuckoos, weaverbirds) have special areas that
contrast with the general color of the oral cavity. The special
colored areas (sometimes modified in structure) are called *directive
marks* because they are presumed to be of additional aid in coordinating the gaping of the young with the feeding response of the
parents. The straw-colored and swollen rictus (page 7) of the
nestling House Sparrow represents another type of directive mark.

The young of many species void their excrement within a whitish
(often black-tipped) fecal sac, which has a gelatinous consistency.
As soon as they are strong enough to do so, the young of passerine
species typically turn around in the nest and elevate their cloacal
region when passing a fecal sac. This behavior tends to result in
deposition of the sac on or over the nest rim, or, in species building
a domed nest (e.g., Ovenbird), at the nest entrance; 14- and 15-day-
old Great Crested Flycatchers that I watched voided at the entrance
to the nestbox. The same instinctive tendency is seen among some
nonpasserine birds (e.g., hawks, herons) in which the feces are not
enclosed in a sac. Most passerine, and some nonpasserine, species
dispose of the fecal sacs; the sacs often are eaten during the first days
of the nestling's life, but later they are carried away. In very
young nestlings especially, feeding is a stimulus to defecation, and
the adults typically pause at the nest after feeding the young as
though removal of fecal sacs were part of the entire feeding complex. Goldfinches, siskins, redpolls, and crossbills remove fecal sacs
regularly only during the first part of the nestling period, with the
result that the outside of the nests later become covered with
fecal sacs.

Parent-Young Recognition

The altricial bird may be unable to raise its head and neck from
the bottom of the nest for an hour or more after hatching. One of
its first responses is gaping for food. With eyes still closed, the
nestling responds to nonvisual stimuli, such as an adult alighting
on the nest, adult call notes, "squeaking," or nest-tapping by an
observer. The gaping of a newly hatched altricial bird is in a
vertical direction without reference to the position of an adult on

the nest rim. Even after their eyes open, the young may not gape toward the adult, but at an age of about 5 to 10 days (depending on the species), the young direct their gaping toward the bill of the adult. There is no evidence to suggest, however, that the young altricial bird recognizes its own parents. A bird in the bottom of the nest may gape wildly at the sight of another nestling perched on the nest rim. The primary stimulus for begging seems to be the movement of another bird at a slightly higher elevation. We do not know whether fledgling passerine birds learn to recognize their parents. Among such precocial and seminidicolous species as coots and terns, it has been shown that older downy young learn to recognize any hostile signs displayed by adults and that they may recognize their own parents.

Experiments show that the adults of some precocial species learn to recognize their own young. Tinbergen found that Herring Gulls learn to recognize their own chicks during the first four or five days after hatching. During this period the adults will accept strange chicks of a similar age that are placed with their own young, but after the fifth day will attack, and even kill, strange young. Passerine birds seem not to recognize their own young. This has been demonstrated by several workers who have transferred nestlings from one nest to another. The new nestlings, either of the same or a different species, usually are accepted by the foster parents. Parmelee (1959) reported that a fledgling Painted Bunting that he placed with three fledglings of another brood a mile away was accepted as a part of that brood. Many New-world passerine species rear young cowbirds and Old-world species rear young cuckoos (Fig. 17). Evidence of a different type is obtained from observations made on the reaction of birds to their own banded young. Bands, being conspicuous on young birds, seem to set off the fecal-sac-removal behavior in the parents. There are records of Horned Larks, Red-eyed Vireos, and Song Sparrows picking up one of their nestlings by a band and carrying the nestling away from the nest. Ormsby Annan wrote about a Veery that removed a four-day-old banded Brown-headed Cowbird from the nest; no attempt was made to remove an unbanded cowbird from the same nest, and this bird was fledged successfully by the Veery. Such "unthinking" behavior is typical of bird activities.

The relationship of imprinting (page 143) to parent-young recognition has been studied in several species of ducks and gallinaceous birds, but much remains to be learned. Different experimental techniques have been used by the several authors, and their results often appear to be contradictory. Thus, Eric Fabricius reported

FIGURE 17. A Meadow Pipit feeding a young European Cuckoo. (Courtesy of Eric Hosking.)

that the readiness to follow a potential parent was greatest in ducklings younger than 12 hours, and that it rapidly decreased thereafter. But, A. O. Ramsay and E. H. Hess (1954) found the critical period for imprinting to be at ages of 13 to 16 hours. Fabricius felt that the species he worked with have a well-developed innate releasing mechanism (page 133) for their instinctive reaction to follow a potential parent bird and that this mechanism "responds to several visual and auditory sign stimuli," which work together in a cumulative way. Ramsay and Hess commented that "it seems very likely . . . that Fabricius was dealing with 2 separate innate releasing mechanisms, and not with 2 key stimuli in the same releasing mechanism. . . ."

One of the most significant studies of imprinting is that of Ramsay (1951). He concluded that "both the adults and the young largely acquire, rather than inherit, the ability to recognize other members of the family to which they belong using color, voice, size and form as cues. Recognition seems to involve several factors, variation in any one of which upsets the recognition behavior of adults and young. In the species studied, auditory cues seem to predominate in recognition, but it is also apparent that these are far from being the only cues involved." He found that young birds could find their hidden parents by vocal cues alone, and that "Muscovy ducklings, removed from their parent a few hours after hatching, could recognize their parent by vocal cues four days later. They remembered her color even longer but showed no memory of her size or form." Behavior also is important: "The adults tended to attack any young birds that retreated from them regardless of whether these were their own young or those of another individual." Ramsay demonstrated for the species he studied that "recognition" for the adult female is primarily a matter of becoming accustomed to whatever comes out of the eggs she is incubating; for the newly hatched bird, it is a matter of becoming accustomed to the bird that hatches it. For example, he reported that a 5-year-old Muscovy Duck that hatched 13 White Rock chicks would not then accept a brood of Muscovy ducklings, even though in previous years she had "mothered several broods of Muscovy ducklings, Mallard ducklings, chicks, and a mixed brood of chicks and ducklings." We know that imprinting is not always irreversible, but we know very little about changes in behavior as imprinted birds mature. This question has considerable significance in relation to pair formation and breeding parasitism in the Redhead (page 269) and the Black-headed Duck, as well as in other parasitic species.

Length of Nestling Period

A young bird is a *nestling* from the time it hatches until it leaves the nest. It is a *fledgling* from the time it leaves the nest until it is independent of all parental care. In practice, the newly hatched young of precocial species usually are referred to as either downy young or chicks, rather than nestlings, even though they may remain in the nest for periods ranging from several hours to more than two days. A very few birds have no fledgling period: the swift *Apus* is completely independent of the adults when it flies from the nest. Young megapodes have neither a nestling nor a fledgling period. When the young birds hatch, they dig out of their "natural" incubators, are able to fly, and are independent.

The nestling period may be about the same length as the incubation period (e.g., Great Crested Flycatcher, Horned Lark), shorter than the incubation period (many wood-warblers and fringillids), or longer than the incubation period (Belted Kingfisher, woodpeckers, swifts, swallows, Cedar Waxwing, Starling). Surprisingly little accurate information is available on the length of the nestling period for the majority of species or on the normal range of variation for a particular species. It is doubtful that any North American passerine bird leaves the nest normally before it is at least eight days old. The Purple Martin (Fig. 18) has one of the longest nestling periods of North American passerines. The young martins usually stay in the nest for 28 days and may remain there as long as 35 days. Bald Eagles remain in the nest for 11 weeks. In what is apparently the only accurate record, a young California Condor was reported to be between 142 and 147 days old when it left the nest site.

Mortality of Young and Adults

The eggs and young are subject to numerous destructive agencies, so many, in fact, that a book could be written about them and the

FIGURE 18. Male Purple Martin feeding young in nest in a gourd. (Courtesy of Samuel A. Grimes.)

survival rates of both young and adults. Elevation of the water level destroys nests of marsh-inhabiting birds. Red-winged Blackbirds sometimes use both dead and living cattails as supports for early nests; new growth may raise one side of the nest so much that the eggs or young are tipped out. The nest of the American Goldfinch is so compact that it will hold water for many hours; not uncommonly this leads to desertion of the nest during the egg-laying period. I found several dead nestlings impaled on thorns when I was studying goldfinch populations in *Crataegus* habitats. K. T. Rogers found a female Brown-headed Cowbird that had been strangled by a loop of horsehair in an old Baltimore Oriole nest (Fig. 19). Migrating birds often are killed by flying into tall buildings, television towers, power lines, and the like.

Several kinds of internal and external parasites cause fatalities among both young and adult birds. Representatives of all classes of vertebrate animals habitually or occasionally prey on eggs, young, or adult birds, and the Praying Mantis has been said to have captured a Ruby-throated Hummingbird. The Bullfrog and Green Frog sometimes capture young birds that fall into the water. The Kingsnake, Ratsnake, Milksnake, Coachwhip, racers, and other bird-eating snakes eat many eggs and young (Fig. 20), and the Water Moccassin has been known to eat birds as large as an adult Pied-billed Grebe. Malcolm W. Coulter (1957) found that the intestinal tract of 42 (out of a total of 171 examined) Snapping Turtles "contained evidence of a minimum of 52 birds including 25 ducks, 11 grebes, 3 rails, and 13 unidentified birds." A few hawks (e.g., Cooper's and Sharp-shinned) kill many birds but most hawks subsist largely on rodents; the House Wren and Blue Jay probably cause more destruction of eggs and young than do most of the hawks. Squirrels, raccoons, skunks, and other mammals often rob nests of eggs or young.

It is important in any life history study to determine the mortality rate during each stage of the nesting cycle, e.g., the percentage of nests that are destroyed during the incubation and nestling periods, the percentage of eggs that hatch, and the percentage of young that survive to nest-leaving time. Because one or more eggs or young may disappear from nests, it should be emphasized that the number of eggs or young found in a nest does not necessarily represent the true clutch size. In order to obtain accurate information, therefore, nests must be visited at least once a day, beginning with the egg-laying period. Mortality data based on nests found after that period are subject to considerable error. To be of much value, survival rates must be based on large numbers of nests. Analyzing 24 studies involving 7788 nests, Nice (1957)

FIGURE 19. Female Brown-headed Cowbird strangled by a loop of horsehair in an old nest of the Baltimore Oriole. (Courtesy of K. T. Rogers and the editor of *The Wilson Bulletin.*)

reported that the success rate of open nests of altricial birds in the North Temperate Zone ranged from 38 to 77 per cent (averaging 49 per cent); in 29 studies involving 21,951 eggs, she found that fledging success ranged from 22 to 70 per cent (averaging 46 per cent).   The survival rate for hole-nesting species averaged 66 per cent, but a wide variation from this average was found: 25.7 per cent for Prothonotary Warblers, 93.7 per cent for Tree Swallows. Moreover, the percentage of young that survive to nest-leaving varies geographically (and locally), seasonally, and annually within the same species. Little attention has been given to possible differences in losses among ground-nesting and tree open-nesting passerine species.

The final criterion of success is the number of young that survive to breed in subsequent years, because the success of a species over long periods of time depends on a reproductive rate adequate to replace losses sustained by the breeding population. Considerable information on longevity and mortality has been obtained from banding studies of certain groups of birds: hawks and owls, because they frequently are shot by an inadequately informed public; game birds; gulls and terns. Austin and Austin (1956) reported a study of the Common Tern that extended from 1923 through 1955: 254,614 chicks and 112,512 adults were banded during this period. Even with the magnitude of this banding program, however, little

FIGURE 20. Blacksnake eating a nestling Rufous-sided Towhee. (Courtesy of Samuel A. Grimes.)

direct information was obtained on the mortality rate during the bird's first year; returns on banded chicks amounted to only 0.28 per cent of the total banded. The authors calculated that at least 20 per cent of the young living to banding age must survive to breed at the age of four years if the population is to maintain itself. The mean annual mortality of the breeding population was constant at 25 per cent from the fourth through the eighteenth years (Table 1). One tern was known to be at least 24 years old when

TABLE 1

Composite Time-Specific Life Table Based on Returns of Common Terns Banded as Chicks and Trapped on Nests, 1940-1955

x Age Interval in Years	lx Alive at Start (July 1)	Per Cent of Population in Each Age Group	dx Calculated Deaths Each Year	qx Mortality Rate per Year, per cent
1-2	41.7	0.8		
2-3	140.4	2.6		
3-4	937.4	17.7		
4-5	1058.6	20.0	263.0	25.0
5-6	795.6	15.0	152.2	19.3
6-7	643.4	12.1	168.9	26.3
7-8	474.5	9.0	129.3	27.3
8-9	345.2	6.5	111.8	32.4
9-10	233.4	4.4	82.4	35.3
10-11	151.0	2.9	33.5	22.2
11-12	117.5	2.2	18.0	15.3
12-13	99.5	1.9	24.8	24.9
13-14	74.7	1.4	21.1	28.3
14-15	53.6	1.0	8.3	15.5
15-16	45.3	0.86	15.7	34.7
16-17	29.6	0.56	7.2	24.3
17-18	22.4	0.42	5.1	22.7
18-19	17.3	0.33	7.9	45.6
19-20	9.4	0.18	5.1	54.4
20-21	4.3	0.08	3.8	88.5
21-22	0.5	0.01	0.5	100.0

Figures for lx are the 16-year averages of numbers of birds taken annually per 100,000 banded in each age class.

Mean annual mortalities: 4 through 22 years = 25.3 per cent.

4 through 18 years = 25.0 per cent.

(By permission of Oliver L. Austin, Jr., from *Bird-Banding,* 27, 1956, page 56.)

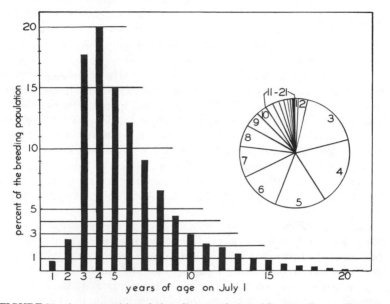

FIGURE 21. Age composition of a breeding population of Common Terns. (Courtesy of Oliver L. Austin, Jr., and the editor of *Bird-Banding*.)

killed, but the maximum reproductive life span of the Common Tern appears to be about 20 years. The authors found that birds from 3 to 10 years old comprise 90 per cent of the breeding population (Fig. 21). Information on the survival rates of gallinaceous birds has been summarized by Hickey (1955) and of many other birds (from penguins to passerines) by Farner (1955).

BREEDING PARASITISM

Some species have become so specialized in their reproductive behavior that they no longer build nests, incubate eggs, or care for their young but lay their eggs in the nests of other species, called the hosts or fosterers. These parasitic species are called *obligate parasites*. Still other species (*nonobligate parasites*) typically incubate their eggs and take care of their young but either rarely or frequently lay one or more eggs in the nest of some other bird. The behavior patterns exhibited by some of the nonobligate parasites suggest ways that obligate parasitism may have evolved.

Nonobligate Parasites

Nonobligate parasites may be divided into two groups: *egg parasites* and *nest parasites*. Nest parasites appropriate the nests of other species in which to lay and incubate their eggs. Nest parasitism is uncommon but some hawks and owls remodel an old nest of another species. The Solitary Sandpiper lays its eggs in the abandoned nests of such birds as the Eastern Kingbird, Gray Jay, Cedar Waxwing, and Robin. The South American nonparasitic Bay-winged Cowbird sometimes builds its own nest or adopts an abandoned nest but more often takes the nest of another species by force. Some authors use the term *nest parasitism* as a synonym for breeding parasitism, thus including both obligate and nonobligate parasitism.

Most nonobligate parasitic species engage in *egg parasitism,* i.e., they lay one or more eggs in the active nest of some other bird (either of the same or a different species). We have very little precise information on most of these species but the data suggest that egg parasitism is much more common in some species than in others. Among those whose eggs are found occasionally in the nests of other birds are these: Eared and Pied-billed grebes, Royal Tern, Virginia Rail, Black-billed and Yellow-billed cuckoos, Roadrunner, Brown Thrasher, Starling, House Sparrow, and House Finch. Several members of the pheasant family occasionally or frequently lay eggs in the nests of other species. Eggs of the California Quail have been found in the nests of several species, including the nest of the Rufous-sided (Spotted) Towhee. Two other members of the pheasant family—Bobwhite and Ring-necked Pheasant—frequently lay eggs in other birds' nests. Samuel A. Grimes found an Eastern Meadowlark nest that held four meadowlark eggs and two of the Bobwhite, and Alexander Blain found Bobwhite eggs in a pheasant's nest. Pheasant eggs have been found in the nests of several species of ducks. Several investigators have concluded that Ring-necked Pheasants often lay eggs in each other's nests, or on the ground, or in "dump" nests in which the eggs are not incubated, and then lay in another nest and carry on normal nesting activities.

It is the duck family, however, that has the largest number of nonobligate parasitic species; some of these have been called semi-parasitic species. The most significant contribution to our knowledge of nonobligate parasitism is that of Milton W. Weller (1959). He tabulated records of 21 different species of ducks whose eggs have been found in nests other than their own (in some instances, the nest of another bird of the same species). This habit reaches its highest development in the Redhead (Figs. 22, 23) and the Ruddy Duck, two species which seem to have a weaker attachment to their nests and eggs than other ducks, and which desert their young at a younger age. Weller found (by trapping) that as many as 13 different Redheads laid eggs in the same nest, which explains the occurrence of "dump" nests containing from 30 to 87 Redhead eggs. More important than this, however, is Weller's conclusion that "three distinct types of nest behavior are found in different individual females: normal nesting, semiparasitism, and complete or obligate parasitism." He estimated that from 5 to 10 per cent of the female Redheads are nonparasitic and nest early in the season. "All other Redhead females apparently lay eggs parasitically at some time. More than half of these hens are semiparasitic and nest after parasitizing while the remainder are probably completely parasitic." Weller pointed out that "in no other species has this range of stages been reported but the simultaneous existence of these stages may be necessary to maintain the population during the development of obligate parasitism." D. F. McKinney watched a Redhead lay an egg in a Canvasback's nest while the hen was incubating her own eggs (Fig. 24).

FIGURE 22. Redhead egg in the nest of an American Bittern at Delta, Manitoba. (Courtesy of Milton W. Weller, from *Ecol. Monog.*, 29, 1959.)

FIGURE 23. Female Mallard brooding four downy Redheads. No Mallard eggs hatched in this nest. (Courtesy of Milton W. Weller, from *Ecol. Monog.*, 29, 1959.)

Obligate Parasites

Obligate parasites are found in five bird families: Anatidae, Cuculidae, Indicatoridae, Icteridae, Ploceidae. Most of the parasitic species inhabit the Old World, but a few are found in Central and South America (e.g., Black-headed Duck, and several genera of cuckoos and cowbirds). The Brown-headed and Bronzed cowbirds are the obligate parasites of North America.

The Bronzed Cowbird inhabits the southwestern United States (parts of Arizona, New Mexico, Texas) and southward to Panama. Its eggs have been found in the nests of about 45 species of birds; little is known of its habits. The Brown-headed Cowbird (including the races formerly called the Nevada and Dwarf cowbirds) is found throughout most of the United States and southern Canada. Its eggs have been found in the nests of about 200 species of birds. For the vast majority of these, however, we have no idea of the incidence of parasitism, the affect on the host species, or which are "good" hosts from the cowbird's standpoint. Some are purely abnormal or accidental hosts (e.g., Blue-winged Teal, Killdeer, phalarope, Mourning Dove) in the sense that they would not feed a nestling cowbird at all or the cowbird would not survive on the food given it. It is possible that the cowbird might survive on food fed by Black-billed and Yellow-billed cuckoos, but there are no reliable records of a cowbird being fledged from nests of these infrequently parasitized species. Because of the lateness of its breeding season, only a small percentage of American Goldfinch nests are parasitized (e.g., 6 out of 536 nests that I studied). There are no records of a cowbird being fledged from a goldfinch nest, and it seems unlikely that the cowbird could survive on regurgitated seeds, the diet of nestling goldfinches. Fledgling cowbirds commonly beg from adults of many species that they encounter, so that an observation of a bird feeding a fledgling cowbird is not proof that the cowbird was raised in that species' nest. There are many other aspects of cowbird breeding behavior about which much needs to be learned: Are the eggs laid at daily intervals? How many eggs constitute a clutch? Is the cowbird a determinate or indeterminate layer? How many eggs are laid during one season? How large is the area over which

FIGURE 24. Canvasback (left) and Redhead both sitting quietly in the Canvasback's nest. The Redhead laid an egg in the nest despite the fact that the Canvasback pecked vigorously at the Redhead's head. (Courtesy of D. F. McKinney and the editor of *The Wilson Bulletin*.)

a female parasitizes nests? Under what circumstances does a female lay more than one egg in a nest? What is the sex ratio at hatching and in the adult population? Are cowbirds monogamous or promiscuous? Is there any evidence for host specificity?

Female cowbirds find nests by watching other birds, either at nest-building time or later, and by actively searching for nests. They usually parasitize open nests but sometimes impose on cavity-nesting species. I once saw a female cowbird enter a horizontal nestbox in which a Great Crested Flycatcher had a nest about half completed; the cowbird did not parasitize this nest, but I did find a cowbird egg in another Great Crested Flycatcher nest that had been deserted for five days. The cowbird usually lays her eggs before sunrise. She apparently does not remove an egg from the nest at the time of laying, but often does so the same day or a day before or after laying, usually during mid-morning, occasionally in the afternoon. The best time for laying, of course, is during the egg-laying period of the host, and the cowbird's laying often is synchronized with the host's egg-laying. Not uncommonly, however, the cowbird lays an egg before a nest has been finished, after incubation is well along, after the host young hatch, and even in deserted nests. I found cowbird eggs in five Song Sparrow nests after they had been deserted for periods ranging from 1 to 26 days. Another Song Sparrow nest contained two cowbirds about 24 hours old and one fully feathered Song Sparrow, which left the nest as I exposed it. One of the cowbirds disappeared but the other fledged eight days after the nest was found. In this instance, the cowbird egg must have been laid after the sparrow egg had been incubated seven or eight days. Mayfield (1960) believes that 10 per cent of all cowbird eggs laid in Kirtland's Warbler nests are laid after incubation begins. If laid too late in the incubation period, cowbird eggs will not hatch. Published reports reveal that cowbirds have laid eggs in nests of the Red-eyed Vireo, Kirtland's Warbler, Indigo Bunting, and Chipping and Field sparrows when they contained nestlings; a Mourning Dove nest I had been observing was parasitized after the dove eggs hatched. Two or more cowbirds frequently lay in the same nest, and as many as eight cowbird eggs have been found in a single nest.

Five passerine families provide most of the cowbird's hosts: tyrant-flycatchers, thrushes, vireos, wood-warblers, finches. Most of the species have not evolved a "defense" against cowbird parasitism. Three reactions exhibited by some hosts are detrimental to the cowbird: ejecting cowbird eggs from the nest, deserting a parasitized nest, and building a new floor over cowbird eggs. The

Yellow Warbler commonly covers cowbird eggs (as well as its own eggs) by building a new lining over them; Traill's Flycatcher, American Goldfinch, and a few other species rarely cover cowbird eggs. Double- and triple-storied Yellow Warbler nests are not unusual; once I found a six-storied nest that held 11 cowbird eggs. In his intensive study of the Yellow Warbler, Daniel S. McGeen found that 86.5 per cent of nonsynchronized cowbird eggs were deserted or covered but that only 22.5 per cent of synchronized eggs were so treated.

Despite the loss of cowbird eggs because of poor synchronization with the host's laying period and the defensive behavior of some hosts, the cowbird is a very successful species. It has not become as specialized as the European Cuckoo, which, during its early nestling life, ejects all eggs and young that occupy the nest (Figs. 25, 26). There is no evidence that the nestling cowbird does this. Destruction of young, especially of the smaller hosts, results primarily from the rapid growth of the cowbird. Hann reported that the weight of the Ovenbird is 81 per cent of that of the cowbird at hatching, but is only 53 per cent of the cowbird's weight at nest-leaving time. Mayfield gave the average weight of three cowbirds on the day of hatching as 3.26 grams; a newly hatched Kirtland's Warbler weighs about 1.5 grams. When three days old, the cowbird weighs about 12.7 grams, which is the weight of an adult warbler.

The incubation period of many hosts is longer than that of the cowbird (average about 11.6 days). Unless the cowbird lays after the host has completed her clutch, and unless the host young hatch before (or on the same day as) the cowbird, the young of most hosts will have little chance of fledging. Occasionally host nestlings do survive when a single cowbird hatches first. Cowbirds often survive even though they hatch several days after the host young. As a rule, only one or two cowbirds are fledged from a single nest, but there is a record of four cowbirds fledging from a Song Sparrow nest (Berger, 1951). Several observers have reported that, in successful parasitized nests, each cowbird is raised at the expense of one host young, but this must be accepted as the broadest of generalizations. In an evolutionary sense, the best hosts for the cowbird should be those which are able to raise both cowbirds and host young.

The amount of cowbird pressure on a species depends on the size of the cowbird population and on the total breeding population of all potential hosts in a given area. It depends also on the relationship of the host's breeding season to that of the cowbird. Thus,

FIGURE 25. Nestling European Cuckoo ejecting egg from a Tree Pipit's nest. (Courtesy of Eric Hosking.)

FIGURE 26. Nestling European Cuckoo ejecting a second egg from a Tree Pipit's nest. (Courtesy of Eric Hosking.)

early and late nests of multibrooded species may escape parasitism entirely. Single-brooded species, as well, may succeed in raising a brood of their own young by renesting after destruction of a parasitized nest. Hence, a simple statement of the percentage of parasitized nests of a species tells little about the effect of parasitism on the production of host young by that species, which is the critical factor. Moreover, one must consider the effects of parasitism over the entire breeding range of a species as well as on local populations.

One of the most thorough analyses of cowbird-host relationships is found in Mayfield's (1960) monograph on the Kirtland's Warbler. The cowbird takes a toll at several stages: 41 per cent of warbler eggs are removed by cowbirds; 10 per cent of warbler eggs present at hatching fail to hatch, presumably because the warbler eggs receive inadequate heat in the presence of the larger cowbird eggs; 59 per cent of warblers hatched do not fledge as a result of cowbird nestlings present. Only 22 per cent of the warbler eggs in parasitized nests produce fledglings as a direct result of the cowbird. "Since 55% of all Kirtland's Warbler nests are parasitized, the cowbird causes the loss of about 43% of all Kirtland's Warbler eggs between laying and fledging in nests not destroyed or abandoned." Furthermore, the fledging success of eggs in nonparasitized nests is only 40 per cent. Consequently, the cowbird is a serious threat to the Kirtland's Warbler, whose total population was estimated to be about 1000 birds in 1951. Mayfield believes that the cowbird discriminates between its own and Kirtland's Warbler eggs and removes only warbler eggs; I am not convinced that this is so.

PROBLEMS FOR STUDY

As long ago as 1887, Alfred Newton wrote: "We have more Natural History Journals than the country can afford, with the result that the numerosity is not only injurious to the Journals themselves but to Natural History itself, as it lowers the tone of the contributions." Newton would be bewildered, indeed, if he were faced with the 200 or more journals that now contain papers dealing with birds. Unfortunately, a high percentage of this great volume of ornithological literature consists of reports on projects that are poorly conceived and superficially executed. A carefully written "general note" often represents more work and has more significance than a "major" paper. The life history of no species of North American bird is so well known that further study is not needed. So inadequate has been the attention given the majority of species that we lack accurate information on such basic items as pair

FIGURE 27. Experimental colony composed of artificial Cliff Swallow nests. The interior of each nest is accessible from above, as shown in Figure 28. (Courtesy of Wilbur W. Mayhew and the editor of *The Condor*.)

FIGURE 28. Observation doors above artificial Cliff Swallow nests open to permit inspection of nest contents. (Courtesy of Wilbur W. Mayhew and the editor of *The Condor*.)

FIGURE 29. Components of an artificial nesting tube designed by William A. Lunk for his study of the Rough-winged Swallow. (Courtesy of William A. Lunk.)

FIGURE 30. Left: Artificial nesting tube for Rough-winged Swallow in place in a dirt bank. Right: Inner lining pulled out in order to examine a nest. (Courtesy of William A. Lunk.)

formation, courtship, incubation and nestling periods, and the period of dependency of the young. The literature contains one precise statement on the time of laying of a single egg for all North American nighthawks. The interval between eggs in a clutch apparently has been determined at two nests of the Black-billed Cuckoo; at no nest of the Yellow-billed Cuckoo.

A thorough approach, which makes full use of available techniques, is prerequisite to obtaining accurate information. Wilbur W. Mayhew and William A. Lunk demonstrated considerable ingenuity in their admirable studies of two difficult species. Mayhew made artificial Cliff Swallow nests and mounted them in such a way that the contents could be examined at any time (Figs. 27, 28). In his study of the Rough-winged Swallow, Lunk designed a nesting tube in which an inner lining could be removed in order to obtain data on incubation and the growth of the young (Figs. 29, 30). Bette J. Johnston trapped three pairs of Brown-headed Cowbirds in three days by baiting a two-compartment trap with an old towhee nest and some House Sparrow eggs. For other techniques, the student is referred to the discussion of "Ornithological Field Methods" in Pettingill's excellent manual (1956).

Anatomy is the study of the structure of an animal (or plant) and the relation of its parts. This broad subject is subdivided into gross anatomy (dealing with structures that can be observed with the naked eye) and microscopic anatomy (dealing with structures so minute they can only be seen with a microscope). Study of the finer anatomy of the body may involve an examination of cells (cytology), tissues (histology), or organs (organology). Neuroanatomy, a special study of the nervous system, deals with both gross and microscopic anatomy. In order to understand adult anatomy, one must consider the development (embryology) of an animal as well. *Physiology* is the study of the functions of living organisms and their parts. A knowledge of the structure of an animal is incomplete without considering function, and a knowledge of function is incomplete without considering structure. It is, in fact, not possible to have a full understanding of one without the other; nor can one understand the behavior of birds without being aware of their anatomical and physiological capabilities. Both anatomy and physiology are vast fields; one can but touch the surface of these subjects in a short chapter. We present here some general principles and selected features of interest to ornithologists.

Structure and Function

THE BIRD IN THE EGG

A female frog lays her gelatinous-covered eggs in the water. After a period of development, a free-swimming tadpole breaks out of the egg mass and breathes by means of external gills. An operculum (a lid) soon grows downward to form a covering (gill sac) over the external gills and the developing internal gills which line visceral arches. These arches separate pharyngeal pouches, several of which rupture to become gill clefts or slits. Water then can pass into the tadpole's mouth, out through the gill clefts, and into the gill sacs; water leaves the interconnected right and left gill sacs through an opening (the spiracle) in the left sac. Oxygen and carbon dioxide exchange takes place as the water flows over the internal gills and the large blood vessels (aortic arches) underlying them, as in fishes. Before the adult form and structure are attained, the tadpole undergoes a process called metamorphosis, involving growth of limbs, loss of tail, degeneration of gills, closure of gill clefts, and development of functional lungs for air breathing.

The embryonic reptile, bird, and mammal repeat or recapitulate many of the stages of their ancient fish and amphibian ancestors, although some of the stages are greatly modified or omitted. All pass through a tailbud stage and develop visceral arches (with their associated aortic arches) and pharyngeal pouches, some of which may actually rupture to form temporary and nonfunctional gill clefts; all go through a metamorphosis, which, however, is not immediately related to changes in physiological processes. After metamorphosis the developing animal is called a fetus. The human embryo at the end of five weeks has the same general structure as a fish or amphibian larva.

Reptiles, birds, and mammals are called *amniotes* because of fetal membranes characteristic of their embryological development (Fig. 1). When one recalls that both birds and mammals evolved from reptilian ancestors (page 1), it is not surprising that each passes through similar developmental stages. Moreover, all develop in a watery environment even though the reptile and bird grow in a hard-shelled egg and the mammal in a uterus. At an early age the embryo becomes enveloped by a closed *amniotic sac* containing amniotic fluid, a watery environment which bathes the embryo. Embryonic cells grow downward to surround the yolk, thus forming a *yolk sac* (a second fetal membrane). Important in reptiles and birds with their large-yolked eggs, a yolk sac also is formed in mammals even though the eggs of most mammals have minimal

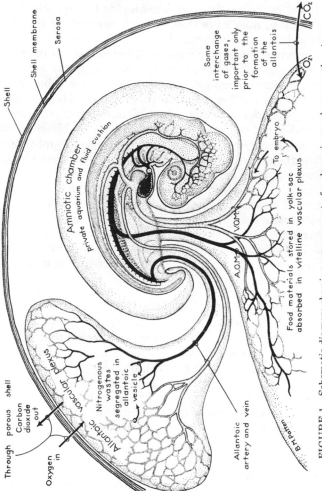

FIGURE 1. Schematic diagram showing arrangement of embryonic membranes and main circulatory channels in a young chick embryo. The sites of some of the extra embryonic interchanges are indicated by the labeling. The vessels within the embryo carry food and oxygen to all its growing tissues, and relieve them of the waste products of metabolism. Abbreviations: A.O.M., omphalomesenteric artery; V.O.M., omphalomesenteric vein. (Courtesy of Bradley M. Patten, from *Amer. Scientist*, 39, April, 1951, p. 224.)

amounts of yolk. The yolk does not pass directly into the body of the embryo; it is digested by the inner surface of the yolk sac and then is carried to the embryo or fetus by special veins. The yolk sac and its contents are drawn through the umbilical opening into the body cavity a day or two before hatching time. Passerine birds do not need food immediately after hatching and a precocial bird, such as the chicken, may have enough food materials in the yolk sac to live four days without eating.

Another important fetal membrane is the *allantois*. It develops as a pouch from the floor of the hind gut, rapidly grows outward through the umbilical opening, and eventually lines the entire inner surface of the shell membrane (page 233). The allantois is both urinary bladder and functional respiratory organ during the fetal period of development. The allantois is richly supplied with blood vessels; oxygen diffuses through the eggshell into these vessels and carbon dioxide passes from them out through the eggshell. Proteins differ from fats and carbohydrates in that they contain nitrogen. Nitrogenous wastes resulting from protein metabolism in birds consist primarily of uric acid salts. These relatively insoluble salts are deposited in the allantois, which dries up near hatching time, leaving the uric acid crystals outside the fetus. Adult birds do not have a urinary bladder, but the proximal part of the allantois remains as the functional bladder in mammals.

THE MAJOR SYSTEMS

A system is composed of various tissues and organs that serve a common function. The organization of the body components into major systems facilitates learning and is, therefore, the traditional approach for the beginning student. However, a regional, rather than a systematic, approach is essential in the study of functional anatomy and medical gross anatomy. The study of function also very quickly leads to a consideration of relationships among the systems.

Integumentary System

The integumentary system includes the skin and all of its specializations (e.g., feathers, wattles, claws, spurs, sensory nerve endings, the oil gland), many of which were discussed in Chapter 1. The skin plays an important role in regulating water loss from the body. In the absence of sweat glands, reduction of body temperature must be effected by increased respiration and by gular flutter-ing (page 256). Body feathers provide an excellent mechanism for conserving body heat. Little is known about the possible role of the skin in the production of vitamin D in birds. Horny spurs, sur-rounding a bony core, are found on the tarsometatarsus (especially in turkeys and some species of pheasants), or on the carpometa-carpus (e.g., Spur-winged Goose, two species of ducks, jaçana, some plovers; Fig. 2). Wing claws have been reported in a number

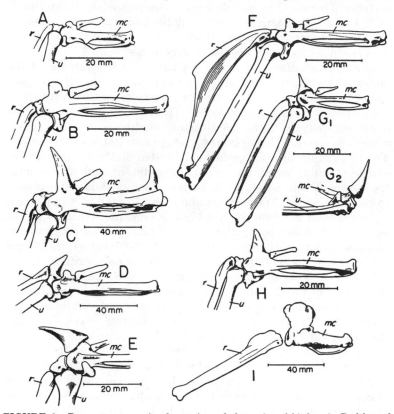

FIGURE 2. Bony structures in the region of the wrist of birds. A. Red-legged Partridge. B. European Oystercatcher. C. Black-necked Screamer. D. Spur-winged Goose. E. Torrent Duck. F. African Jaçana. G_1. Jaçana. G_2. Another view to show the curve of the spur. H. Southern Lapwing. I. Solitaire (an extinct bird related to the pigeons). A and B show the "normal" process on metacarpal I; in C, E, G, and H this process is elongated into a spur (drawn with a horny sheath in E and G); C has an extra spur; D has the spur on a carpal bone; F has a thickened radius; I has a swollen knob on both metacarpal and radius. Abbreviations: r, radius; u, ulna; mc, meta-carpal. (Courtesy of Austin L. Rand and the editor of The Wilson Bulletin.)

of nonpasserine birds and in several passerines (Kiskadee Flycatcher, White-necked Crow, Red-winged Blackbird).

Skeletal System

The skeletal system is the internal framework of the body. Cartilage is a type of supporting tissue that lacks the strength and rigidity of bone; it is associated particularly with the articulating surfaces of bones. The bird skeleton is specialized for strength and for lightness. Strength is attained by the fusion of bones. Resorption of bone marrow and its replacement by extensions of the air sac system decrease the weight of some bones.

The *appendicular skeleton* (see Chapter 1) is composed of the bones of the forelimb and hind limb and their supporting arches, the pectoral and pelvic girdles. The pectoral girdle is formed by the scapula, coracoid, and clavicle. The right and left clavicles are fused ventrally to form the furcula (wishbone) in most birds. Superiorly the three bones bound a bony canal (foramen triosseum). The large supracoracoideus muscle, located on the ventral surface of the sternum, sends its tendon dorsally through the foramen triosseum, which serves as a pulley, thus enabling the muscle to raise the wing. The scapula and coracoid take part in forming a glenoid fossa in which the head of the humerus articulates. The pelvic girdle is formed by the fusion of three paired bones (ilium, ischium, pubis) with the synsacrum. The head of the femur articulates in the acetabulum, a socket in the pelvic girdle.

The *axial skeleton* consists of the skull, vertebral column, ribs, sternum, and hyoid elements (the support for the tongue). The vertebral column is composed of a series of bones (vertebrae; sing., vertebra). The several regions are designated cervical, dorsal, synsacral, free caudal, and pygostyle. As in other vertebrates, the first (anteriormost) vertebra is called the atlas (since it supports the globe of the head); the second vertebra is called the axis because of its importance in pivoting the head. The most frequent number of cervical vertebrae in birds is 14 or 15, but among the different groups the number ranges from 13 to 25. The dorsal (or back) vertebrae are those that are connected by ribs with the sternum and that do not fuse with the synsacrum. Two or more (commonly 3 to 5) of the dorsal vertebrae fuse to form a rigid *notarium* in some genera. The synsacrum is formed by the fusion of a series (10 to 23 bones) of vertebrae. Four to 9 free caudal vertebrae lie between the synsacrum and the pygostyle, the terminal bone in the vertebral column. Formed by the fusion of several embryonic vertebrae, the pygostyle is the support for the tail feathers.

True ribs consist of a dorsal element that has two articulations with a dorsal vertebra and a ventral segment which articulates with the sternocostal process of the sternum. Thoracic ribs articulate dorsally with the anterior synsacral vertebrae; a sternal segment may be present or absent.

The sternum or breastbone (Fig. 3) of most birds (carinates) has a projecting keel (carina), which serves as an area of attachment for the major flight muscles (pectoral muscles). Ratite birds lack a keel and, therefore, have a flat sternum; examples are the ostrich, rhea, cassowary, emu, and kiwi.

Sesamoid bones, located where tendons cross joints, protect tendons from wear and increase their angle of pull. An *os opticus,* a small cancellous bone surrounding the entrance of the optic nerve into the eyeball, is found in many species of birds. All birds have a *sclerotic ring* embedded in the outer wall of the eyeball. Composed of 10 to 18 overlapping plate-like bones, the "ring" is actually a tube-like structure in owls and some hawks (Fig. 4).

Muscular System

The muscular system is composed of specialized cells whose contractility produces movement. Muscles are bundles or sheets of muscle cells (called fibers) which are held together and surrounded by fascia (sheets of connective tissue). Three types of muscles are skeletal (striated), smooth, and heart (cardiac) muscle. Smooth muscle fibers are long, spindle-shaped cells containing a single nucleus. Because they are under the control of the autonomic nervous system, smooth muscles are called involuntary muscles. Typically arranged in sheets or layers, smooth muscles are found in the integumentary, respiratory, circulatory, digestive, and urogenital systems. Skeletal muscles are formed of bundles of multinucleate fibers. Dense membranous sheets (aponeuroses) or tough cord-like tendons attach the muscles to bones. The *origin* of a skeletal muscle is the more proximal or the relatively more fixed attachment; the *insertion* is the more distal or the more movable attachment. Cardiac muscle is similar to skeletal muscle because both have striations, but cardiac muscle has the property of innate rhythmicity, i.e., it can contract without being stimulated by nerves to do so. The nerves to the heart do not initiate muscular contraction; they regulate the rate of heart beat.

A muscle can only pull; it cannot push. When it contracts, a skeletal muscle becomes shorter and thicker. Most skeletal muscles cross joints and, upon contracting, move one bone on another. Special terms are used to describe the different actions that muscles

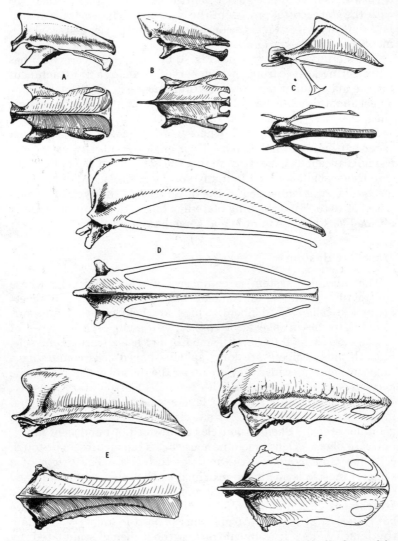

FIGURE 3. Selected examples of the avian sternum. A. Alfred's Oropendola. B. Belted Kingfisher. C. Scaled Quail. D. Great Tinamou. E. Limpkin. F. Scarlet Macaw. (By permission from *Fundamentals of Ornithology* by Josselyn Van Tyne and Andrew J. Berger, published by John Wiley & Sons, Inc. Copyright, 1959.)

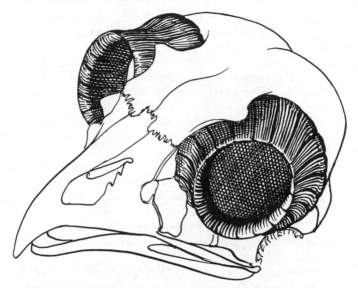

FIGURE 4.   Skull of Snowy Owl to show tubular sclerotic rings.

perform. *Flexion* is the act of bending or of reducing the angle between two bones; *extension* increases the angle or moves the bones toward a straight position. *Adduction* is the movement of a part toward the longitudinal axis of the body (or of a specified digit); *abduction* moves the part away from that axis. In *pronation,* the palm of the hand is turned downward; in *supination,* the palm is turned upward. Pronation and supination result from the *rotation* of the radius around the ulna. One can analyze the individual actions of muscles, but muscles almost invariably act in groups rather than alone. When one flexes the forearm (draws the hand toward the shoulder), for example, the flexing action of the biceps and brachialis muscles is regulated by the triceps muscle, whose contraction extends the forearm. These flexor and extensor muscles act together to produce a smooth, regulated movement. In order to understand the functions of a particular muscle, one must consider the origin, the insertion, and the nature of the joint that the muscle crosses. One must think, also, in terms of nerve-muscle relationships because skeletal muscles do not contract unless stimulated by nerves.

The Latin name of a muscle often is a compact description of its location or action. Mm.* extensor digitorum longus and extensor

---

* "Musculus" before names of muscles is commonly abbreviated M; plural, Mm.

digitorum brevis are two muscles (one long and one short) that extend the toes. Pairs of muscles whose functions and positions are similar are distinguished by being called superior and inferior, medialis and lateralis, or superficialis and profundus. The name may describe the muscle's shape (deltoideus, shape of the Greek letter delta), its location (brachialis, in the arm), its structure (semimembranosus, half-membranous), its attachments (sterno-coracoideus: origin, sternum; insertion, coracoid), its action (pronator profundus), or the number of its heads or bellies (biceps, digastricus).

About 175 different muscles (most of which are paired) have been described in birds. These may be grouped for convenience as follows: muscles of the skull and jaws; orbit and ear; tongue, trachea, and syrinx; upper limb; lower limb; vertebral column; and body wall. Muscles of four of these groups have been used in the classification of birds: muscles of the trachea, jaws, and the two limbs (Fig. 5).

For many years people have written about the mechanism that enables a bird to hold its grasp on a perch while sleeping. The tendons of muscles that cross the back of the "heel" joint are said to be stretched so much that the toes are "locked" to the branch. I have watched sleeping Kirtland's Warblers many times, and they (and probably other passerine birds) do not maintain a vise-like hold on a branch. At relatively short intervals (usually 10 to 30 seconds), the sleeping bird takes one foot off the perch, quickly extends and flexes the toes, and then grasps the perch again. The bird may thus relax the muscles of the legs alternately, or the same foot may be raised from the perch several times in succession. Occasionally a bird may raise one foot and then the other in a matter of two or three seconds.

Nervous System

The nervous system integrates the activities of the body. It receives and interprets stimuli from the interior and the exterior of the body and then effects adjustments to these stimuli. It is composed of supporting elements and of nerve cells (neurons) that are specialized to conduct impulses. A neuron has a cell body and several processes (nerve fibers) which conduct an impulse either toward (dendrite) or away from (axon) the cell body. Specialized endings on the nerve fibers determine both the direction and the type of impulse conducted. Thus a "pain" nerve fiber, with its freely branched ending, conducts impulses which we interpret as

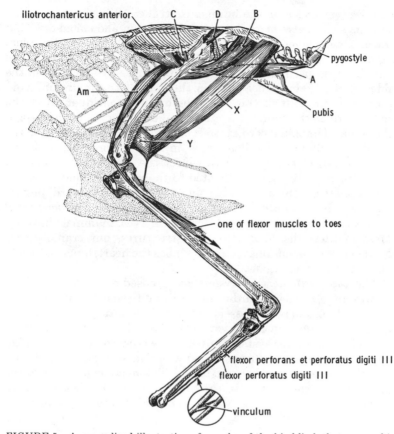

FIGURE 5. A generalized illustration of muscles of the hind limb that are used in the classification of birds. Abbreviations: A, piriformis, pars caudofemoralis; B, piriformis, pars ileofemoralis; C, iliotrochantericus medius; D, gluteus medius et minimus; X, semitendinosus; Y, accessory semitendinosus; AM, ambiens; V, vinculum. (By permission from *Fundamentals of Ornithology* by Josselyn Van Tyne and Andrew J. Berger, published by John Wiley & Sons, Inc. Copyright, 1959.)

pain. Other types of nerve endings account for the special senses and for the activation of muscles and glands (Fig. 6). A "nerve" is a collection of many nerve fibers (both axons and dendrites) held together and surrounded by connective tissue.

The brain and spinal cord form the *central nervous system.* Both exhibit a characteristic pattern of gray matter and white matter. Gray matter contains a concentration of nerve cell bodies; white matter contains mostly nerve fibers. Cerebrospinal fluid fills cavities (ventricles) in the brain, a central canal in the spinal cord, and the space between the surface of the brain and spinal cord and the arachnoid layer of their protective coverings. The cerebrospinal fluid serves as a shock absorber for these vital structures. The bird brain is peculiar in that the optic lobes are located at the sides of the brain rather than in the roof of the midbrain, as in reptiles and mammals (Fig. 7). The brain is continuous with the spinal cord at the foramen magnum, a large opening in the base of the skull. The spinal cord extends backward through a canal in the vertebral column. Swollen areas in two regions (cervical and lumbosacral) of the spinal cord reflect the increase in amount of nerve tissue there; they are related to the wing and hind limb.

Cranial (from the brain) and spinal (from the spinal cord) nerves, together with their sensory and motor endings, form the *peripheral nervous system*. Birds have 11 cranial nerves, mammals have 12. Most of these distribute to head structures, but cranial nerve X (vagus, the "wandering" nerve) supplies the heart, lungs, stomach, and other visceral organs.

The *autonomic nervous system* is composed of motor fibers that distribute to glands, to cardiac muscle, and to smooth muscle of the viscera, skin, and blood vessels. It is an involuntary system in that it regulates functions over which we have little or no conscious control. This motor system consists of two-neuron chains (preganglionic and postganglionic neurons) which involve both the central and the peripheral nervous systems. The nerve cell bodies of the preganglionic neurons lie in the brain or spinal cord; their axons leave the central nervous system as one of several types of nerve

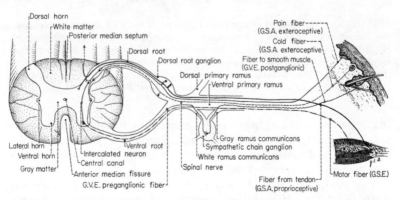

FIGURE 6. Cross section of a human spinal cord and spinal nerve to emphasize different types of nerve fibers. (By permission from *Essentials of Human Anatomy* by Russell T. Woodburne, published by Oxford University Press. Copyright, 1957.)

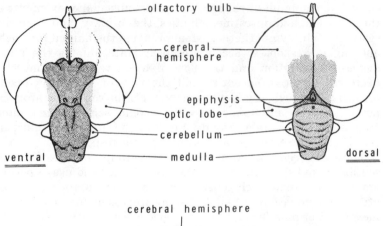

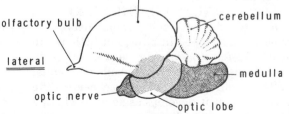

FIGURE 7. A generalized bird brain to show relationships of the several parts; the stippled area in the lower three drawings is the "brain stem" as designated by Adolphe Portmann in his studies of comparative brain development in birds. (By permission from *Fundamentals of Ornithology* by Josselyn Van Tyne and Andrew J. Berger, published by John Wiley & Sons, Inc. Copyright, 1959.)

fibers in spinal and certain cranial nerves. The axons form synapses* with the dendrites of postganglionic neurons, whose axons carry the stimulus to the organ innervated. The cell bodies of the postganglionic neurons tend to be concentrated in special regions, called ganglia, which are located along the vertebral column (chain ganglia) or some distance from it (collateral and terminal ganglia).

Two anatomical or physiological parts of the autonomic system are described: (1) *craniosacral* or *parasympathetic,* associated with cranial nerves III, VII, IX, and X and the sacral portion of the spinal cord, and (2) *thoracolumbar* or *sympathetic,* which has its origin in cervical, thoracic, and upper lumbar segments of the spinal cord in birds. Visceral organs are innervated both by sympathetic and parasympathetic fibers; there is no parasympathetic supply to the limbs or surface of the body. In general, parasympathetic innervation controls vegetative activities: slows heart rate, constricts the pupil of the eye, increases muscular movements of the stomach and intestine, empties the urinary and digestive systems. The sympathetic system prepares the animal for "fight and flight" responses: accelerates heart rate, dilates the pupil, increases respiration and the flow of blood to skeletal muscles, decreases digestive activities and the flow of blood to visceral organs. Although, by definition, not considered an anatomical portion of the autonomic nervous system, sensory (and inter-mediate) neurons are an essential part of the functional reflex arc that involves a sensory stimulus and a motor response.

The *sense organs* are considered in two groups: organs of general sensibility and special sense organs. Specialized endings of periph-eral nerves mediate such general sensations as pain, touch, temper-ature discrimination, pressure, and awareness of the position and movement of muscles and joints. Special senses are mediated by certain cranial nerves (I, II, VII, VIII, IX, X).

Olfaction, the sense of smell (cranial nerve I), appears to be relatively poorly developed in birds, but little reliable information is available. *Vision* (nerve II), on the other hand, is highly developed in birds, and the two eyeballs may equal or exceed the weight of the brain itself. The optic nerve differs from other cranial nerves in that it develops as an outpocketing of the embry-onic brain; it is more properly referred to as a fiber tract of the brain.

---

* A synapse is the region where an impulse is transmitted from the axon of one neuron to the dendrite of another neuron. The method of transmission is in debate, but we know that the synapse controls the direction in which the impulse is directed, i.e., it is polarized.

Movement of the bird's eyes is restricted as compared to mammals, and in owls the eyes are immovably fixed in the orbits by the enlarged sclerotic rings. In order to look from one side to the other, an owl must turn its head. Hawks and owls have their eyes placed anteriorly in the skull so that there is considerable overlap (50° to 70°) in the fields of vision of the two eyes. This binocular vision is advantageous for judging distance in the pursuit of prey. According to Gordon Walls, the Woodcock's eyes are set so far back in the skull that the posterior binocular field of vision probably is much wider than the anterior binocular field. The *pecten,* a folded structure containing many blood vessels, projects into the eyeball from the head of the optic nerve. It appears to function in nourishing the retina, the inner lining of the eyeball that is sensitive to light rays. In rare instances, one or both eyes fail to develop normally. R. D. Lord, for example, reported adult Rough-legged and Red-tailed hawks having only one functional eye. These birds were able to adapt to monocular vision, although it was not known whether they were forced to change their diets.

Taste, like smell, is a type of chemoreception. Details are lacking but nerves VII, IX, and X are thought to carry taste fibers in birds. Birds, as compared to mammals, have few taste buds, especially on the tongue; some birds have taste buds along the edges of the mandibles. The role of taste in food selection by birds is unknown.

The bird's *auditory system* has three parts: external auditory canal, middle ear cavity, and internal ear. An external ear flap (pinna) is absent and the opening of the external auditory canal is hidden by feathers. The external auditory canal ends at the eardrum (tympanic membrane). The middle ear extends from the eardrum to the outer bony wall of the internal ear; it contains a single ear bone (columella); it is connected with the pharynx by the pharyngotympanic tube. The internal ear is a series of membranous channels housed in the temporal bone of the skull. The columella converts the sound waves striking the eardrum into mechanical energy and transmits it to the cochlea of the internal ear for the sense of hearing. Three semicircular canals are responsible for the sense of balance, which involves the coordination of impulses arising in the semicircular canal systems of both inner ears with other sensory stimuli and the subsequent association with motor neurons so that compensatory body movements (head, neck, limbs) can be effected as necessary. Cranial nerve VIII (acoustic nerve), therefore, has two components, one for hearing, the other for equilibrium.

Circulatory System

The circulatory system is composed of the blood-vascular system (heart, arteries, veins, and capillaries) and the lymphatic system (a series of nodes and channels). The heart and blood vessels form a closed system of tubes through which blood is carried to all parts of the body. Blood is composed of a watery fluid (plasma), blood cells (corpuscles), and platelets. Red corpuscles (erythrocytes) carry most of the oxygen that is picked up in the lungs and is distributed to the body cells. Several types of white corpuscles are important in combatting infections. Blood platelets, which are much smaller than corpuscles, play a role in coagulation of the blood. Most of the carbon dioxide (one of the waste products of metabolism) is carried by the plasma to the lungs, where it is discharged. The plasma also carries food materials, hormones, enzymes, antibodies, and waste products.

The heart lies in the anterior part of the body cavity (deep to the sternum), enclosed in a protective sac. Arteries carry blood away from the heart; veins bring blood back to the heart from all parts of the body. A system of microscopic capillaries is interposed between the arterial and venous channels. Capillaries are thin-walled blood channels so small in diameter that they may permit the passage of a single corpuscle at a time. Plasma and some of the white corpuscles pass through the capillary walls and into the spaces between cells, which are bathed by tissue fluid. Some of the fluid passes back into the venous end of the capillary network and thence into the veins.

The heart is a muscular pump which provides the propelling force for the blood. Birds, like mammals, have a four-chambered heart which is divided into completely separated right and left halves. Venous blood from all parts of the body enters the "right heart," passing from its atrium through a right atrioventricular opening into the right ventricle. Contraction of the right ventricle forces the blood through the pulmonary artery and into the right and left lungs, where carbon dioxide is released and oxygen is picked up by the red corpuscles. Pulmonary veins conduct oxygenated blood to the left atrium, from which the blood passes into the left ventricle. Contraction of the left ventricle pumps the blood out through the right aortic arch, whose branches carry blood to all parts of the body except the lungs. Correlated with the greater work necessary to pump the blood throughout the body, the left ventricle has a much thicker muscular wall than the right ventricle. Right and left brachiocephalic arteries, arising from the aortic arch, divide into branches which supply the head, neck, wing, and part of the thorax. The aortic arch turns to the right and dorsally to continue as the dorsal aorta, which courses between the lungs and into the abdominal cavity. The celiac, superior mesenteric, and inferior mesenteric arteries are large, unpaired branches that carry blood to the liver, pancreas, spleen, stomach, and intestine. Paired branches of the aorta supply the esophagus, intercostal muscles, kidneys, reproductive organs, abdominal and pelvic walls, and hind limb.

Blood from the head, neck, chest, and wings drains into the right and left precaval veins, which empty into the right atrium. Blood from the lower half of the body reaches the right atrium via the single postcaval vein. Most of the arterial branches are accompanied by veins bearing the same name as the arteries. A notable exception is the hepatic portal* vein, which receives tributaries from the abdominal portion of the digestive tract and ends in the liver. Large hepatic veins then carry the blood from the liver into the postcaval vein.

Tissue fluid, occupying interstices between the cells of the body, is called lymph when it is absorbed by lymphatic capillaries, which conduct the lymph to progressively larger channels. The largest lymph trunks are paired thoracic ducts which carry most of the lymph from the lower half of the body to the jugular veins at the base of the neck. Emulsified fats resulting from fat digestion are absorbed by special lymphatic channels (lacteals) in the intestine and then are carried to the venous system by way of the thoracic ducts. Lymph nodes (which produce lymphocytes) are said to be uncommon in birds, but lymphatic tissue is found in the thymus gland, the spleen, and in the wall of the intestine.

Respiratory System

The respiratory system consists of the lungs and a series of channels that conducts air to them. In sequence these channels are: nasal cavities, nasopharynx, larynx, trachea, and bronchi (page 164). The external nares, or nostrils, are simple openings into the nasal cavities in most birds, but the opening is modified as a horny tube in albatrosses and their relatives, and as a soft flexible tube in some nightjars. In adult anhingas, cormorants, gannets, and frigatebirds, the nostrils are completely closed (obsolete),

---

*A "portal" system is one that begins and ends in a capillary network. Thus, the hepatic portal vein has its beginnings in the capillaries of the gut wall; the vein again breaks up into capillaries in the liver.

so that the birds presumably must breathe through their mouth. A protective cover (operculum) is attached above the nostrils in some passerines and in gallinaceous birds. The nostrils are exposed in most birds but in some (e.g., grouse, crows) feathers of the forehead extend forward to conceal them.

The trachea is a long tube, located ventral to the esophagus, supported by a series of cartilaginous and bony rings. The entrance (glottis) to the trachea is surrounded by a series of cartilages that form the larynx. The trachea ends by dividing into right and left bronchi, which enter the lungs as mesobronchi. These divide many times to form a complete parabronchial capillary network, which allows a continuous circuit of air through the lungs; consequently, oxygen and carbon dioxide exchange takes place during both inspiration and expiration. Birds are unique in this respect. Another peculiar feature of the avian respiratory system is the presence of thin-walled air sacs which are intricately related to the parabronchial network. Three or four paired sacs are located among the viscera and an unpaired interclavicular sac lies between the two halves of the furcula. Diverticulae (pouches leading off from the main channels) extend into many of the bones, particularly the humerus, femur, ribs, and vertebrae. There is much variation in the amount of pneumatization of bones among different species and individuals of the same species (Fig. 8).

Digestive System

The digestive system begins with the bill and oral cavity and ends at the vent. Correlated with feeding habits, both bill and tongue exhibit many different patterns of shape and structure. The bill varies from the needle-like bill of a hummingbird to the powerful hooked beak of a hawk, from the chisel-like bill of a woodpecker to the flattened spatulate bill of the Roseate Spoonbill (Figs. 9, 10). The bill may be straight, curved upward (recurved), or curved downward (decurved). The crossbill gets its name because the tips of the two mandibles cross each other rather than fitting together. The lower mandible of the skimmer is longer than the upper mandible. In shape the tongue, which may serve as a probe, a capillary tube, a sieve, a brush, or a rasp, may be rectangular, cylindrical, lanceolate, spoon-shaped, flat, cupped, grooved, tubular, bifid; it may be fleshy, horny, spiny, "feathery," brush-tipped, or rudimentary. The tongue and its supporting bones (hyoid apparatus) are specially modified in some woodpeckers in which the long tongue can be protruded some distance beyond the tip of the

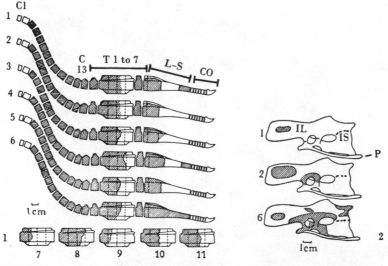

FIGURE 8. Left: Diagrams of vertebral columns of six specimens of the domestic chicken and of the second to fifth dorsal ("thoracic") vertebrae in five additional specimens to show the pneumatized (aerated) bones. Right: Diagrams of left halves of the pelvic girdles of three specimens, showing the pneumatized areas (hatched). The dotted lines show the approximate boundaries between the ilium (IL) and ischium (IS). Other abbreviations: P, pubis; C1 to 13, the 13 cervical vertebrae; T1 to 7, the 7 dorsal vertebrae; L-S, lumbosacral vertebrae, forming the synsacrum; CO, coccygeal vertebrae, including the pygostyle. (Courtesy of A. S. King, from *Acta Anatomica*, 31, 1957, p. 223.)

bill; when the tongue is withdrawn, the posterior hyoid elements curve upward and forward to follow the contour of the skull (Fig. 11).

The oral cavity and the two nasal cavities open into the pharynx. The glottis lies in the floor of the pharynx. Dorsal to the glottis, the pharynx leads into the esophagus, a musculomembranous tube which conveys food from the pharynx to the stomach. A permanent dilation (crop) in the lower part of the esophagus is a reservoir for food in gallinaceous birds, pigeons, doves, and in some passerine birds. The stomach typically is divided into a glandular proventriculus and a muscular ventriculus (gizzard). The proventriculus secretes digestive enzymes; the gizzard aids in grinding up the food. Seed-eating birds eat grit (quartz, pebbles, small shells, etc.), which facilitates the grinding process. Grit may be an important source for such minerals as calcium and phosphorus. Owls, which swallow small mammals whole, are especially noted for regurgitating pellets of indigestible portions (hair and bones), but herons, gulls, and some passerine birds also cast pellets at times.

FIGURE 9. The Caracara, a falcon found in southern Texas and Arizona and central and southern Florida. (Courtesy of Samuel A. Grimes.)

The stomach leads into a short U-shaped duodenum, the first part of the small intestine, which receives the bile duct from the liver and pancreatic ducts from the pancreas. The pancreas lies between the two arms of the duodenum. The long coiled ileum is the second part of the small intestine; it leads into the large intestine (usually called the "rectum" in birds). A pair of caeca mark the junction between the small and large intestine. The large intestine, a short straight tube in most birds, empties into the coprodeum, the innermost compartment of the cloaca. The cloaca (Latin, a sewer) is the common chamber which receives the products of the digestive, excretory, and reproductive systems. It is characteristic of most vertebrate animals; exceptions are some

FIGURE 10. A Roseate Spoonbill. (Courtesy of Samuel A. Grimes.)

fishes and the higher mammals. In birds and reptiles, especially, the cloaca is incompletely separated into three compartments. The large intestine empties into the ventral *coprodeum;* the ureters and genital ducts (oviducts and ductus deferentia), into a dorsal *urodeum.* The coprodeum and urodeum communicate with the

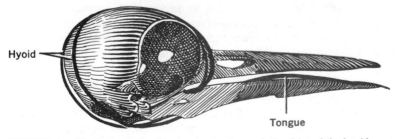

FIGURE 11. Skull of a Hairy Woodpecker to show relationships of the hyoid apparatus to the tongue and the skull.

proctodeum, which opens to the exterior through the vent (often called "anus," which, strictly speaking, is the external opening of the digestive tract, as in most mammals). A cloaca is present during the embryonic development of man and other mammals, but a transverse shelf develops to divide the chamber into a dorsal rectum and a ventral urogenital sinus.

Urogenital System

The urogenital system includes the excretory and the reproductive organs. The nitrogenous wastes of protein metabolism are synthesized to uric acid in the liver and then are excreted by the kidney. Most of the water excreted with the uric acid is reabsorbed during its passage through the kidney tubules and in the proctodeum, where the whitish uric acid is mixed with the feces. The kidneys are long, irregular-shaped structures occupying spaces between the transverse processes of synsacral vertebrae. Tubular ureters carry urine from the kidneys to the urodeum.

The main features of the female reproductive system were discussed on pages 227–230. Male birds possess two functional testes; they often differ in size and shape. Deferent ducts (ductus deferentia) carry sperm cells from the testes to the urodeum. The caudal end of each duct expands into a thick-walled ampullary duct, which passes through the wall of the urodeum as an ejaculatory duct. The highly coiled deferent ducts develop to form seminal vesicles (seminal glomera) during the breeding season. The seminal vesicles in passerine birds hypertrophy to such an extent that they cause an enlargement and protrusion of the cloacal region (Fig. 12). The cloacal protuberance thus formed aids in identifying male birds and in determining the stage of the reproductive cycle. Wolfson (1954) reported that the temperature in the cloacal protuberance averaged about 7° F. cooler than body temperature in several species of sparrows, and he suggested, therefore, that one of the functions of the protuberance might be to provide a region where the sperm can mature at a more favorable temperature. One should recall in this connection that the testes of most mammals are located in the scrotum, where the temperature is lower than body temperature, and that normal spermatogenesis seems to depend on this lower temperature. In some mammals (e.g., squirrels) the testes are retracted into the pelvic cavity during the nonbreeding season but they descend into the scrotum at the onset of the breeding period.

FIGURE 12. The cloacal protuberance of an adult male Swamp Sparrow. Anterior is toward the left and the bird is lying on its back. The cloacal opening is not visible, but it is surrounded by the anal tuft of feathers; usually it is centrally located in the protuberance. Measurements of the protuberance were: anterior wall 6.2 mm.; posterior wall 6.7 mm.; largest diameter 7.0 mm. Photographed June 23, 1952. (Courtesy of Albert Wolfson.)

A copulatory organ develops from the floor of the proctodeum in such birds as the ostrich, ducks, tinamous, gallinaceous birds, storks, and flamingos. This cloacal penis, which can be protruded and retracted by special muscles, facilitates the transfer of sperm to the female's cloaca during copulation.

Endocrine System

The endocrine system is composed of a group of widely scattered "ductless" glands. These endocrine glands secrete chemical substances (hormones; Greek, to set in motion) which, diffusing directly into the blood stream, are carried to other parts of the body to stimulate or regulate the activities of other glands or organs. Thus, hormones, like the nervous system, integrate physiological processes. The pituitary, thyroid, parathyroid, and suprarenal (adrenal) glands are exclusively endocrine glands. The duodenum, pancreas, and the gonads perform both endocrine and exocrine functions. As an endocrine gland, the pancreas secretes hormones (e.g., insulin) which pass into the blood stream and are especially important in carbohydrate metabolism. As an exocrine gland, the pancreas secretes digestive enzymes which reach the duodenum via pancreatic ducts. The secretory activity of the pancreas is controlled by parasympathetic nerves and by a hormone produced in the duodenum. Ova and spermatozoa are the exocrine products of the ovary and the testes. Both gonads also secrete sex hormones which control secondary sex characters and interact with other endocrine glands.

The pituitary gland, suspended from the bottom of the brain, has been called the "master" gland because its several hormones regulate activities of the other major endocrine glands. A lactogenic hormone stimulates the crop glands of pigeons to secrete "pigeon's milk." The thyroid and parathyroid glands lie in the base of the neck in relation to the jugular veins and carotid arteries. The parathyroid hormone controls calcium and phosphorus metabolism. The thyroid hormones influence many metabolic and growth processes (e.g., oxidation, bone formation, feather development, molting). The suprarenal glands lie near the anterior ends of the kidneys and between them and the gonads. Each suprarenal gland is actually a double gland, composed of an inner medulla and an outer cortex. The secretions of the medulla (e.g., adrenaline) produce the same general effects as does stimulation of the sympathetic nervous system. This is not surprising because the medulla and the sympathetic nerve cells develop from the same type of neuroectoderm cells. The cortex, developing from mesoderm, is essential to life. It secretes a number of steroid-type hormones which control fluid and electrolyte balance and protein and carbohydrate metabolism and which regulate bodily reactions to stress. There is an intricate interrelationship among the hormones secreted by the suprarenals, the pituitary, and the gonads, which influences anatomical structures, physiological processes, and behavior. For example, it has been demonstrated, by injecting sex hormones and by castration, that female sex hormones in ducks inhibit development of the male-type syrinx and the penis. When female canaries are injected with male sex hormones, they may sing as well as adult males. Injected females also achieve peck dominance over untreated females and exhibit male-type courtship behavior. Other examples of the role of endocrine organs in life processes were given in Chapters 4 and 8.

WATER AND SALT

All animals must be adapted in some way to maintain a proper water balance with their particular environment, for the protoplasm of most animal cells is about 75 per cent water. Terrestrial animals are faced with the problem of controlling the loss of water from the body. The skin, with its appendages (e.g., hair, feathers, scales), not only protects an animal but is essential for preventing an excessive loss of body fluids beyond that lost in urine and in respiration. Birds lose very little water in excretion because most of the water filtered through the kidneys is reabsorbed, leaving semisolid uric acid salts. However, birds may lose a considerable amount of water in respiration, especially when high air temperatures require evaporative cooling (page 256). In a study of 12 species of desert birds, Bartholomew and Dawson (1953) found that the birds lost more water than was produced by the metabolism of their food, even at moderate air temperatures, and that the loss was much greater for small than for large birds. In order to occupy desert habitats, therefore, the birds must have access to water or to foods that contain large amounts of water. Desert-inhabiting pigeons and doves, which subsist largely on dry seeds, may fly many miles each day in order to obtain water. Bartholomew and Dawson (1954) reported that captive Mourning Doves kept at an air temperature of 39° C. drank four times as much water per day as those kept at 23° C. Doves held without water for 24 hours at the higher temperature might lose 15 per cent of their weight, but could regain this weight within a few minutes after water was made available again. This capacity to endure high temperature and dehydration, plus their strong flight, makes it possible for the doves to inhabit desert areas.

Physiological processes maintain a concentration of salts in the blood stream within certain narrow limits which vary in different animals. Excess salts in mammals are excreted by the kidneys and by sweat glands. A pathological imbalance of the salt-regulating mechanism might result in a drastic increase in the concentration of salts in the blood. Because of the nature of cell membranes, dehydration would result as water passed from the cells of the body into the blood. Death would result if the imbalance were prolonged or extreme. The salt-regulating mechanism of man and other mammals is such that they cannot survive on sea water, and available evidence suggests that even marine mammals do not drink sea water but obtain their water from the foods they eat. For a long time ornithologists have speculated about how sea birds are able to survive without fresh water for drinking. Schmidt-Nielsen and his co-workers were the first to study this problem experimentally, using such birds as penguins, gulls, cormorants, and pelicans. Schmidt-Nielsen and Fange (1958) summarized the problem this way:

In order to profit from the ingestion of sea water it is necessary for an animal to excrete salts in a concentration at least as high as that in the water ingested. The elimination of the salt would otherwise require an additional amount of water which would be taken from the body tissues. Therefore, if the organism cannot excrete a highly concentrated salt solution, the drinking of sea water only will lead to a progressive dehydration or a harmful accumulation of salt.

The bird kidney is able to excrete salts in a concentration only about one-half that found in sea water. Hence, if the bird kidney should excrete the salts from a given amount of sea water, it would be necessary to produce twice as much urine as the amount of water ingested. Thus, the kidney is not able to keep a marine bird in a favorable water balance if it drinks sea water.

Schmidt-Nielsen discovered that a gland (Fig. 13) located in the orbit can secrete a fluid with a higher salt concentration than that in sea water, thereby leaving a net gain of water for the bird. The salt gland (or nasal gland) reaches its highest development in marine birds, and the size of the gland is directly correlated with "the extremeness of the marine habitat." Thus, this provision for

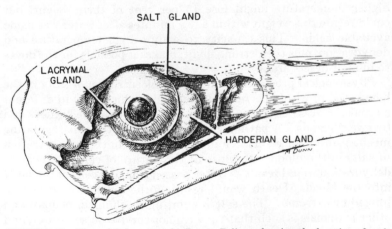

FIGURE 13. The orbital region of a Brown Pelican showing the location of major glands. (Courtesy of Knut Schmidt-Nielsen and the editor of *The Auk*.)

extrarenal salt excretion makes it possible for marine birds to survive without fresh water. It should be noted that one of the functions of the "head-shaking" movements propounded by behavior theorists is to discard the accumulation of salt secretion, which accumulates at the tip of the bill, and, in some instances, this may be its only function.

Among land birds, some species are noted for their habit of eating salt. This habit appears to be characteristic of species which subsist largely on seeds or fruit during certain periods of the year, e.g., quail, doves, the African colies, crossbills, siskins, Purple Finches, and the Evening and Pine grosbeaks.

HIBERNATION AND TORPIDITY

The idea persisted for centuries that swallows and other birds hibernated in mud and that some species even flew to the moon to spend the winter months. These old wives' tales were, of course, without basis in fact, but Edmund C. Jaeger (1949) began a series of observations on Poor-wills in 1946 that revealed that some birds are indeed capable of true hibernation. Jaeger found a Poor-will in a small rock crypt in the Chuckawalla Mountains in southeastern California during December, 1946; so deep was the bird's torpid state that it could be handled and weighed without being aroused. When Jaeger visited the site again in November, 1947, he found a Poor-will in the same spot (Fig. 14). He examined the bird at two-week intervals over a period of 88 days. The bird's temperature varied from 64.4° to 67° F., in contrast to a body temperature of about 106° F. in an active bird. An extreme reduction of general metabolic activities was indicated by the fact that no heart beat or respiration could be detected, and by a slow but continual loss of weight during the hibernation period. The same banded bird was found in the same place the following two winters. Only a few wild hibernating Poor-wills have been found, but much information on physiological activities has been obtained from captive birds. Howell and Bartholomew (1959), for example, discovered that Poor-wills could be induced to enter a torpid state at air temperatures ranging from 2° to 19° C. (35.6° to 66° F.), and that "it seems probable that daily periods of torpor may be interspersed between longer periods of hibernation." The calculated metabolic rate of a hibernating Poor-will is such that 10 grams of stored fat could sustain the bird for 100 days if its body temperature remained at 10° C.

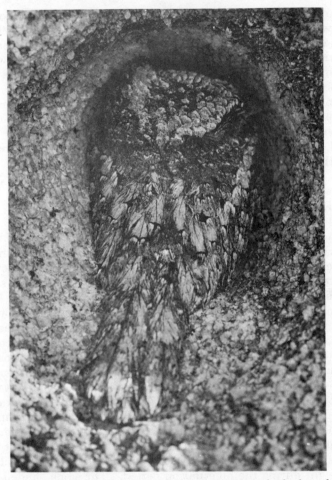

FIGURE 14. Close-up of a Poor-will in its hibernation crypt in the face of granite rock; Chuckawalla Mountains, Riverside County, California. (Courtesy of Edmund C. Jaeger and the editor of *The Condor;* photograph by Kenneth Middleham.)

In the discussion of temperature control (page 253), we pointed out that most adult birds maintain a high body temperature despite low air temperatures. A few species, however, can enter a state of torpor in the face of adverse environmental conditions, and hummingbirds may exhibit a daily cycle involving nocturnal torpidity. In addition to the Poor-will, torpid states have been described for the Lesser Nighthawk, several species of swifts and hummingbirds, and the Old-world coly. Bartholomew, Howell, and Cade (1957) reported that low environmental temperatures are not necessary for the development or maintenance of torpidity in swifts and hummingbirds, but that lowered body temperatures (hypothermia) occurred in two genera of swifts (*Apus* and *Aëronautes*) only after considerable loss of weight. They summarized the advantages to these primarily insectivorous birds of the physiological adaptations permitting a lowering in metabolic activities by stating that "reduced body temperature and torpor provide a means of energy conservation and are associated with high metabolic rates during activity (hummingbirds) or survival during long periods of fasting (swifts and Poor-will)." It should be noted, however, that Howell and Dawson (1954) reported that a female Anna's Hummingbird did not become torpid at any time while incubating the eggs or brooding the nestlings. How the nesting female maintains a fairly constant body temperature (and nest temperature) at night is unknown.

10

Conservation

Conservation is a philosophy. It is a way of life—one that is foreign to much of the ultimately destructive philosophy that pervades government, industry, and society in the United States. Although it seems to be impossible for any political party to sacrifice party interests for the greater good of the entire country, it is fortunate, indeed, that there are (and have been) a few leaders of vision who do place country first. For conservation is far more than a matter of interest to bird watchers and butterfly chasers. Conservation does not imply conserving in the sense of hoarding, or of storing until rot and decay set in. Conservation is the *wise use* of all natural resources: minerals, fuels, soil, water, food, forests, and animals. It must in the future be concerned, as well, with the wise use of manpower.

It is because of the undeniable significance of a sound conservation philosophy for the future welfare of the United States and the world, as well as for wildlife, that we have the temerity to include this short chapter for students of ornithology. It is clear, at the same time, that the student cannot understand birds until he learns how their lives are inextricably related to their environment. Moreover, the education of biologist or nonbiologist cannot be considered complete unless it develops an awareness of man's place in nature and of man's responsibilities to his environment and to society. Freedom without responsibility is a mockery and an illusion.

The ancient Persians and Hebrews recognized to some extent the importance of taking care of the land. Careful land use has been practiced in parts of Europe for many years. George Washington, Thomas Jefferson, and Patrick Henry were aware of the necessity for wise use of resources. In all the years that have followed since their time, however, only one American president has been fully aware of the imperative nature of a sound conservation philosophy for the United States. In 1908 Theodore Roosevelt commented: "Facts which I cannot gainsay force me to believe that the conservation of our natural resources is the most weighty question now before the people of the United States. If this is so, the proposed conference [Governor's Conference] which is the first of its kind will be among the most important gatherings in our history in its effect upon the welfare of our people." Owing to Theodore Roosevelt's dynamic leadership, the foundation was laid for a sound conservation policy for the United States. Unfortunately, his successors have, at best, demonstrated only a superficial comprehension of the nature of the problem (except where it applied to war materials), or a complete disinterest in it save where it was politically expedient to satisfy the strongest pressure group of the moment. The same can be said for the majority of other so-called "public servants."

Fred Smith (1956) put it this way:

THOSE WHO WOULD DESPOIL THE NATION, usurp its resources, and endanger its future for immediate gain more often than not depend upon politics to get their way. Conservationists traditionally have hoped that wide-spread public education would undermine such efforts at exploitation; but important as it is, leisurely education is becoming progressively less dependable in the tight spots because—well, because it is amazing how a talented wordsmith can confuse the most genuinely interested layman by somehow making an out-and-out theft of resources ring out as a thoughtful, considered measure to advance the cause of Conservation.

One would hope that taxpayers eventually would become concerned enough to take action as a result of reports in various periodicals on the waste and folly of some federal programs: a farm program* amounting to $7 billion in fiscal year 1959 alone; $1.5 million spent

---

* Information taken from three articles on "The Farm Surplus You're Paying For," which appeared in the November 30, December 7, and December 14, 1959, issues of *LIFE* magazine; cited here by permission of LIFE, copyright 1959 by Time, Inc.

every day for wheat subsidies; buying crops from farmers and then paying them to store them; paying millionaire farmers up to $40,000 a year for not planting their land, i.e., for doing nothing (Fig. 1). What does this have to do with conservation? Except for the farmers who receive such handsome incomes, this is waste, and, therefore, it is the antithesis of conservation. Wealth cannot be legislated; it must be produced. Waste, whether of soil, manpower, or tax money, can work only to the detriment of the country. This tragic situation can be corrected only when conscientious and informed taxpayers accept their responsibilities.

POPULATION AND THE LAND

The population explosion in the United States and throughout the world has been well publicized. The United States supported about 76 million people in 1900; it has been estimated that the population will number 300 million by the year 2000. And the crisis is already with us, subtle and unrecognized by the uninformed and the disinterested. For some time we have been faced with conditions of overcrowded classrooms and a shortage of competent teachers at all levels; little improvement is in sight. There is a crying need for gifted scientists in *all* disciplines, but the need is less for narrow-minded specialists than for those scientists who, competent in their fields, also are conversant with history, the arts, and the nature of civilizations. By the same token, we need lawyers, sociologists, and artists who have some knowledge of the physical and biological world of which they are a part. There is, as well, a drastic need for more statesmen and for fewer politicians; a broad education for them would not be detrimental.

A mineral and fuels crisis faces us now. Clarence Cottam (1958) reported that

in 1950, the United States comprised about 9.5% of the Free World's population. At that time our consumption of petroleum, rubber, manganese, and iron was 24% to 85% higher than elsewhere outside the Iron Curtain. We also consumed nearly as much zinc, copper, and lead as did all the rest of the non-communist world. Generally our per capita consumption of raw materials other than food is slightly more than ten times as high in the United States as in the rest of the Free World. . . . Since 1914 the United States alone has consumed as much irreplaceable mineral and fuel resources as had been used by the entire world from the time of the first cave man to 1914. (See also Spengler, 1956.)

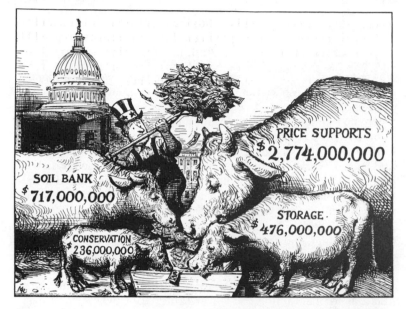

FIGURE 1.   Federal Government supports for 1959.   Another $2.5 billion were required to carry on other Department of Agriculture functions.   Note the small percentage spent for conservation.   It should be pointed out that the Government has no money of its own; these are YOUR tax dollars.   (Reproduced by permission of Michael Ramus and LIFE magazine, copyright 1959 by Time, Inc.)

Cottam further reminded us that

America's large number of ghost towns that were once thriving communities are nothing more than tombstones to dead resources.   They are monuments to short sighted exploitive policies in such businesses as lumbering, grazing, mining, fishing, and farming with accompanying land booms and unwise drainage.

Similar monuments exist in the form of hills of devastation where strip-mining has been practiced in recent years.

The crisis is already with us in the shortage of camping and fishing sites and of other types of outdoor recreational areas (Clawson, 1959).   The crisis is with us in the "simple" things of life: water, the land, and even the air about us.   And this is where we must start in the battle against the "so what?" attitude toward nature and conservation.

WATER

Water is essential to life. The human body is 66 per cent water. The supply of usable water is not inexhaustible. We are dependent ultimately for fresh water on rain and snow, but the distribution of precipitation is very irregular over the earth. There are areas where no rain may fall at all for long periods and other areas where as much as 100 inches may fall in a single month. The amount and kind of vegetation in any area is related to the soil, to temperature, and to the average annual precipitation and its seasonal distribution. Little of the rainfall, whatever the amount, is wasted in areas where man has not disturbed the climax communities, for these tend to be in equilibrium with the total environment (page 77). In a deciduous forest, for example, the layers of leaves and humus covering the ground, and the tree roots in the ground, inhibit the runoff of water, so that it soaks into the soil. Here some of the water (capillary water) is held and is utilized by the plants. Part of the water (gravitational water) percolates downward through the soil and aids in maintaining the water table. But, where the forest is leveled by ax or by fire, the rain pounds the surface and runs off in torrents, carrying with it the soil and inexorably eroding larger and larger ditches and gullies (Figs. 2, 3, 4, 5). It has been estimated that as much as a half million acres of fertile soil are thus carried away each year. Floods cause loss of life and great destruction to land and property. Water tables fall with long-term effects.

Water is essential to industry. Smith (1956) pointed out that

water is a basic raw material common to almost every refining, manufacturing, and fabricating process. Industry alone uses more water than all the other elements of our population could use if everyone went on the water wagon, if we bathed until we grew scales and fins, if we made swamps of our front-yards, if we drenched our fields to the point where only water lilies would grow.

Water is nondestructible, but through pollution our society makes large quantities of it unfit for use. Also, when many of the waste products of industrial processes are dumped into streams and rivers, conditions become intolerable for most aquatic life, whether vegetable or animal. To be sure, we cannot eliminate industry, but we can educate and we can conduct research into methods for making the waste products nontoxic to living things. We repeat that the goal of the conservationist is to make the best use of all resources within the framework of our industrial society. It is imperative,

FIGURE 2. Severely gullied land in Hall County, Georgia. (Courtesy of the U.S.D.A. Soil Conservation Service.)

FIGURE 3. The same field shown in Figure 2, 2½ years after kudzu had been planted. (Courtesy of the U.S.D.A. Soil Conservation Service.)

FIGURE 4. An old gully that is gradually eroding back into better land; Marion County, Iowa. Willows have been planted in the bottom and black locust and other hardwoods on the sides of the gully. (Courtesy of the U.S.D.A. Soil Conservation Service.)

FIGURE 5. The same gully shown in Figure 4, two years later. (Courtesy of the U.S.D.A. Soil Conservation Service.)

however, that industries become increasingly aware of their responsibilities for a serious problem and that they demonstrate a willingness to cooperate with professional conservationists in working out the best solutions. Not all the answers are known, but the forester, the soil scientist, and the game manager have learned a great deal about the intricate interrelations of soil and water and forests and animals.

Millions of fishermen are disinterested in the soil or forests because they fail to realize that good fishing requires more than water. When the ground cover is inadequate, heavy rains fill the streams with silt. As Durward Allen (1954: 79) stated, this

has broadened and shallowed many a northern river, whereas trout need deep holes, plant beds, and riffles. To keep it cool (except at high altitudes), trout water should have plenty of shade, but stream-bank logging and grazing have let the sun into long stretches. Fish also need the cover of bank brush, stumps, snags, and dead-heads; and for many years salvage operations have snaked old pine logs out of the beds of northern rivers and sent them to the mill.

The introduced carp will flourish in these streams when they no longer are suitable for trout or other good game fishes, but what fisherman wants carp? It has been demonstrated clearly that the nature of the soil of the watershed itself is important in determining the productivity of a lake or stream. Good fishing is to be found where the soil is fertile, and poor fishing where the soil is poor. The harvest of fish from artificially fertilized waters has been known to be over 300 per cent higher than in unfertilized waters, when the artificial fertilizing has been done by experts.

THE LAND

Poor land not only makes poor plants and poor people; in general, it makes poor animals. We have mentioned the effect of a calcium-deficient soil on the survival of young pheasants (page 75). An extensive study revealed that rabbits living in areas with a fertile soil were a third larger than those raised on poor land. Not only did these big rabbits have larger leg bones but the bones contained more phosphorus and calcium and were over a third stronger than the bones of the smaller rabbits. Durward Allen has pointed out that muskrats living in streams that drain good farmland have better pelts than those living where the land is poor. Thus it would seem that what is good for the land is good for its animal (and

plant) inhabitants, including man.   As a simple example of the relationship of soil and diet to health in man, we may recall that a high
incidence of endemic goiter is correlated to iodine-deficient areas.

It is fortunate that many good soil conservation practices work
not only to the advantage of those who depend upon the land for
their livelihood but also to the advantage of wildlife.   Contour farming, crop rotation, and land conversion inhibit erosion and enrich
the soil, thereby increasing productivity.   The wise use of farm
wood lots involves protection from fire and grazing and the selective cutting of mature trees.   Such a wood lot provides a continuing income, and it also supports bird and mammal populations from
two to four times higher than a heavily grazed woods can support
(Dambach, 1944).   It would be incorrect to suggest, however, that
all good land use, from the agricultural viewpoint, also is good wildlife management practice.   Drainage of a marsh, for example, might
be advantageous for a farmer but not for muskrats and ducks.
Warbach (1958) reported the changes in songbird populations on
an experimental farm in Maryland over a six-year period.   Drainage of swampy thickets, clearing of brush, and planting changed
the area from a partially abandoned farm with 34 acres in cultivation to a modern conservation farm with 134 acres under cultivation
(Figs. 6, 7).   About 10 per cent fewer species and 40 per cent fewer

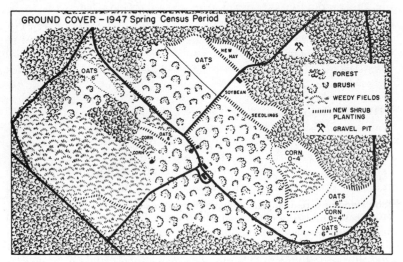

FIGURE 6.   The experimental farm in Maryland at the time of the first census of
songbirds: 34 acres are cropped; 40 acres of two- to three-year-old abandoned fields;
63 acres of fields abandoned 10 or more years.   (Courtesy of Oscar Warbach.)

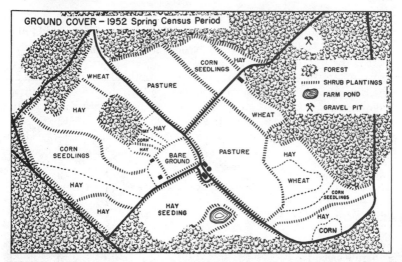

FIGURE 7. The experimental farm in Maryland at the time of the sixth spring census; all fields were being tilled and five miles of plantings had been made as multiflora rose hedges, field borders, and contour hedges. (Courtesy of Oscar Warbach.)

nesting pairs were found during the last three years as compared to the first three years of the study (Table 1).

Overgrazing, whether of wood lot, eastern pasture, or western range, does more than destroy vegetation and reverse the trend of ecological succession. When, for example, desirable perennial grasses are destroyed in the southwestern part of the United States by overgrazing, they tend to be replaced by annual weeds and by cacti. There is at the same time a great increase in rodents, prairie dogs, and other small mammals. As Graham (1947: 186–187) explained the process:

Not only does it appear to be true that misuse of land is the primary cause of the increase in range rodents that compete with livestock for forage; it is conversely true that better land use will decrease their numbers. If grazing cattle are decreased to a number that will permit the range to remain in a good stand of perennial grasses—and this protects the land from erosion and yields better beef—the rodents do not thrive in great numbers. Good range has few rodents, poor range has many.

In other parts of the country, as well, overgrazing destroys the nutritive plants and encourages the invasion by weeds and other plants that are unsuitable as food for grazing animals.

TABLE 1
Changes in Songbird Populations on an Experimental Maryland Farm

Species	Number of Pairs in Each Year					
	1947	1948	1949	1950	1951	1952
Prairie Warbler	34	26	22	6	6	1
Yellowthroat	33	24	27	25 ·	20	19
Field Sparrow	19	23	20	15	12	12
Rufous-sided Towhee	17	16	15	11	12	11
White-eyed Vireo	15	10	13	3	2	2
Catbird	13	19	10	6	5	4
Yellow-breasted Chat	12	8	12	7	3	4
Indigo Bunting	12	15	18	14	20	20
Song Sparrow	4	2	5	2	2	5
Chipping Sparrow	4	4	4	5	5	3
Cardinal	3	5	5	6	6	4
Henslow's Sparrow	3	4	0	3	0	1
Eastern Kingbird	2	3	3	3	3	3
Eastern Bluebird	2	2	1	1	3	+*
Blue Jay	2	2	1	1	1	+
Mockingbird	1	0	1	1	3	2
Grasshopper Sparrow	1	2	1	1	2	3
Robin	+	+	1	1	3	1
Red-winged Blackbird	+	0	+	+	2	3
Eastern Meadowlark	0	0	0	3	4	3

* The symbol + means recorded on fewer than four of the eight census trips of this year. (From Warbach, 1958.)

WILDLIFE

We discussed in the chapter on bird habitats the several environmental factors that influence the distribution of animals. This was, in a sense, an introduction to the broader subject of conservation. Of the environmental factors, we cannot control temperatures over broad areas but we can, by proper land use, control the land, and thereby conserve and control water. We can, therefore, control habitats if we have a mind to do so. Let us consider now some of the things that game managers have learned about environment and animal populations. Game management is only one phase of conservation, but it is important because of the millions of hunters and fishermen who derive recreation from these sports. It is important economically because of the large sums of money spent (and often wasted) by sportsmen and by private, State, and Federal agencies in the attempt to increase the numbers of game animals. It is important also because a host of devoted field biologists have amassed a large amount of information on the relations between good land use and animal populations. Although we speak primarily in terms of game animals, the principles of management apply to songbirds and other animals. The principles are well established. Much needs to be learned about details for different species and ecological conditions, as game managers state repeatedly. They need only time, money, and an informed public and government in order to find more answers.

Reproductive (Biotic) Potential

The rate at which animal populations could increase in a perfect habitat where no mortality occurred would vary with differences in reproductive behavior. For birds, the rate of increase would vary with the number of eggs per clutch and the number of broods raised per year. Thus, a pair of Royal Albatrosses, which care for a single egg in alternate years, would produce only two young by the end of a three-year period. If all adults and young survived, one pair of Bobwhite, with an average clutch of 14 eggs per year, would increase to 1024 birds during three breeding seasons. This innate capacity to reproduce is the *reproductive potential* of a species. However, habitats are not "perfect" and mortality does occur. Some eggs are infertile, embryos die in fertilized eggs, nests are destroyed, and both young and adult birds die or are killed. Inadequate diets lower, or inhibit completely, the physiological capacity to reproduce. The entire complex of factors that prevents the full expression of reproductive potential is called *environmental resistance*. Two examples illustrate the tremendous rates of increase that can occur in nature under favorable conditions. In 1937, Arthur S. Einarsen released two cock and six hen pheasants on a 400-acre island off the coast of Washington, where there were no pheasants and no ground predators. A census made at the end of the fifth breeding season revealed that the population of pheasants exceeded 1500. The full import of reproductive potential is often demonstrated when animals are introduced into areas where their usual diseases, parasites, and predators are absent, as witness the spread and success of the European Starling and the House Sparrow in North America, or the European rabbit in Australia. Near the end of 1859, 24 rabbits were released on an estate in Australia. About 20,000 rabbits were killed during the next six years, yet the rabbit has continued to be a serious problem in Australia ever since.

Carrying Capacity

The concept of the carrying capacity of habitat is the basis for any conservation program involving animals, and it is important whether one is thinking of game animals or songbirds. Briefly, this recognizes that there is an upper limit to the size of population of any species that can be supported by a unit of habitat. The maximum population density varies both with the species and with the habitat itself. An acre of land may support several pairs of nesting Song Sparrows or one pair of Bobwhite, whereas a square mile of good habitat may be necessary to support a breeding population of three or four pairs of hawks. A given habitat may have a high carrying capacity for one species and a low carrying capacity for another species, but the breeding potential of any species cannot be realized on suboptimal habitats. Furthermore, there may be a single *limiting factor* that makes a given habitat suboptimal for a species. A good habitat must provide certain necessities for a non-migratory species throughout the year: suitable breeding sites, adequate food supplies, good winter cover, a balanced predator pressure, and certain conditions of rainfall and temperature. A deficiency in breeding sites or in food or cover at any time of the year might be the limiting factor which makes a potentially good habitat inferior. It is necessary, also, that there be a certain relationship between the environmental components that form good habitat for a species; for Bobwhite or pheasants, for example, food, water, and dusting areas must be close to good cover. This brings us back to the edge effect mentioned in Chapter 3. A wide variety of herbaceous plants, shrubs, and trees interspersed with open areas provide excellent food and cover for many species. It should be recalled, as well, that the limiting factor to population size might be social pressures due to territorial behavior. Moreover, extremes in temperature or precipitation from average conditions, or a drastic increase in predator pressure, may result in considerable fluctuation in populations from year to year even in the best habitat; i.e., the carrying capacity of a given habitat may vary from year to year.

Either limiting or favorable factors may be *density-dependent* or *density-independent.* The effects of density-dependent factors vary directly with the density of the population. As the density increases, for example, competition for food, cover, and safe breeding sites increases. Epidemics of disease may take a higher toll when densities are high. The effects of density-independent factors remain essentially constant (absolutely or proportionally) irrespective of population size. There are exceptions, but, in general, climatic factors exert a density-independent effect and biotic factors a density-dependent effect. "Density-independent aspects of the environment tend to bring about variations, sometimes drastic, in population density and to cause a shifting of upper asymptotic or carrying-capacity levels, while density-dependent natality and mortality tend to maintain a population in a 'steady-state' or to hasten the return to such a level" (Odum, 1959: 208–209).

Limiting factors, of course, not only limit population size; they may make an area totally unsuitable for a species. A species can be established by stocking only where a suitable habitat exists. This has been demonstrated many times by unsuccessful attempts (at great cost) to establish a breeding population by stocking areas with game-farm animals. The carrying capacity of cultivated areas can, in some instances, be improved by following good agricultural practices. Food, cover, and nesting sites are provided when thickets are allowed to develop along fence rows and roads. Where conditions are suitable, multiflora rose forms excellent stockproof fences and wildlife cover.

Ecological succession plays an important part in determining carrying capacity in uncultivated areas. The carrying capacity is greatest for deer and many other species in the early stages of forest development, when there is an abundant ground cover, shrubby growth, and young trees. This optimal habitat also is very susceptible to the destructive effects of an overpopulation of deer.

Harvesting the Crop

Many sentimental people abhor the thought of hunting any wild animal. Yet these same people seem not to be disturbed by the thousands of white-tailed deer that die of starvation every winter. These deer die because the populations are larger than the habitat can support during the critical winter period. The overabundance of deer (as found in many states) results in deterioration of the habitat as the deer eat all of the browse within their reach. Reproduction of shrubs and trees (including the more desirable timber species) may be virtually impossible in areas of large deer populations. Deer on overpopulated areas also tend to be smaller and less fecund. Hence, it is good conservation practice to harvest the surplus crop. Because of public pressure (uninformed, as usual), however, only rarely can enough of the crop be harvested to reduce the population to the carrying capacity of the range (see Durward Allen's excellent discussion of this problem, 1954, Chapter 9).

The reproductive potential of a species is expressed in the tend-

ency to leave as many offspring as possible, and the largest populations occur toward the end of the breeding season. Environmental
resistance begins to take its toll as soon as a bird lays its eggs, or
as soon as a mammal gives birth to young, and continues throughout the fall and winter. As a very broad generalization, one can say
that, regardless of how many offspring a pair of birds produces
during one breeding season, only two birds will be alive to breed
the following year. A population can maintain itself so long as this
breeding stock exists. The animals that the hunter takes are part
of the loss that would occur as a result of the factors that make up
the environmental resistance; these animals would not survive to
reproduce the following year anyway. The hunter actually may
improve the chances of survival for the remaining animals by reducing the population and thus conserving food supplies.

The size of the harvestable crop varies with the species and with
the habitat. A larger crop can be taken from good habitat than
from poor habitat. It has been demonstrated by several investigators that up to 90 per cent of the cock pheasants on good range
in the fall can be killed without adversely affecting the population
the following year, because a spring ratio of 1 cock to 10 hens seems
to be adequate for maintaining the population. Similarly, it is
safe to take a fall harvest of about 50 per cent of a Bobwhite population. The extent of the harvestable crop is known for a few
additional species but much research is still needed on others.

It must be emphasized that we have been talking about abundant
species in good habitat. Annual fluctuations in population size are
to be expected, but a steady decline in numbers of even a large
population (such as ducks) is a warning that a limiting factor is
operating during some stage of the life cycle. Reduction of the
numbers of breeding sites because of drainage of ponds and marshes
appears to be largely responsible for the serious decline in waterfowl populations; in addition, drainage activities along migration
routes concentrate migrants in smaller areas, thus subjecting them
to greater hunting pressure. Decimation of a species can occur
very rapidly in a declining population, so that strict hunting regu-
lations may be necessary until the cause for the decline can be
ascertained and corrected. Rare species, such as the Whooping
Crane, Trumpeter Swan, and California Condor, must be protected
at all times. Even full protection from man, however, may be in
vain after the total population of a species has been reduced to very
low numbers, because there seems to be a minimum population size
below which a species cannot recover despite protection or habitat
improvement.

Predators and Bounties

Some states continue to waste public money by paying bounties for the destruction of certain carnivorous animals despite the overwhelming evidence indicating this to be a futile practice for the control of predators. Moreover, it is doubtful that predator control has any real value as a game management technique. To refer to a species as a "predator" is to damn it at once in the eyes of the uninformed. The fact is that many thousands of species are predators in the sense that their food consists largely of smaller animals. The "bad" predators are those that feed on Bobwhite, pheasants, rabbits, and other animals that man himself wishes to prey upon. In reality, inadequate habitat rather than predation usually is responsible when the sportsman fails to find his limit of any game species. Moreover, the hunter of predators rarely discriminates between the highly beneficial and the less beneficial predators. We use the phrase "less beneficial" for those species (e.g., Cooper's and Sharp-shinned hawks) that may subsist almost exclusively on birds (most of them nongame species) because predation is but one of the factors which contribute to environmental resistance.

It should be realized that the staple diet for most hawks, owls, and the smaller predatory mammals consists of rodents, and that the rodents relieve the predator pressure on other species. Rodent populations are characterized by striking and rapid fluctuations in numbers. At the peak of their population cycle, the animals may cause great destruction to their habitat as well as to farm crops. Considerable evidence indicates a direct relationship between the availability of rodents and the number of young produced by predatory species. Clutch sizes are considerably larger when food is abundant, and some species apparently suspend breeding activities entirely during years when rodents are scarce.

As part of the total environment, predators play a role in maintaining a biotic equilibrium. John and Frank Craighead (1956: 184) defined biotic equilibrium as a "dynamic state in which interrelated animal population densities fluctuate about a mean in such a manner that extremes either do not occur or if they do are quickly limited by natural regulating forces of the environment." Their extensive studies of predator-prey relations led them to conclude (page 245) that "predation operates as a stabilizing or regulating force—a balance of nature process—both under wilderness conditions, where the members of the fauna have relatively few drastic ecological adjustments to make, and on intensively utilized land, where the fauna is altered and its members are adjusted to rapid man-made changes."

Refuges, Sanctuaries, and Wilderness Areas

The establishment of private, State, and Federal refuges and sanctuaries is one management technique that has received considerable publicity. All such areas are established to protect one or more species of animal. The term "sanctuary" usually is applied to an area (either private or public) in which all plants and animals are protected. The implication of the word "refuge" is that legal protection from hunting is provided. Game managers have become skeptical of the value of this kind of refuge because they are convinced that for most species the gun is not a limiting factor. In fact, the function of some waterfowl refuges is not necessarily to benefit the species but to hold birds in an area to provide local hunters an opportunity which they would not otherwise have. The decline in waterfowl populations appears to be due in large measure not to hunting but to insufficient breeding grounds as a result of wholesale drainage of marsh areas. Refuges and sanctuaries make possible the preservation of breeding and feeding sites, the improvement of habitat, and, in some instances, the increased propagation of breeding stocks that may be used for repopulating other regions.

It must be emphasized that the successful development of any protected area depends primarily on the preservation of existing suitable habitat and the improvement of suboptimal habitat. In one sense protected areas (whatever they are called) are necessary because of the long years of irresponsible land (and water) management. They are not an adequate substitute for wise land use throughout the country or for an informed public. In a second sense, however, the preservation of native habitat and wilderness areas in all parts of the country becomes increasingly important in view of our expanding population and the millions of people who now derive great pleasure from visiting national parks and other wilderness areas each year. Our physical standard of living is higher than that in any other part of the world, but our philosophical standard of living has lagged far behind. The esthetic value of wilderness areas must yet be recognized for its true worth before such areas will be free from continuing pressures to invade or destroy them for temporary financial gain. A concerted effort is now being made by several conservation-minded organizations to inform legislators and the public about the long-term significance of the wise use of natural resources, but in many instances these organizations must concentrate on preserving some area that previously had been thought to be inviolate.

A significant and encouraging step was taken in 1956 when the Michigan Conservation Commission voted to set aside and manage some State forest lands for the Kirtland's Warbler, in what appears to be the first management program established for the benefit of a songbird species (Figs. 8, 9).   This decision was made by an informed and alert Commission after considering a realistic and sound proposal prepared by Harold Mayfield, long a student of Michigan's "own bird."   The Michigan Audubon Society was then invited to name an advisory committee to work with the Michigan Department of Conservation, whose responsibility it was to establish and manage the reserve.   The advisory committee, with Mayfield as chairman, filed its recommendations with Mr. G. S. McIntire, Chief of the Forestry Division, in July, 1957.   Plantings, in accordance with the committee's recommendations, were made the following spring, less than two years after the original decision had

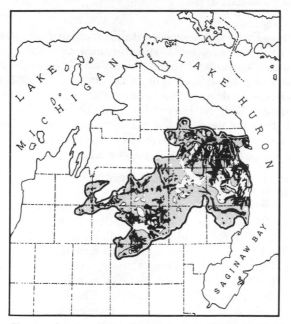

FIGURE 8.   The complete known breeding range of the Kirtland's Warbler is an area less than 100 by 60 miles in Michigan.   (By permission from *Fundamentals of Ornithology* by Josselyn Van Tyne and Andrew J. Berger, published by John Wiley & Sons, Inc.   Copyright, 1959.)

FIGURE 9. Kirtland's Warbler habitat in an area of natural jack pine growth.
(Courtesy of Harold Mayfield.)

been made. Three areas, each containing about four square miles,
were selected as being most suitable and available within the
present breeding range of the Kirtland's Warbler. Over 100,000
jack pines were planted in each of two of the areas in 1958; the third
area was left to be developed at a later date when the present jack
pines would be ready for harvesting as pulpwood. The committee
suggested that the needs of the warbler could be met best by developing semiopen lands with trees in three age groups, providing a
21-year cycle in three steps of 7 years each:

1. Trees 5 to 8 years old: just becoming suitable as breeding
habitat for Kirtland's Warblers.
2. Trees 12 to 15 years old: prime habitat for the warblers.
3. Trees 19 to 22 years old: habitat no longer suitable for the
warblers; area ripe for burning and replanting. Available evidence
suggests that openings are as important as conifers in producing a
suitable habitat for this warbler. Consequently, the plantings were
made in strips one chain (66 feet) in width, separated by un-
planted strips, also one chain in width. The Forestry Division, as
a matter of course, made all plantings in rows curving to follow the
edge of existing stands of trees (Fig. 10).

A census made in 1951 indicated that the total population of the
Kirtland's Warbler amounted to fewer than 1000 birds. It is con-

ceivable that this species might not recover from a serious reduction in the population because of a catastrophe either on the breeding grounds or in the winter home. A continuing decrease in breeding habitat because of more efficient fire control and the demands of an expanding population might also prove disastrous to the species. This experiment in the management of a nongame species of considerable scientific interest will provide information not only on the biology of the Kirtland's Warbler and associated species but also on forestry techniques in the relatively sterile pine barrens of central Michigan.

Pesticides

A pesticide (herbicides and insecticides) is a chemical agent that is used to kill any plant or animal that proves to be a nuisance to man. Pesticides have been employed for many years, but only since World War II, when DDT became available, has their use developed into a national problem. The public in general was ob-

FIGURE 10. The beginning of jack pine planting on a Kirtland's Warbler reserve in Crawford County, Michigan, April, 1958; 2½ strips completed. A few pairs of warblers occupied the habitat in the upper part of the picture. (Courtesy of the Michigan Conservation Department.)

livious to the dangers inherent in the indiscriminate application of chemicals until the sale of cranberries was banned just before Thanksgiving in 1959. In this instance, the Secretary of Health, Education, and Welfare was condemned from many sides for his courageous action; but it was time that the public became aware of the problem. However, the magnitude and the insidious nature of this problem are appreciated by all too few people, including those in industry and government who are in a position to do something about it. Thousands of different pesticides are now sold, many of them far more dangerous than DDT.

The situation is not unlike that encountered immediately after the "wonder" drugs became available. Penicillin and some of its successors were used indiscriminately by many physicians, and some patients even insisted that they be treated with one of the antibiotics. Most of these drugs, however, have a far greater specificity than the insecticides. Failure to isolate and identify the cause of the human infection meant that the drug used often had absolutely no effect on the causative agent but it did play havoc with the normal and beneficial organisms in the digestive tract, which constitute part of the body's defense system against infection and disease. More significantly, in a sense, some human disease organisms developed strains that were resistant to certain drugs, and, in some instances, these resistant strains were more virulent than the previous strains. This serious, even fatal, problem was recognized in a relatively short time because man was directly concerned.

Unfortunately, as has often been the case where wildlife and conservation are concerned, the earliest and most vociferous outcries against insecticides came from sentimentalists and extremists who were concerned primarily about the death of a few songbirds, and who would almost go so far as to propose a ban on the use of all insecticides. Moreover, self-styled "authorities," whether "scientists" or not, typically based their statements on pure subjective impressions or on studies so superficial in scope that they did not warrant being called research at all. Therefore, not only was their stand unrealistic and unsound but it was based on evidence so flimsy that no responsible leader in industry, government, or science could accept it. We do not mean to suggest that leaders in these fields were alert to the gravity of the situation, but we do mean to insist that a careful and scholarly approach is imperative in attacking any complex problem related to conservation, health, and the public welfare. The mediocrity that characterizes our society and much so-called "research" (whatever the source of funds) is indefensible, particularly in these times.

If we ignore the intentional distortions in the literature and the exaggerated, emotional, and sensational predictions, we can set down some statements that seem to have a basis in fact. Insecticides are poisons. Most of them will kill any animal, including man, providing the dosage is large enough (and this can often be very small). Many are cumulative in their effects; once taken into the body they are stored there permanently. Very little reliable information is available on the indirect or long-term effects of these poisons. Most insecticides are nonspecific in their action; they kill friend and foe alike—the beneficial and the harmful insects, as well as mammals, birds, fishes, crabs, etc. More than 40 species of insects have already developed a resistance to one or more of the insecticides. It has been demonstrated that some hydrocarbon compounds can produce fatal human diseases (e.g., leukemia). Not only are hydrocarbon compounds the basic ingredient of many of the newer and more potent insecticides but, as petroleum distillates, they are used as suspension agents. This would seem to have significance to the human population and its food supply when one reflects that over 2 billion pounds of such chemicals may be sprayed over 100 million acres of land in a single year. One needs to bear in mind, also, that the human population encounters many other petroleum distillates in its environment. Among these are gasoline, dry-cleaning solvents, paint thinners, fuel oils, and various industrial solvents.

Insecticides are here to stay. They are necessary for the protection of the health of man and domestic animals and for the protection of crops. But it is imperative that they be used wisely.

Even in the light of this conservative estimate of the situation, one would fully expect that responsible leaders in both industry and government would proceed with utmost caution in their programs and would take every possible measure to inform the public of the dangers inherent in the use of insecticides. This, however, has not been the case. Perhaps the most revealing, and well-documented, example, is the program of the U. S. Department of Agriculture for the "eradication" of the fire ant in the southern part of the United States, although no insect has ever been eradicated in this country. Two potent insecticides (dieldrin and heptachlor) have been broadcast from the ground or from airplanes over several hundred thousand acres. These insecticides are effective in killing the ants as well as most other animals. Congress appropriated $2.4 million for the eradication program for the fiscal year of 1958; no money was appropriated for research. The same amount for eradication was appropriated for 1959; $125,000 was appropriated to the Fish and Wildlife Service for research on the effect of pesticides on wildlife. At the time that the Department of Agriculture requested its first funds for this program, however, very little was known about the fire ant. John L. George wrote (1958):

> Knowledge of both the biology and the economic significance of the fire ant is limited. Although it is commonly stated that the ant is a serious agricultural pest, little concrete evidence is available of actual damage to crops and forests. It would seem that the fire ant is more a nuisance than a crop pest. . . . The insecticides being used are highly effective against the fire ant, but the program was initiated with little knowledge of the overall effects upon the environment of the widespread aerial applications. No study has been made of the probable benefits of pest eradication as against probable damages to wildlife and possible hazards to agriculture and to man.

One of the most heavily infested states is Alabama, yet during 1959 the Alabama legislature refused to appropriate matching funds to continue this unsound program in that state. But there is an even more insidious part of the story. In referring to the fire ant program, Clarence Cottam (1959) said that "attempts have been made in four states, through legislative and congressional representatives and by other means, to have wildlife research men fired or transferred because their conclusions were contrary to the claims and desires of the proponents of control. Do we need better proof that this subject needs a public airing?" One may ask a further question: Is it any wonder that some of the most competent and respected leaders in the conservation and wildlife management fields have resigned from Federal service in recent years?

An important step was taken in 1960 when the National Academy of Sciences–National Research Council established a Committee on Pest Control and Wildlife Relationships. Some of the objectives of the committee are these:

1. To provide technical advice and guidance to government agencies, industries, and other public and private organizations and individuals on problems involved in the maximum control of pests with a minimum of damage to other forms of plant and animal life.

2. To provide critical evaluation of information concerning the effects (direct and indirect) of various pest control operations on plants and animals, particularly fish and wildlife.

3. To stimulate and encourage research to obtain factual information as a basis for sound guiding principles and policy determinations.

This committee faces a formidable task. Success can be achieved only with the full cooperation of the Federal Government and industry.

The need for a much more concerted effort toward conservation education at all levels of American society is essential. The conservation of natural resources is an integral part of the over-all economic, social, and moral mobilization plan that is imperative in the continuing struggle between the free world and the Communist world. Failure in any part of this plan could be catastrophic for our society and for the free world.

Systematics, or taxonomy, is the science of arranging or classifying the forms of life. A system of classification attempts to reflect the evolution and relationships of animals, and it provides categories of names which permit the interchange of information among biologists. Although modern systems of classification are based on phylogeny, it is to be emphasized that phylogeny and classification are not the same thing. Phylogeny is the actual evolutionary history of animals. Systems of classification represent man's attempt to reconstruct the evolutionary history and to express the relationships among living animals.

THE TAXONOMIC HIERARCHY

We pointed out in Chapter 2 that the species is the basic taxonomic category that every student must learn because the species is what he actually observes in the field, in the laboratory, and in the museum collection. In order to appreciate the place of the species in the entire scheme of things, however, the student needs to be familiar with the taxonomic hierarchy. This consists of a series of obligatory groupings for all animals: kingdom, phylum, class, order, family, genus, and species. Other categories sometimes are used in the at-

11

Systematics

tempt to express natural relationships more clearly. These are formed by adding the prefixes super, sub, and infra to certain terms of the basic hierarchy. The classification of the Blue-winged Warbler in hierarchic order is:

Kingdom	Animalia
Phylum	Chordata
Class	Aves
Subclass	Neornithes
Superorder	Neognathae
Order	Passeriformes
Suborder	Passeres
Family	Parulidae
Genus	*Vermivora*
Species	*pinus*

Every student would like to have a list of taxonomic characters that would distinguish all the orders, another list applicable to families, a third list for recognizing subfamilies, etc. Unfortunately, it is not possible to prepare such lists. We said on page 34 that the different kinds of nuthatches are placed in the genus *Sitta* to suggest that they are closely related and that they are presumed to have evolved from a common ancestor. Similarly, the Common Crow and several other large black birds are placed in the genus *Corvus* to suggest their close relationship. However, the features which characterize the nuthatches are not the same as those which characterize the crow-like birds; and so we find, at the beginning, that the characteristics of the genera differ from each other. Inasmuch as subfamilies are composed of groups of genera, and families are composed of groups of subfamilies, the diagnostic features will vary among the subfamilies, the families, and the orders. This means that the taxonomist must find the diagnostic characters by studying the birds. One must bear in mind that only the species are found in nature; the other categories are conceived by man.

"The use of taxonomic characters in classification is based on the simple fact that some characters change very rapidly in evolution, while others only change slowly. The rapidly changing characters are used to distinguish subspecies and species; the slowly changing ones are used to characterize the higher categories" (Mayr et al., 1953: 123). Let us now examine this "simple fact." Theoretically, taxonomic characters fall into five main groups: morphological, physiological, ecological, ethological, and geographical. In actual practice, every classification of the world's birds has been based almost exclusively on morphological and geographical criteria. This has not led to unanimity on the number of orders of birds. Wetmore (1951, 1960) recognized 27 orders; Mayr and Amadon (1951) recognized 28 orders. Erwin Stresemann placed the birds of the world into 49 orders in 1934, into 51 orders in 1959. The situation does not improve if one considers the different classifications of families, subfamilies, and genera. The student must recognize that the avian taxonomist is dealing with a complicated subject, and he must realize that systems of classification are not as final as they appear in printed form. Basically, two systems of classification are used in the United States: that proposed by Ernst Mayr and that proposed by Alexander Wetmore and all other American ornithologists who have published on the subject.

SPECIES AND SUBSPECIES

No phase of avian taxonomy causes as much confusion to the beginning student—and to the world at large—as the concepts of the species and the subspecies. This confusion is aided and abetted by the taxonomist's boundless confidence in his own writing and thought processes. Precise definitions are, of course, important in taxonomy as in any other branch of science, and the taxonomist expects nontaxonomists to use these precise definitions even though he may disdain to be fettered by precise definitions from other disciplines. For example, the anatomical definition of the term "arm," as given on page 12, has been ignored by taxonomists, who use this word to mean any part of the upper limb except possibly the hand and fingers.

A species may be defined as a population of similar individuals occupying a definite (and usually continuous) geographical range and breeding among themselves but normally not breeding with individuals of other species. We have said that Robins, Blue Jays, Cardinals, and Song Sparrows are examples of species (page 34). We have pointed out that variation is characteristic of all animals, and (page 233) that the inheritance of variations has far-reaching implications that involve survival and speciation (i.e., the formation of new species).

The Song Sparrow and the Swamp Sparrow are two closely related species whose breeding ranges coincide over a large portion of the eastern United States. These two species remain distinct because they do not interbreed. They are described as being *reproductively isolated*. Reproductive isolation may be effected because of ethological factors (differences in advertising song or call notes, or in display and other types of behavior patterns), as mentioned in Chapters 5 and 7. The Song Sparrow and the Swamp Sparrow tend to be ecologically isolated as well, because, in general, they select different types of breeding habitats. These two species of sparrows are examples of *sympatric species:* both are found in the same general areas but they do not interbreed. *Allopatric species* are those whose breeding ranges do not coincide or overlap at all, so that interbreeding is impossible.

The Song Sparrow has an extensive breeding range, from the Aleutian Islands and Newfoundland southward into Mexico and much of the United States. If one examines specimens collected throughout the breeding range, one is impressed by differences in size and intensity of coloration (Fig. 1). There is no doubt that all are Song Sparrows, but the differences between some specimens are so striking that populations from different parts of the range are called *subspecies* or geographical races. They are identified by adding a subspecies name to the generic and specific name. For example, the race of Song Sparrow that breeds in Michigan and adjacent areas is identified by the name *Melospiza melodia euphonia;* a resident race in the Aleutian Islands, as *Melospiza melodia maxima.* In all, 31 different subspecies of Song Sparrow are listed in the American Ornithologists' Union Check-List (1957). These subspecies are recognized because each is more or less morphologically distinct from each of the other races and because it is assumed that reproductive isolating mechanisms have not yet evolved—i.e., it is assumed that fertilization of eggs would result from the interbreeding between birds from any of the populations. The differences in size and color are, so far as is known, examples of hereditary variation. It should be noted that superficial morphological differences are only external manifestations of possible gene changes, which influence physiological processes in the animal, and of these we know very little. The degree of morphological difference is not necessarily a reliable indicator of the extent of physiological modification produced by gene change. Profound internal modifications might result from gene mutation, with little or no change in the external appearance of the animal.

The theory of *geographical speciation* postulates that new species arise because of gene changes which effect reproductive isolating mechanisms when subspecies are geographically isolated for long periods of time. Sibley (1957) and others have suggested that speciation might also take place in situations brought about by a breakdown of barriers so that a secondary contact occurs between two populations before reproductive isolating mechanisms have

FIGURE 1. Some geographical races of the Song Sparrow. From top downward: *Melospiza melodia sanaka,* Aleutian Islands, Alaska; *M. m. caurina,* southeastern Alaska; *M. m. samuelis,* Vallejo, California; *M. m. montana,* Chiricahua Mountains, Arizona; *M. m. saltonis,* Oak Creek, Arizona; *M. m. mexicana,* Lerma, Mexico.

developed. These mechanisms then are presumed to develop as a result of sexual dimorphism and various sorts of species-specific signal characters (the social signals discussed in Chapter 7).

The subspecies concept is a cherished one, especially by those who like to see their own name perpetuated as part of the scientific name of a bird, and by those who revel in examining bird skins and then giving free reign to their imagination. This approach has certain advantages because one deals primarily with theories and is not hampered by considering facts. The conjuring up of theory has a real place in ornithology if it is based on adequate data and on accurate concepts concerning the biological responses of living animals to the total environment. Some of these responses are known but their significance is imperfectly known, at best. There is in general an inverse relationship between the force of an author's positive statements about taxonomic relationships and the amount of data available to support those statements. A typical description of a newly proposed subspecies often begins with this sort of statement (from a 1958 paper): "Similar to . . . but decidedly paler in color and averaging smaller in size." Such a specimen usually is "unquestionably" an example of one or another population; in most instances, nothing is known about the breeding behavior of either population. A statistical approach (generally on too few specimens) then follows, whereupon the author concludes that two populations may be "subspecifically separable" on the basis of bill size, etc., and then names a new subspecies. Sometimes this is done because the author feels it "desirable" to publish "preliminary taxonomic findings" before completing a major paper on the same subject.

THE TAXONOMIC METHOD

As pointed out above, morphological, physiological, ecological, ethological, and geographical features may be used in attempting to determine the relationships among birds. Obviously, therefore, the beginning student should not initiate taxonomic studies (at the subspecies level or higher categories) until he learns something about anatomy, physiology, behavior, and the nature of living populations of animals. At the same time, the beginning student should not allow himself to be overwhelmed by taxonomic papers. Perhaps he will be encouraged if we express the opinion that it is doubtful that over a third of all the avian taxonomic papers published during the past 60 years are worth the paper they are written on.

Instead of discussing the methods theoretically used by taxonomists, therefore, it seems more pertinent to give the student some idea of the basis for current systems of classification and to give him some insight into the nature of the typical taxonomic study.

The distinguished German ornithologist Erwin Stresemann commented (1959) that on the whole all the avian systems presented in the standard works in this century are similar to each other, since they are all based on the works of Max Fürbringer and Hans Gadow, two brilliant German anatomists and ornithologists of the last century. Stresemann pointed out that "Fürbringer, with his incomparable practical experience, has frankly admitted that the decision in questions of relationship is very often based on rather subjective considerations," for Fürbringer himself had written: "At the present time only very little is completely certain, some is highly probable, the majority of the groupings are however probable only to a medium degree." Although Fürbringer and Gadow apparently studied the anatomy of more birds than anyone before or since their time, they could dissect representatives of only a few of the more than 8000 species of birds. In fact, most birds are allocated to families not because their anatomy (or breeding behavior) is known but because they "look like" some other species. As Stresemann remarked: "In many cases the systematist who wants to place an aberrant species of song bird is essentially forced to rely on intuition and courage. I am amazed at the courage which is apparent in some of the most recent attempts to classify the Oscines." He might have added that authors who use their "intuition" in this way rarely state that this is their basis for classification. More often they add a muscle formula, a reference to the syrinx or some other anatomical structure, and then clinch the argument by stating that two forms are "obviously related." An important difference between Fürbringer and many contemporary ornithologists is that the latter have immeasureably more confidence in inadequate data. Further studies of bones, muscles, and feather tracts have shown that there is no easy solution to the question of the phylogeny of birds. Thorough anatomical studies of all the members of any given taxonomic unit are needed in order to provide more information on the functional and taxonomic significance of anatomical differences. It is clear that the search for a few "reliable" diagnostic anatomical characters is in vain. Stresemann suggested that the systematist

confine his comparative studies to representatives of the same order, family, or genus, the close relationship of which facilitates separation of relatively recent *functional* modifications from the more stable and taxonomically more important structures. He will be fascinated by this topic, for every true naturalist has been uplifted by the discovery of interrelations between form and function. In this field he is sure to move on firm ground and does not need to bridge the gaps in our knowledge by flimsy speculations.

Most taxonomic work in recent years has involved subspecies, species, and genera. Interest in speciation was kindled by Ernst Mayr's stimulating publications on geographical speciation and the biological concept of the species and subspecies (in contrast to a static morphological concept). Few of the ornithologists who jumped on this bandwagon possessed Mayr's background, however, and many poorly conceived speculations on hereditary variation and presumed relationships have been published after the examination of museum skins. Some taxonomists have considered the significance of courtship patterns and nesting behavior for revealing relationships. Lack (1956a, b) correlated his extensive knowledge of the breeding behavior of swifts with external features that typically are used to characterize genera of birds. Under a discussion of critical taxonomic characters in swifts, Lack concluded that "some of the morphological characters previously relied upon for classifying swifts give misleading results." For example, he found feathering of the toes, position of the toes, furcation of the tail, and the size of the birds to be unreliable characters for determining relationships. On the other hand, color pattern, geographical range, and nesting habits proved extremely useful to Lack in reclassifying these birds. However, taxonomic approaches that seem significant to one person may not appear significant to another. Hence, referring to Lack's work, Johnston (1956) commented: "I grant that a systematist's insight is perhaps his most valuable tool and that statistics are only a means of gaining additional insight, but there seems to be no excuse for the author's anachronistic presentation. His views may be the very best possible at this time on the genus *Apus;* if this is true, they represent probably the last triumph of 19th-century taxonomy."

Bock (1956) used a different approach in his study of the herons. He noted that "color by itself is one of the poorest characters on which to base generic or higher groups," but, on the other hand, "color pattern is more conservative than color alone and is useful in grouping species of herons at the generic level." Bock also found the structure of feather plumes (Figs. 2, 3) useful in judging relationships, although "plumes, like many other characters because of their function . . . , are not constant within a genus; indeed, it is the rule rather than the exception for the plumes to break down as a

FIGURE 2. A Reddish Egret, showing specialized feather plumes on head, neck, and back. (Courtesy of Samuel A. Grimes.)

diagnostic generic character in a genus containing more than one biogeographic species." However, if one considers their function, "plumes, although very variable, can serve as valuable characters at all levels in the family, but are most useful at the specific and generic levels." Bock also considered other external features (powder down patches; bill shape; toes and claws; proportions—e.g., some herons are short-legged and chunky-bodied birds), calls, and courtship and nesting habits (although knowledge of the biology of herons "is still very sparse"). In his complete reclassification of the herons in order to "keep systematics in accord with the recent advances in knowledge of the principles of evolution, phylogeny, and related fields," Bock reduced the number of genera from 32 to 15 and the number of species from 70 to 64. He then reported: "I am continuing study of the relationships of the Ardeidae and have started an investigation of the comparative and functional anatomy of the herons." Thus, the student should note that although anatomy is the primary basis for classification, the taxonomist apparently feels no need to consider the internal anatomy of the group he is classifying.

There can be little doubt that some behavior patterns may be used to advantage as clues to relationship, providing the patterns are understood and are employed in conjunction with anatomical and other criteria. Taxonomists, ever on the alert for new clues to bird relationships, welcomed the suggestion that fixed-action patterns (page 133) were "just as stable as anatomical structures," and sometimes asserted that certain birds were related because they

FIGURE 3. A Snowy Egret. (Courtesy of Samuel A. Grimes.)

"always" performed a given action in the same way. However, further study has shown that behavior patterns, like anatomical structures, must be analyzed very carefully if they are to advance our knowledge of phylogenetic relationships. K. E. L. Simmons stated in 1957 that "birds scratch their heads in one only of two ways, either directly or indirectly, and one method is used by all members of the same family." A bird is said to scratch its head "directly" when its foot is brought up under the wing; in "indirect" scratching, the wing is drooped and the foot is brought up over it. Nice and Schantz (1959) reported that "the method of head-scratching proves to be less stereotyped than has been assumed. Diversity may exist within a family, a genus, or among individuals of the same species, and the same individual may use both methods." Hence, another "perfect" taxonomic character proves to be unreliable.

One of the most recent fads in avian taxonomy is the electrophoretic analysis of egg-white and blood-serum proteins. Ornithologists owe a debt of gratitude to Sibley and Johnsgard (1959), who initiated a study to determine both the uses and the *limitations* of this technique for determining closeness of relationship. They concluded:

> If reliable quantitative measurements of avian sera are desired, sample size must be large, the birds must be healthy, and they must be separated by age and sex, just as in studies of morphological characters.
>
> Quantitative characteristics in avian sera are less reliable than qualitative ones, thus more weight should be given to the latter if comparative studies are undertaken.
>
> Blood serum profiles of different species of birds tend to be more alike in their qualitative composition than are egg albumen profiles, thus serum provides fewer sources of qualitative specific variation upon which to base taxonomic decisions than does egg white.

These conclusions should serve as a deterrent to the initiation of a rash of superficial electrophoretic studies and subsequent untenable taxonomic conclusions.

CONVERGENCE AND DIVERGENCE

By this time, the student must wonder why authorities, who are presumably equally competent, do not agree on the taxonomy of birds. Van Tyne and Berger (1959) summarized a number of factors that complicate the analysis of bird relationships, but two related phenomena probably cause most of the difficulty: *conver-gence* and *divergence*. Most ornithologists agree that each species is more or less adapted for life in a particular ecological niche (Fig. 4), and that most ecological niches are occupied. As a simple explanation of divergence (or adaptive radiation), we may assume that a single species invaded two islands and that the birds then remained on their respective islands. We may assume, also, that mutations of genes occurred over a period of time and that the mutations in the population on island A were different from those in the population on island B. We will assume that the two popu-lations became more and more dissimilar in external appearance and that reproductive isolating mechanisms evolved. We would then

FIGURE 4. A Spoon-bill Sandpiper, an example of remarkable specialization of the bill.

have two new species, both of which were unlike the parent or
ancestral species from which the original invasion had come. Let
us assume that on only one occasion a part of species A left island
A and invaded island B. Species A and B could live on island B
without competing with each other because each was adapted to a
particular habitat, ecological niche, or feeding habit. With the
passage of time and additional mutations, ecological isolating mechanisms might evolve in the population of species A on island B so
that we would have a third species distinct from its sister species
on island A. By means of this process of speciation when populations are geographically isolated, one might, theoretically, populate
each habitat with a different species, each of which had evolved
from a single parent species. These daughter species, however,
might be so unlike each other and the parent species that one might
not suspect the relationship among them. The Hawaiian honeycreepers (Drepaniidae) and the Galápagos finches (Geospizinae)
offer two good examples of adaptive radiation. The differences in
bill development among the Hawaiian honeycreepers, for example,
are so striking that the several species once were assigned to several
different families (Fig. 5).

Similarly, competition for food and other necessities leads, as a
result of natural selection, to convergence in structure and habits
of species from unrelated families. In this instance, the birds may
look superficially very much alike although they are not related
(Figs. 6, 7). These well-known examples of divergence and conver-
gence are those that ornithologists have recognized; how many
remain unrecognized is anyone's guess.

A BIRD'S CORRECT NAME

The neophyte is often understandably confused when he finds
that a particular bird is given one name in one book and a different
name in another book. If he wants to look up information on
British loons, for example, he must look up the family Colymbidae.
If he refers to the family Colymbidae in an American book, however, he will find a discussion of the grebes; to find the loons, he
must refer to the family Gaviidae. This situation immediately increases the student's awe for taxonomy! This is but one of many
examples that could be cited to demonstrate the perversity of man
and his strong desire to live up to the letter of the law while disre-
garding completely the spirit of the law.

The Swedish naturalist Linnaeus (1707–1778) was the father of

FIGURE 5. Divergence as illustrated by bill gradation in Hawaiian Honeycreepers (family Drepaniidae, subfamily Psittirostrinae). Left to right: *Loxops v. virens, Hemignathus o. obscurus, H. lucidus affinis, H. wilsoni, Pseudonestor xanthophrys, Psittirostra psittacea, P. cantans, P. kona.* (Courtesy of Dean Amadon and the American Museum of Natural History.)

modern taxonomy. His binomial system of Latin names is the foundation for nomenclature, and the tenth edition (1758) of his *Systema Naturae Regnum Animale* is the starting point for zoological nomenclature. Linnaeus adopted two Latin words for naming animals: one name to indicate the general kind (the genus) of animal; the other, the particular kind (the species). (The subspecies concept was added much later.) Because many problems arose over the years, a permanent International Commission on Zoological Nomenclature was established in 1901. This committee was charged with refining and interpreting an International Code for

FIGURE 6.   Left: Male Eastern Meadowlark (family Icteridae).   Right: Male African pipit, *Macronyx capensis* (family Motacillidae), Cape Province, South Africa.   In addition to the striking similarity in color and pattern (both ventrally and dorsally) of these representatives of two different families, the birds inhabit the same type of open grassy area and build semidomed nests of grasses on the ground.

FIGURE 7. Some examples of convergence. From top to bottom: *Zosterops japonica* (family Zosteropidae), Izu Islands, Japan; *Vireo flavifrons* (Vireonidae), Michigan; *Eulampis jugularis* (Trochilidae), St. Lucia; *Chalcomitra senegalensis* (Nectariniidae), Transvaal, South Africa; *Certhia familiaris* (Certhiidae), Cambridge, England; *Lepidocolaptes affinis* (Dendrocolaptidae), Colombia, South America.

Zoological Nomenclature.   Some of the principal provisions of the
International Code are:

1. Zoological nomenclature is independent of botanical nomenclature.

2. Family and subfamily names are formed by adding *idae* and
inae, respectively, to the stem name of the type genus; they must
be changed if the name of the type genus is changed or if, on the
basis of priority, a new type genus is designated (e.g., the family
name of the American wood-warblers has been, in turn, Sylvicolidae,
Mniotiltidae, Compsothylypidae, and Parulidae).

3. Names of subgenera and all higher categories are uninomial;
names of species are binomial; of subspecies, trinomial.   All names
must be Latin or Latinized words.   The generic name must be
unique in zoology.   The specific name must be unique in the genus;
it may be a Latin adjective, noun, or patronym.   Generic and sub-
generic names are capitalized; specific and subspecific names are
uncapitalized (formerly, names derived from surnames often were
capitalized).   The generic, specific, and subspecific names are underlined in manuscripts, italicized in published works.

4. The Law of Priority states that the generic and specific names
of a particular animal shall be the name proposed by Linnaeus in
1758, or the name first proposed after that date.   However, a
recognizable description of the animal must be *published* together
with a binomial or trinomial name (preferably but not necessarily
appropriate).

5. The author of a name is the one who first publishes it in conjunction with a suitable description of the animal.   The author's
name follows the trivial name without punctuation (and without
being underlined or italicized) unless the species has been transferred to a genus other than that in which it was first described, in
which event the author's name is enclosed in parentheses, e.g.,
Dendroica graciae Baird, *Vermivora pinus* (Linnaeus).

The confusing situation about the loons and grebes resulted because Linnaeus described both loons and grebes under the generic
name *Colymbus,* and British ornithologists insisted that the name
should be used for the loons, whereas American ornithologists insisted that the name be used for the grebes.   Finally, it was
announced in 1956 that the International Commission had agreed
to suppress (i.e., eliminate) the generic name *Colymbus* (and, thus,
the family name Colymbidae), and had recommended that the

generic name *Gavia* (family Gaviidae) be used for the loons and the generic name *Podiceps* be used for the typical grebes. Most authors will follow this recommendation, so that books and papers written after the announcement will be in agreement on this nomenclature. However, depending upon the book that one examines, the family name for the grebes may be given as Podicipedidae, Podicipitidae, or Podicipidae.

Nomenclature may be a means to an end or it may become a fetish, an end in itself. A few taxonomists take great delight in poring through old literature in the hope that they can find an earlier description for a particular species or genus so that a change can be proposed in contemporary nomenclature. Theoretically, this practice demonstrates true scholarship, but in the opinion of many people the value of the finding is frequently outweighed by the confusion which results. The value of any name change is directly related to the thoroughness and reliability of the taxonomic study upon which it is based. Ideally, increased knowledge and changing concepts of speciation are the bases for proposed name changes. The student must learn to expect changes in the names of some species and genera, realizing that the ultimate goal is a taxonomy that comes closer to indicating true phylogenetic relationships than do past systems.

The standard reference for both scientific and common names of North American birds is the *Check-List of North American Birds,* published by the American Ornithologists' Union in 1957. This list, prepared by a distinguished committee of 11 American ornithologists under the chairmanship of Alexander Wetmore, also summarizes information on the breeding range and winter range for each species and subspecies. Common names are given only to species (and not to subspecies), because the committee hoped that this procedure would "help to restore emphasis to the species—the unit usually involved in most studies made outside the museum or laboratory." The committee saw fit to state on the title page that "Zoölogical Nomenclature is a means, not an end, of Zoölogical Science." Revisions of ranges or recommended name changes are published periodically in *The Auk,* the quarterly journal of the American Ornithologists' Union. Any author, at his own discretion, may or may not follow this, or any other, check-list, but acceptance of the check-list makes possible a greater uniformity in the use of both scientific and common names for American birds. The check-list also represents the best conservative thinking on the taxonomy of American birds as of 1957.

ORDERS AND FAMILIES OF NORTH AMERICAN BIRDS

A listing of the orders and families of birds serves the practical use of being an aid to memory. The student should bear in mind that a family is supposed to be a monophyletic group—all of its species have evolved from a single ancestral species. He can learn quickly which birds belong to the duck family, the parrot family, and the hummingbird family. Some species, however, are placed in a given family largely by conjecture. This is true, especially, for a number of passerine families. There is considerable disagreement among ornithologists as to how many families should be recognized, what species they should contain, and in what sequence they should be listed. We adopt here the classification proposed by Josselyn Van Tyne (Van Tyne and Berger, 1959), which is very close to that in the AOU Check-List.

Gaviiformes
    Gaviidae—Loon family
Podicipediformes
    Podicipedidae—Grebe family
Procellariiformes
    Diomedeidae—Albatross family
    Procellariidae—Shearwater family
    Hydrobatidae—Storm-petrel family
Pelecaniformes
    Phaëthontidae—Tropicbird family
    Pelecanidae—Pelican family
    Sulidae—Booby family
    Phalacrocoracidae—Cormorant family
    Anhingidae—Anhinga family
    Fregatidae—Frigatebird family
Ciconiiformes
    Ardeidae—Heron family
    Ciconiidae—Stork family
    Threskiornithidae—Ibis family
    Phoenicopteridae—Flamingo family
Anseriformes
    Anatidae—Duck family
Falconiformes
    Cathartidae—American Vulture family
    Accipitridae—Hawk family
    Falconidae—Falcon family
Galliformes
    Cracidae—Curassow family

Tetraonidae—Grouse family
Phasianidae—Pheasant family
Meleagrididae—Turkey family
Gruiformes
Gruidae—Crane family
Aramidae—Limpkin family
Rallidae—Rail family
Charadriiformes
Jacanidae—Jaçana family
Haematopodidae—Oystercatcher family
Charadriidae—Plover family
Scolopacidae—Sandpiper family
Recurvirostridae—Avocet family
Phalaropodidae—Phalarope family
Stercorariidae—Skua family
Laridae—Gull family
Rynchopidae—Skimmer family
Alcidae—Auk family
Columbiformes
Columbidae—Pigeon family
Psittaciformes
Psittacidae—Parrot family
Cuculiformes
Cuculidae—Cuckoo family
Strigiformes
Tytonidae—Barn-owl family
Strigidae—Typical-owl family
Caprimulgiformes
Caprimulgidae—Nightjar family
Apodiformes
Apodidae—Swift family
Trochilidae—Hummingbird family
Trogoniformes
Trogonidae—Trogon family
Coraciiformes
Alcedinidae—Kingfisher family
Piciformes
Picidae—Woodpecker family
Passeriformes
Suborder Tyranni
Cotingidae—Cotinga family
Tyrannidae—Tyrant-flycatcher family
Suborder Passeres ("Oscines" of many authors)
Alaudidae—Lark family
Hirundinidae—Swallow family
Corvidae—Crow family
Paridae—Titmouse family

Sittidae—Common Nuthatch family
Certhiidae—Creeper family
Cinclidae—Dipper family
Troglodytidae—Wren family
Mimidae—Mockingbird family
Turdidae—Thrush family
Sylviidae—Old-world Warbler family
Motacillidae—Pipit family
Bombycillidae—Waxwing family
Ptilogonatidae—Silky-flycatcher family
Laniidae—Shrike family
Sturnidae—Starling family
Vireonidae—Vireo family
Parulidae—American Wood-warbler family
Icteridae—Troupial or blackbird family
Thraupidae—Tanager family
Ploceidae—Weaverbird family
Fringillidae—Finch family

CHAPTER 1

Beebe, C. W. 1906. *The Bird, Its Form and Function.* Henry Holt & Co., New York.*Dover reprint.*

Berger, A. J. 1953. The pterylosis of *Coua caerulea. Wils. Bull.,* 65: 12–17.

———— 1956. Two albinistic Alder Flycatchers at Ann Arbor, Michigan. *Auk,* 73: 137–138.

Coues, E. 1903. *Key to North American Birds.* Vol. 1. Dana Estes & Co., Boston.

Gilliard, E. T. 1958. *Living Birds of the World.* Doubleday & Co., New York.

Kortright, F. H. 1943. *The Ducks, Geese and Swans of North America.* Amer. Wildlife Inst., Washington, D. C.

Mayr, E., and M. Mayr. 1954. The Tail Molt of Small Owls. *Auk,* 71: 172–178.

Mewaldt, L. R. 1958. Pterylography and natural and experimentally induced molt in Clark's Nutcracker. *Condor,* 60: 165–187.

Romer, A. S. 1949. *The Vertebrate Body.* W. B. Saunders Co., Philadelphia.

Sutton, G. M. 1935. The juvenal plumage and postjuvenal molt in several species of Michigan sparrows. *Cranbrook Inst. Sci. Bull. No. 3.*

———— 1941. The juvenal plumage and postjuvenal molt of the Vesper Sparrow. *Occ. Pap. Univ. Michigan Mus. Zool. No. 445.*

Thomson, J. A. 1923. *The Biology of Birds.* Macmillan Co., New York.

Wagner, H. O. 1957. The molting periods of Mexican hummingbirds. *Auk,* 74: 251–257.

Weller, M. W. 1957. Growth, weights, and plumages of the Redhead, *Aythya americana. Wils. Bull.,* 69: 5–38.

Wetherbee, D. K. 1957. Natal plumages and downy pteryloses of passerine birds of North America. *Bull. Amer. Mus. Nat. Hist.,* 113: 339–436.

Wetmore, A. 1931. Birds. *Warm-blooded Vertebrates, Birds and Mammals.* Vol. 9. *Smiths. Inst., Sci. Ser.,* Washington, D. C.

General References

CHAPTER 2

Allen, A. A. 1930. *The Book of Bird Life.* D. Van Nostrand Co., New York.

American Ornithologists' Union. 1957. *Check-List of North American Birds.* 5th ed. Amer. Ornith. Union, Baltimore, Md.

Hickey, J. J. 1943. *A Guide to Bird Watching.* Oxford Univ. Press, New York.
Peterson, R. T. 1941. *A Field Guide to Western Birds.* Houghton Mifflin Co., Boston.
———— 1947. *A Field Guide to the Birds.* Houghton Mifflin Co., Boston.
———— 1960. *A Field Guide to the Birds of Texas.* Texas Game and Fish Commission, Austin, and Houghton Mifflin Co., Boston.
Pettingill, O. S., Jr. 1951. *A Guide to Bird Finding East of the Mississippi.* Oxford Univ. Press, New York.
———— 1953. *A Guide to Bird Finding West of the Mississippi.* Oxford Univ. Press, New York.
———— 1956. *A Laboratory and Field Manual of Ornithology.* 3rd ed. Burgess Publ. Co., Minneapolis.
Pough, R. H. 1946. *Audubon Bird Guide. Eastern Land Birds.* Doubleday & Co., New York.
———— 1951. *Audubon Water Bird Guide.* Doubleday & Co., New York.
———— 1957. *Audubon Western Bird Guide.* Doubleday & Co., New York.
Saunders, A. A. 1951. *A Guide to Bird Songs.* Doubleday & Co., New York.
Sutton, G. M. 1928. The birds of Pymatuning Swamp and Conneaut Lake, Crawford County, Pennsylvania. *Ann. Carnegie Mus.,* 18: 19-239.

CHAPTER 3

Aldrich, J. W. 1945. Birds of a deciduous forest aquatic succession. *Wils. Bull.,* 57: 243-245.
Chatfield, P. O., C. P. Lyman, and L. Irving. 1953. Physiological adaptation to cold of peripheral nerve in the leg of the Herring Gull (*Larus argentatus*). *Amer. Jour. Physiol.,* 172: 639-644.
Dale, F. H., and J. B. DeWitt. 1958. Calcium, phosphorus and protein levels as factors in the distribution of the pheasant. *Trans. 23rd North American Wildl. Conf.,* pp. 291-295.
Dawson, W. R., and H. B. Tordoff. 1959. Relation of oxygen consumption to temperature in the Evening Grosbeak. *Condor,* 61: 388-396.
Dixon, K. L. 1959. Ecological and distributional relations of desert scrub birds of western Texas. *Condor,* 61: 397-409.
Hensley, Max. 1954. Ecological relations of the breeding bird population of the desert biome of Arizona. *Ecol. Monog.,* 24: 185-207.
Hine, R. L., and K. G. Flakas. 1957. Stress response and survival time in three wildlife species. *Jour. Wildl. Manag.,* 21: 239-240.
Johnston, D. W., and E. P. Odum. 1956. Breeding bird populations in relation to plant succession on the Piedmont of Georgia. *Ecol.,* 37: 50-62.
Klonglan, E. D. 1955. Factors influencing the fall roadside pheasant census in Iowa. *Jour. Wildl. Manag.,* 19: 254-262.
Lack, David. 1954. *The Natural Regulation of Animal Numbers.* Oxford Univ. Press, London.
Marshall, J. T., Jr. 1957. Birds of pine-oak woodland in southern Arizona and adjacent Mexico. *Pacific Coast Avi. No. 32.*
Mayfield, H. F. 1960. The Kirtland's Warbler. *Cranbrook Inst. Sci. Bull. 40.*
Mayhew, W. W. 1955. Spring rainfall in relation to Mallard production in the Sacramento Valley, California. *Jour Wildl. Manag.,* 19: 36-47.
Middleton, D. S. 1957. Notes on the summering warblers of Bruce Township, Macomb County, Michigan. *Jack-Pine Warbler,* 35: 71-77.

Odum, E. P. 1959. *Fundamentals of Ecology.* 2nd ed. W. B. Saunders Co., Philadelphia.

Pettingill, O. S., Jr. 1956. *A Laboratory and Field Manual of Ornithology.* 3rd ed. Burgess Publ. Co., Minneapolis.

Shelford, V. E., and R. E. Yeatter. 1955. Some suggested relations of Prairie Chicken abundance to physical factors, especially rainfall and solar radiation. *Jour. Wildl. Manag.,* 19: 233–242.

Sutton, G. M., and D. F. Parmelee. 1954. Survival problems of the Water-Pipit in Baffin Island. *Arctic,* 7: 81–92.

Van Tyne, J., and A. J. Berger. 1959. *Fundamentals of Ornithology.* John Wiley & Sons, New York. *Dover reprint.*

CHAPTER 4

Bagg, A. M. 1955. Airborne from gulf to gulf. *Bull. Mass. Audubon Soc.,* 39: 106–110, 159–168.

————, W. W. H. Gunn, D. S. Miller, J. T. Nichols, W. Smith, and F. P. Wolfarth. 1950. Barometric pressure-patterns and spring bird migration. *Wils. Bull.,* 62: 5–19.

Baird, James, C. S. Robbins, A. M. Bagg, and J. V. Dennis. 1958. "Operation Recovery"—the Atlantic Coastal netting project. *Bird-Banding,* 29: 137–168.

Baldwin, S. P. 1931. Bird banding by systematic trapping. *Sci. Publ. Cleveland Mus. Nat. Hist.,* 1: 125–168.

Farner, D. S. 1955. The annual stimulus for migration: experimental and physiologic aspects. In *Recent Studies in Avian Biology.* Univ. Illinois Press, Urbana, pp. 198–237.

———— 1959. Photoperiodic control of annual gonadal cycles in birds. In *Photoperiodism and Related Phenomena in Plants and Animals.* Amer. Assoc. Advan. Sci., Publ. No. 55, Washington, D. C., pp. 717–750.

Griffin, D. R. 1952. Bird navigation. *Biol. Rev.,* 27: 359–400.

———— 1955. Bird navigation. In *Recent Studies in Avian Biology.* Univ. Illinois Press, Urbana, pp. 154–197.

Hochbaum, H. A. 1955. *Travels and Traditions of Waterfowl.* Univ. Minnesota Press, Minneapolis.

Irving, Laurence. 1960. Birds of Anaktuvuk Pass, Kobuk, and Old Crow. *U. S. Natl. Mus. Bull. 217.*

Kramer, Gustav. 1957. Experiments on bird orientation and their interpretation. *Ibis,* 99: 196–227.

———— 1961. Long-distance orientation. In *Biology and Comparative Physiology of Birds,* ed. by A. J. Marshall, Vol. 2, Academic Press, New York.

Lack, David. 1960. The influence of weather on passerine migration. A review. *Auk,* 77: 171–209.

Lincoln, F. C. 1950. Migration of birds. *Fish & Wildlife Serv. Circ. 16.*

Lowery, G. H., Jr., and R. J. Newman. 1955. Direct studies of nocturnal bird migration. In *Recent Studies in Avian Biology.* Univ. Illinois Press, Urbana, pp. 238–263.

Moreau, R. E. 1951. The migration system in perspective. *Proc. 10th Internatl. Ornith. Congr.,* 1950: 245–248.

Sauer, E. G. F. 1958. Celestial navigation by birds. *Sci. Amer.,* Aug. 1958: 42–47.

Van Tyne, Josselyn. 1932. Winter returns of Indigo Buntings in Guatemala. *Bird-Banding,* 3: 110.

Vleugel, D. A. 1960. On the temporal pattern of nocturnal migration in thrushes. *Auk,* 77: 10–18.

Williamson, Kenneth. 1955. Migrational drift. *Acta XI Congr. Internatl. Ornith.,*
1954, pp. 179–186.
Wolfson, Albert. 1959. The role of light and darkness in the regulation of spring
migration and reproductive cycles in birds. In *Photoperiodism and Related Phe-*
nomena in Plants and Animals. Amer. Assoc. Advan. Sci., Publ. No. 55, Washington, D. C., pp. 679–716.

CHAPTER 5

Beach, F. A. 1951. Instinctive behavior: reproductive activities. In *Handbook of*
Experimental Psychology, ed. by S. S. Stevens. John Wiley & Sons, New York.
Darling, F. Fraser. 1952. Social behavior and survival. *Auk,* 69: 183–191.
Frazier, Anita, and Val Nolan, Jr. 1959. Communal roosting by Eastern Bluebirds in
winter. *Bird-Banding,* 30: 219–226.
Hinde, R. A. 1953. Appetitive behaviour, consummatory act, and the hierarchical
organisation of behaviour—with special reference to the Great Tit (*Parus major*).
Behaviour, 5: 189–224.
Lehrman, D. S. 1953. A critique of Konrad Lorenz's theory of instinctive behavior.
Quart. Rev. Biol., 28: 337–363.
Lorenz, K. Z. 1958. The evolution of behavior. *Sci. Amer.,* 199, Dec. 1958: 67–78.
Moynihan, M. 1955a. Remarks on the original sources of displays. *Auk,* 72: 240–246.
———— 1955b. Types of hostile display. *Auk,* 72: 247–259.
Tinbergen, Niko. 1952. "Derived" activities; their causation, biological significance,
origin, and emancipation during evolution. *Quart. Rev. Biol.,* 27: 1–32.
———— 1953. *The Herring Gull's World.* Collins, London.
Whitaker, Lovie. 1957. A résumé of anting, with particular reference to a captive
Orchard Oriole. *Wils. Bull.,* 69: 195–262.

CHAPTER 6

Borror, D. J. 1961. Intraspecific variation in passerine bird songs. *Wils. Bull.,*
73: 57–78.
Dilger, W. C. 1956. Hostile behavior and reproductive isolating mechanisms in the
avian genera *Catharus and Hylocichla. Auk,* 73: 313–353.
Frings, Hubert, and Mable Frings. 1959. The language of crows. *Sci. Amer.,* 201,
Nov. 1959: 119–131.
Kellogg, P. P., and R. C. Stein. 1953. Audio-spectrographic analysis of the songs of
the Alder Flycatcher. *Wils. Bull.,* 65: 75–80.
Marshall, A. J. 1950. The function of vocal mimicry in birds. *Emu,* 50: 5–16.
Miskimen, Mildred. 1951. Sound production in passerine birds. *Auk,* 68: 493–504.
Nice, M. M. 1943. Studies in the life history of the Song Sparrow. II. *Trans. Linn.*
Soc. N. Y., 6. *Dover reprint.*
Smith, R. L. 1959. The songs of the Grasshopper Sparrow. *Wils. Bull.,* 71: 141–152.
Stein, R. C. 1958. The behavioral, ecological and morphological characteristics of two
populations of the Alder Flycatcher, *Empidonax traillii* (Audubon). *New York State*
Mus. Bull. No. 371, Albany.
Weeden, J. S., and J. B. Falls. 1959. Differential response of male Ovenbirds to
recorded songs of neighboring and more distant individuals. *Auk,* 76: 343–351.

CHAPTER 7

Armstrong, E. A. 1947. *Bird Display and Behaviour.* Lindsay Drummond, London.

Bent, A. C. 1919–1961. Life. Histories of North American Birds. . . . *U. S. Natl. Mus. Bulls. Dover reprint.*

Coues, E. 1903. *Key to North American Birds.* 5th ed. Dana Estes & Co., Boston.

Dilger, W. C. 1956. Hostile behavior and reproductive isolating mechanisms in the avian genera *Catharus* and *Hylocichla. Auk,* 73: 313–353.

Friedmann, Herbert. 1950. The breeding habits of the weaverbirds: a study in the biology of behavior patterns. *Smiths. Rept. for 1949,* 1950: 293–316.

Hann, H. W. 1937. Life history of the Oven-bird in southern Michigan. *Wils. Bull.,* 49: 145–237.

Headstrom, Richard. 1949. *Birds' Nests, A Field Guide.* Ives Washburn, New York.

———— 1951. *Birds' Nests of the West.* Ives Washburn, New York.

Kilham, Lawrence. 1958. Pair formation, mutual tapping and nest hole selection of Red-bellied Woodpeckers. *Auk,* 75: 318–329.

Laskey, A. R. 1948. Some nesting data on the Carolina Wren at Nashville, Tennessee. *Bird-Banding,* 19: 101–121.

Mayr, Ernst. 1951. Speciation in birds. Progress report on the years 1938–1950. *Proc. 10th Internatl. Ornith. Congr. 1950:* 91–131.

Mengel, R. M. 1957. A catalog of an exhibition of landmarks in the development of ornithology. . . . Univ. Kansas Libraries.

Nice, M. M. 1937. Studies in the life history of the Song Sparrow. I. *Trans. Linn. Soc. N. Y.,* 4. *Dover reprint.*

———— 1943. Studies in the life history of the Song Sparrow. II. *Trans. Linn. Soc. N. Y.,* 6. *Dover reprint.*

Nickell, W. P. 1958. Variations in engineering features of the nests of several species of birds in relation to nest sites and nesting materials. *Butler Univ. Bot. Studies,* 13: 121–139.

Pettingill, O. S., Jr. 1942. The birds of a bull's horn acacia. *Wils. Bull.,* 54: 89–96.

Sutton, G. M., and O. S. Pettingill, Jr. 1942. Birds of the Gomez Farias region, southwestern Tamaulipas. *Auk,* 59: 1–34.

Tinbergen, N. 1954a. The origin and evolution of courtship and threat display. In *Evolution as a Process,* ed. by J. Huxley et al. George Allen & Unwin, London.

———— 1954b. The courtship of animals. *Sci. Amer.,* 191, Nov. 1954: 42–46.

Wolfson, Albert. 1959. Ecologic and physiologic factors in the regulation of spring migration and reproductive cycles in birds. In *Comparative Endocrinology,* ed. by Aubrey Gorbman, John Wiley & Sons, New York.

CHAPTER 8

Austin, O. L., and O. L. Austin, Jr. 1956. Some demographic aspects of the Cape Cod population of Common Terns (*Sterna hirundo*). *Bird-Banding,* 27: 55–66.

Bartholomew, G. A., Jr., and W. R. Dawson. 1954. Temperature regulation in young pelicans, herons, and gulls. *Ecol.,* 35: 466–472.

———— and E. J. O'Neill. 1953. A field study of temperature regulation in young White Pelicans, *Pelecanus erythrorhynchos. Ecol.,* 34: 554–560.

Berger, A. J. 1951. The cowbird and certain host species in Michigan. *Wils. Bull.,* 63: 26–34.

Breckenridge, W. J. 1956. Nesting study of Wood Ducks. *Jour. Wildl. Manag.*, 20: 16–21.

Coulter, M. W. 1957. Predation by snapping turtles upon aquatic birds in Maine marshes. *Jour. Wildl. Manag.*, 21: 17–21.

Davis, D. E. 1955. Determinate laying in Barn Swallows and Black-billed Magpies. *Condor*, 57: 81–87.

Dawson, W. R., and F. C. Evans. 1957. Relation of growth and development to temperature regulation in nestling Field and Chipping Sparrows. *Physiol. Zoöl.*, 30: 315–327.

Farner, D. S. 1955. Birdbanding in the study of population dynamics. In *Recent Studies in Avian Biology*, Univ. Illinois Press, Urbana, pp. 397–449.

Graber, R. R. 1955. Artificial incubation of some non-galliform eggs. *Wils. Bull.*, 67: 100–109.

Hanson, H. C. 1959. The incubation patch of wild geese: its recognition and significance. *Arctic*, 12: 139–150.

————— and C. W. Kossack. 1957. Methods and criteria for aging incubated eggs and nestlings of the Mourning Dove. *Wils. Bull.*, 69: 91–101.

Hickey, J. J. 1955. Some American population research on gallinaceous birds. In *Recent Studies in Avian Biology*, Univ. Illinois Press, Urbana, pp. 326–396.

Irving, Laurence, and John Krog. 1956. Temperature during the development of birds in Arctic nests. *Physiol. Zoöl.*, 29: 195–205.

Kilham, Lawrence. 1959. Early reproductive behavior of Flickers. *Wils. Bull.*, 71: 323–336.

Lack, David. 1954. *The Natural Regulation of Animal Numbers*. Oxford Univ. Press, London.

————— 1958. The significance of the colour of turdine eggs. *Ibis*, 100: 145–166.

————— and Elizabeth Lack. 1954. The home life of the swift. *Sci. Amer.*, July 1954: 60–64.

Mayfield, H. F. 1960. The Kirtland's Warbler. *Cranbrook Inst. Sci. Bull. 40*.

Mayhew, W. W. 1958. The biology of the Cliff Swallow in California. *Condor*, 60: 7–37.

Mewaldt, L. R. 1956. Nesting behavior of the Clark Nutcracker. *Condor*, 58: 3–23.

Nice, M. M. 1953. The question of ten-day incubation periods. *Wils. Bull.*, 65: 81–93.

————— 1954. Problems of incubation periods in North American birds. *Condor*, 56: 173–197.

————— 1957. Nesting success in altricial birds. *Auk*, 74: 305–321.

Noble, G. K., and D. S. Lehrman. 1940. Egg recognition by the Laughing Gull. *Auk*, 57: 22–43.

Nolan, Val, Jr. 1958. Anticipatory food-bringing in the Prairie Warbler. *Auk*, 75: 263–278.

Parmelee, D. F. 1959. The breeding behavior of the Painted Bunting in southern Oklahoma. *Bird-Banding*, 30: 1–18.

Pettingill, O. S., Jr. 1956. *A Laboratory and Field Manual of Ornithology*. 3rd ed. Burgess Publ. Co., Minneapolis.

Putnam, L. S. 1949. The life history of the Cedar Waxwing. *Wils. Bull.*, 61: 141–182.

Ramsay, A. O. 1951. Familial recognition in domestic birds. *Auk*, 68: 1–16.

————— and E. H. Hess. 1954. A laboratory approach to the study of imprinting. *Wils. Bull.*, 66: 196–206.

Romanoff, A. L., and A. J. Romanoff. 1949. *The Avian Egg*. John Wiley & Sons, New York.

Skutch, A. F. 1949. Do tropical birds rear as many young as they can nourish? *Ibis*, 91: 430–458.

Tinbergen, Niko. 1953. *The Herring Gull's World*. Collins, London.

Vosburgh, F. G. 1948. Easter egg chickens. *Natl. Geographic Mag.*, 94: 377–387.

Wagner, H. O. 1957. Variation in clutch size at different latitudes. *Auk*, 74: 243–250.

Weller, M. W. 1959. Parasitic egg laying in the Redhead (*Aythya americana*) and other North American Anatidae. *Ecol. Monog.*, 29: 333–365.

Witschi, Emil. 1956. *Development of Vertebrates*. W. B. Saunders Co., Philadelphia.

CHAPTER 9

Bartholomew, G. A., Jr., and W. R. Dawson. 1953. Respiratory water loss in some birds of southwestern United States. *Physiol. Zoöl.*, 26: 162–166.

———— 1954. Body temperature and water requirements in the Mourning Dove, *Zenaidura macroura marginella*. *Ecol.*, 35: 181–187.

Bartholomew, G. A., Jr., T. R. Howell, and T. J. Cade. 1957. Torpidity in the White-throated Swift, Anna Hummingbird, and Poor-will. *Condor*, 59: 145–155.

Howell, T. R., and G. A. Bartholomew. 1959. Further experiments on torpidity in the Poor-will. *Condor*, 61: 180–185.

Howell, T. R., and W. R., Dawson. 1954. Nest temperatures and attentiveness in the Anna Hummingbird. *Condor*, 56: 93–97.

Jaeger, E. C. 1949. Further observations on the hibernation of the Poor-will. *Condor*, 51: 105–109.

King, A. S. 1957. The aerated bones of Gallus domesticus. *Acta Anat.*, 31: 220–230.

Rand, A. L. 1954. On the spurs on birds' wings. *Wils. Bull.*, 66: 127–134.

Schmidt-Nielsen, Knut, and Ragnar Fange. 1958. The function of the salt gland in the Brown Pelican. *Auk*, 75: 282–289.

Schmidt-Nielsen, Knut, and W. J. L. Sladen. 1958. Nasal salt secretion in the Humboldt Penguin. *Nature*, 181: 1217–1218.

Wolfson, Albert. 1954. Sperm storage at lower-than-body temperature outside the body cavity in some passerine birds. *Science*, July 9, 1954: 68–71.

CHAPTER 10

Allen, D. L. 1954. *Our Wildlife Legacy*. Funk & Wagnalls Co., New York.

Clawson, Marion. 1959. The crisis in outdoor recreation. *Amer. Forests*, 65: 22–31, 40–41.

Cottam, Clarence. 1958. Science and resources in America. Address presented at the North American Wildl. Conf., St. Louis, Mo., Mar. 4, 1958.

———— 1959. Chemical pesticides and conservation problems. Address presented before the National Wildl. Fed., New York, N. Y., Feb. 27, 1959.

Craighead, J. J., and F. C. Craighead. 1956. *Hawks, Owls, and Wildlife*. Wildl. Manag. Inst., Washington, D. C. *Dover reprint*.

Dambach, C. A. 1944. A ten-year ecological study of adjoining grazed and ungrazed woodlands in northeastern Ohio. *Ecol. Monog.*, 14: 255–270.

Gabrielson, I. N. 1959. *Wildlife Conservation*. Macmillan Co., New York.

George, J. L. 1958. The program to eradicate the imported fire ant. Conservation Foundation, New York.

Graham, E. H. 1947. *The Land and Wildlife*. Oxford Univ. Press, New York.

Leopold, Aldo. 1933. *Game Management.* Charles Scribner's Sons, New York.

Odum, E. P. 1959. *Fundamentals of Ecology.* 2nd ed. W. B. Saunders Co., Philadelphia.

Rogers, J. P. 1959. Low water and Lesser Scaup reproduction near Erickson, Manitoba. *Trans. 24th North American Wildl. Conf.,* pp. 216–224.

Smelser, M. A. 1959. Uncontrollable "Control." *Nature Mag.,* Jan. 1959: 33–40, 50.

Smith, Fred. 1956. The critical need for statesmanship in conservation. Address presented before the Recreation, Conservation and Park Council, Pittsburgh, Pa., Nov. 27, 1956.

Spengler, J. J. 1956. Population threatens prosperity. *Harvard Bus. Rev.,* 34: 85–94.

Warbach, Oscar. 1958. Bird populations in relation to change in land use. *Jour. Wildl. Manag.,* 22: 23–28.

Weller, M. W., B. H. Wingfield, and J. B. Low. 1958. Effects of habitat deterioration on bird populations of a small Utah marsh. *Condor,* 60: 220–226.

CHAPTER 11

American Ornithologists' Union. 1957. *Check-List of North American Birds.* 5th ed. Amer. Ornith. Union, Baltimore, Md.

Bock, W. J. 1956. A generic review of the family Ardeidae (Aves). *Amer. Mus. Novitates No. 1779.*

Johnston, R. F. 1956. Review of Lack's, The species of Apus. *Auk,* 73: 470.

Lack, David. 1956a. The species of Apus. *Ibis,* 98: 34–62.

———— 1956b. A review of the genera and nesting habits of swifts. *Auk,* 73: 1–32.

Mayr, Ernst, and Dean Amadon. 1951. A classification of recent birds. *Amer. Mus. Novitates No. 1496.*

Mayr, Ernst, E. G. Linsley, and R. L. Usinger. 1953. *Methods and Principles of Systematic Zoology.* McGraw-Hill Book Co., New York.

Nice, M. M., and W. E. Schantz. 1959. Head-scratching movements in birds. *Auk,* 76: 339–342.

Sibley, C. G. 1957. The evolutionary and taxonomic significance of sexual dimorphism and hybridization in birds. *Condor,* 59: 166–191.

———— and P. A. Johnsgard. 1959. Variability in the electrophoretic patterns of avian serum proteins. *Condor,* 61: 85–95.

Simmons, K. E. L. 1957. The taxonomic significance of the head-scratching methods of birds. *Ibis,* 99: 178–181.

Storer, R. W. 1960. The classification of birds. In *Biology and Comparative Physiology of Birds,* ed. by A. J. Marshall, Vol. 1, Academic Press, New York.

Stresemann, Erwin. 1959. The status of avian systematics and its unsolved problems. *Auk,* 76: 269–280.

Van Tyne, J., and A. J. Berger. 1959. *Fundamentals of Ornithology.* John Wiley & Sons, New York. *Dover reprint.*

Wetmore, Alexander. 1951. A revised classification for the birds of the world. *Smiths. Misc. Coll. 117.*

———— 1960. A classification for the birds of the world. *Smiths. Misc. Coll. 139.*

Albatross, Royal, *Diomedea epomophora*
———, Wandering, *Diomedea exulans*
Anhinga, *Anhinga anhinga*
Ani, Groove-billed, *Crotophaga sulcirostris*
———, Smooth-billed, *Crotophaga ani*
Baldpate, see Widgeon, American
Becard, Rose-throated, *Platypsaris aglaiae*
Bittern, American, *Botaurus lentiginosus*
———, Least, *Ixobrychus exilis*
Blackbird, Brewer's, *Euphagus cyanocephalus*
———, European, *Turdus merula*
———, Red-winged, *Agelaius phoeniceus*
———, Rusty, *Euphagus carolinus*
———, Tricolored, *Agelaius tricolor*
———, Yellow-headed, *Xanthocephalus xan-*
thocephalus
Bluebird, Eastern, *Sialia sialis*
———, Mountain, *Sialia currucoides*
———, Western, *Sialia mexicana*
Bobolink, *Dolichonyx oryzivorus*
Bobwhite, *Colinus virginianus*
Budgerigar, *Melopsittacus undulatus*
Bufflehead, *Bucephala albeola*
Bunting, Indigo, *Passerina cyanea*
———, Lark, *Calamospiza melanocorys*
———, Lazuli, *Passerina amoena*
———, Painted, *Passerina ciris*
———, Snow, *Plectrophenax nivalis*
Bushtit, Common, *Psaltriparus minimus*
Canvasback, *Aythya valisineria*
Caracara, *Caracara cheriway*
Cardinal, *Richmondena cardinalis*
Catbird, *Dumetella carolinensis*
Chaffinch, *Fringilla coelebs*
Chat, Yellow-breasted, *Icteria virens*
Chickadee, Black-capped, *Parus atricapillus*
———, Carolina, *Parus carolinensis*
———, Mexican, *Parus sclateri*
———, Mountain, *Parus gambeli*
Chicken, Greater Prairie, *Tympanuchus cupido*
Chuck-will's-widow, *Caprimulgus carolinensis*
Coly, *Colius striatus*
Condor, California, *Gymnogyps californianus*
Coot, American, *Fulica americana*
Cormorant, *Phalacrocorax*
Cowbird, Bay-winged, *Agelaioides badius*
———, Bronzed, *Tangavius aeneus*
———, Brown-headed, *Molothrus ater*

Common and Scientific Names of Birds

Flycatcher, Alder, see Flycatcher, Traill's
————, Ash-throated, *Myiarchus cinerascens*
————, Boat-billed, *Megarynchus pitangua*
————, Buff-breasted, *Empidonax fulvifrons*
————, Coues', *Contopus pertinax*
————, Derby, see Flycatcher, Kiskadee
————, Dusky, *Empidonax oberholseri*
————, Gray, *Empidonax wrightii*
————, Great Crested, *Myiarchus crinitus*
————, Hammond's, *Empidonax hammondii*
————, Kiskadee, *Pitangus sulphuratus*
————, Least, *Empidonax minimus*
————, Olivaceous, *Myiarchus tuberculifer*
————, Olive-sided, *Nuttallornis borealis*
————, Scissor-tailed, *Muscivora forficata*
————, Social, *Myiozetetes similis*
————, Sulphur-bellied, *Myiodynastes luteiventris*
————, Traill's, *Empidonax traillii*
————, Vermilion, *Pyrocephalus rubinus*
————, Western, *Empidonax difficilis*
————, Wied's Crested, *Myiarchus tyrannulus*
————, Yellow-bellied, *Empidonax flaviventris*
Frigatebird, Magnificent, *Fregata magnificens*
Fulmar, *Fulmarus glacialis*
Gallinule, Purple, *Porphyrula martinica*
Gannet, *Morus bassanus*
Garden-warbler, *Sylvia borin*
Gnatcatcher, Black-tailed, *Polioptila melanura*
————, Blue-gray, *Polioptila caerulea*
Goldfinch, American, *Spinus tristis*
————, Lawrence's, *Spinus lawrencei*
————, Lesser, *Spinus psaltria*
Goose, Canada, *Branta canadensis*
————, Spur-winged, *Plectropterus gambensis*
Goshawk, *Accipiter gentilis*
Grackle, Boat-tailed, *Cassidix mexicanus*
————, Common, *Quiscalus quiscula*
Grebe, Eared, *Podiceps caspicus*
————, Pied-billed, *Podilymbus podiceps*
————, Western, *Aechmophorus occidentalis*
Grosbeak, Black-headed, *Pheucticus melanocephalus*
————, Blue, *Guiraca caerulea*
————, Evening, *Hesperiphona vespertina*
————, Pine, *Pinicola enucleator*
————, Rose-breasted, *Pheucticus ludovicianus*
Ground-tyrant, Rufous-backed, *Lessonia rufa*
Grouse, Blue, *Dendragapus obscurus*
————, Ruffed, *Bonasa umbellus*

Grouse, Sage, *Centrocercus urophasianus*
————, Sharp-tailed, *Pedioecetes phasianellus*
————, Spruce, *Canachites canadensis*
Gull, Black-headed, *Larus ridibundus*
————, California, *Larus californicus*
————, Great Black-backed, *Larus marinus*
————, Heermann's, *Larus heermanni*
————, Herring, *Larus argentatus*
————, Laughing, *Larus atricilla*
————, Ring-billed, *Larus delawarensis*
Hawk, Broad-winged, *Buteo platypterus*
————, Cooper's, *Accipiter cooperii*
————, Ferruginous, *Buteo regalis*
————, Marsh, *Circus cyaneus*
————, Red-shouldered, *Buteo lineatus*
————, Red-tailed, *Buteo jamaicensis*
————, Rough-legged, *Buteo lagopus*
————, Sharp-shinned, *Accipiter striatus*
————, Sparrow, *Falco sparverius*
————, Swainson's, *Buteo swainsoni*
Hawk-Owl, *Surnia ulula*
Heron, Black-crowned Night, *Nycticorax nycticorax*
————, Great Blue, *Ardea herodias*
————, Green, *Butorides virescens*
————, Little Blue, *Florida caerulea*
Hummingbird, Allen's, *Selasphorus sasin*
————, Anna's, *Calypte anna*
————, Black-chinned, *Archilochus alexandri*
————, Blue-throated, *Lampornis clemenciae*
————, Broad-tailed, *Selasphorus platycercus*
————, Costa's, *Calypte costae*
————, Rivoli's, *Eugenes fulgens*
————, Ruby-throated, *Archilochus colubris*
————, Rufous, *Selasphorus rufus*
Ibis, White, *Eudocimus albus*
————, Wood, *Mycteria americana*
Jaçana, *Jacana spinosa*
————, African, *Actophilornis africanus*
Jackdaw, *Corvus monedula*
Jaeger, Parasitic, *Stercorarius parasiticus*
Jay, Blue, *Cyanocitta cristata*
————, Canada, see Jay, Gray
————, Gray, *Perisoreus canadensis*
————, Mexican, *Aphelocoma ultramarina*
————, Piñon, *Gymnorhinus cyanocephala*
————, Scrub, *Aphelocoma coerulescens*
————, Steller's, *Cyanocitta stelleri*
Junco, Gray-headed, *Junco caniceps*

Oriole, Baltimore, *Icterus galbula*
————, Black-headed, *Icterus graduacauda*
————, Bullock's, *Icterus bullockii*
————, Hooded, *Icterus cucullatus*
————, Lichtenstein's, *Icterus gularis*
————, Orchard, *Icterus spurius*
————, Scott's, *Icterus parisorum*
Oropendola, Alfred's, *Ostinops angustifrons*
————, Wagler's, *Zarhynchus wagleri*
Osprey, *Pandion haliaetus*
Ovenbird, *Seiurus aurocapillus*
Owl, Barred, *Strix varia*
————, Burrowing, *Speotyto cunicularia*
————, Elf, *Micrathene whitneyi*
————, Flammulated, *Otus flammeolus*
————, Great-horned, *Bubo virginianus*
————, Long-eared, *Asio otus*
————, Pygmy, *Glaucidium gnoma*
————, Saw-whet, *Aegolius acadicus*
————, Screech, *Otus asio*
————, Snowy, *Nyctea scandiaca*
————, Spotted, *Strix occidentalis*
————, Whiskered, *Otus trichopsis*
Oystercatcher, American, *Haematopus palliatus*
————, European, *Haematopus ostralegus*
Palm-swift, *Cypsiurus parvus*
Parakeet, Brown-throated, *Aratinga pertinax*
————, Gray-breasted, *Myiopsitta monachus*
Parrot, Thick-billed, *Rhynchopsitta pachyrhyncha*
Partridge, Hungarian, *Perdix perdix*
————, Red-legged, *Alectoris rufa*
Pauraque, *Nyctidromus albicollis*
Pelican, Brown, *Pelecanus occidentalis*
————, White, *Pelecanus erythrorhynchos*
Penguin, Gentoo, *Pygoscelis papua*
————, King, *Aptenodytes patagonica*
Petrel, Wilson's, *Oceanites oceanicus*
Pewee, Eastern Wood, *Contopus virens*
————, Western Wood, *Contopus sordidulus*
Phainopepla, *Phainopepla nitens*
Phalarope, Northern, *Lobipes lobatus*
Pheasant, Edward's, *Lophura edwardsi*
————, Ring-necked, *Phasianus colchicus*
Phoebe, Eastern, *Sayornis phoebe*
Pigeon, Band-tailed, *Columba fasciata*
Pintail, *Anas acuta*
Pipit, American, see Pipit, Water
————, Meadow, *Anthus pratensis*

Pipit, Sprague's, *Anthus spragueii*
————, Tree, *Anthus trivialis*
————, Water, *Anthus spinoletta*
Plover, American Golden, *Pluvialis dominica*
————, Black-bellied, *Squatarola squatarola*
————, Ringed, *Charadrius hiaticula*
————, Upland, *Bartramia longicauda*
————, Wilson's, *Charadrius wilsonia*
Poor-will, *Phalaenoptilus nuttallii*
Ptarmigan, Rock, *Lagopus mutus*
————, White-tailed, *Lagopus leucurus*
————, Willow, *Lagopus lagopus*
Pyrrhuloxia, *Pyrrhuloxia sinuata*
Quail, California, *Lophortyx californicus*
————, Gambel's, *Lophortyx gambelii*
————, Harlequin, *Cyrtonyx montezumae*
————, Mountain, *Oreortyx pictus*
————, Scaled, *Callipepla squamata*
Rail, Clapper, *Rallus longirostris*
————, King, *Rallus elegans*
————, Sora, *Porzana carolina*
————, Virginia, *Rallus limicola*
Raven, Common, *Corvus corax*
Razorbill, *Alca torda*
Redhead, *Aythya americana*
Redpoll, Common, *Acanthis flammea*
Redstart, American, *Setophaga ruticilla*
————, Painted, *Setophaga picta*
Roadrunner, *Geococcyx californianus*
Robin, *Turdus migratorius*
————, British, *Erithacus rubecula*
————, European, see Robin, British
Rook, *Corvus frugilegus*
Sanderling, *Crocethia alba*
Sandpiper, Pectoral, *Erolia melanotos*
————, Purple, *Erolia maritima*
————, Red-backed, See Dunlin
————, Semipalmated, *Ereunetes pusillus*
————, Solitary, *Tringa solitaria*
————, Spoon-bill, *Eurynorhynchus pygmeum*
————, Spotted, *Actitis macularia*
Sapsucker, Williamson's, *Sphyrapicus thyroideus*
Scoter, White-winged, *Melanitta deglandi*
Screamer, Black-necked, *Chauna chavaria*
Shearwater, Manx, *Puffinus puffinus*
————, Sooty, *Puffinus griseus*
Shrike, Loggerhead, *Lanius ludovicianus*
————, Northern, *Lanius excubitor*

Siskin, Pine, *Spinus pinus*
Skimmer, Black, *Rynchops nigra*
Skylark, *Alauda arvensis*
Solitaire, *Pezophaps solitaria*
————, Townsend's, *Myadestes townsendi*
Song-Thrush, British, *Turdus ericetorum*
Sparrow, Bachman's, *Aimophila aestivalis*
————, Baird's, *Ammodramus bairdii*
————, Black-chinned, *Spizella atrogularis*
————, Black-throated, *Amphispiza bilineata*
————, Brewer's, *Spizella breweri*
————, Cassin's, *Aimophila cassinii*
————, Chipping, *Spizella passerina*
————, Clay-colored, *Spizella pallida*
————, Desert, see Sparrow, Black-throated
————, English, see Sparrow, House
————, Field, *Spizella pusilla*
————, Fox, *Passerella iliaca*
————, Golden-crowned, *Zonotrichia atricapilla*
————, Grasshopper, *Ammodramus savannarum*
————, Harris', *Zonotrichia querula*
————, Henslow's, *Passerherbulus henslowii*
————, House, *Passer domesticus*
————, Ipswich, *Passerculus princeps*
————, Lark, *Chondestes grammacus*
————, Lincoln's, *Melospiza lincolnii*
————, Rufous-crowned, *Aimophila ruficeps*
————, Sage, *Amphispiza belli*
————, Savannah, *Passerculus sandwichensis*
————, Sharp-tailed, *Ammospiza caudacuta*
————, Song, *Melospiza melodia*
————, Swamp, *Melospiza georgiana*
————, Tree, *Spizella arborea*
————, Vesper, *Pooecetes gramineus*
————, White-crowned, *Zonotrichia leucophrys*
————, White-throated, *Zonotrichia albicollis*
Spoonbill, Roseate, *Ajaia ajaja*
Starling, *Sturnus vulgaris*
Stilt, Black-necked, *Himantopus mexicanus*
Swallow, Bank, *Riparia riparia*
————, Barn, *Hirundo rustica*
————, Cliff, *Petrochelidon pyrrhonota*
————, Rough-winged, *Stelgidopteryx ruficollis*
————, Tree, *Iridoprocne bicolor*
————, Violet-green, *Tachycineta thalassina*
Swan, Mute, *Cygnus olor*
————, Trumpeter, *Olor buccinator*
————, Whistling, *Olor columbianus*

Swift, Chimney, *Chaetura pelagica*

———, Common, *Apus apus*

Tanager, Hepatic, *Piranga flava*

———, Scarlet, *Piranga olivacea*

———, Summer, *Piranga rubra*

———, Western, *Piranga ludoviciana*

Teal, Blue-winged, *Anas discors*

Tern, Arctic, *Sterna paradisaea*

———, Black, *Chlidonias niger*

———, Common, *Sterna hirundo*

———, Fairy, *Gygis alba*

———, Forster's, *Sterna forsteri*

———, Least, *Sterna albifrons*

———, Noddy, *Anoüs stolidus*

———, Royal, *Thalasseus maximus*

———, Sooty, *Sterna fuscata*

Thrasher, Bendire's, *Toxostoma bendirei*

———, Brown, *Toxostoma rufum*

———, California, *Toxostoma redivivum*

———, Crissal, *Toxostoma dorsale*

———, Curve-billed, *Toxostoma curvirostre*

———, Sage, *Oreoscoptes montanus*

Thrush, Gray-cheeked, *Hylocichla minima*

———, Hermit, *Hylocichla guttata*

———, Russet-backed, see Thrush, Swainson's

———, Swainson's, *Hylocichla ustulata*

———, Wood, *Hylocichla mustelina*

Tinamou, Great, *Tinamus major*

Tit, Great, *Parus major*

———, Long-tailed, *Aegithalos caudatus*

Titmouse, Bridled, *Parus wollweberi*

———, Plain, *Parus inornatus*

———, Tufted, *Parus bicolor*

Towhee, Abert's, *Pipilo aberti*

———, Brown, *Pipilo fuscus*

———, Green-tailed, *Chlorura chlorura*

———, Rufous-sided, *Pipilo erythrophthalmus*

Trogon, Coppery-tailed, *Trogon elegans*

Turkey, *Meleagris gallopavo*

Veery, *Hylocichla fuscescens*

Verdin, *Auriparus flaviceps*

Vireo, Bell's, *Vireo bellii*

———, Black-capped, *Vireo atricapilla*

———, Black-whiskered, *Vireo altiloquus*

———, Gray, *Vireo vicinior*

———, Hutton's, *Vireo huttoni*

———, Philadelphia, *Vireo philadelphicus*

———, Red-eyed, *Vireo olivaceus*

Vireo, Solitary, *Vireo solitarius*
————, Warbling, *Vireo gilvus*
————, White-eyed, *Vireo griseus*
————, Yellow-throated, *Vireo flavifrons*
Vulture, Turkey, *Cathartes aura*
Wagtail, Yellow, *Motacilla flava*
Warbler, Audubon's, *Dendroica auduboni*
————, Bachman's, *Vermivora bachmanii*
————, Bay-breasted, *Dendroica castanea*
————, Black-and-white, *Mniotilta varia*
————, Blackburnian, *Dendroica fusca*
————, Blackpoll, *Dendroica striata*
————, Black-throated, *Gerygone palpebrosa*
————, Black-throated Blue, *Dendroica caerulescens*
————, Black-throated Gray, *Dendroica nigrescens*
————, Black-throated Green, *Dendroica virens*
————, Blue-winged, *Vermivora pinus*
————, Canada, *Wilsonia canadensis*
————, Cape May, *Dendroica tigrina*
————, Cerulean, *Dendroica cerulea*
————, Chestnut-sided, *Dendroica pensylvanica*
————, Colima, *Vermivora crissalis*
————, Connecticut, *Oporornis agilis*
————, Golden-cheeked, *Dendroica chrysoparia*
————, Golden-winged, *Vermivora chrysoptera*
————, Grace's, *Dendroica graciae*
————, Hermit, *Dendroica occidentalis*
————, Hooded, *Wilsonia citrina*
————, Kentucky, *Oporornis formosus*
————, Kirtland's, *Dendroica kirtlandii*
————, Lucy's, *Vermivora luciae*
————, MacGillivray's, *Oporornis tolmiei*
————, Magnolia, *Dendroica magnolia*
————, Mourning, *Oporornis philadelphia*
————, Myrtle, *Dendroica coronata*
————, Nashville, *Vermivora ruficapilla*
————, Olive, *Peucedramus taeniatus*
————, Orange-crowned, *Vermivora celata*
————, Palm, *Dendroica palmarum*
————, Parula, *Parula americana*
————, Pine, *Dendroica pinus*
————, Prairie, *Dendroica discolor*
————, Prothonotary, *Protonotaria citrea*
————, Red-faced, *Cardellina rubrifrons*
————, Swainson's, *Limnothlypis swainsonii*
————, Tennessee, *Vermivora peregrina*
————, Townsend's, *Dendroica townsendi*
————, Virginia's, *Vermivora virginiae*

Warbler, Wilson's, *Wilsonia pusilla*

————, Worm-eating, *Helmitheros vermivorus*

————, Yellow, *Dendroica petechia*

————, Yellow-throated, *Dendroica dominica*

Waterthrush, Northern, *Seiurus noveboracensis*

Waxwing, Bohemian, *Bombycilla garrula*

————, Cedar, *Bombycilla cedrorum*

Weaver, Sociable, *Philetairus socius*

Weaverbird, Philippine, *Ploceus philippinus*

Wheatear, *Oenanthe oenanthe*

Whip-poor-will, *Caprimulgus vociferus*

Whitethroat, Lesser, *Sylvia corruca*

Widgeon, American, *Mareca americana*

Willet, *Catoptrophorus semipalmatus*

Woodcock, American, *Philohela minor*

Woodpecker, Acorn, *Melanerpes formicivorus*

————, Arizona, *Dendrocopos arizonae*

————, Black-backed Three-toed, *Picoïdes arcticus*

————, Downy, *Dendrocopos pubescens*

————, Gila, *Centurus uropygialis*

————, Great Spotted, *Dryobates major*

————, Hairy, *Dendrocopos villosus*

————, Ivory-billed, *Campephilus principalis*

————, Northern Three-toed, *Picoïdes tridactylus*

————, Nuttall's, *Dendrocopos nuttallii*

————, Pileated, *Dryocopus pileatus*

————, Red-bellied, *Centurus carolinus*

————, Red-cockaded, *Dendrocopos borealis*

————, Red-headed, *Melanerpes erythrocephalus*

Wren, Bewick's, *Thryomanes bewickii*

————, Cactus, *Campylorhynchus brunneicapillum*

————, Carolina, *Thryothorus ludovicianus*

————, Guiana House, *Troglodytes musculus*

————, House, *Troglodytes aedon*

————, Long-billed Marsh, *Telmatodytes palustris*

————, Short-billed Marsh, *Cistothorus platensis*

————, Winter, *Troglodytes troglodytes*

Wrentit, *Chamaea fasciata*

Wryneck, *Jynx torquilla*

Yellowlegs, Greater, *Totanus melanoleucus*

————, Lesser, *Totanus flavipes*

Yellowthroat, *Geothlypis trichas*

Index

A CATALOGUE OF SELECTED DOVER BOOKS
IN ALL FIELDS OF INTEREST

A CATALOGUE OF SELECTED DOVER
BOOKS IN ALL FIELDS OF INTEREST

CONDITIONED REFLEXES, Ivan P. Pavlov. Full translation of most complete statement of Pavlov's work; cerebral damage, conditioned reflex, experiments with dogs, sleep, similar topics of great importance. 430pp. 5⅜ x 8½.   60614-7 Pa. $4.50

NOTES ON NURSING: WHAT IT IS, AND WHAT IT IS NOT, Florence Nightingale. Outspoken writings by founder of modern nursing. When first published (1860) it played an important role in much needed revolution in nursing. Still stimulating. 140pp. 5⅜ x 8½.   22340-X Pa. $3.00

HARTER'S PICTURE ARCHIVE FOR COLLAGE AND ILLUSTRA-TION, Jim Harter. Over 300 authentic, rare 19th-century engravings selected by noted collagist for artists, designers, decoupeurs, etc. Machines, people, animals, etc., printed one side of page. 25 scene plates for backgrounds. 6 collages by Harter, Satty, Singer, Evans. Introduction. 192pp. 8⅞ x 11¾.   23659-5 Pa. $5.00

MANUAL OF TRADITIONAL WOOD CARVING, edited by Paul N. Hasluck. Possibly the best book in English on the craft of wood carving. Practical instructions, along with 1,146 working drawings and photographic illustrations. Formerly titled *Cassell's Wood Carving*. 576pp. 6½ x 9¼.
                                              23489-4 Pa. $7.95

THE PRINCIPLES AND PRACTICE OF HAND OR SIMPLE TURN-ING, John Jacob Holtzapffel. Full coverage of basic lathe techniques—history and development, special apparatus, softwood turning, hardwood turning, metal turning. Many projects—billiard ball, works formed within a sphere, egg cups, ash trays, vases, jardiniers, others—included. 1881 edition. 800 illustrations. 592pp. 6⅛ x 9¼.   23365-0 Clothbd. $15.00

THE JOY OF HANDWEAVING, Osma Tod. Only book you need for hand weaving. Fundamentals, threads, weaves, plus numerous projects for small board-loom, two-harness, tapestry, laid-in, four-harness weaving and more. Over 160 illustrations. 2nd revised edition. 352pp. 6½ x 9¼.
                                              23458-4 Pa. $6.00

THE BOOK OF WOOD CARVING, Charles Marshall Sayers. Still finest book for beginning student in wood sculpture. Noted teacher, craftsman discusses fundamentals, technique; gives 34 designs, over 34 projects for panels, bookends, mirrors, etc. "Absolutely first-rate"—E. J. Tangerman. 33 photos. 118pp. 7¾ x 10⅝.   23654-4 Pa. $3.50

HISTORY OF BACTERIOLOGY, William Bulloch. The only comprehensive history of bacteriology from the beginnings through the 19th century. Special emphasis is given to biography-Leeuwenhoek, etc. Brief accounts of 350 bacteriologists form a separate section. No clearer, fuller study, suitable to scientists and general readers, has yet been written. 52 illustrations. 448pp. 5⅝ x 8¼. 23761-3 Pa. $6.50

THE COMPLETE NONSENSE OF EDWARD LEAR, Edward Lear. All nonsense limericks, zany alphabets, Owl and Pussycat, songs, nonsense botany, etc., illustrated by Lear. Total of 321pp. 5⅜ x 8½. (Available in U.S. only) 20167-8 Pa. $3.95

INGENIOUS MATHEMATICAL PROBLEMS AND METHODS, Louis A. Graham. Sophisticated material from Graham *Dial*, applied and pure; stresses solution methods. Logic, number theory, networks, inversions, etc. 237pp. 5⅜ x 8½. 20545-2 Pa. $4.50

BEST MATHEMATICAL PUZZLES OF SAM LOYD, edited by Martin Gardner. Bizarre, original, whimsical puzzles by America's greatest puzzler. From fabulously rare *Cyclopedia*, including famous 14-15 puzzles, the Horse of a Different Color, 115 more. Elementary math. 150 illustrations. 167pp. 5⅜ x 8½. 20498-7 Pa. $2.75

THE BASIS OF COMBINATION IN CHESS, J. du Mont. Easy-to-follow, instructive book on elements of combination play, with chapters on each piece and every powerful combination team—two knights, bishop and knight, rook and bishop, etc. 250 diagrams. 218pp. 5⅜ x 8½. (Available in U.S. only) 23644-7 Pa. $3.50

MODERN CHESS STRATEGY, Ludek Pachman. The use of the queen, the active king, exchanges, pawn play, the center, weak squares, etc. Section on rook alone worth price of the book. Stress on the moderns. Often considered the most important book on strategy. 314pp. 5⅜ x 8½. 20290-9 Pa. $4.50

LASKER'S MANUAL OF CHESS, Dr. Emanuel Lasker. Great world champion offers very thorough coverage of all aspects of chess. Combinations, position play, openings, end game, aesthetics of chess, philosophy of struggle, much more. Filled with analyzed games. 390pp. 5⅜ x 8½. 20640-8 Pa. $5.00

500 MASTER GAMES OF CHESS, S. Tartakower, J. du Mont. Vast collection of great chess games from 1798-1938, with much material nowhere else readily available. Fully annoted, arranged by opening for easier study. 664pp. 5⅜ x 8½. 23208-5 Pa. $7.50

A GUIDE TO CHESS ENDINGS, Dr. Max Euwe, David Hooper. One of the finest modern works on chess endings. Thorough analysis of the most frequently encountered endings by former world champion. 331 examples, each with diagram. 248pp. 5⅜ x 8½. 23332-4 Pa. $3.75

THE CURVES OF LIFE, Theodore A. Cook. Examination of shells, leaves, horns, human body, art, etc., in *"the* classic reference on how the golden ratio applies to spirals and helices in nature . . . . "—Martin Gardner. 426 illustrations. Total of 512pp. 5⅜ x 8½.   23701-X Pa. $5.95

AN ILLUSTRATED FLORA OF THE NORTHERN UNITED STATES AND CANADA, Nathaniel L. Britton, Addison Brown. Encyclopedic work covers 4666 species, ferns on up. Everything. Full botanical information, illustration for each. This earlier edition is preferred by many to more recent revisions. 1913 edition. Over 4000 illustrations, total of 2087pp. 6⅛ x 9¼.   22642-5, 22643-3, 22644-1 Pa., Three-vol. set $25.50

MANUAL OF THE GRASSES OF THE UNITED STATES, A. S. Hitchcock, U.S. Dept. of Agriculture. The basic study of American grasses, both indigenous and escapes, cultivated and wild. Over 1400 species. Full descriptions, information. Over 1100 maps, illustrations. Total of 1051pp. 5⅜ x 8½.   22717-0, 22718-9 Pa., Two-vol. set $15.00

THE CACTACEAE,, Nathaniel L. Britton, John N. Rose. Exhaustive, definitive. Every cactus in the world. Full botanical descriptions. Thorough statement of nomenclatures, habitat, detailed finding keys. The one book needed by every cactus enthusiast. Over 1275 illustrations. Total of 1080pp. 8 x 10¼.   21191-6, 21192-4 Clothbd., Two-vol. set $35.00

AMERICAN MEDICINAL PLANTS, Charles F. Millspaugh. Full descriptions, 180 plants covered: history; physical description; methods of preparation with all chemical constituents extracted; all claimed curative or adverse effects. 180 full-page plates. Classification table. 804pp. 6½ x 9¼.
23034-1 Pa. $12.95

A MODERN HERBAL, Margaret Grieve. Much the fullest, most exact, most useful compilation of herbal material. Gigantic alphabetical encyclopedia, from aconite to zedoary, gives botanical information, medical properties, folklore, economic uses, and much else. Indispensable to serious reader. 161 illustrations. 888pp. 6½ x 9¼. (Available in U.S. only)
22798-7, 22799-5 Pa., Two-vol. set $13.00

THE HERBAL or GENERAL HISTORY OF PLANTS, John Gerard. The 1633 edition revised and enlarged by Thomas Johnson. Containing almost 2850 plant descriptions and 2705 superb illustrations, Gerard's *Herbal* is a monumental work, the book all modern English herbals are derived from, the one herbal every serious enthusiast should have in its entirety. Original editions are worth perhaps $750. 1678pp. 8½ x 12¼.
23147-X Clothbd. $50.00

MANUAL OF THE TREES OF NORTH AMERICA, Charles S. Sargent. The basic survey of every native tree and tree-like shrub, 717 species in all. Extremely full descriptions, information on habitat, growth, locales, economics, etc. Necessary to every serious tree lover. Over 100 finding keys. 783 illustrations. Total of 986pp. 5⅜ x 8½.
20277-1, 20278-X Pa., Two-vol. set $11.00

AMERICAN BIRD ENGRAVINGS, Alexander Wilson et al. All 76 plates. from Wilson's *American Ornithology* (1808-14), most important orchithological work before Audubon, plus 27 plates from the supplement (1825-33) by Charles Bonaparte. Over 250 birds portrayed. 8 plates also reproduced in full color. 111pp. 9⅜ x 12½. 23195-X Pa. $6.00

CRUICKSHANK'S PHOTOGRAPHS OF BIRDS OF AMERICA, Allan D. Cruickshank. Great ornithologist, photographer presents 177 closeups, groupings, panoramas, flightings, etc., of about 150 different birds. Expanded *Wings in the Wilderness*. Introduction by Helen G. Cruickshank. 191pp. 8¼ x 11. 23497-5 Pa. $6.00

AMERICAN WILDLIFE AND PLANTS, A. C. Martin, et al. Describes food habits of more than 1000 species of mammals, birds, fish. Special treatment of important food plants. Over 300 illustrations. 500pp. 5⅜ x 8½. 20793-5 Pa. $4.95

THE PEOPLE CALLED SHAKERS, Edward D. Andrews. Lifetime of research, definitive study of Shakers: origins, beliefs, practices, dances, social organization, furniture and crafts, impact on 19th-century USA, present heritage. Indispensable to student of American history, collector. 33 illustrations. 351pp. 5⅜ x 8½. 21081-2 Pa. $4.50

OLD NEW YORK IN EARLY PHOTOGRAPHS, Mary Black. New York City as it was in 1853-1901, through 196 wonderful photographs from N.-Y. Historical Society. Great Blizzard, Lincoln's funeral procession, great buildings. 228pp. 9 x 12. 22907-6 Pa. $8.95

MR. LINCOLN'S CAMERA MAN: MATHEW BRADY, Roy Meredith. Over 300 Brady photos reproduced directly from original negatives, photos. Jackson, Webster, Grant, Lee, Carnegie, Barnum; Lincoln; Battle Smoke, Death of Rebel Sniper, Atlanta Just After Capture. Lively commentary. 368pp. 8⅜ x 11¼. 23021-X Pa. $8.95

TRAVELS OF WILLIAM BARTRAM, William Bartram. From 1773-8, Bartram explored Northern Florida, Georgia, Carolinas, and reported on wild life, plants, Indians, early settlers. Basic account for period, entertaining reading. Edited by Mark Van Doren. 13 illustrations. 141pp. 5⅜ x 8½. 20013-2 Pa. $5.00

THE GENTLEMAN AND CABINET MAKER'S DIRECTOR, Thomas Chippendale. Full reprint, 1762 style book, most influential of all time; chairs, tables, sofas, mirrors, cabinets, etc. 200 plates, plus 24 photographs of surviving pieces. 249pp. 9⅞ x 12¾. 21601-2 Pa. $7.95

AMERICAN CARRIAGES, SLEIGHS, SULKIES AND CARTS, edited by Don H. Berkebile. 168 Victorian illustrations from catalogues, trade journals, fully captioned. Useful for artists. Author is Assoc. Curator, Div. of Transportation of Smithsonian Institution. 168pp. 8½ x 9½. 23328-6 Pa. $5.00

YUCATAN BEFORE AND AFTER THE CONQUEST, Diego de Landa. First English translation of basic book in Maya studies, the only significant account of Yucatan written in the early post-Conquest era. Translated by distinguished Maya scholar William Gates. Appendices, introduction, 4 maps and over 120 illustrations added by translator. 162pp. 5⅜ x 8½.
23622-6 Pa. $3.00

THE MALAY ARCHIPELAGO, Alfred R. Wallace. Spirited travel account by one of founders of modern biology. Touches on zoology, botany, ethnography, geography, and geology. 62 illustrations, maps. 515pp. 5⅜ x 8½.
20187-2 Pa. $6.95

THE DISCOVERY OF THE TOMB OF TUTANKHAMEN, Howard Carter, A. C. Mace. Accompany Carter in the thrill of discovery, as ruined passage suddenly reveals unique, untouched, fabulously rich tomb. Fascinating account, with 106 illustrations. New introduction by J. M. White. Total of 382pp. 5⅜ x 8½. (Available in U.S. only)   23500-9 Pa. $4.00

THE WORLD'S GREATEST SPEECHES, edited by Lewis Copeland and Lawrence W. Lamm. Vast collection of 278 speeches from Greeks up to present. Powerful and effective models; unique look at history. Revised to 1970. Indices. 842pp. 5⅜ x 8½.   20468-5 Pa. $8.95

THE 100 GREATEST ADVERTISEMENTS, Julian Watkins. The priceless ingredient; His master's voice; 99 44/100% pure; over 100 others. How they were written, their impact, etc. Remarkable record. 130 illustrations. 233pp. 7⅞ x 10 3/5.   20540-1 Pa. $5.95

CRUICKSHANK PRINTS FOR HAND COLORING, George Cruickshank. 18 illustrations, one side of a page, on fine-quality paper suitable for watercolors. Caricatures of people in society (c. 1820) full of trenchant wit. Very large format. 32pp. 11 x 16.   23684-6 Pa. $5.00

THIRTY-TWO COLOR POSTCARDS OF TWENTIETH-CENTURY AMERICAN ART, Whitney Museum of American Art. Reproduced in full color in postcard form are 31 art works and one shot of the museum. Calder, Hopper, Rauschenberg, others. Detachable. 16pp. 8¼ x 11.
23629-3 Pa. $3.00

MUSIC OF THE SPHERES: THE MATERIAL UNIVERSE FROM ATOM TO QUASAR SIMPLY EXPLAINED, Guy Murchie. Planets, stars, geology, atoms, radiation, relativity, quantum theory, light, antimatter, similar topics. 319 figures. 664pp. 5⅜ x 8½.
21809-0, 21810-4 Pa., Two-vol. set $11.00

EINSTEIN'S THEORY OF RELATIVITY, Max Born. Finest semi-technical account; covers Einstein, Lorentz, Minkowski, and others, with much detail, much explanation of ideas and math not readily available elsewhere on this level. For student, non-specialist. 376pp. 5⅜ x 8½.
60769-0 Pa. $4.50

THE ANATOMY OF THE HORSE, George Stubbs. Often considered the great masterpiece of animal anatomy. Full reproduction of 1766 edition, plus prospectus; original text and modernized text. 36 plates. Introduction by Eleanor Garvey. 121pp. 11 x 14¾.   23402-9 Pa. $6.00

BRIDGMAN'S LIFE DRAWING, George B. Bridgman. More than 500 illustrative drawings and text teach you to abstract the body into its major masses, use light and shade, proportion; as well as specific areas of anatomy, of which Bridgman is master. 192pp. 6½ x 9¼. (Available in U.S. only)
22710-3 Pa. $3.50

ART NOUVEAU DESIGNS IN COLOR, Alphonse Mucha, Maurice Verneuil, Georges Auriol. Full-color reproduction of *Combinaisons ornementales* (c. 1900) by Art Nouveau masters. Floral, animal, geometric, interlacings, swashes—borders, frames, spots—all incredibly beautiful. 60 plates, hundreds of designs. 9⅜ x 8-1/16.   22885-1 Pa. $4.00

FULL-COLOR FLORAL DESIGNS IN THE ART NOUVEAU STYLE, E. A. Seguy. 166 motifs, on 40 plates, from *Les fleurs et leurs applications decoratives* (1902): borders, circular designs, repeats, allovers, "spots." All in authentic Art Nouveau colors. 48pp. 9⅜ x 12¼.
23439-8 Pa. $5.00

A DIDEROT PICTORIAL ENCYCLOPEDIA OF TRADES AND IN-DUSTRY, edited by Charles C. Gillispie. 485 most interesting plates from the great French Encyclopedia of the 18th century show hundreds of working figures, artifacts, process, land and cityscapes; glassmaking, paper-making, metal extraction, construction, weaving, making furniture, clothing, wigs, dozens of other activities. Plates fully explained. 920pp. 9 x 12.
22284-5, 22285-3 Clothbd., Two-vol. set $40.00

HANDBOOK OF EARLY ADVERTISING ART, Clarence P. Hornung. Largest collection of copyright-free early and antique advertising art ever compiled. Over 6,000 illustrations, from Franklin's time to the 1890's for special effects, novelty. Valuable source, almost inexhaustible.
Pictorial Volume. Agriculture, the zodiac, animals, autos, birds, Christmas, fire engines, flowers, trees, musical instruments, ships, games and sports, much more. Arranged by subject matter and use. 237 plates. 288pp. 9 x 12.
20122-8 Clothbd. $14.50

Typographical Volume. Roman and Gothic faces ranging from 10 point to 300 point, "Barnum," German and Old English faces, script, logotypes, scrolls and flourishes, 1115 ornamental initials, 67 complete alphabets, more. 310 plates. 320pp. 9 x 12.   20123-6 Clothbd. $15.00

CALLIGRAPHY (CALLIGRAPHIA LATINA), J. G. Schwandner. High point of 18th-century ornamental calligraphy. Very ornate initials, scrolls, borders, cherubs, birds, lettered examples. 172pp. 9 x 13.
20475-8 Pa. $7.00

ART FORMS IN NATURE, Ernst Haeckel. Multitude of strangely beautiful natural forms: Radiolaria, Foraminifera, jellyfishes, fungi, turtles, bats, etc. All 100 plates of the 19th-century evolutionist's *Kunstformen der Natur* (1904). 100pp. 9⅜ x 12¼. 22987-4 Pa. $5.00

CHILDREN: A PICTORIAL ARCHIVE FROM NINETEENTH-CENTURY SOURCES, edited by Carol Belanger Grafton. 242 rare, copyright-free wood engravings for artists and designers. Widest such selection available. All illustrations in line. 119pp. 8⅜ x 11¼. 23694-3 Pa. $4.00

WOMEN: A PICTORIAL ARCHIVE FROM NINETEENTH-CENTURY SOURCES, edited by Jim Harter. 391 copyright-free wood engravings for artists and designers selected from rare periodicals. Most extensive such collection available. All illustrations in line. 128pp. 9 x 12. 23703-6 Pa. $4.50

ARABIC ART IN COLOR, Prisse d'Avennes. From the greatest ornamentalists of all time—50 plates in color, rarely seen outside the Near East, rich in suggestion and stimulus. Includes 4 plates on covers. 46pp. 9⅜ x 12¼. 23658-7 Pa. $6.00

AUTHENTIC ALGERIAN CARPET DESIGNS AND MOTIFS, edited by June Beveridge. Algerian carpets are world famous. Dozens of geometrical motifs are charted on grids, color-coded, for weavers, needleworkers, craftsmen, designers. 53 illustrations plus 4 in color. 48pp. 8¼ x 11. (Available in U.S. only) 23650-1 Pa. $1.75

DICTIONARY OF AMERICAN PORTRAITS, edited by Hayward and Blanche Cirker. 4000 important Americans, earliest times to 1905, mostly in clear line. Politicians, writers, soldiers, scientists, inventors, industrialists, Indians, Blacks, women, outlaws, etc. Identificatory information. 756pp. 9¼ x 12¾. 21823-6 Clothbd. $40.00

HOW THE OTHER HALF LIVES, Jacob A. Riis. Journalistic record of filth, degradation, upward drive in New York immigrant slums, shops, around 1900. New edition includes 100 original Riis photos, monuments of early photography. 233pp. 10 x 7⅞. 22012-5 Pa. $7.00

NEW YORK IN THE THIRTIES, Berenice Abbott. Noted photographer's fascinating study of city shows new buildings that have become famous and old sights that have disappeared forever. Insightful commentary. 97 photographs. 97pp. 11⅜ x 10. 22967-X Pa. $5.00

MEN AT WORK, Lewis W. Hine. Famous photographic studies of construction workers, railroad men, factory workers and coal miners. New supplement of 18 photos on Empire State building construction. New introduction by Jonathan L. Doherty. Total of 69 photos. 63pp. 8 x 10¾. 23475-4 Pa. $3.00

THE DEPRESSION YEARS AS PHOTOGRAPHED BY ARTHUR ROTH-STEIN, Arthur Rothstein. First collection devoted entirely to the work of outstanding 1930s photographer: famous dust storm photo, ragged children, unemployed, etc. 120 photographs. Captions. 119pp. 9¼ x 10¾.

23590-4 Pa. $5.00

CAMERA WORK: A PICTORIAL GUIDE, Alfred Stieglitz. All 559 illustrations and plates from the most important periodical in the history of art photography, Camera Work (1903-17). Presented four to a page, reduced in size but still clear, in strict chronological order, with complete captions. Three indexes. Glossary. Bibliography. 176pp. 8⅜ x 11¼.

23591-2 Pa. $6.95

ALVIN LANGDON COBURN, PHOTOGRAPHER, Alvin L. Coburn. Revealing autobiography by one of greatest photographers of 20th century gives insider's version of Photo-Secession, plus comments on his own work. 77 photographs by Coburn. Edited by Helmut and Alison Gernsheim. 160pp. 8⅛ x 11.

23685-4 Pa. $6.00

NEW YORK IN THE FORTIES, Andreas Feininger. 162 brilliant photographs by the well-known photographer, formerly with Life magazine, show commuters, shoppers, Times Square at night, Harlem nightclub, Lower East Side, etc. Introduction and full captions by John von Hartz. 181pp. 9¼ x 10¾.

23585-8 Pa. $6.95

GREAT NEWS PHOTOS AND THE STORIES BEHIND THEM, John Faber. Dramatic volume of 140 great news photos, 1855 through 1976, and revealing stories behind them, with both historical and technical information. Hindenburg disaster, shooting of Oswald, nomination of Jimmy Carter, etc. 160pp. 8¼ x 11.

23667-6 Pa. $5.00

THE ART OF THE CINEMATOGRAPHER, Leonard Maltin. Survey of American cinematography history and anecdotal interviews with 5 masters—Arthur Miller, Hal Mohr, Hal Rosson, Lucien Ballard, and Conrad Hall. Very large selection of behind-the-scenes production photos. 105 photographs. Filmographies. Index. Originally Behind the Camera. 144pp. 8¼ x 11.

23686-2 Pa. $5.00

DESIGNS FOR THE THREE-CORNERED HAT (LE TRICORNE), Pablo Picasso. 32 fabulously rare drawings—including 31 color illustrations of costumes and accessories—for 1919 production of famous ballet. Edited by Parmenia Migel, who has written new introduction. 48pp. 9⅜ x 12¼. (Available in U.S. only)

23709-5 Pa. $5.00

NOTES OF A FILM DIRECTOR, Sergei Eisenstein. Greatest Russian filmmaker explains montage, making of Alexander Nevsky, aesthetics; comments on self, associates, great rivals (Chaplin), similar material. 78 illustrations. 240pp. 5⅜ x 8½.

22392-2 Pa. $4.50

HOUSEHOLD STORIES BY THE BROTHERS GRIMM. All the great Grimm stories: "Rumpelstiltskin," "Snow White," "Hansel and Gretel," etc., with 114 illustrations by Walter Crane. 269pp. 5⅜ x 8½.
21080-4 Pa. $3.50

SLEEPING BEAUTY, illustrated by Arthur Rackham. Perhaps the fullest, most delightful version ever, told by C. S. Evans. Rackham's best work. 49 illustrations. 110pp. 7⅞ x 10¾.
22756-1 Pa. $2.50

AMERICAN FAIRY TALES, L. Frank Baum. Young cowboy lassoes Father Time; dummy in Mr. Floman's department store window comes to life; and 10 other fairy tales. 41 illustrations by N. P. Hall, Harry Kennedy, Ike Morgan, and Ralph Gardner. 209pp. 5⅜ x 8½.
23643-9 Pa. $3.00

THE WONDERFUL WIZARD OF OZ, L. Frank Baum. Facsimile in full color of America's finest children's classic. Introduction by Martin Gardner. 143 illustrations by W. W. Denslow. 267pp. 5⅜ x 8½.
20691-2 Pa. $3.50

THE TALE OF PETER RABBIT, Beatrix Potter. The inimitable Peter's terrifying adventure in Mr. McGregor's garden, with all 27 wonderful, full-color Potter illustrations. 55pp. 4¼ x 5½. (Available in U.S. only)
22827-4 Pa. $1.25

THE STORY OF KING ARTHUR AND HIS KNIGHTS, Howard Pyle. Finest children's version of life of King Arthur. 48 illustrations by Pyle. 131pp. 6⅛ x 9¼.
21445-1 Pa. $4.95

CARUSO'S CARICATURES, Enrico Caruso. Great tenor's remarkable caricatures of self, fellow musicians, composers, others. Toscanini, Puccini, Farrar, etc. Impish, cutting, insightful. 473 illustrations. Preface by M. Sisca. 217pp. 8⅜ x 11¼.
23528-9 Pa. $6.95

PERSONAL NARRATIVE OF A PILGRIMAGE TO ALMADINAH AND MECCAH, Richard Burton. Great travel classic by remarkably colorful personality. Burton, disguised as a Moroccan, visited sacred shrines of Islam, narrowly escaping death. Wonderful observations of Islamic life, customs, personalities. 47 illustrations. Total of 959pp. 5⅜ x 8½.
21217-3, 21218-1 Pa., Two-vol. set $12.00

INCIDENTS OF TRAVEL IN YUCATAN, John L. Stephens. Classic (1843) exploration of jungles of Yucatan, looking for evidences of Maya civilization. Travel adventures, Mexican and Indian culture, etc. Total of 669pp. 5⅜ x 8½.
20926-1, 20927-X Pa., Two-vol. set $7.90

AMERICAN LITERARY AUTOGRAPHS FROM WASHINGTON IRVING TO HENRY JAMES, Herbert Cahoon, et al. Letters, poems, manuscripts of Hawthorne, Thoreau, Twain, Alcott, Whitman, 67 other prominent American authors. Reproductions, full transcripts and commentary. Plus checklist of all American Literary Autographs in The Pierpont Morgan Library. Printed on exceptionally high-quality paper. 136 illustrations. 212pp. 9⅛ x 12¼.
23548-3 Pa. $12.50

GEOMETRY, RELATIVITY AND THE FOURTH DIMENSION, Rudolf Rucker. Exposition of fourth dimension, means of visualization, concepts of relativity as Flatland characters continue adventures. Popular, easily followed yet accurate, profound. 141 illustrations. 133pp. 5⅜ x 8½.
23400-2 Pa. $2.75

THE ORIGIN OF LIFE, A. I. Oparin. Modern classic in biochemistry, the first rigorous examination of possible evolution of life from nitrocarbon compounds. Non-technical, easily followed. Total of 295pp. 5⅜ x 8½.
60213-3 Pa. $4.00

PLANETS, STARS AND GALAXIES, A. E. Fanning. Comprehensive introductory survey: the sun, solar system, stars, galaxies, universe, cosmology; quasars, radio stars, etc. 24pp. of photographs. 189pp. 5⅜ x 8½. (Available in U.S. only)
21680-2 Pa. $3.75

THE THIRTEEN BOOKS OF EUCLID'S ELEMENTS, translated with introduction and commentary by Sir Thomas L. Heath. Definitive edition. Textual and linguistic notes, mathematical analysis, 2500 years of critical commentary. Do not confuse with abridged school editions. Total of 1414pp. 5⅜ x 8½.   60088-2, 60089-0, 60090-4 Pa., Three-vol. set $18.50

Prices subject to change without notice.

Available at your book dealer or write for free catalogue to Dept. GI, Dover Publications, Inc., 31 East Second Street, Mineola, N.Y. 11501. Dover publishes more than 175 books each year on science, elementary and advanced mathematics, biology, music, art, literary history, social sciences and other areas.